The World Turned Upside Down

ASIA PERSPECTIVES

Asia Perspectives
History, Society, and Culture

A series of the East Asian Institute,
Columbia University, and Columbia University Press
Carol Gluck, Editor

Comfort Women: Sexual Slavery in the Japanese Military During World War II, Yoshimi Yoshiaki

The World Turned Upside Down

MEDIEVAL JAPANESE SOCIETY

Pierre François Souyri
Translated by Käthe Roth

COLUMBIA UNIVERSITY PRESS

NEW YORK

Columbia University Press
Publishers Since 1893
New York Chichester, West Sussex

Columbia University Press wishes to express its appreciation for assistance
given by the government of France through the Ministère de la Culture
in the preparation of this translation.

Library of Congress Cataloging-in-Publication Data
Souyri, Pierre
  [Monde a l'envers. English]
  The world turned upside down : medieval Japanese society /
Pierre-François Souyri ; translated by Käthe Roth.
     p. cm. — (Asia perspectives)
  Includes bibliographical references and index.
ISBN 978-0-231-11842-2 (cloth : alk. paper) – 978-0-231-11843-9 (pbk. : alk. paper)
    1. Japan—History—1185-1600. I. Title. II. Series.
DS857 S6813
952'.02—dc21

00–066026

Today, those among the local barons of Yamashiro Province who are between fifteen and sixty years of age have met to hold counsel. The peasants of the province are doing the same on their side. The purpose is to force the armies of Hatakeyama Masanaga and Hatekeyama Yoshinari, who are waging war and making the region their battlefield, to retreat. This is completely reasonable. And yet one might also say that this is truly the lower commanding the upper.

—*Jinson, abbot of the Daijōin, personal journal, eleventh day of the twelfth lunar month of year 17 of Bunmei (1485)*

Japan is a world in total opposition to what is happening in Europe; all is so different and contrary that we almost don't recognize it. . . . And I admire the fact that on the whole they govern themselves as a prudent, well-regulated nation, although there would be no reason to be surprised if they conducted themselves like barbarians.

—*Father Valignano* (Missionary Relations, 1583)

CONTENTS

MAPS

AUTHOR'S NOTE

The first version of this text was published in 1990 in *L'Histoire du Japon*, edited by Francine Hérail, for Éditions Horvath. That book is now out of print, and this volume is an expanded and revised edition of that part of the book dealing with the Middle Ages.

Many parts of the original text have been revised and expanded. Chapter 2 is completely new. Notes also have been provided, along with a greater number of citations, a bibliography, a chronology, and a glossary of Japanese terms. The notes cite sources and/or recent works that discuss the respective issues or offer a different point of view. On the whole, I have avoided referring to purely scholarly works. Although most of the notes cite works in Japanese, I also provide a bibliography of related works in English and French. The book's overall critical framework should make general readers aware of the importance of Japanese historiography, which is, unfortunately, little known in the West.

Japanese words have been romanized according to the Hepburn system. Following Japanese usage, the family name precedes the first name.

I would like to thank Francine Hérail for allowing this work to be published, and Fujiki Hisashi, Ishii Susumu, Ninomiya Hiroyuki, Satō Kazuhiko, and Yoshie Akio for their assistance and valuable advice while I was in Japan. I would also like to thank Carol Gluck, who encouraged publication of this book in English. My deepest gratitude goes to Abe Takeshi, who patiently introduced me to the strange world that was medieval Japan.

A CHRONOLOGY OF JAPANESE HISTORY, WITH AN EMPHASIS ON THE MIDDLE AGES

Jōmon civilization (ca. 8000–ca. 300 B.C.): neolithic period, coiled pottery, beginnings of agriculture.

Yayoi civilization (ca. 300 B.C.–ca. A.D. 300): pottery made on wheels, metallurgy, flooded-field rice cultivation.

"Ancient land" civilization: (third–fourth century): appearance of an embryonic state in Yamato.

ANCIENT JAPAN (SEVENTH–TWELFTH CENTURY)

Asuka period (seventh century)

- 592–622: Rapid adoption of Chinese culture by the Yamato court under the aegis of Shōtoku Taishi.
- 646: Coup d'état that eliminates the Soga clan, followed by the Taika reforms inspired by Tang-dynasty China.
- Beginning of the code system of government; the first attempt to create a centralized, bureaucratic monarchy.

Nara period (710–92)

- Creation of a capital in Nara.
- 712–20: Compilation of ancient myths.
- Development of Buddhism and its influence on the government.
- Ca. 760: Compilation of the *Man'yōshū* anthology of poetry.

Heian period (794–1185)

- Creation of a new imperial capital in Heian (today's Kyoto).

- Spiritual renewal of Buddhism in the early ninth century; creation of the Tendai and Shingon schools of Buddhism.
- Expansion of the Fujiwara family's political influence on the court.
- Ca. 1000: Court under the complete control of Fujiwara no Michinaga.

Slow economic and political emergence of the provinces.

- 935–41: Uprising led by Taira no Masakado in Kanto; the first evidence of an autonomous warrior grouping.
- 1051–87: Pacification wars in the northern provinces, with Minamoto no Yoshiie emerging as one of the most powerful warlords.

Late tenth–early eleventh century: Spread of faith in Amida Buddha to aristocratic circles.

- 1068: Ascension of Emperor Go Sanjō to the throne, the first break with the Fujiwara family.
- 1086: Inauguration by Emperor Shirakawa of the cloistered-emperor system.

Expansion of the imperial household's economic base and its clientele, sometimes at the expense of the Fujiwara clan.

- 1156–59: Court torn apart by factional struggles, with Emperor Go Shirakawa, allied with Taira no Kiyomori, defeating the opposing forces.
- 1160–80: Rise of Taira no Kiyomori as the all-powerful head of the state.
- 1180–85: Civil war between the Taira and Minamoto warrior clans.
- Fall 1180: Uprising by the Minamoto vassals and the installation by Minamoto Yoritomo of an illegal feudal-style government in Kamakura, in Kanto.
- 1183: Withdrawal of the defeated Taira from Kyoto to the western provinces, which are under their control, and the retired emperor's grant to Yoritomo of absolute control over eastern Japan (and thus legitimacy).
- 1185: Definitive victory by the Minamoto, who destroy the Taira clan, and the appointment by Yoritomo of *shugo* (military governors) and *jiō* (military estate stewards); he is now the only person entitled to maintain a public armed force.

Medieval Japan (late twelfth–late sixteenth century)

Kamakura period (1185–1333)
The first warrior regime (Kamakura bakufu).

- 1192: Yoritomo given the official title of *seii tai shōgun* ("barbarian-subduing generalissimo").
- 1199: After Yoritomo's death, the succession of his son, Yoriie, as shogun, but with the power remaining in the hands of a council of vassals led by the Hōjō (distant relatives of the shogun).

- 1213: After elimination of the Miura, the Hōjō's consolidation of their position at the head of the bakufu.
- 1219: Assassination of the third shogun, Sanetomo, and thus the end of the direct family line of the Minamoto and the ascension of the Hōjō.
- 1221: Jōkyū disturbance between the forces allied with the retired emperor Go Toba and those allied with the Hōjō, with the victory of the Hōjō, who control the Kamakura regime until it collapses in 1333.

Emergence of new religious forms: Zen, Amidism, Lotus sect.

- 1191: Introduction by the monk Eisai of Zen of the Rinzai school when he returns from China and, in around 1240, the creation by Dōgen of the Sōtō sect.
- Thirteenth and fourteenth centuries: Construction of monasteries by Zen monks, some of them from China, with the support of the shogunal authorities.
- Introduction by Hōnen of the doctrine of Amida Buddha, after which, in 1207, Hōnen is expelled from Kyoto, but his disciples found the sect of the Pure Land (Jōdoshū).
- Radicalization of the Amida doctrine by Shinran in 1232 and his disciples' founding of the True Sect of the Pure Land (Jōdo shinshū).
- Teaching by Nichiren of the Lotus sutra in the 1260s and 1270s and the founding of the Hokke sect (Nichiren sect).
- Warrior literature: around 1215, completion of the *Heike monogatari* (Tale of the Heike), the masterpiece of medieval literature.
- 1232: Goseibai shikimoku, a legal code, compiled at the request of the shogunal regent Hōjō Yasutoki.
- 1274 and 1281: Failure of the Mongolian invasions of Kyushu; extension of the Kamakura bakufu's control over the western provinces, though its inability to reward the warriors causes a crisis in the regime.
- Development of piracy and a rise in violence; split of the imperial dynasty into two branches, each of which claims the power to reign.
- 1324–31: Several attempts by Emperor Go Daigo to overthrow the Kamakura regime.
- Kenmu restoration (1333–36).
- Overthrow by a coalition of the Kamakura bakufu and the restoration of the imperial family, personally led by Emperor Go Daigo.

Period of the Northern and Southern Courts (1333–92)

- Civil war between followers of the Southern Court, exiled in southern Yamato, and followers of the Northern Court, installed in Kyoto and supported by the Ashikaga shogun.
- 1336: Beginning of civil war lasting almost a half century; the creation by Ashikaga Takauji of a new warrior regime with the support of the emperors of the Northern Court.

- 1338: Appointment of Takauji as shogun.
- 1349–52: Armed conflicts among factions within the bakufu.
- 1358–67: Gradual control assumed by Ashikaga Yoshiakira, the second shogun; economic development of the countryside.
- Expansion of piracy in western Japan toward Korea after 1350, with Japanese pirates, the *wakō*, ravaging the Korean coast and contributing to the collapse of Korean Koryŏ dynasty in 1392.
- Culmination of Zen Buddhism.
- 1378: Inauguration by the third shogun, Yoshimitsu, of his Muromachi "palace of flowers" in Kyoto and support of a new form of theater, nō, with the playwright Zeami the shogun's favorite; peace almost completely reestablished.
- 1392: Surrender of the Southern Court, with Yoshimitsu now ruling the entire country.

Muromachi period (1392–ca.1490)

- Peak of the shogunal regime in the late fourteenth and early fifteenth centuries.
- 1397: Retirement of Yoshimitsu to his villa, the Golden Pavilion, near Kyoto.
- 1401: Official mission sent to the Ming court in China.
- 1403: Acceptance by Yoshimitsu of the Chinese title that makes him "king of Japan" but also vassal of the Ming emperor.
- Development of trade, beginning of a monetary economy (based on Chinese coins), emergence of new social groups in Kyoto; emergence of merchants, moneylenders, bankers, and so on.
- 1403: Beginning of official "seal" trade between China and Japan, which continues, with interruptions, to 1547.
- Growing social instability; the time of revolts (*do-ikki*) and the "lower commanding the upper" (*gekokujō*).
- 1416: Disturbances in the eastern part of the archipelago, with the lords of Kanto gradually slipping beyond the control of Kyoto; Kanto in a state of feudal anarchy for more than a century.
- 1428–29: First major peasant revolt, around Kyoto, for the abolition of debts.
- 1441: New political and social crises; assassination of the shogun Ashikaga Yoshinori by one of his vassals; submission by the government to insurgent peasants, resulting in more peasant revolts.
- 1462: New wave of revolts around the capital.

High point of medieval Japanese culture: nō theater, the notion of yūgen, *"the obscure charm of mystery," Zen gardens, and a new aesthetic of simplicity.*

- 1467–77: The Ōnin War between the feudal chiefs Hosokawa and Yamana, each at the head of a vast coalition, in the streets of Kyoto, which is devastated.

- 1474: Expulsion of the Kaga lords by the Amidist *ikkō* leagues, composed of disciples of the monk Rennyo; creation of a religious commune that lasts for a century.
- 1483: Move by the shogun Ashikaga Yoshinori to the Silver Pavilion.
- 1485–93: Uprising south of Kyoto by low-ranking local warriors and peasants; birth of an autonomous regional commune.
- 1493: Coup d'état by Hosokawa Masamoto in Kyoto that forces the shogun to abdicate.

Sengoku period (ca. 1490–1573): Period of the Warring States

- Growing movement toward rural and urban autonomy, with villages and city neighborhoods in central Japan organizing to provide self-defense and self-administration.
- 1532–36: Kyoto under control of urban districts (*machigumi*), influenced by the armed leagues of the Hokke sect, which are defeated in 1536 by a coalition of lords and monk-warriors, with the capital remaining under the political and administrative control of autonomous residents' organizations.
- Cultural peak of the late Middle Ages in the first half of the sixteenth century, with the aesthetic notions of *sabi* (sad beauty, patina of time), *wabi* (simplicity and solitude), and *seijaku* (serenity in simplicity).

New regional potentates

- 1491: Attack by Hōjō Sōun, an obscure warrior, the deputy shogun of Kanto; creation of a new, independent estate in the Izu Peninsula, where he establishes himself as a *sengoku daimyō* (warlord). The "later" Hōjō hold southern Kanto for a century.
- After 1550: Battles for supremacy by Takeda Shingen, Uesugi Kenshin, Mōri Motonari, and others.
- Increase in trade and production, making Japan a major commercial power in the Far East.
- Introduction to Japan of Europeans, firearms, and Christianity.
- 1543: First landing of Portuguese on Tanegashima.
- 1549: First time that Francis Xavier preaches in Kagoshima.
- 1560: Surprise victory by the young Oda Nobunaga over his powerful neighbor, Imagawa Yoshimoto; beginning of the rise of Nobunaga.
- 1568: Entrance of Nobunaga into Kyoto.
- Starting in 1570: Crushing by Nobunaga, in an alliance with Tokugawa Ieyasu, of the lords opposing his hegemony in central Japan, and waging of war against the Buddhist monasteries that have armed forces.
- 1573: Nobunaga's expulsion of the last Ashikaga shogun from Kyoto, thereby ending the shogunal regime.

PREMODERN JAPAN

Azuchi-Momoyama epoch (1573–1603)

- Formation of a new state.
- Gradual defeat or vassalization of the warlords.
- Defeat of religious organizations that have armed forces; the crushing of peasant leagues.
- Creation of free markets by Nobunaga and his successor, Hideyoshi, leading to the breakup of the merchants' and artisans' guilds and the rise of new bourgeois strata.
- Readjustment of tax base through a systematic land survey; increased profitability of the fiefs.
- Transformation of the warrior class into an urban class by the daimyo, by separating the warriors from the peasants and forcing them to live near the castles.
- 1575: Nobunaga's defeat of the Takeda cavalry.
- 1581: Reception by Nobunaga, in conflict with the Buddhist monasteries, of Father Valignano, visiting brother of the Jesuits of Japan.
- 1582: Suicide by Nobunaga after betrayal by vassal, and succession by Hideyoshi, one of his generals.
- 1587: Hideyoshi's defeat of the lords of Kyushu.
- 1590: Hideyoshi's defeat of the Hōjō and subjugation of Kanto; move by Tokugawa Ieyasu to Edo.
- 1592–97: Failure of Japanese military campaigns in Korea.
- 1598: Death of Hideyoshi.
- 1600: Victory of Tokugawa Ieyasu's coalition opposing the western lords in their war of succession.

EDO PERIOD (1603–1867)

From Edo (today's Tokyo), the government by the Tokugawa shogun of a country fractured into fiefdoms (han) held by daimyo.

MODERN JAPAN

- Meiji period (1868–1912)
- Taishō period (1912–25)
- The first twenty years of the Shōwa period (1925–45)

CONTEMPORARY JAPAN

- Second part of the Shōwa period (1945–89)
- Heisei period: from 1989

The World Turned Upside Down

Chapter 1

THE CURTAIN RISES

It was early autumn in 1180, and night was falling on the Izu Peninsula, obscuring the smoke that constantly hovered over Mount Fuji. A small group of horsemen in full armor—menacing in their helmets and breastplates, with bows slung over their shoulders and full quivers—were making their way from the village of Hōjō to Izu, the seat of the provincial government, near Mishima Shrine.

On that evening, a celebration was under way at the province's biggest shrine to thank the gods for the abundant harvest. Afterward, at the Kise Inn, a short distance away on the Tōkaidō (road), dancers, puppeteers, and storytellers entertained travelers, low-ranking warriors, and local peasants. Games of chance were in full swing, and the betting was lively. Surveillance of the residence of the provincial governor's agent, Yamaki Kanetaka, was relaxed.

Suddenly, horsemen appeared at full gallop around the residence buildings, which were protected by only a single bamboo hedge. The guards were taken by surprise. Soon, as the ceremonies reached a peak, the residence of the governor's agent of Izu Province was ablaze, and Yamaki Kanetaka, a vassal of the Taira clan, was killed in his own home.

In the late twelfth century, such an incident was not unusual. Night attacks and the burning of buildings, in fact, were common criminal offenses.[1] This time, however, it was neither a simple settling of accounts nor an act of banditry perpetrated by some outlaw warrior holing up deep in the mountains and living by pillaging. Instead, this event was to be an important one in Japan's history. It was the seventeenth day of the eighth lunar month of the fourth year of the Jishō era. The uprising of warriors of the Kanto Plain had begun.[2]

The commando operation had been organized by Hōjō Tokimasa, a local notable, on behalf of the heir to the Minamoto family line, Yoritomo, whom he was supposed to be keeping under surveillance. Less than five years later, in the spring of 1185, Yoritomo, the rebel, was the most powerful man in Japan: the conqueror of the powerful Taira, the "pillar" (*tōryō*), and the supreme leader of the Minamoto *bushidan*, the largest vassal-warrior organization in the country. He was recognized by the imperial court in Kyoto as the guarantor of order in the empire. In 1192, the emperor appointed Yoritomo *seii tai shōgun*, "barbarian-subduing generalissimo," a title later shortened to *shogun*. The title legitimized a new state of affairs: Yoritomo, with his general quarters in Kamakura, in southern Kanto, was now the only person authorized by the Kyoto court to use his armed forces to keep order in the empire.

JAPANESE MEDIEVAL SOCIETY

THE AGE OF THE WARRIORS

The age of the warriors with its shogun and vassals launched Japan into what is now called the Middle Ages, a new term for this period in Japan's history. In the late twelfth century, people called the transitional period in which they were living the "age of the warriors."[3] The term *Middle Ages* (*chūsei*) was used for the first time by Hara Katsurō, a professor at Kyoto Imperial University who published a history of the Japanese Middle Ages in 1906.[4] He chose the term to signify the intermediary period between two stable societies: the ancient period, dominated by the imperial court in Heian (today's Kyoto), and the modern period (*kinsei*), dominated by the Tokugawa *bakufu* (literally, "tent government")[5] based in Edo (today's Tokyo). Between these two periods, the government's power was decentralized. Since the late nineteenth century, Western dictionaries have translated the word *hōken* (*feng-jiang* in Chinese) as "feudalism." The age of the warriors thus designates the beginning of the feudal period in Japan—or, if one prefers, the beginning of the medieval period. By using the term Middle Ages, Hara Katsurō tried to establish a correspondence between the major periods in Western history—antiquity, the Middle Ages, the modern period, and the contemporary period—and those in Japanese history. As Hara was writing, Japan was at war with czarist Russia at Port Arthur and demonstrating its modern technological power by sinking the Russian fleet at Tsushima, so he felt it necessary to compare historical development in the West and in Japan.

For Japanese medievalists in the early twentieth century, the "age of the warriors" was a significant turning point in Japanese history, comparable to what might have been the beginning of the Middle Ages in the West. Like medieval Europe, Japan was marked by a crumbling of power, a militarization of the upper social classes in the provinces, the rise of vassal relationships linking lords to their retainers, and the creation of feudal estates that dominated the land and those who worked on it. In fact, the shogunal state of the late twelfth century was similar in some respects to Western feudal monarchies: the shogun of the Minamoto clan was invested by the emperor, who was descended from the Sun Goddess, just as the king of France was consecrated by the bishop of Reims, a representative of the Christian Church and the delegate of the pope in Rome, and just as the king of England was crowned in Canterbury cathedral. As it "invented" new social forms in the Middle Ages, Japan gradually distanced itself from the Asian — especially Chinese — social models, becoming less "Asiatic" and more "European." The Middle Ages seemed to reveal a European-style society springing up in the very heart of Japan.

Far from stagnating, as did other Asian societies — at least as Westerners of the time portrayed them — Japanese society had a dynamic that led it, with the emergence of feudalism, to follow in the footsteps of Western European societies. Japan's intrinsic industrial and military superiority over the other Asian nations had its source in late-twelfth-century Kanto, where the *bushi*, warriors in the eastern part of the country, overthrew the old forms of aristocratic domination and swept the country into feudalism.[6] It is easy to understand the ideological stakes in such historical discourse in that epoch of triumphant imperialism.

In the hands of the warriors, the bakufu — the new state power — coexisted with the old imperial state until the fourteenth century, when it took over completely. The warriors' customs were codified in 1232, when a collection of laws, the Goseibai shikimoku, replaced the court law inherited from the old codes (themselves inspired by the models of Tang-dynasty China) and was gradually imposed on all of society. Imperial prerogatives passed into the hands of landowners, whose objective was to create estates out of parcels of contiguous land. These local lords, who were armed, formed groups of vassals called *kenin* (housemen), bound to them by a system of reciprocal obligations. The Japanese Middle Ages also saw the emergence of new values arising from the early warrior ethic, which was "refined" by teachings brought from China — mainly Zen Buddhism and Neo-Confucianism.

For many prewar historians, the Middle Ages was a decisive time in Japan's history because it confirmed the country's national identity. New forms of cultural expression (storytelling, poetry, theater, garden design, the tea ceremony, flower arranging, illustrated scrolls, the aesthetic of asceticism, architectural styles, and the like), conveyed a unique sensibility, sometimes in opposition to the Chinese models championed by the old nobility. Through these forms, Japan in the warrior age "finally found itself"—that is, for observers from the early twentieth century, it became culturally autonomous.[7]

A similar view may also explain the significance of the Edo period, which followed the Middle Ages. The Edo period was a Japanese version of the French *ancien régime*, and some of the Tokugawa shogun, such as Yoshimune, played the role of enlightened despot perfectly.[8]

The rise of the warriors, the *bushi*—at first armed servants of the court nobility (samurai) and then lords in their own right with extensive local powers—is a phenomenon specific to the internal development of Japanese society and is not found, at least on a comparable scale, in other Asian societies. Accordingly, a number of historians see in the appearance and then the expansion of these warrior classes, whose workings and values are reminiscent of those of the feudal classes of the West, the motive for a unique historical evolution.[9]

SOCIAL MOBILITY, REVOLTS, AND GROWTH

The rise of the warrior classes, the creation of a shogunal state, and the gradual collapse of the political system established by the imperial rule in the ancient period were prominent phenomena of this period, as was social mobility—or, rather, social instability. In the fifteenth century, this social instability was described with the colorful expression *gekokujō*, "the lower commanding the upper," signifying a time of civil disobedience and the inversion of social hierarchies, in which the world was "upside down." We might also translate this expression as "revolution," in the sense not of a great social upheaval but of an age-old movement constantly challenging state or regional powers, an attempt by the lower classes to reject the inevitability of their condition when the ruling classes proved incapable of maintaining stable institutions. The existence of *gekokujō* explains why the state had such difficult keeping order in the provinces.

The lack of a precise definition of landownership, unclear rights to the land, a multiplicity of jurisdictions, and the practice of shared land inheritance among descendants under the authority of a clan leader created tensions among social groups, within social classes, and even within families. Violent conflicts broke out between neighboring landowners. Private wars became common. Not only were they fights over real control of the land and the rents paid by peasants, they also were excuses for pillaging and doing battle for its own sake in a society that remained largely dominated by an ethic of warfare.

These feudal wars were complicated by real social conflicts between landowners and peasant communities. These communities, closely structured around rice cultivation, resisted the taxes levied by the upper classes, often successfully. The amount and nature of the annual payment of rents and the duration and purpose of corvées were frequent sources of dispute. In the fifteenth century, peasant communities began to challenge the very nature of the landowners' power and claimed the right to self-government, including legal rights, which until then had left up to the lords. Other conflicts, produced by the development of a cash economy, arose between rural dwellers and usurious moneylenders living in the towns. In addition to the factional struggles within vassal families for control of inheritances and the class struggles between rural peasant communities and warlords or urban absentee landowners, there were conflicts among the peasant communities themselves, which Japanese historians term "disputes over boundaries"(kyōkai no funsō). These were sometimes heated quarrels over the control and distribution of irrigation water and the exploitation of forests and uncultivated land. Despite their seemingly trivial motivations, some of these incidents quickly escalated, with each community seeking the protection of, and sometimes military assistance from, its lord.[10]

These conflicts spread during the fifteenth century, dragging entire provinces into civil war. The bakufu was unable to impose its will on or, if necessary, to arbitrate between the parties. As a result, villages, town districts, and regions ended up creating autonomous local government structures and communes based on federations of villages or even on entire provinces. The ensuing social upheaval and desire for autonomy and local power, stemming from the feudal structures unable to function and increasingly seen as superfluous, explain the difficulty that authorities in the late Middle Ages had in maintaining order. The inability of duly constituted powers to impose their will in the face of constant destabilization from below casts a new light on the unceasing war throughout most of the period.[11]

Even though the Middle Ages was an age of warriors, revolts, and social insubordination, Japanese society during this time was relatively dynamic and open, bringing in its wake a period of exceptional cultural creativity and enormous economic potential. As an active participant in the increased trade and creation of new merchant networks in East Asia following the collapse of the Mongol empire, Japan began to experiment with a commercial cash economy. Although the use of money was still, of course, in its infancy, it was the first step toward accumulating capital. Furthermore, an investigation of the port archives of Hyōgo (the future Kobe) from the fifteenth century reveals that trade in the Inland Sea was equivalent to that in the Baltic Sea in the late Middle Ages.[12] Christian missionaries who arrived in the Japanese archipelago in the sixteenth century could not help but compare Sakai, with its international port, ruling bourgeois hierarchy, and many artisans, with Venice.[13]

Long considered a dark time in the history of the country because of its anarchy and frequent usurpations,[14] the medieval period is now being reconsidered by Japanese historians. These four centuries (late twelfth to late sixteenth) are now seen as the time when the country first "took off." Its economic growth and social dynamism made the "Cipango" about which Marco Polo wrote, if not a legendary country overflowing with gold, at least one of the Far East's strongest commercial powers. Despite the civil wars and chronic political instability, Japanese society was well enough structured to learn from its early Western visitors what it needed to know about the rest of the world without becoming technically and culturally dependent on Europe. The Portuguese reached the archipelago in 1542, but they never came close—much as they tried—to equaling the conquests of the Spanish in America. Although they were faced with European firearms, Japanese metallurgists were not completely unprepared. They had inherited a strong craft-based tradition and had developed bellows techniques that enabled their forges to attain temperatures unknown in any other culture.[15] Japan was the region's main exporter of arms, and Japanese swords were the equal of the best blades from Toledo; more than 20,000 swords were exported to China in the fifteenth century by the only official trade intermediary between the two countries. Now, in an attempt to advance their weapons expertise, the artisans of Tanegashima, Negoroji, Sakai, and other towns immediately set out to study these amazing firearms, which had in fact long been known elsewhere in Southeast Asia. The first firearms made in Japan were produced in 1545,[16] and the advantage that these new weapons provided was quickly understood. Around 1570, the warlord Oda Nobunaga positioned soldiers behind palisades, with their backs to the hills, to discharge their weapons against the enemy's cavalry. In the battle of Nagashino in 1575, Nobunaga destroyed the cream of the cavalry of the Takeda feudal clan with his muskets, thereby eliminating one of his most powerful rivals.[17]

The arrival of the Europeans presented a new challenge to Asian countries. Although the Portuguese had ships able to stay at sea for months, possessed effective firearms, and were driven by an unshakable faith, they were not facing passive societies,[18] most of which knew perfectly well how to keep out invaders. This was particularly true of Japan, which was strikingly "modern" for a society that had been somewhat isolated from the world for centuries. That is, the uniqueness of its social organization explained its ability to respond as it did, and it was this organization that was no doubt behind the formidable internal expansion that completely reshaped the archipelago in the seventeenth century.[19]

THE SOURCES

Contemporary historians have access to an abundance and wide variety of sources—critiques, journals, and other publications—that provide knowledge and understanding of Japanese medieval society.

WRITTEN SOURCES

Written sources—especially archival materials but also compilations, chronicles, personal notes, and so on—are an easily accessible group of documents (though not necessarily so accessible when it comes to comprehension!),[20] because they have been classified and annotated since at least the seventeenth century. These sources have enabled Japanese historians to reconstruct political events, understand how institutions worked, untangle the mechanisms of property ownership and taxation, and so on. They include official documents (edicts, laws, various regulations, and so on) produced by the court, the bakufu, aristocratic households, monasteries, shrines, and warlords' households. Prominent figures also wrote more personal documents, such as *nikki* (diaries), notes, chronicles, commentaries on the classics and on etiquette, and *kakun* (house codes), which have been preserved and compiled according to a system imported from China. A few analytical works, such as Jien's *Gukanshō* (early thirteenth century) and Kitabatake Chikafusa's *Jinnō shōtoki* (1339),[21] are proof that some thinkers attempted to understand the nature of historical events. The very early establishment in Japan of a philological tradition with a smattering of Neo-Confucianism led to the compilation of some of these archives when the lord of Mito, Tokugawa Mitsukuni, organized a group of scholars in 1657 to produce the *History of Greater Japan* (*Dai Nihon shi*). This monumental work, whose origins are more or less contemporary with the Benedictine tradition of Saint Maur, was completed only in the early twentieth century. Very old collections of archival records, such as the *Gunsho ruijū*, date from between 1779 and 1819. In 1869, the Meiji government appointed a bureau of experts, who, using methods still little influenced by Western critical history, founded the Shiryō hensanjo (Institute for the compilation of historical documents), which was situated at Tokyo Imperial University in 1888. This institute produced *Dai Nihon shiryō* (Archives of greater Japan) in 1901 and also published a critical edition of the ancient archives of greater Japan (*Dai Nihon komonjo*). As a site for research, preservation of archival materials, and critical publications of the archives, the Shiryō hensanjo is still one of the major centers of historical research in Japan. Sources from the Kamakura period, published by the historian Takeuchi Rizō, contain an invaluable group of documents,[22] and the *Chūsei hōsei shiryō shū* (Anthology of medieval juridical sources) and the *Nihon shisō taikei* (The major texts of Japanese thought) are indispensable.[23] Volumes 21 and 22 of the latter collection, titled *Chūsei seiji shakai shisō* (Political and social thought in the Middle Ages) (1971–81), are particularly useful for providing access to written traces left by commoners, those inhabitants of domains protesting against too-high taxes, village communes decrying new internal regulations (*mura no okibumi*), and so on.

Another type of written documentation comes from works of fiction written in the medieval period (novels, edifying stories, plays, poems), which may be considered indirect sources. The corpus is considerable and provides readers with insights into the attitudes and sensibilities of the times. To the many poetry collections, some compiled by imperial order,[24] we could add literary sources such as the great warrior epics,[25] collections of stories, tales,[26] miracles, marvelous stories relating the lives of saints or the foundation of monasteries, and treatises of religious theology.[27] Some rarer and more personal works, such as the *Hōjōki* and the *Towazugatari*,[28] offer a glimpse into the private lives of their authors. The world of fiction is highlighted by the performance arts, which were very popular in the Middle Ages—the scripts for some plays have been preserved—and constitute an inexhaustible source for studying the attitudes of the times.[29]

In contrast to the rest of the Far East, few epigraphs were written in Japan: the inscription by Yagyū testifies to the peasants' gratitude to their gods in 1428 after they led a successful insurrection to cancel their debts.[30]

OTHER TYPES OF HISTORICAL MATERIALS

To this group of written sources, we must add the numerous illustrated scrolls, paintings, and sculptures that portray medieval society. These iconographic sources, especially scrolls, carefully preserved in monasteries and museums and recently reproduced in high-quality collections,[31] have drawn the interest of historians—and not just art historians—because they evoke, among other things, the world of ordinary people and ordinary crafts as well as attitudes, gestures, and symbols that do not necessarily appear in traditional written sources.[32] In a different vein, plans and maps constitute a source of raw information on urban areas, palaces, and provincial estates.[33]

It is useful to compare these sources with the findings of medieval archaeology, a field that has been growing for some thirty years. Vanished towns, abandoned ports, destroyed castles, and forgotten cemeteries are slowly being rediscovered in archaeological excavations, and these give us a better grasp of material life and symbolic structures in Japan. In the 1960s, Kusado Sengen, a site near Fukuyama, was discovered in the alluvia left by a flood in 1673. Its excavation led to a reconstruction of some physical aspects of the daily life of commoners in the late Middle Ages and a reevaluation of the scope of international trade at the time, which was greater than written sources indicate. Excavations started in 1967 to reconstruct the Ichijōdani citadel built by the Asakura lords in 1458 and the town that grew at its feet (which was reduced to ashes by Oda Nobunaga in 1573). This dig has enabled us, among other things, to understand better the process that led to the creation of feudal towns "at the foot of the castle" (*jōkamachi*) in the seventeenth century. Excavations in Hiraizumi, in northern Japan, and in the lagoon of Tsugaru Tosa harbor have led to a reassessment of the economic importance of the regions of northern Japan and their direct links with Kyoto and central Japan. Work done in the 1980s in Mitsuke (Ichinotani) on the Tōkaidō has taught historians much about the symbolic structuring of the space and about burial rites for commoners in the provinces.[34]

Finally, a comparison of the results of research in folklore ethnology and anthropology—active disciplines since they were launched around 1910 by Yanagita Kunio—with the historical data offers an essential key to the psychological and technical world of the lower social classes, particularly in Japan. Here, interdisciplinary research is at its best. Ethnologists such as Shibusawa Keizō and Miyamoto Tsune'ichi, literary scholars such as Iwasaki Takeo, experts in religious studies such as Gorai Shigeru, and unconventional historians such as Inoue Toshio have, in different ways, helped the scientific community turn to other methodologies for studying social groups and practices that are difficult to discern through written texts alone.[35] The creation in 1984 of the journal *Rettō no bunkashi* (History of the cultures of the archipelago), with contributions by historians, ethnofolklorists, and anthropologists, illustrates the trend toward historical anthropology.[36]

THE PEOPLE OF JAPAN

At the beginning of the Middle Ages, Japan—that is, the group of countries under the authority of the court—was a smaller area than today's Japan.[37] Neither Hokkaido to the north nor the Ryukyu Islands to the south were under the control of Kyoto, the imperial capital. Contrasts in population density, economic and cultural activities, strategic political importance, and geographic distance created strong regional inequalities. It is easy to imagine that in the late eleventh century, there were sizable differences between the central provinces around the capital, where the Japanese state was born, and the faraway provinces of Tōhoku, in the north part of the main island, conquered in ancient times, whose inhabitants were considered half barbarian and not well integrated culturally. These differences were exacerbated by the difficulty of traveling in these regions. Land and sea routes had existed since ancient times, but the sea was always dangerous, and in the mountainous areas that made up a large part of the territory, communications remained difficult and the population was very sparse.

Historical demographers have tried to estimate the population of medieval Japan. The sources for these periods are fragmentary, making calculations—even guesswork—difficult, but researchers seem to have agreed that around 1150, the population was 7 million or perhaps a little less (twenty-four inhabitants per square kilometer).[38] The population distribution throughout the territory was uneven, but two regional centers were already quite large. The first was Kinai, more or less corresponding to today's Kansai region, which contained the capital, Kyoto: 1.4 million people lived in this small region, and the population density was already more than sixty per square kilometer. The second center was Kanto, with 1.6 million inhabitants in a larger area and a population density of about fifty per square kilometer. These two regions alone represented 40 percent of Japan's total population in the mid-twelfth century.[39] Throughout the Middle Ages, political power alternated between these two poles: Kinai, with the imperial capital of Kyoto, and Kanto, with the shogunal capital of Kamakura.

Kinai, containing the imperial court, was truly the heart of the country. Here, Japanese society crystallized over the centuries. The landscape of these regions bears age-old marks of human works. The Nara basin, with its ancient capital and the Buddhist Kōfukuji and Tōdaiji temples, the plain through which the Yodo River flows from the southern suburbs of Kyoto to the Inland Sea, and the area around Lake Biwa have been cultivated for more than a millennium. The systematic division of rice paddies into parcels of equal area is a remnant of the *jōri* system instituted in the seventh century, and it marked the landscape prominently in medieval times. Kinai was a center of rice cultivation, and the yields were already high.

North of Kinai, in the plains east of Wakasa Bay, the former provinces of Echizen, Kaga, and Etchū (today's Fukui and Kanazawa regions) communicated directly with Kyoto via Lake Biwa, a major travel route throughout the medieval period. These plains were in fact a sort of rice-growing hinterland of the capital. East of Lake Biwa, the former Mino, Owari, and Mikawa Provinces (today's Gifu and Nagoya regions) were only two or three days' walk from Kyoto and also integrated into the capital's zone of influence, as were the southwestern regions bordering the Inland Sea toward Harima and Bizen Provinces (today's Himeji and Okayama regions). Kyoto was, in fact, in the heart of the most developed region of the time, where rice cultivation dominated agriculture. About 2 million people probably lived in this fairly small area (30,000 to 35,000 square kilometers), with the imperial court at its center.

These central provinces were linked to the rest of the country by roads. In the early Middle Ages, the best-traveled road was the San'yōdō, linking the capital to northern Kyushu. This land route along the coast was paralleled by a sea route that linked the harbors of Kanzaki and Eguchi, at the mouth of the Yodo River (the site of today's Osaka), to Dazaifu, the seat of the general government of the large western island. Dazaifu was located near the port of Hakata (both now part of Fukuoka), where ships sailing the high seas between the archipelago and the mainland arrived and departed. The sea route between Kyushu and Kinai was essential to shipping the rents charged by nobles in the capital on estates located in the western part of the country. Most of Japan's salt, a strategic staple for the conservation of foods, was produced in these regions. The ships, many of them barely larger than boats, that sailed this "Jap-

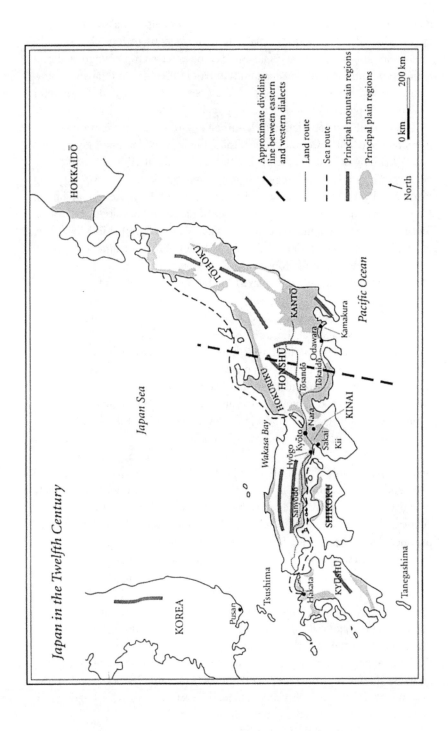

Japan in the Twelfth Century

Approximate dividing
line between eastern
and western dialects

Land route

Sea route

Principal mountain regions

Principal plain regions

North

0 km   200 km

HOKKAIDŌ

TŌHOKU

KANTŌ

Pacific Ocean

Kamakura

Odawara

Tōkaidō

Tōsandō

HONSHŪ

HOKURIKU

KINAI

Nara

Kyōto

Sakai

Kii

Hyōgo

Sanyōdō

Wakasa Bay

Japan Sea

SHIKOKU

KYŪSHŪ

Hakata

Tanegashima

Tsushima

KOREA

Pusan

anese Mediterranean" were coastal vessels, and they helped make this maritime area, sprinkled with islands, a relatively homogeneous region. Occasionally, junks belonging to merchants of the Song empire crossed from Ningbo to Japan with cargo from the Middle Kingdom (China). In these western Japanese provinces, the sea, boats, and fishing played an essential role, as did the more or less endemic piracy.

This maritime Japan, deliberately turned toward the open sea, was the most important regional power base of the Taira, the warrior clan that took over the court's main functions after the coup d'état in 1159. About 2 million people lived in western Japan (Chūgoko region, Kyushu, and Shikoku), for an average population density of twenty per square kilometer. Most of them lived in the littoral plains, along the shores, and on the islands of the Inland Sea and in northwest Kyushu, where the population density was about as high as that in Kinai. Elsewhere, in the southern part of Shikoku, southwest of Kyushu, and on the north side of the western part of Honshu bordering the Japan Sea, there were fewer people, and these regions thus played a more marginal role in the history of medieval Japan.

The other major route that linked the capital to eastern Kanto was the Azuma region, as it was called at the time. In the late twelfth century, the Tōsandō (road) was the most frequently traveled, since it led directly to the northern part of the plain, where agriculture was oldest and best developed. This area, composed of the former Kōzuke, Shimotsuke, and Hitachi Provinces (today's Gunma, Tochigi, and Ibaraki Prefectures) and Shimōsa Province (northern Chiba Prefecture), was the most highly developed and had the best land and crop yields. The population densities in northern Kanto seem to have been relatively high, and rice cultivation had taken over the lower parts of the easily flooded plain. Those who cleared the land in the eastern provinces apparently were skilled at planting rice in wet lowlands, an art that did not spread widely in the western part of the country before the second half of the thirteenth century. The cultivation of silkworms also was widespread. Alluvial terraces provided ideal pastures for horses, and on the highlands, overlooking their operation, the estate administrators-become-warriors built their manors.[40]

The rest of Kanto, especially the central part—the Musashi Plain (now Tokyo, southern Saitama Prefecture, and northern Kanagawa Prefecture)—was, in contrast, very little developed in the Middle Ages. Grassy, marshy in many places, and a paradise for deer, boars, and ducks, it was uninhabited between the northern parts of the plain and the southern regions near Kamakura where the Minamoto had established their headquarters, although some crops were grown in dry fields. To the west, in the foothills toward Chichibu, and on the plateaus of Kai Province (today's Yamanashi Prefecture), dryland agriculture and horse breeding were the main activities.

The Tōkaidō, the other road linking Kyoto to the east via the Pacific coast, ended in a cul-de-sac, the Miura peninsula, from where one took a boat to cross the bay and continue toward Kazusa and Shimōsa Provinces (Chiba Pre-fecture). This road, whose landscapes the painter Hiroshige immortalized in prints in the early nineteenth century (*The Fifty-five Stations of the Tōkaidō*, 1833–34) serves as the spine of the Japanese economy today, but it did not play a vital role at the start of the Middle Ages. It began to be important only in the mid-thirteenth century, with the development of political centers in southern Kanto: Kamakura, the shogunal capital, then Odawara, the town at the foot of the Hōjō lords' castle in the sixteenth century, and Edo, the capital of the Tokugawa shogun starting in the seventeenth century.

People in the east felt remote from the capital and its culture. They loved to gallop through the open spaces and hunt with bows and arrows. Their lan-guage, with a strong, somewhat harsh accent, was quite different from that of the inhabitants of Kinai, who found that "the people of Azuma have a language that twists the tongue," and their manners, considered crude in Kyoto, were based on different values. In addition, the people of the east and the west did not trust each other. In *Tsurezuregusa*, written around 1330, the author, Yoshida Kenkō, has a man of the eastern provinces say, "You can trust what a man from the east says. People from the capital are good at making promises, but they're not to be trusted." Kenkō also introduces the opposite point of view: in the capital, "they are so gentle and warmhearted," while in the east, they "lack such gentleness in their hearts or sympathy for others."[41]

Thus, in contrast to a western Japan of sea, ships, and piracy was a more continental eastern Japan, a land of plains and horses, of warriors practicing the "way of the bow and the horse."[42] It was in eastern Japan that Japanese chivalry, whose values slowly spread to the rest of the country, was born.

In medieval times, Japan grew up around the roads built by the state in the late seventh century when the provinces were administratively grouped into circuits.[43] The capital ruled the empire, and in the late twelfth century there was no other city to compete with it. The few towns, markets, and ports located along trade routes had, at most, several hundred sedentary inhabitants. Japan at the beginning of the Middle Ages was thus a rural society, to which Kyoto was the only magnificent exception.

To control the provinces, the court appointed administrators for a fixed term whose mission was to ensure order and collect public rents. Under these con-ditions, the routes assumed strategic importance. Traffic on the roads, which were very narrow (just wide enough for two horses to pass each other), was heavy, with convoys carrying rents from the provinces to the capital, function-aries and their retinues traveling to or from some distant post, couriers (it nor-mally took seven or eight days for a courier to travel from Kyoto to Kamakura in the thirteenth century, and three to four days for an urgent official message), and pilgrims, rich and poor, going to a temple or shrine to make their devotions. Inns were established in seaports, near bridges, fords, and ferryboat moorings, and at the foot of hills to provide shelter for travelers. Sites of intense sociability, they often hosted puppeteers (*kugutsu*), jugglers, magicians, and storytellers—itinerant "artists" who went from inn to inn. The performers' wives (*kugutsume*) sang *imayō*—improvised songs, appreciated both at the court and by the lower classes—and danced wearing colorful, shimmering costumes and makeup in the style then popular. The *kugutsume* were also prostitutes.[44] Ōe no Masafusa, a great scholar of the late eleventh century, describes these characters in *Kugutsu ki* as people "who ignored the state, did not fear the provincial administrators, did not pay rents, and lived for pleasure."[45]

Was there indeed a marginal and wandering population beyond the state's control? Sailing boats down the rivers or along the coasts and traveling the roads were fishermen and prostitutes, peddlers and storytellers, preaching monks and professional performers, magicians and salt merchants, fortune-tellers and iron-mongers, thieves, merchants selling oils and Chinese medicines, musicians, horse dealers, slave traders—an entire mobile society of people of ill-defined status. They were "those who have an art, a path," whom the medievalist Amino Yoshihiko characterized as "the wandering world" (*henreki no sekai*)[46]—an almost nomadic population with no close tie to the land. They did not yet seem to suffer from discrimination, and they offer evidence of a society that was more diversified than one might think. Between a peasantry bound to the soil and the ruling classes—court nobles, abbots of major temples, wealthy warriors—was a fluctuating population that usually had service ties to the court, spread folk culture throughout Japan, disseminated beliefs and fashions, and ultimately helped make the peoples who lived on the archipelago a group more homogeneous than fragmented.

Beyond the regions located near the two or three major routes that linked Kyoto to northern Kyushu, the Kanto Plain, and the Hokuriku regions—which were within easy reach of the capital via Lake Biwa—Japan was more sparsely populated, its inhabitants less in evidence in political and social life at the beginning of the Middle Ages. Mountains were difficult to cross and were populated with mysterious, sometimes monstrous deities feared by the peasants of the plains and valleys. Only the forest dwellers, who worshiped the mountain gods, and a few hermits who practiced Shugendō esoteric asceticism dared enter these remote woods. The entire Kii Peninsula, from Yoshino (south of Nara) to Kumano, seems to have been very isolated from Kinai, despite the relative proximity of the capital. A few pilgrims crossed these regions to reach Mount Kōya, the great monastery of the Shingon school, or the Kumano Shrine,[47] but they were difficult to penetrate and formed autonomous, uncontrolled areas, some of them bandits' refuges. Mountains were not the only obstacle, however; geographic distance also was a constraint. Some parts of the archipelago were thus frontiers. The southern and eastern parts of the distant island of Kyushu remained beyond the major trade routes for a long time, as did the vast north-eastern provinces that comprised the Tōhoku region, which were still semi-independent in the twelfth century. Because they were located more than a thousand kilometers from the capital, it took several weeks to reach them, and heavy snow in winter slowed travel still more. The quickest way to reach Tōhoku was by boat. Although there was no direct sea route, the Japan Sea linked the small ports in Wakasa Bay and trading posts such as Tsugaru Tosa harbor, in Dewa (today's Akita and Aomori Prefectures). Perhaps 600,000 people lived in these territories, and the population density was fewer than ten per square kilometer.

Although it was isolated, Japan was definitely not closed. Sea travel somewhat mitigated the difficulties and distances of the land routes within the archipelago, linking remote regions and providing contact between people from island to island. The passage from Honshu, the main island, to Kyushu was easy, and from there it was not difficult to reach Tsushima, the small Japanese island midway between the archipelago and the Korean peninsula. From Tsushima, the coast of Korea around Pusan was visible in good weather. As Amino Yoshihiko points out, it is difficult to see why the sea, which somewhat unified the archipelago, would present such an formidable obstacle between Japan and other countries.[48] From Hokkaido, Tsushima, or the southern Ryukyu Islands, the mainland could be reached by leapfrogging from island to island. For a seagoing people, there were no "borders." In fact, in the early fifteenth century, the lords of Tsushima, the Sō, were official vassals of the Ashikaga shogun and at the same time paid allegiance to the king of Koryŏ.

The people of Tōhoku went to Hokkaido from where they could reach the northern islands. Although no formal documents have survived, archaeologists' discoveries of Song currency show that there was trade linking intermediaries to intermediaries, northern Japan to China, no doubt via northern China—the Jürchet kingdom at the time—Sakhalin, and Hokkaido. These northern islands were inhabited by semi-nomadic peoples of North Asian origin who lived mainly from trade and catching sea mammals. From the eleventh to the thirteenth century, these populations constituted the "culture of the Sea of Okhotsk." On Hokkaido, non-Japanese populations descended from the Ainu hunted and gathered but also knew about dryland agriculture; they formed a northern cultural area called Satsumon. These cultures, which had no written language, no doubt did have some influence on the "awakening" of Tōhoku at that time.[49]

At the other end of the archipelago, an embryonic state developed in Okinawa in the twelfth century. Excavations have revealed a large quantity of Song-dynasty porcelain, indicating trade with the Chinese mainland. Ryukyu culture thus seemed closer to that of China than to that of Japan. Indeed, as late as the fifteenth century, people from the Ryukyu Islands were considered foreigners in Kyoto.[50] Less isolated from the rest of Asia than the written sources indicate and more complex in its social workings, Japan in the late twelfth century was on the brink of political changes reflecting the rise of new social classes and the new social and cultural importance of the eastern regions. This movement marked the beginning of the decline of the court nobles' influence on the empire's political destiny, the close of an era in which the court easily governed a vast territory from the capital, and the end of a peaceful order in which civil war was the exception.[51] Japan was now entering a period of great turbulence.

Chapter 2

SOCIAL DYNAMICS IN THE LATE HEIAN PERIOD

At the end of the ancient period, Japanese society was undergoing many changes, all of them tending to distance it from the Chinese bureaucratic models that the state had attempted to apply in the seventh and eighth centuries under what has come to be called the "regime of codes." The Fujiwara clan had largely dominated the bureaucracy in the court at Kyoto in the tenth and early eleventh centuries. But starting in 1068 (beginning with the reign of Emperor Go Sanjō) and especially after 1086 (when Emperor Shirakawa abdicated to gain control over the fate of the imperial family), the Fujiwara had to learn to share power with a serious competitor, the imperial family itself, organized around its patriarchal leader, the retired emperor. Some of the imperial family's newfound strength lay in the economic power that it had obtained by increasing the number of the provincial estates, or *shōen*, and managing them through a private administrative apparatus, the In no chō. In the eleventh and twelfth centuries, the imperial family expanded its sources of revenue, diversified its clientele, and broadened its networks in the provinces.[1]

The awakening of the provinces was the other factor in this social evolution.[2] By "awakening," I mean a slowly growing sense of independence among the local gentry. They began systematically to clear new land and replant abandoned rice paddies, building themselves properties that they "commended" (*kishin*) to those more powerful than them: large monasteries, the Fujiwara nobles, the retired emperors. In addition, the gentry in the eastern part of the country also armed themselves. In the second half of the eleventh century, following hard-fought wars in the provinces of Tōhoku between the leaders of the Minamoto clan and local chiefs rebelling against the central authority, the gentry broke away from the dominant cultural patterns established by the court. They built local feudal organizations, *bushidan* (warrior groups), and then affiliated themselves with one of the two large warrior vassal organizations, the Taira and the Minamoto.

In the second half of the eleventh century, the Fujiwara family saw its undisputed hegemony in the court being challenged by the imperial family. Along with the large monasteries, the Taira and Minamoto families formed a series of networks, with support from the newly formed large warrior organizations, that enabled them to control most of the estates being created in the provinces. But these great aristocratic and warrior families were also divided into influence groups that sought outside support, with the result that the factions that formed in the mid-twelfth century were in fact overlapping alliances competing for power. Consequently, during the Hōgen coup d'état in 1156, both the Taira and the Minamoto camps contained people close to the retired emperor and to the Fujiwara.[3]

The faction led by the retired emperor Go Shirakawa took control in 1156 and again in 1159. But it depended too heavily on its alliance with the leader of the Taira clan, Kiyomori, who ultimately ousted his main rivals and in 1167 found himself in a position to control the court. But then some of the Fujiwara, the retired emperor, and several monasteries turned against him. This was the opportunity that the leader of the Minamoto, exiled in the eastern part of the country, had been waiting for.

THE COURT'S DOMINATION OF THE PROVINCES

Implementation of the estate system (*shōen sei*)[4] led to a number of changes in provincial society. These converged to destroy the real-estate system as it had been defined in the "regime of codes," which was based on the public ownership of cultivated land, particularly the rice paddies. Estates (*shōen*) were based on a series of complex mechanisms that ultimately resulted in the private appropriation of the land. Benefiting from tax relief that turned into permanent exemptions, the *shōen* were sometimes converted into zones in which intervention by representatives of the state became difficult or even illegal.[5]

During the Heian period, the key figure at the center of the land privatization was the provincial governor (*kokushi*), who held the highest position in the local administration. Under the regime of codes, one of the governor's main functions was to protect the farmers (*kōmin*) who worked on the public estates (*kōchi*).[6] In the eighth century, the governors abandoned their basic official mission, which was to oversee agricultural production and harvests, and took charge of collecting taxes, thus gaining new powers. Despite the court's attempts to stop this extortion, the governors' power grew, and they began to appropriate land for themselves. Because they had a firm grasp on provincial administrative power, even the smallest tax exemption became impossible to obtain without their support. In other words, it became difficult to form and administer a *shōen* without the involvement of the highest official in the local administration, the governor, who was gradually taking total responsibility for taxation in his province. Provincial governors thus slowly became the masters of their domains.

This expansion of the provincial governors' powers can be seen in the light of the monopolization of important functions in the court by the Fujiwara family, who increasingly excluded the aristocracy from access to the most remunerative positions. Consequently, as it became impossible to envisage a decent career in the court, members of noble families and the imperial family, low- and middle-ranking nobles, and others saw the position of provincial governor as a means of guaranteeing an ascent that now would be blocked if they stayed in Heian. Many people therefore left the capital to try their luck in the provinces. They had only one thing in mind: to enrich themselves as quickly as possible and return to Heian. Not all of them, however, had the determination or talent to choose this route to prosperity. Instead, taking advantage of other offices that they had accumulated in the capital, they sent to the provinces under their jurisdiction professional administrators from their households or among their clients. These resident deputies, or governor's agents (*mokudai*) ran the province for the governor, who remained in Heian for the duration of their administrative mandate. Indeed, some went to their province only when their rents were collected. Under these circumstances, governorships became so profitable that middle-ranking court nobles began to compete for them, rushing to spend their fortunes on repairs to the imperial palace or a temple in hopes of being noticed and rewarded by the central government. The potential for bribery and corruption mushroomed. Some governors went to their province accompanied by their own men, who took over the local administrative positions; others assigned these positions to the local gentry in order to gain allies in the area. The goods that they accumulated (horses, rice, silk, and so on) they sent to the capital, though first making sure to distribute some of them among the high-ranking aristocrats who had secured their appointment so that they could consolidate their position and curry new favor.

In the eleventh century, these wealthy governors were called *zuryō*, and they were known for their rapaciousness. Some moved to the provinces, where the profits were more certain than in the capital. They married the daughters of the powerful local gentry, forming a network of alliances that ensured their control over their province. They usually appropriated a growing portion of the rents, used peasant labor for their own purposes in the name of public corvées, confiscated the most valuable products under the guise of taxes, and sent to the capital an ever-shrinking portion of the tax revenues. Their hired hands oversaw the peasants during the harvest and created land cadastres that overestimated the area of the rice paddies in order to justify the increased taxes.

This exploitation provoked the peasants in some provinces to respond. They were sometimes encouraged by local low-ranking notables, who were infuriated by the arrogance of the new masters. These notables' complaints began to be recorded in the late tenth century. In 988, peasants and low-ranking local managers lodged a complaint in Owari Province against the governor and his men,[7] listing thirty-one transgressions over a three-year period.

THE BIRTH OF THE WARRIOR CLASS

The transformation of governors into *zuryō* (often translated as "tax managers") reflected a major change in the real-estate system. Previously, public lands owned by the state had formed the basis for the court's domination—a clearly identifiable form of social order, centralized and bureaucratic, with its own rules. But this system was dissolving in favor of another system of tax sharing that involved private appropriation and modes of payment based on influence, client relationships, and rewards. For this new system to develop, even with the complicity of the powerful, physical force had to be used—that is, a favorable balance of power had to be imposed, through violence if necessary. It thus became easier to use an armed force to solve problems than to count on the law and political mechanisms for a peaceful resolution of conflicts of interest.[8]

This was the reason that in the provinces—especially those farthest from the capital, where the court's control was weak—the local lords, who were responsible for paying the rents and controlling and organizing peasant labor, sought to strengthen their family ties, thus reinforcing the social role of clans as a means of resistance. These new social configurations then began to maintain permanent armed forces, local warrior groupings called *bushidan*.

The local gentry operated parcels of land on which they had acquired rights that enabled them to draw on and command peasant labor. How they came to do so, however, is a complex process that is difficult to recreate in detail (owing to the lack of sources). It seems to have varied widely in nature and scope in different regions of the country and to have developed more rapidly in Kanto and Kyushu than elsewhere, as if the imperial state worked less well in outlying areas than at the center. This operation also signified the beginning of a kind of social differentiation: On the one hand were those originally from court families who became warriors, found salvation in emigrating to the provinces, and drew along in their wake the provincial upper classes. On the other hand was militarization from below: wealthier peasants and low-ranking gentry were gradually transformed into warriors. And so the sword was never very far from the rice paddy.[9]

Model A. Local lords, both organized and militarized, held an important degree of regional power. Many of them held or had held administrative titles and offices in provincial or district bureaucracies. These local provincial officials were called *zaichō kanjin* and were often ranked: *suke, jō, sakan* (deputy governor, middle-ranking bureaucrat, field officer), and so on. Most were descendants of former governors from the middle-ranking nobles who had come from the capital to settle locally and had prospered by forming alliances with the local gentry. Others were from families that had ruled districts (*gunji*) for several generations.

These powerful men owned *konden*—rice paddies that their ancestors had had cleared or reseeded. The lands had once been farmed by slaves or fleeing peasants, who were attracted by the prospect of land and better working conditions. This labor pool, mobile and not always very motivated, was organized by bosses called *tato* ("captains of the rice paddies"), whom the gentry bound to the soil by making them responsible for paying rents on land that had been given a name. The members of this wealthier peasant middle class were called *myōshu*, "head of a named rice paddy." When they controlled many paddies, they were called *daimyo*. The *myōshu* became the managers of local farming operations. Thus, the system progressed gradually from direct ownership based on large farming properties to indirect ownership based on smaller farming operations. The *myōshu* were obliged to collect the rents required by the provincial governor or his henchmen. In the early eleventh century, the most powerful *myōshu* (the daimyo) began to escape this obligation by "commending" (*kishin*) their lands to high-ranking aristocrats in the capital (the Fujiwara, the imperial family, and so on) or to powerful religious institutions.

The local gentry were thus caught in a squeeze between provincial governors from the nobility, who created powerful domination structures and settled in the provinces (that is, the *zuryō*), and the former peasant bosses, who had become *myōshu* and gradually freed themselves, strengthened their leadership over the peasants, and kept increasingly large portions of the rents for themselves. To escape this predicament, the gentry usually maintained their own groups of armed men, reinforced their clan links, and maintained their domination over the peasants—by terror, if necessary—by physically forcing the *myōshu* to pay rent and take part in corvées. At the same time, they rewarded the *myōshu* by allowing them to rise to the lower echelons of their military hierarchy, thus integrating them (or their sons) into the warrior society. Little by little, all of rural society found itself in a new world in which physical and military protection was the dominant element.[10] The local gentry were able to hold together the provincial bureaucracy through the functions they performed and their armed forces on the estates they controlled. At best, they had complete authority over a district, or even an entire province, which became, in a sense, their private domain. They also had at their disposal warrior organizations of several hundred to several thousand armed men.

Model B. Some *tato* and *myōshu* managed to escape the grasp of the local lord. If they were able to free themselves from agricultural work and be promoted to the manager of the farm for which they were responsible, they could, in turn, dominate a group of small-scale farmers, slaves, and various agricultural workers and became owners of small estates. On the one hand, they resisted the fiscal pressure of the *zuryō* and the domination of the local lords. But on the other hand, they subjugated poor peasants, transforming them into "their men" or "men of their household" (*ie no ko, kenin*) and arming them. They also created family or clan structures with reinforced solidarity to the point that they formed territorial alliances. Some of these "managers" based their power on the responsibilities that they had obtained from their superiors on the estates, whereas others held their position purely through the military strength of the organization they had developed.[11]

The main warrior organizations created in northern Kanto belonged to model A: the Chiba, the Kazusa, the Satake, the Nitta, the Ashikaga, and others. Those organizations in Kyushu were the Shimazu and the Ōtomo. The smaller, though not necessarily less effective, warrior groupings created in western Kanto and the mountainous regions, such as the "seven bands of Musashi" (*Musashi no shichitō*), belonged to model B.[12] This model was also more common in central Japan, where it took longer for warriors to gain their freedom. Nevertheless, between the tenth and twelfth centuries (depending on the region), these warrior organizations became an essential element in the provinces' political and social importance.

Local *bushidan* often banded together, and by the tenth century, they formed vast alliances. This process was facilitated when imperial princes with aristocratic family names left the court, where their way to a high-level career had been blocked. These nobles, with blood ties to the emperor (ties that became more tenuous with each generation), had great prestige in the provinces, and some of them took over warrior organizations as their uncontested leaders. This was the case for two families of imperial origin: the Kammu Taira and the Seiwa Genji. The Taira (or Heike) line was descended from Imperial Prince Takamochi, descendant of Kammu (who reigned in the late eighth and early ninth centuries), who was given the family name Taira and went to Kazusa Province in Kanto as *suke* (deputy governor). Similarly, in the mid-tenth century, a descendant of Emperor Seiwa (r. 858–76) obtained the family name Minamoto (Gen) and was appointed governor of several provinces (Musashi, Shinano, Iyo) before settling in Kinai as the head of a *bushidan*. During the Jōhei and Tengyō uprisings (935–41), these two clans showed their power at the Heian court.

In Shimōsa Province in eastern Kanto, Taira no Masakado, a local notable from the Kammu Taira clan, had a fight with his uncle, who held an administrative office in the neighboring Hitachi Province, and killed him. Openly opposed to the provincial governor, Masakado rallied a number of discontented local landowners, attacked and set fire to the headquarters of the Hitachi administration, and took the governor prisoner. He then appropriated some of the governor's possessions, took over the administration of the neighboring Shimōsa and Kazusa Provinces, and assumed all the royal prerogatives in the regions he occupied. In 939, Masakado's rebellion expanded to the eight provinces of Kanto. The court was concerned about this turn of events because Masakado had also assumed the title of *shinnō* (new emperor) and set about establishing a new monarchy in the eastern part of the country. He appointed governors to administrative positions in Kanto and planned to construct a capital in Shimōsa, decree a new era, and form an imperial court with administrative departments similar to those of the Heian court. Was this simply a provincial replica of a model created several centuries before, or a dress rehearsal for what was to occur in the late twelfth century—an emancipative thrust by the eastern provinces against domination of the country by the Heian court? Japanese experts have long debated this question, despite the risk of falling into historical misinterpretation by attributing too much significance to the sources. It is nevertheless probable that Masakado rallied to his side not only a large number of local lords from the region, to whom he promised rapid promotion, but also part of the population, who were outraged by their high taxes. The veneration of Masakado—still very much alive today—shows that the popularity of the movement he started has endured through the centuries.[13]

At the same time, Fujiwara no Sumitomo, a low-ranking bureaucrat in Iyo Province, near the Inland Sea, took command of groups of seafaring warriors— designated pirates by the court—seized the governor's headquarters, and ransacked his storehouses. With a fleet of, reportedly, 1,500 boats, Sumitomo attacked the headquarters of Bizen and Sanuki and burned down the headquarters of Dazaifu, in Kyushu, in 941, sowing disorder throughout the Inland Sea.

Caught by surprise by the scope and coincidence of these attacks, the court was late in reacting, and when it finally sent troops, they arrived after the combat had ended. Other military forces put down the rebels on the Kanto Plain and the Inland Sea. Masakado and Sumitomo were finally defeated and killed by warriors acting for the court.[14] Nevertheless, it was a great shock to the court to discover how important the *bushidan*, organized as vassals, had become; that is, they were capable of starting or repressing a revolt. A century later, other rebellions, similar in nature and size, broke out in eastern Kanto, in a movement started by Taira no Tadatsune in 1028–31.

Not until the second half of the eleventh century, during the wars conducted in the northern provinces by the leaders of the Seiwa Genji clan, did truly solid, stable *bushidan* emerge. The Abe were the chiefs of the Ezo tribes in northern Japan—populations not yet culturally integrated into Japanese society but attached to the court since the early ninth century. In the eleventh century, they established their domination in the Koromo valley and resisted the governors' claim on the region. Refusing to cooperate with Minamoto no Yoriyoshi, the representative of the imperial court sent to subdue the rebels in 1051, the Abe brothers began a particularly bloody guerrilla war against Yoriyoshi's troops, most of whom were from Kanto. With the support of another local clan, the Kiyohara, Yoriyoshi managed to reestablish peace in the region in 1062. But not long after, in 1083, Minamoto no Yoshiie, Yoriyoshi's son, personally intervened in the quarrels that had broken out within the Kiyohara family, hoping to draw some profit for his *bushidan* from the wars fought by his father by installing his vassals in the northern part of the country. The battles were extremely bitter and provided storytellers of the Middle Ages with many edifying anecdotes on the prowess of fierce warriors. After coming close to defeat, the Kiyohara troops supported by Yoshiie finally won in 1087, and Yoshiie's reputation became legendary.[15] In these battles, the Minamoto consolidated their charismatic influence over the warriors of Kanto, and the head of the Minamoto clan was identified as the suzerain, the "pillar" (*tōryō*) of the *bushidan* of the eastern warriors.

But the warriors were only warriors. The court aristocracy refused to let them be anything but men in its service. Despite his reputation, Yoshiie was forbidden to benefit from "commended" estates, and he was barred from the triumph he sought: entering Kyoto at the head of his troops. He was still only a samurai—an armed man serving the nobles of the imperial court.

THE REGIME OF THE RETIRED EMPERORS

For the first time in 170 years, the prince who ascended the imperial throne in 1068, Go Sanjō, was not the son of an imperial wife of Fujiwara blood. Designated emperor against the advice of Yorimichi, the chief of the Fujiwara clan, Go Sanjō had a free hand, and to the highest positions at court, he appointed nobles—among them, Ōe no Masafusa—who were opposed to the Fujiwara's hold on the court's most important functions. In addition, Go Sanjō implemented a new policy, which was put into effect the following year, 1069, with the publication of a ruling to review the estate titles.

The policy consisted of strong measures aiming to eliminate estates that did not have exemptions founded in law, and it affected both those estates formed since 1045 and also those that were older. To apply this sweeping revision, a special commission "for the registration of estate titles" was formed to examine the deeds of all those who claimed to own a *shōen*. In accordance with the judgment rendered, estates were either eliminated or preserved. The new emperor's intention was to slow the overly rapid formation of private tax-exempt estates, which reduced the court's revenues. But he also wanted to contest the supremacy of the northern branch of the Fujiwara family over newly acquired estates, which had enabled this clan to become more powerful than the imperial family itself. Finally, Go Sanjō wanted to gain the support of the provincial *zuryō*, who looked favorably on any measure taken to slow the formation of estates that they could not control.

In 1073, Go Sanjō was succeeded by his son, Shirakawa, who, like his father, was not the son of a Fujiwara princess. Shirakawa named as crown prince one of his young sons, whose mother was one of his concubines, and then he abdicated in 1086. The eight-year-old prince became emperor under the name Horikawa. Shirakawa, of course, preserved his political prerogatives as father of the emperor. The preceding system, under which the maternal Fujiwara uncle governed in the name of the emperor, was now replaced by a system in which the emperor's father's role was preeminent.[16] Shirakawa retired to a monastery (*in*), from where he controlled the political affairs of the government (*insei*, "cloister government"). He created a private administration, the In no chō, that defended the imperial family's interests and became a partial substitute for the official administration. Freed from the official constraints of being emperor, the retired emperor now was free to influence appointments and propose laws for imperial approval—that is, for the approval of his young son. Some nobles missed the old system, feeling that the Fujiwara had acted more prudently and that the new regime was despotic.[17] Although reduced, the Fujiwara's influence did remain considerable.

The middle-ranking court nobility, which had been unhappy with the arrogance of the Fujiwara, followed the example of the *zuryō* in more actively supporting the new imperial regime. They sent gifts to the In no chō administration to obtain confirmation of their prerogatives and began to insinuate themselves into its machinery. Thus, the center of power gradually moved from the court to the Fujiwara family and then from the Fujiwara family to the imperial household.

But another center of influence rose within the In no chō. To ingratiate themselves with the new authority, the chiefs of the *bushidan* offered their services to the retired emperor and gradually formed his armed escort, a private army at his service. Because these chiefs lived near the north gate of the retired emperor's palace, they were named after it (*hokumen no bushi*). Under Shirakawa, the North Gate was made up of warriors organized by the Seiwa Genji, with Minamoto no Yoshiie as their leader. These warriors were in no way a praetorian guard for the retired emperor. Rather, their first loyalty was to their suzerain, who was a client of the retired emperor. They thus were situated within the framework of vassal relations and not a bureaucratic world. So if their chief were to be banished by the retired emperor, they would follow him. It was because the retired emperor soon forgot this that he lost real power in the late twelfth century.

At the beginning of the twelfth century, however, it was in fact the administration of the retired emperor—via the registration commission—that granted or refused tax exemptions on lands and authorized the creation of estates. The only means that a local lord had to escape the invasive power of a *zuryō* was to "commend" his land to the retired emperor himself—in other words, to become his client, to beg for his protection. But even though the imperial household amassed a huge number of estates and a far-reaching network of indebted people in the provinces, it did not keep the Fujiwara and some monasteries from gathering a great number of *shōen* for themselves.

Around this time, the provinces formed a new system of assigning power. The In no chō granted to its vassals the right to propose someone to carry out the official functions of provincial governor and to collect tax revenues. In other words, the retired emperor's household controlled the opportunity to create *shōen*, lands exempted from official rents (in whole or in part), and reserved the right to appropriate them for itself or its confederates. It also granted the right to control public lands in the provinces through "provincial fiefdoms" (*chigyōkoku*), which, for a period of time, accorded a monopoly to a particular person. The imperial family thus owned a gigantic private estate and held the real rights to tax exemption on public lands. This system, obviously, brought to an end the old regime of codes.

Until his death in 1129, Shirakawa presided over the imperial household through the reigns of three emperors. Then from 1129 to 1156, Toba succeeded him, also governing through the reign of three emperors.

The alliance formed among the retired emperors, the low-ranking nobility, and some *bushidan* chiefs would not have been strong enough to hold on to power over the long term if it had not been extended to the major Buddhist monasteries. In effect, although the imperial household benefited from its granting of *shōen* in the twelfth century, some large monasteries also saw their economic strength expand considerably during this period when many low-ranking provincial lords "commended" their estates to them. One might think that these notables were sincerely trying to buy their salvation in the hereafter, but the fact was that the monasteries were relatively efficient managers of their properties, and they knew how to defend their material interests by taking advantage of their sacred character and how to press their point of view in the capital. Some large monasteries, such as the Kōfukuji, in Nara, and the Enryakuji, located on Mount Hiei near the capital, began to maintain bands of armed men who were tonsured and dressed like monks. Monks versed in theological studies and concerns ran the institution, and others were assigned to maintaining the monastery buildings, managing the lands that provided the community with its livelihood, and providing armed defenders. Quick to defend their assets by force and hold demonstrations in the streets of the capital to obtain their due, the monks were also quick to demand reparation from *zuryō* who tried to seize any of the rents owed to their monastery.[18] Thus the monasteries provided a brake on the all-powerful *zuryō*, whose hands the regime of the retired emperors had freed.

THE RISE OF THE TAIRA

Whether it was monks holding demonstrations in the streets of the capital or complaints being lodged against provincial administrators, the only institution able to calm tensions was the In no chō. And the In no chō had its own armed force, the North Gate. Gradually, the retired emperors allowed the suzerains of the warrior groups that escorted and protected them also to have direct access to them. Minamoto no Yoshiie obtained this privilege late in life. It was obviously a considerable advantage, for it enabled certain affairs to be settled at the highest level.

After Yoshiie's death in 1106, crippling disagreements broke out among the Minamoto *bushidan*, and another warrior clan grew in strength: the Taira from Ise. Taira no Tadamori distinguished himself between 1129 and 1135 by dispatching the pirates who were once again plundering on the Inland Sea. He thus gained for his men the privilege of being the new North Gate, obtained responsibility in provincial administrations in the western regions where he had been victorious, and consolidated his clan's position. In 1151, the Taira in their turn were finally allowed direct access to the palace of the retired emperor Toba.

In the mid-twelfth century, the concentration of power in Toba's hands gave rise to deep antagonisms in the Heian court between those who had his support and those who did not. By changing the rules of the political game that had been played peacefully since the Fujiwara had been in power and creating a more despotic authority, Shirakawa and then Toba created an opportunity for opposing forces to confront each other beyond the reach of the law or traditional political practices. As the strength of the head of the imperial household ebbed, these factions were now positioned to use force.

After the death of Toba, who ran the "cloister government" with an iron fist, coalitions with divergent interests began to form. Emperor Go Shirakawa, with the backing of the grand chancellor, Fujiwara no Tadamichi, tried to take over the cloister government, pitting him against the ex-emperor Sutoku and the minister of the right, Fujiwara no Yorinaga, who had support of factions in the Minamoto *bushidan* led by Tameyoshi. Go Shirakawa's faction was supported by the warriors of Taira no Kiyomori, who controlled the North Gate; was allied with another faction of the Minamoto *bushidan*, led by Yoshitomo; and was backed by most of the forces that had traditionally supported the regime of retired emperors. In 1156, the factions clashed in the streets of the capital for the first time. Blood flowed; Sutoku's faction was defeated; and Sutoku was exiled. Yorinaga was killed in the fighting, as were the military leaders who had been loyal to him. These events are known as the Hōgen uprising.

Power relations shifted immediately after the uprising. Taira no Kiyomori and Minamoto no Yoshitomo were no longer lowly samurai and members of the emperor's escort. They had been the main protagonists in his camp's victory, intervening decisively on behalf of the imperial and Fujiwara families, and they wanted rewards at the highest levels of government for themselves and their families. Quickly, however, the victorious faction split into two antagonistic groups. Go Shirakawa, who "retired" in 1158, still had the support of the Taira who formed his guard, but Fujiwara no Nobuyori turned to the powerful Minamoto warriors, led by Yoshitomo. Taking advantage of Kiyomori's departure from the capital, Nobuyori launched an uprising in 1159. He held Go Shirakawa under house arrest and had one of his loyal men, the monk Shinzei (himself a member of the Fujiwara clan), killed. Kiyomori quickly returned to Kyoto and rescued Go Shirakawa. The Minamoto troops were defeated, and Nobuyori and Yoshitomo were killed. The Taira, led by Kiyomori, were victorious. These events are known as the Heiji uprising.

The outcome of these violent battles, which lasted only a few days, was that power relations had once again been completely reversed. Go Shirakawa and his rescued Fujiwara chiefs knew that their power was now gone. Kiyomori, master of the battlefield and of an illustrious warrior organization, now set out to increase his prerogatives through his claim on the In no chō. Without Go Shirakawa or anyone else to oppose him, Kiyomori obtained various positions in the court, and in 1167, he received the most prestigious title, *dajōdaijin*, prime minister. In an aristocratic society deeply attached to its titles of nobility, this rapid promotion of a parvenu could only signal the end of an era. To cap it off, in 1171, Kiyomori arranged for his daughter Tokuko to marry Emperor Takakura, Go Shirakawa's son, and for the son born of this union to be proclaimed crown prince. The child would reign under the name Antoku.

In a few years, the Taira took over from the Fujiwara the external family relations with the imperial family, and they plotted in the court to have their clansmen and vassals appointed to high positions in the provinces. The Taira were everywhere. Through the *zuryō* and "provincial fiefdoms," it was reported, they controlled thirty of the sixty-six provinces in the empire and held almost five hundred *shōen*. But by insinuating themselves into the structures of the old state without creating new ones, they committed a fatal error, as Japanese historians have frequently pointed out[19] — an error that a member of the Minamoto clan, the young Yoritomo, would not repeat.

Thus, an entire social order was on the verge of collapse during the crisis of the late twelfth century. As the great historian Ishimoda Shō wrote,

> The formation of the Middle Ages was the crumbling of ancient Japan. The decline of the world of antiquity was inseparable from the birth of a new order. The Middle Ages was the antithesis of ancient society; it repudiated it. At the same time, it could not arise anywhere but from it. The continuity between the two societies, simultaneous with their antagonism, explains the formation of the medieval world, which could develop only on the basis of a critique of the ancient society.[20]

Chapter 3

THE CRISIS IN THE LATE TWELFTH CENTURY

WAR

Minamoto no Yoritomo's strike against the local representative of the Taira in the Izu Peninsula, where he had been living in exile for about twenty years, was the result of careful planning. For a number of months, emissaries and travelers from Kyoto had been reporting tension in the court. A group of nobles, led by the retired emperor Go Shirakawa and supported by most of the large monasteries—including those on Mount Hiei and in Nara—were preparing to oppose the Taira, who had taken over most of the important functions in the court in the 1170s and created conflict and jealousy, especially among those who believed that they held hereditary power. The court nobles feared and mistrusted the newcomers from the warrior groups because they considered them of low birth. Nonetheless, they had to submit to the iron hand of Kiyomori, the clan chief: "Other men obeyed his commands as grass bends before the wind. People everywhere looked toward him for aid as soil welcomes moistening rain."[1]

In 1177, an attempted coup d'état failed, and the leaders of the plot, all of them close to Go Shirakawa, were executed or exiled. Kiyomori was planning to transfer the capital to one of his estates in Fukuhara, on the Inland Sea. According to the *Heike monogatari*, he wanted to shield the court from the violent demonstrations regularly held by the warrior-monks of the great Nara and Mount Hiei monasteries to protest political decisions that they felt were not in their interest. Today, however, historians believe that he wanted to place the new capital both within his sphere of influence and near a port in order to strengthen his control over the warrior groups of the Inland Sea and over trade with the Chinese merchants from the Song empire, a source of wealth and profits.[2] But this plan was wholeheartedly opposed, for the construction of a new capital would mean huge expenditures. In any case, in 1179, Kiyomori began a series of strikes against the opposition and placed the retired emperor under house arrest.

From then on, events moved quickly. In the fifth lunar month of the year corresponding to 1180, an imperial prince, Mochihito, issued a proclamation calling on forces hostile to the Taira, including the warriors linked as vassals to the Minamoto, to rise up against Kiyomori's dictatorship. The response was swift. Although Mochihito was killed, his emissaries were already on their way, carrying his message of rebellion to the provinces. This appeal, coming from an eminent person in the court, served as a justification and legitimization to those who had been looking for an opportunity to take up arms. Some monasteries, such as the Kōfukuji in Nara, mobilized their warrior-monks, and unrest in the provinces was widespread. Yoritomo, heir to the chief of the great Minamoto *bushidan*, felt that the moment had come to take revenge.

The three eventful months that followed the surprise attack at Izu added to the discontent in the eastern provinces. Hōjō Tokimasa had only thirty horsemen for his nighttime surprise attack on the residence of the governor's agent in Izu. Two weeks later, Yoritomo, with three hundred warriors, had to face the thousand men that the Taira vassals of the region had mobilized. The battle took place at Mount Ishibashi, near the site of today's Atami. Although Yoritomo was defeated, he managed to escape with the help of a long-standing network of accomplices among the people of his clan in southern Kanto and crossed the sea to the provinces east of what is now Tokyo Bay. In less than one month, Yoritomo was able to rally local warriors led by powerful lords, some of whom, such as the Chiba, were traditional vassals of the Minamoto. From all directions, warriors flocked to his side, and he soon found himself at the head of a sizable army. Ishii Susumu estimated that he had 27,000 men![3] On the sixth day of the tenth lunar month, barely fifty days after the Izu attack, Yoritomo marched triumphantly into Kamakura to give thanks to the god of war at the Hachiman Shrine as leader of the Minamoto clan.

At about the same time—in the fall of 1180—warrior uprisings broke out all over the country: in Kinai and along the Tōkaidō; in the mountainous province of Shinano, where the revolt was led by Yoritomo's cousin and rival, Kiso Yoshinaka; and in Kai Province, north of Mount Fuji, where the warriors of the small Takeda *bushidan* were restless. Given the scope of the revolts, the Taira decided to send an army from the capital to quash them. After a very difficult month's march, the army arrived near the Fuji River, just west of the Izu Peninsula, where Yoritomo's warriors, allied with reinforcements from the Takeda, awaited it. The first clash between the two camps resulted in little fighting. Indeed, since its departure from Kinai, the Taira's warriors had deserted in increasing numbers as they moved eastward. Then, faced with an enemy, they fled. According to the *Heike*, in the night, they confused the roosters' crowing with a surprise attack:

> [The Taira] could not retreat quickly enough. In their haste and hurry, he who took his bow forgot his arrows, he who took his arrows forgot his bow; one mounted someone else's horse and left that person his own horse; another jumped onto a horse that was tied and went endlessly in circles around the stake. The courtesans and pleasure girls whom they had sent for from the neighboring inns, some with their skulls cracked from a kick, others with their backs broken under the horses' hooves, cried and whimpered on all sides.[4]

After this decisive victory, Yoritomo wanted to enter Kyoto to pursue the remnants of the Taira army, but his highest-ranking vassals counseled him instead to return to Kamakura, consolidate his authority over the warriors of the east, and dispatch the *bushidan* of northern Kanto that had been indecisive or hostile, such as the Satake. Above all, he should reward the warriors who had rallied to his cause by confirming their rights to their estates or granting them lands confiscated from those whom they had defeated. Yoritomo followed the advice of the Minamoto chiefs.

The next two years were quiet. The Taira warded off what they perceived as their greatest threat, the discontented monks in the old capital (Nara), entrenched with their warrior-monks in the Kōfukuji and Tōdaiji monasteries, bastions of anti-Taira sentiment. To the great displeasure of the nobles at court, Taira warriors set fire to these venerable institutions: "If the warrior-monks be crushed, so be it! But must the monasteries also be destroyed?"[5]

Kiyomori died in early 1181, leaving the Taira clan with no real leader. Unrest swirled through Kyushu, and bands of armed pirates from around Kumano took advantage of the disarray to ravage the coasts of the Inland Sea. Yoritomo's cousin, Kiso Yoshinaka, managed to gain control of some of the provinces bordering the Japan Sea, and the power base shifted. Now Yoritomo ruled Kanto; Yoshinaka held the mountainous area around the Tōsandō; and the Taira still held Kinai and the western part of the country. In the distant provinces of Tōhoku, the descendants of the Kiyohara, who had taken the family name Fujiwara, carefully maintained their neutrality.

Things changed again in 1183 when the Taira decided to attack Yoshinaka, but they were severely beaten. They retreated to the western provinces, pursued by Yoshinaka, who met no resistance as he entered Kyoto. In their flight, the Taira swept up the young emperor Antoku, Kiyomori's grandson, and the three symbols of imperial legitimacy—the sword, the mirror, and the jewel. Then Yoshinaka made the mistake that Yoritomo had avoided after the battle at Mount Fuji. Once in Kyoto, what could he do there? His army of rebellious warriors, tempted by the booty, plundered as they pleased, and Yoshinaka was unable to control them. He rushed westward in pursuit of the Taira, but they were victorious on their home turf, and Yoshinaka was forced to retreat to Kyoto. Yoritomo now had a second chance.

The retired emperor Go Shirakawa was now rid of the Taira but had to put up with Yoshinaka's boorish soldiers in his city. He thus decided to make an official appeal to Yoritomo, who asked his brothers Noriyori and Yoshitsune to lead an army to the west. Yoritomo, however, stayed in Kamakura, seeing himself more as a politician and an organizer than a warlord. With a few battles, Yoshitsune made short work of Yoshinaka's last warriors, and Yoshinaka, defeated, committed suicide in early 1184. Then Yoshitsune decided to march immediately toward the western provinces, where the Taira were reassembling their forces and plotting their return to Kyoto. He won a brilliant tactical victory at Ichinotani, forcing the Taira to retreat to Yajima and Shikoku. Finally, in the spring of 1185, in a masterful campaign using blitzkrieg tactics, Yoshitsune definitively defeated the Taira, whose fleet, ambushed at Yajima, was completely destroyed at the naval battle of Dannoura. The Taira chiefs were killed or committed suicide, and the young emperor perished at sea. The Minamoto had finally eliminated their enemies. According to the *Heike monogatari*, there was no doubt that Kiyomori's outsize pride had been responsible for the disaster that befell the Taira: "The man who had held the whole country in the palm of his hand and executed and banished as he pleased . . . [had] no concern either for society or for individuals. There seemed no room for doubt that the evil deeds of a father must be visited on his offspring."[6]

The account of military events summarized here leaves a number of questions unanswered: What were Yoritomo's intentions in Kanto? What incited the warriors to wage war? Why were there times of intense activity and long periods of truce? How can the Minamoto's military superiority be explained?

FAVORABLE CONDITIONS IN THE EASTERN PROVINCES

The first factor in explaining this eventful history, with its spectacular reversals, is cyclical and related to climatic disturbances. Research conducted by historians studying the climate, particularly those specializing in dendrochronology (the study of growth rings in trees to date events and changes in environment), shows that the second half of the twelfth century was one of the hottest periods in Japan's history.[7] We now understand the effects of apparently tiny climatic variations on the precarious balance of a country with a traditional economy:

violent rains following a dry season produce floods, and food shortages—even famine—are the result, aggravated by epidemics quickly spreading among weakened populations. Phenomena similar to those well understood in medieval and modern Europe have been found in Japan. Famine was a recurrent calamity in every generation. Unfortunately, although the sources do not enable us to measure accurately the demographic consequences of these crises, contemporary accounts do reveal their frequency and their ultimate social repercussions.

In 1134, following strong rains that caused flooding, Kyoto suffered a famine, and its residents fell victim to an epidemic, probably exacerbated by malnutrition. In 1153–54, death prowled the city once again: this time it was another disease, perhaps smallpox, that mowed down the inhabitants. In the spring of 1154, crowds of people overwhelmed by adversity went to the Murasakino Shrine, on the northern outskirts of the city, to rid themselves of the demons that had apparently caused the disease. The ancient Japanese thought that illness was caused by evil spirits possessing the body and that these spirits could be exorcised by dancing. Men and women, commoners, nobles, and outcasts all gathered in front of the Murasakino Shrine, where they danced, accompanied by flutes, bells, and tambourines, and sang an old song:

Hama yasa kitaru	The flowers have bloomed
Yasuraya	As if everything is peaceful.
Hana yasa kiraruya	Have the flowers bloomed?
Yasurai hanaya	Are they flowers of peace?[8]

Young servants of the shrine, dressed in ceremonial robes, performed acrobatics while the crowd danced and stamped their feet on the ground to expel the demons. The dances lasted day and night. The people seemed to have gone mad, perhaps hoping that their madness would cure both fear and illness. But the authorities began to be concerned about these excesses, and the dances were finally banned by imperial edict.

Famine struck in 1181–82 and returned in 1231 and again in 1259. The poet and philosopher Fujiwara no Sadaie (Teika) recounted in his personal notes, Meigetsuki, that floods and typhoons destroyed the harvests in the fields in 1230. So as a hedge against future shortages, he had his servants plant wheat in the garden of his villa. The following year, as he had predicted, the famine returned. Bands of starving people crowded into the temples, hoping that the monks would distribute free food. Nobles were robbed on the roads. In the panic, thieves started fires to distract the authorities so that they could attack and pillage the estates of the wealthy. In the streets, bodies rotted; even the palace servants died. That year, one document noted that on an estate in Ise Province, sixty-two people died in ten days.[9]

A curious rumor ran through Kyoto: "Long ago, stones were thrown during festivals in the shrines. The bakufu has banned stone throwing, and this is why famine has broken out." The regent, Hōjō Yasutoki, forced to react to this silly rumor, stated that stone throwing (*tsubute*) was not actually banned but that it was forbidden to aim stones at someone because it might cause injury! The medievalist Amino Yoshihiko noted that Yasutoki was forced to justify official policy before crowds driven hysterical by their hardships.[10]

In these times of crisis, populations became difficult to control. Urban dwellers fled to the countryside in hopes of finding something to steal, or to the mountains, where it was still possible to survive by hunting and gathering berries and wild vegetables in season. Others went to the seashore to subsist on seaweed and shellfish. Meanwhile, rural dwellers flooded into the city, hoping that it held the key to survival. As the seat of political power and a symbol of wealth, the city fascinated people from the country, as did the rumors that a particular noble or monastery was handing out rice to the people. The authorities tried to restrain these movements of people, since by leaving their fields, the peasants put the harvest at risk and caused further rents in the social fabric. With the specter of death lurking, uncontrollable forces, menacing because of their sheer irrationality, seemed to well up from the depths of society.

In wetland rice-growing areas, very hot weather combined with drought has catastrophic consequences, since rice needs a great deal of water. Conversely, heat accompanied by humidity leads to abundant harvests. It seems that the years between 1167 and 1176, which more or less corresponded to the height of the Taira regime, were hot, humid years with good harvests. However, 1177 to 1186, a time of acute political crisis, were hot but very dry in Kinai and the west. Under these conditions, it was impossible to raise rice.

In Kanto, the summers had a normal level of humidity and the eastern warriors were ready for war as soon as the crops were in. In the west, however, the harvest was poor, and the Taira army was not well prepared. Because of the poor harvest in the summer of 1180, famine broke out in Kinai in 1181. In the *Hōjōki*, Kamo no Chōmei recalls this catastrophic year:

> There was a famine in the country . . . a most terrible thing. A drought persisted through the spring and summer, while the autumn and winter brought storms and floods. One disaster followed another, and the grains failed to ripen. . . . Some of the people as a result abandoned their lands and crossed into other provinces; some forgot their homes and went to live in the mountains. . . . Many beggars lined the roads, and their doleful cries filled the air.[11]

The harvest in the autumn of 1181 was as bad as the preceding one. Thus the situation, already abysmal, became tragic. In addition, political crisis was dividing the country, and there was no question of sending provisions from regions where the harvest had been good. Malnourished peasants no longer paid their rent, and then they were hit again, by an epidemic.

> It was thought that the new year would see an improvement, but it brought instead the additional affliction of epidemics. . . . The people were starving, and with the passage of days approached the extremity, like fish gasping in insufficient water. . . . Overwhelmed by misery, they would walk in a stupor, only presently to collapse. The number of those who died of starvation outside the gates or along the roads may not be reckoned. There being no one even to dispose of the bodies, a stench filled the whole world, and there were many sights of decomposing bodies too horrible to behold. Along the banks of the Kamo River there was not even room for horses and cattle to pass. . . . In an attempt to determine how many people had died, [the priests] made a count during the fourth and fifth months, and found within the boundaries of the capital over 42,300 corpses lying in the streets. What would the total have been had it included all who died . . . both within the city and in the suburbs? And what if all the provinces of Japan had been included?[12]

In the west, the warriors could barely summon the energy to fight, so 1181 and 1182 were years of forced truce. Consequently, Yoritomo was able to fortify his political base in Kanto without opposition. Likewise, from the mountains of Shinano, Yoshinaka extended his influence to the Hokuriku plain on the Japan Sea. It was not until the spring of 1183 that the Taira could react. But Yoshinaka defeated them and moved to Kyoto with his mountain warriors, who saw this adventure as tantamount to a raid on the capital. At the end of the summer of 1183, however, they began to drift home to help with the harvest on their estates. Whereas in the spring of 1183, Yoshinaka had seemed all-powerful, six months later, he was only a shadow of himself, "barbarian though [he] seemed."[13] Indeed, Yoshitsune's army, marching from Kanto, swept Yoshinaka aside with no problem and then conquered the Taira. But the Minamoto showed their prudence once again by not pursuing their adversaries. Instead, they consolidated the political base of their newly won hegemony in Kinai by rallying the local warriors to their cause, making them vassals of Yoritomo, and promising to reward them for their support. The next campaign took place the following year, 1185.

The warriors left for battle with their own retinue—servants, grooms, porters, pages, and others—and horses. The question of provisions thus became central as the campaign dragged on, for each warrior had to provide food and supplies for both his men and his animals. Furthermore, these warriors had to return to their estates when the crops were harvested and the rents were paid. Therefore, war could not begin until after the harvest, and only on condition that it was a good one. The duration of combat also was limited, and the generals' room for maneuver was reduced. When the lines of communication were stretched thin, when warriors found themselves in unknown or hostile territory and harvest time was approaching, they felt an irresistible urge to return home, and armies dissolved. This explains the apparent chaos of military campaigns in the Middle Ages, of the wars between the Taira and Minamoto and between Ashikaga Takauji and the generals of the Southern Court in the mid-fourteenth century.

In late 1184, Noriyori, one of Yoritomo's brothers, was waging war at the western end of the main island, trying to link up with the warrior groups of Kyushu who had sided with the Minamoto. His army, far from its base, was not advancing and soon found itself in a precarious situation. Noriyori sent a desperate message to Yoritomo in Kamakura, the content of which was reported in *Azuma kagami*, a thirteenth-century historical chronicle: "Because of the lack of food, the men were divided; each pined for his country and more than half of them decided to desert to go home."[14] This episode shows the limits of the supposedly exemplary loyalty of the Japanese warrior: as soon as the going got rough, he was ready to betray and desert. What attracted him was the prospect of victory and rewards; he was, above all, an opportunist. The poor climatic conditions that affected central and western Japan thus played into Yoritomo's hands by helping slow, or even stop, his enemy's advance. Conversely, because the Taira's territorial bases and networks of alliances were in those regions suffering most from the food crisis, they were the losers.

TO THE DEATH FOR THE ESTATE!

Economic hardships in the central and western provinces linked to a series of poor harvests cannot, by themselves, explain the Minamoto's victories. The reasons for Yoritomo's success were also structural; that is, the organization of warrior society in eastern Japan played a decisive role.

Who were the warriors of the eastern provinces?

Just before the battle at Mount Fuji, Koremori, the commander in chief of the Taira army, asked Saitō Sanemori, a warrior from Musashi Province in the east who served as his guide, to tell him about the fierce warriors of the eight provinces of Kanto:

> "Tell me, Sanemori, how many men in the Eight Provinces can wield a strong bow as well as you do?" . . .
>
> "Any number of warriors in the east can equal that. . . . A strong bow is held to be one that requires six stout men for the stringing. One of those powerful archers can easily penetrate two or three suits of armor when he shoots.

"Every big landholder commands at least five hundred horsemen. Once a rider mounts, he never loses his seat; however rugged the terrain he gallops over, his horse never falls. If he sees his father or son cut down in battle, he rides over the dead body and keeps on fighting. In west-country battles, a man who loses a father leaves the field and is seen no more until he has made offerings and completed a mourning period; someone who loses a son is too overwhelmed with grief to resume the fight at all. When westerners run out of commissariat rice, they stop fighting until after the fields are planted and harvested. They think summertime is too hot for battle, and wintertime too cold. Easterners are entirely different. . . .

"I don't expect to return to the capital alive from the fight we face." All the Taira warriors trembled at his words.[15]

Even if the *Heike monogatari* exaggerated Sanemori's words, it was clear that the warriors of eastern Japan were skilled horsemen and archers, fierce and tireless. In addition, the powerful daimyo, in charge of huge areas of cultivated land (*myō*), could mobilize large fighting forces.

The warriors of the late twelfth century, especially those in the east, had three functions. First, they were low-ranking officials in provincial or estate administrations, and in this sense they were part of the state bureaucracy. Their office was "public" if exercised on a public estate (*kokugaryo*) or "private" if exercised on an estate belonging to a noble of the court or a Buddhist or Shinto religious institution (*shōen*). Second, they ran agricultural operations as descendants of local gentry who, in the late eleventh and early twelfth centuries, had cleared or replanted the land. They lived on their land, sometimes alongside the peasants, as landowners—although this term may seem inappropriate, since the notion of property in medieval Japan was not the same as it is today. Third, they were military leaders, specialists in combat, who had been professional soldiers for several generations.

In the eastern provinces, warriors lived in manors built on hills and surrounded by palisades and ditches or moats. Inside the manor walls were the residences of the master and his companions, stables, barns and kennels, a weapons depot, a forge, weaving workshops, and outbuildings where workmen and servants lived in slavelike conditions. Around the manor were pastures for the horses; farther out were the lands where the master and his companions hunted.[16] Leaseholds were farmed by relatively well-off peasants living in houses (*zaike*) who hired laborers called *genin*, "inferiors." In the western provinces, they often were also *myōshu*—managers of tax-generating cultivated lands who were responsible for collecting rents.

The lord's manor was thus in the middle of lands farmed by peasants. The ensemble formed a unit, a small-scale center of production. In the weaving workshops, where the women worked, ordinary clothes were made, as were luxurious silk kimono often used as gifts or even to pay rent. As in the West, the women made the valuable fabrics and were, to quote Jacques le Goff, "the textile workers of the feudal group." Around the agricultural area, the warriors trained in riding, archery, and sword fighting. The lord of the manor commanded the armed force, which enabled him to control the peasants, oversee the tax collection and the payment of rents, and defend the estate against attacks.

At first, the lords (or their forebears) held a bureaucratic position in the provincial administration, which helped them obtain authorization to develop uncultivated public land. In more practical terms, this meant that they could draft peasants to do the hard labor of clearing land, digging wells and canals, and building dikes and walls and that they could redirect water to flood the new rice paddies.

The lord received a three-year exemption from paying the annual rents on the newly developed lands. But after this period was over, he had to levy on the peasants the taxes that had to be paid to the state. This was why the lord tried to obtain an official position in the tax district where his lands were, such as the office of *gunji*, district chief. Once he had secured such a position, he was responsible for imposing taxes and organizing corvées in his region. The lord's domain thus extended well beyond his own estate. He was compensated for this responsibility by supplementary tax exemptions on his own land, and he was authorized to keep for himself part of the public rents he collected. He interacted with and commanded the peasants in the environs, whom he came to see as "his" men. On both the political and economic fronts, obtaining administrative responsibility in the zone where his property was could only help the lord strengthen his hold on the land.

Over time, the lord established his brothers, sons, and other relatives in strategic spots in the countryside. Small manors were built, and members of his extended family moved in. Nonetheless, they recognized the supremacy of the head of the family in a united community of blood ties. The lord remained at the head of the main family (*honke*), and members of the other families formed secondary branches (*bunke*). This *sōryōsei*, "system of global control" (by the family head), enabled the fiefdoms to be expanded and their domination over the territory to be consolidated. It resembled the hierarchy of feudal times in northern France, as the law historian Nakada Kaoru noted in the early twentieth century.[17] The head of the family's main branch was responsible for ancestor worship and maintained the family altar. This vast clanlike family organization was also a warrior grouping that accepted the suzerainty of its leader. As the holder of a title and the head of a large economic producer, the lord was a warlord, and his position as the family head gave him the right—or privilege— to lead his men in battle.

As the historian Ishii Susumu has shown, the manor was at once a protected defensive unit, a center of agricultural and craft activities, and the starting point from which the lord extended his domination over the surrounding territory.[18] The warrior was inclined to invest in land in order to increase his sphere of influence. This inclination, however, had its limits—the properties of other lords. Another obstacle was the governor or his agent. In effect, the governor— a noble of the court or his delegate, and thus his client—could appoint, maintain in office, and fire the members of the provincial administration. If the lord of an estate became too powerful and was no longer trusted or if other local lords became jealous of his influence and conspired against him, he could lose some of his land. Or he might have to resign as district chief, and his office could be given to a rival lord. Thus deprived of the right to raise public rents for the administration, this lord would be powerless if a rival intruded on what he considered his property. In other words, the local lord's power was closely linked to the bureaucratic title he held, and the governor or his delegate could take away this power. This was a constant threat. If the lord had a disagreement with the head of the local administration, he would have to back down and hope that the appointment of a new administrator would be more favorable to him. He could appeal to local justice in the case of obvious aggression, but the outcome was never certain. Even being patient was difficult. Therefore, it is not surprising that some particularly powerful lords were tempted to use force to fend off neighbors' intrusions on their property. Intimidation and violence thus became more common. Everything depended on local power relations and the amount of support that the governor or his agent could count on from the court.

Rather than stand by as outside forces took over his land, the owner would sometimes prefer to "commend" all or part of it to a prestigious person or institution with influence in the court (the retired emperor, a Fujiwara dignitary, a major monastery or shrine, and the like)—in other words, to obtain protection from his superiors. The local lord's property then became a *shōen*, benefiting from tax exemptions or, sometimes, immunities. For example, the Chiba in Kanto—who were, despite their Taira ancestry, longtime loyal vassals of the Minamoto—traditionally held the office of district administrator of Sōma in Shimōsa. They handed over the entire district, in which they had great influence, to the great Ise Shrine, and Sōma became a *mikurya* (term referring to an estate belonging to a particular shrine).[19]

When a property was "commended," the head of the estate became its resident manager, a hereditary title. As the military steward (*jitō*) for the nominal owner of the land, the local lord made a compromise: he preserved the integrity of his property and continued to exercise real control over it, but he had to pay part of his revenue to the absentee owner and undergo inspection tours when the owner decided to send someone to look over his real estate. In fact, the steward actually could remain the master of his domain as long as the new owner lived far away—as was the case in Kanto. Nothing fundamental changed in local power relations except that the lord, protected by the influence of an eminent owner in the court, was now beyond the governor's grasp.

But what would happen if the power relations in the court in Kyoto changed and the owner of the estate lost his influence? He would find that his control over his land had once again been put at risk. This was what happened when the Taira suddenly rose to power in the court after 1160. In just a few years, the factions and the political landscape in the capital had changed. The Taira temporarily claimed sovereignty over some thirty provinces, which enabled them not only to appropriate part of the revenues but also to appoint trusted lieutenants to key positions in the provincial administrations. The local lords had to be constantly on their guard and keep abreast of political developments at court. For many reasons, their room for maneuver vis-à-vis the provincial governors and their agents remained limited.

Although these local lords held administrative positions, because they were more warriors than bureaucrats, the head of the Minamoto *bushidan*—the suzerain of most warriors in Kanto—suddenly seemed to offer a possible recourse as the only authority who might let them enjoy their properties in peace. This was what the warriors felt on the eve of their revolt: "In the province, we must obey the governor's agent. In the estates, we must obey the managers [*azukaridokoro*] sent by the eminent landlords. We are buried under rents and corvées. No more rest, day or night."[20]

Despite the defeat in 1160, the Minamoto clan was regarded highly by warriors in the region. By proposing to unify them under his banner against the common enemy, the Taira, Yoritomo was thus responding to their anxiety and discontent. It was not by chance that everything started with the attack on the manor of the provincial governor's agent in Izu, for he was a vassal of the Taira. Yoritomo's first act of rebellion had an added value: he attacked not the first Taira warrior he encountered but the one responsible for administering the province.

After the defeat at Mount Ishibashi, Yoritomo came close to catastrophe.[21] But with the help of the Miura warrior clan, he escaped across the bay to Awa Province, where he had arrested all the representatives of the court under the governor's agent, that is, those sent from Kyoto. He then forced the administration's local, low-ranking bureaucrats to recognize his authority and work for him. Next, he confiscated the properties of the warriors who had opposed him and validated the properties of those who had supported him. Finally, he gave the warriors who had been his most loyal supporters the lands confiscated from the defeated warriors.

Some essential aspects of the future shogun's policy were evident in the way in which he proceeded in Awa.[22] After each campaign, Yoritomo integrated the local warriors into the Minamoto *bushidan*. He provided written assurance that they would have "peaceful possession" (*ando*) of their stated rights to the estates that they had inherited from their forebears, and he compensated them for their services and bravery by granting them estates confiscated from the enemy.[23]

Assured of their rights to the land and granted new estates—these were decisive motivations for warriors, and they lined up under the Minamoto banner, feeling that the lands cleared by their ancestors did in fact belong to them. Their clans often bore the name of those lands—Hōjō, Miura, Ōba, and Chiba were place-names before they were warrior-family names—and the warriors did not want to lose them. Indeed, if the outcome of war looked unfavorable, many warriors resorted to treason to guarantee perpetual title to the estate on which their family lived. Most of the 3,000 Taira warriors commanded by Ōba Kagechika after the battle of Mount Ishibashi were to fight the Minamoto army in the following weeks when it appeared that Yoritomo had the stronger force. Kazusa Hirotsune, an eminent functionary and powerful warrior of Kazusa Province, was to lead the battle against Yoritomo and his "20,000" warriors. But instead he defected to the Minamoto side without a fight, delivering his province and warriors to his new suzerain.

One day, Yoritomo was surprised when Hirotsune spoke to him without bothering to dismount from his horse. Hirotsune told him, "The Kazusa have never saluted anyone for at least three generations."[24] This anecdote, showing the independent nature of the Kanto warriors, exemplifies the relationship between the suzerain, Minamoto no Yoritomo, and his principal vassals. They were free men, and they knew that Yoritomo owed his success to their help. "Who made you duke? Who made you king?" they might have asked. The military chiefs, the daimyo, did not hesitate to disagree with one another. They needed a leader to settle their disputes and with enough authority to recognize their power, but they no longer wanted to depend on the goodwill of the men in the capital. An egalitarian spirit and pride were even stronger among the low-ranking warriors, who did not have the means to mobilize hundreds or thousands of horsemen and had to fight on the frontlines.

One example is often cited (from the *Azuma kagami*): Kumagai Naozane was a low-ranking warrior from Musashi Province who rallied to Yoritomo's side late, after the battle of the Fuji River. Although Yoritomo recognized Naozane's right to the Kumagai estate after his exploits in the battles against the Satake in northern Kanto, Naozane was a man of little means. One day, Yoritomo and his vassals were practicing their archery and ordered him to set up the targets. Naozane retorted to Yoritomo, "All vassals have the same rank. Setting up the targets is the work of foot soldiers. I am a horseman, and I draw a bow. This is unfair. I will not obey the order." Disturbed by his loyal supporter's reaction, Yoritomo felt bound to explain that setting up the targets was not a degrading task, and he confiscated some land from Naozane for his insubordinate response."[25]

Low-ranking warriors formed the frontlines in battle. For these men, whose sliver of land was always under threat by a more powerful neighbor, obtaining a letter of confirmation from the Minamoto suzerain was essential. They did not have the means, as did daimyo such as the Kazusa, to go to war with hundreds of soldiers; instead, they went alone, accompanied by one or two sons or brothers. The only way they had to gain Yoritomo's recognition as vassals was to distinguish themselves in battle, for courage would be rewarded. On the eve of the battle of Ichinotani, a low-ranking warrior, Narita Gorō, declared outright, "Don't be in a hurry to attack first. . . . Nobody will know how you acquitted yourself unless you have friends watching in the rear. What would be the use of dashing to your death in the middle of an enemy host?" In other words, a warrior who risked his life with no one watching was stupid! Kumagai Naozane summarized his philosophy of battle in a similar way: "Fame depends on the adversary. It does not come from meeting just any fellow who happens along."[26]

Being noticed in battle and defeating a high-ranking enemy — these were the objectives.[27] If the low-ranking warriors of Kanto were fierce fighters, it was because it represented their only way to ascend the social ladder. For them, *isshokenmei* — risking one's life to keep (or expand) one's estate — was the stake in these wars. In modern Japanese, this expression is used to mean ardor, zeal, and focusing one's energy, in the image of the warriors of Kanto who risked their lives in battle to hold onto their land.[28]

In western Japan, the social situation of the warrior class was different for several reasons. In Kinai and the regions around the Inland Sea, the power and domination of the court nobles and religious institutions were manifestly greater. The warriors were samurai in the original sense of the term — armed servants of the nobility, responsible for guarding the nobles' manors and providing an escort. They fought on command, and because many did not have an estate of their own to defend, they were not as independent as their counterparts in the east. When they did own a piece of land, it was generally smaller and in a narrow valley. They did not resemble the local chiefs who controlled a piece of land on which peasant labor worked, even if this was sometimes the case. Rather, their power was usually based not on property but on a network of links with craftsmen who saw them as leaders and whom they ultimately defended. Those people who made their living from the sea — gatherers of seafood and seaweed, salt makers, fishermen, seamen — had patrons who specialized in weaponry, who ultimately established a feudal domination over their communities. Relations of this type were found among certain groups of artisans, fishermen, and suppliers of fresh produce for the emperor's table.[29]

In both west and east, warriors formed groups for the purpose of combat. But the groups in the west were quite different from those in the east. The warrior groups in Kanto used a hierarchical system that meant that their descendants and extended family members who had been "taken care of" on the estate owed absolute obedience to their suzerain, who led them into battle. In the west, the relations among warriors were based on matrilineal links that were more horizontal and resulted in alliances among warriors living in a particular region rather than a vassal grouping. On a military level, it might seem that this organization would be less powerful.

The social position of warriors in the western provinces seemed much less precarious than that of warriors in the east, where the hostility between the local gentry and representatives of the court nobility had reached a peak. Building on favorable economic circumstances, Yoritomo took over the leadership of discontented warriors in eastern Japan at a moment when the political power in Kyoto was in full crisis. What were his objectives?

ESTABLISHMENT OF THE BAKUFU

Japanese historians do not agree on the date when the new regime took over, for in fact, there were three distinct periods in the process of establishing the bakufu.

First, following his early victories, including the decisive one at Mount Fuji, Yoritomo returned to Kamakura, where he had a new residence constructed. A ceremony in late 1180 was an occasion for gathering together his principal retainers (*gokenin*). Acting as a feudal suzerain, Yoritomo gave himself the title lord of Kamakura (Kamakura *dono*). His 311 supporters, lined up in two rows, had to write their names in a register kept by the head of the Bureau of Samurai (Samurai dokoro), which had recently been created to govern the warrior vassals. And acting as a virtual ruler, Yoritomo appointed many of his retainers to provincial administrative positions and others as estate stewards. By placing his warriors in positions that fell under the sole authority of the court or of eminent landowners, Yoritomo was acting in utter contempt of the law, taking imperial prerogatives for himself, and placing himself in a position of power rivaling that of the court. In short, he was creating a small independent state in the east. Some historians see Yoritomo's "crowning" in Kamakura in 1180 as marking the birth of the new regime.

During this period, which lasted until autumn of 1183, Yoritomo's legitimacy was not very strong. He was only the chief of a huge group of warriors, and his only official authority flowed from the call to arms issued by Prince Mochihito in early 1180. Yoritomo stressed this proclamation and claimed to be acting in Mochihito's name. But as soon as Mochihito died and his plot failed, the court nobility, still under the sway of the Taira, branded Yoritomo as a common rebel and, furthermore, declared him to be an enemy. Under these conditions, he had little choice but to form a new regime. His vassal Kazusa Hirotsune proclaimed that in Kanto, orders from outside would no longer be obeyed: "Why worry about something so insignificant as the imperial court? We live in the east, and so who can command us?"[30]

In 1181, the name of the era was changed to Kyoto. But Yoritomo refused to adopt the court's official calendar; that is, he rejected Kyoto's supremacy. It was a symbolic act, but it presented Kamakura as an autonomous power, even though Yoritomo was not interested in going that far. According to the *Gyokuyō* (the personal notes of Kujō Kanezane, a court noble and future regent), Yoritomo maintained a secret correspondence with the retired emperor Go Shirakawa, in which he spoke of his loyalty and his desire simply to reestablish his clan's position by ridding the court of the abhorred Taira.

Meanwhile, Yoritomo was consolidating his hold on the provinces under his control in Kanto and the regions east of the Tōkaidō. In 1180, his vassals began to build residences in Kamakura, where a sort of shogunal court was being established. Roads were built between Kamakura and the seats of provincial administrations in Kanto.

The second period began in the autumn of 1183. After the hard years of poor harvests, the court nobility and the population of Kinai could no longer bear Yoshinaka's arrogance and his warriors acting like boors in the capital. Negotiations were held between retired emperor Go Shirakawa and Yoritomo during the time that Yoshinaka was fighting the Taira. The court was in a truly difficult situation: "With all the checkpoints closed, those in the provinces could deliver neither official tax goods nor private rents, and people of all degrees in the capital resembled fish in shallow water. Such were the parlous circumstances under which the old year [1183] ended."[31] Finally, Go Shirakawa promulgated an edict known as the Edict of the Tenth Month (of 1183). According to the *Gyokuyō*, this document more or less said, "In the provinces around the Tōkaidō and Tōsandō Roads [that is, the regions controlled by both Yoritomo and Yoshinaka], rents collected in the past must be brought in again. Yoritomo is charged with applying this edict."[32]

At the same time, Yoritomo shed his dishonorable title of "enemy of the court" and regained his fifth court rank, of which he had been stripped in 1160 when he was just a child, after the events of the Heiji era. The last sentence of the text is particularly important: Yoritomo was charged with applying an imperial edict in the provinces in question. Not only was the lord of Kamakura recognized, but he also was to enforce an imperial edict in the eastern part of the country. Kyoto and Kamakura had reached an accommodation: Kamakura would collect the rents due to the court nobles from public and private estates, and in exchange, the court would recognize the supremacy of the Minamoto throughout the eastern part of the country and thus legitimize the ousting of all rival warrior groups. Collecting the rents without which it could not subsist was the court's main objective. For this to happen, there had to be order. With Yoritomo on the court's side, the threat of secession suddenly faded. Yoritomo would not found an independent monarchy in the east; he would be the delegate of imperial authority. The bakufu, a form of political power unique to Japan, was formed on the basis of this compromise in the autumn of 1183.[33]

From the point of view of the court and Go Shirakawa, the advantages were not insignificant: the east, which had seemed lost, returned to Kyoto's orbit, and the public and private rents would flow in once again. For Yoritomo, official recognition of his hegemony by the court brought great relief, for it was proof of the immense prestige that the court still had. The emperor, even if he was a retired emperor acting in the name of the titular emperor, benefited from an almost religious aura, a magical and sacred power that was not easily circumvented. But Yoritomo now had extended his reach: by means of the autumn 1183 compromise, he obtained a sort of military imperium over one-third of the empire. Although he commanded the army in the eastern provinces in the name of the emperor, no one was fooled. Yoritomo was not simply a new type of high-ranking functionary; he had gained this power by armed victory, and no one, not even the emperor, could make him step down except by force.

In the fall of 1183, Yoritomo's prerogatives began to expand. After the defeat of Yoshinaka in early 1184, he was officially charged by the court with pursuing the Taira in the west. Following the battle of Ichinotani, he obtained a new concession from the emperor: he was the only one authorized to use arms throughout the country to subdue warriors who tried to use violence or usurp titles. Yoritomo thus had a hold on the entire warrior class, not just on his own warriors, and he incorporated them into the Minamoto *bushidan*, which became, in effect, a state army.[34] In the same year, he established the Bureau of Administration and Finance and the Chamber of Inquiries, a court of justice that ruled on conflicts among followers of the lord of Kamakura.[35]

As a sign of these new times, Yoritomo had Kazusa Hirotsune, whose mistrust of the court and insolent behavior exasperated him now that he had made his peace with Kyoto, arrested and executed. Yoritomo, the "first among equals" of the Kanto warriors, was becoming a despot.

Finally in 1185, after the historic victory of the Minamoto over the Taira, relations quickly deteriorated between the lord of Kamakura and his half brother Yoshitsune, who, as a young victorious general, had some prestige of his own. Yoshitsune may have been a brilliant military strategist, but he was a political dunce. He was manipulated by the retired emperor, who saw him as someone capable of stemming Yoritomo's growing power and so heaped honors on him. The tension between the brothers quickly grew into open conflict. But Go Shirakawa, an expert on court intrigues, did not understand warrior society well. Yoshitsune was only a general, not a suzerain, and the warriors refused to follow him. Without an army, he was compelled to flee and take refuge in Tōhoku with the Fujiwara lords of the northern provinces.

By supporting Yoshitsune too openly, Go Shirakawa had put himself in a weak position. Yoritomo took advantage of this by extending his prerogatives in the court even further. In late 1185, the edict of the Bunji era gave him authorization to appoint his vassals as *shugo*, protectors of a province or provincial military governors, and as *jitō*, military stewards of estates.[36] The goals were simple: to maintain order, to control overly disruptive local warriors, and to collect the rents. Yoritomo usually appointed loyal local warriors to these new positions. He also attempted to gain control over the lower-ranking provincial administrators of the public estates and imposed on Go Shirakawa a council of nobles partial to Kamakura, led by the imperial regent Kujō Kanezane.

Many Japanese medievalists feel that the 1185 edict, which was issued a few months after the destruction of the Taira *bushidan*, marked the real beginning of the bakufu. In 1189, Yoritomo had his men attack the Fujiwara in the north, and afterward, all the provinces in Tōhoku were under his rule. Officially, his powers now extended throughout Japan. The following year, he went to Kyoto for the first time and was received at the court—a major concession. Yoritomo's powers, up to then granted temporarily during a crisis situation, were confirmed definitively and became hereditary. After Go Shirakawa died in 1192, the regent Kujō Kanezane had Yoritomo appointed—in the name of the young emperor— to the official position of *seii tai shōgun*, the ancient title of "barbarian-subduing generalissimo" that was conferred on the commander responsible for repressing the revolts of the Ezo people, who lived in the eastern and northern provinces and did not recognize the court's authority. Although the title of shogun did not add anything to Yoritomo's real power—he had several other titles—it did mark him as the person who exercised military power in Japan in the name of the emperor. The bakufu founded by Minamoto no Yoritomo between 1180 and 1192 was to constitute the government's institutional framework, ensuring the warrior classes of political domination of the country for almost seven centuries. The system was not completely abolished until 1867.

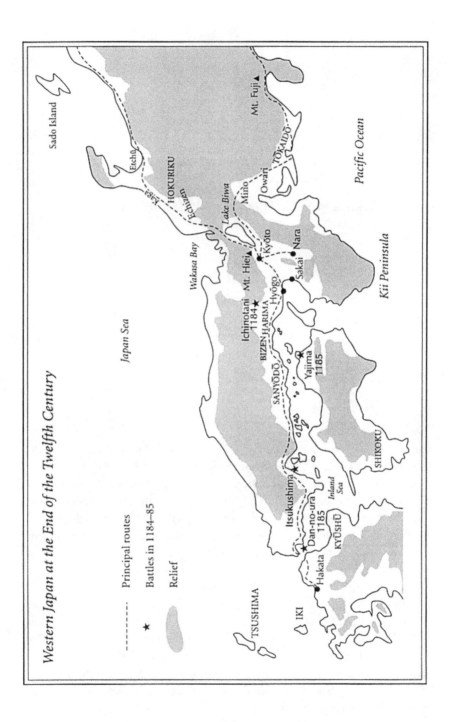

Western Japan at the End of the Twelfth Century

Principal routes
★ Battles in 1184–85
Relief

Sado Island

Japan Sea

Echo

HOKURIKU
Echizen
Wakasa Bay
Lake Biwa
Mino
Owari
TOKAIDŌ
Mt. Fuji

Kyōto
Mt. Hiei
Nara
Sakai
Hyōgo

Ichinotani
1184 ★
BIZEN HARIMA
SANYŌDŌ

Yajima
1185 ★

Itsukushima ★

Dan-no-ura
1185 ★

Hakata

KYŪSHŪ

Inland
Sea

SHIKOKU

Kii Peninsula

Pacific Ocean

TSUSHIMA

◁ IKI

Chapter 4

KAMAKURA: THE WARRIOR REGIME

Founded by Minamoto no Yoritomo following epic battles and after a decade of social and political crisis, the bakufu in Kamakura was the first locus of power in Japanese history established outside the central provinces of the Kinai and away from the imperial court. The upper ranks of the warrior class turned Kamakura into a true political and cultural capital that often rivaled Kyoto in the thirteenth century before the "old capital" regained its hegemony in the following century. This period, which began around 1185 and ended abruptly in 1333 with the destruction of the regime by the descendants of the very people who founded it, might well be called the Kamakura century.

Although the period began and ended in war, it also was a time of relative civil peace. Notwithstanding the bloody conflicts when the regime began, this peace was the result of a compromise between the court nobility and the warrior classes, notably those in the east, who dominated the bakufu's institutions. It can also be credited to the political wisdom of the *shikken* (shogunal regents) of the Hōjō family, who dominated the political scene in Kamakura throughout the period. Until 1284, when Tokimune died, the Hōjō were composed of people with a great political sense, who left their mark on the century. The Kamakura century could also, therefore, be called the Hōjō century.

THE RISE OF THE HŌJŌ FAMILY

When Yoritomo died in 1199, many questions arose. Could the new regime survive the death of its charismatic founder? Could the shogun remain an all-powerful figure, a despot reigning over his vassals? Or would the vassals force a new distribution of power? Would the court nobility accept the new power relations imposed by the compromise of 1185, even though Yoritomo's heir was only seventeen years old? Would the new retired emperor, Go Toba, abide by the decisions made in Kamakura?

The twenty years between the death of the first shogun and the military defeat of Go Toba's supporters in 1221 were filled with tension and power struggles—years of crises, plots, and assassinations, testifying to the bitterness of the conflicts. In Kamakura, the Hōjō family quickly came to be seen as the main beneficiary of these often bloody incidents.[1]

Who were the Hōjō? In the mid-twelfth century, they were vassals of the Taira and obscure bureaucrats in the local government of Izu, a province where they owned an estate. In 1160, they found themselves the guardians of the young Yoritomo, who had been rescued by Taira Kiyomori and placed under house arrest. In those times, the imprisonment of opponents and criminals was common in the Izu Peninsula. Yoritomo grew up among the Hōjō, and in 1177 he married one of the household's daughters, Hōjō Masako. They had a number of children, including two sons. In 1180, Yoritomo took up arms with the blessing of his father-in-law, Tokimasa, who thereby betrayed the confidence of the Taira. Tokimasa played an important role during the war years. He was an implacable politician who negotiated the famous Bunji edict with the court in 1184. His daughter, Masako, had a strong personality and was an adviser to her husband. After his death, she played a central role in the bakufu as a sort of queen mother who ruled over her husband's vassals and sons. Indeed, until her death in 1225, she was the true leader of the regime.

The character of Masako, the nun-shogun (*ama shōgun*), as she was called, gives us a good picture of the status of women of the warrior classes in the early Middle Ages. Masako continued her husband's work after his death, following in the path of other women of the warrior classes who often assumed their men's leadership of estates and clans when they died. As mistresses, nurses, wives, and widows, they were central to all political maneuvers. Whereas women in the aristocracy had no real power or influence—except literary—and were only pawns in power struggles, women in the warrior classes often acted as interested parties in the early Kamakura period, taking an active role in political circles and promoting the careers of their sons or protégés. Although they were excluded from official positions, they nevertheless did have real power—and, in Masako's case, a feared power.

Masako began her political career by eliminating her own son, Yoriie, in

1203. This young man, tyrannical and sickly, was manipulated by the Hiki clan, a powerful vassal group in Kanto. Because Yoritomo had been raised by a nurse from the Hiki family, to whom he felt a filial gratitude, he insisted that his oldest son also be raised by a woman of the Hiki family. Later, Yoriie married a Hiki woman, with whom he had a son. A fierce battle for control of the bakufu then broke out between the Hiki and the Hōjō families. Masako and her father took the initiative and had the vassal warriors of the Hiki massacred, along with Yoriie's young son. Yoriie himself was deposed and died a few months later, no doubt assassinated by a hit man hired by the Hōjō.

Masako then installed as shogun her second son, Sanetomo, whose nurse had been a Hōjō, Masako's younger sister. In 1205, she had her own father, Tokimasa, arrested; besotted with his latest young wife, he had let his family's interests slide. Then in 1213, Masako and her brother Yoshitoki led a coup d'état against Wada Yoshimori, of the Miura clan, who held the key position of chief of the Bureau of Samurai, which controlled the bakufu's vassals. After they eliminated Wada Yoshimori and his supporters—around 170 men from southern Kanto who were hostile to the Hōjō—Masako and Yoshitoki seized their estates. The Hōjō clan, whose power was linked mainly to Masako's position but whose economic foundations were fragile, thereby expanded its authority by broadening its territorial base, as a large number of estates around Kamakura were now controlled by the Hōjō or their private vassals.[2]

This series of coups propelled Hōjō Yoshitoki, Masako's brother and chief of the Hōjō clan, into a position of power within the bakufu. Yoshitoki became chief of the Bureau of Samurai and the Bureau of Administration and Finance, and he took the title of *shikken*, regent of the shogun, through which the Hōjō were to exercise real power in Kamakura.

Weak willed, sensitive, sickly, and ill at ease in Kamakura, the third shogun, Minamoto no Sanetomo, inherited none of the political skills of his father, Yoritomo, and his mother, Masako. Rather, he had other talents, being an excellent writer of *waka*-style poems. In fact, Teika, one of the great poets of that time, recognized him as one of his best disciples. The retired emperor Go Toba, himself a lover of poetry, contacted the young shogun, and they maintained a literary correspondence. Though fascinated by the world of the imperial court, Sanetomo was a dreamer, and political intrigues interested him not at all. He refused to marry a woman from a vassal family and wed instead a court princess who was a cousin of the retired emperor. This marriage, which led to a rapprochement between Kyoto and the bakufu, was not, however, appreciated by certain retainers. Recall that Go Toba was the leader of the anti-Kamakura faction in the court, and so Sanetomo might have been manipulated by Go Toba and the revanchist nobles. Furthermore, the literary friendship between the retired emperor and the young shogun might have been a cover for a conspiracy against Kamakura.

Sanetomo was horrified by the idea of being in the grip of a power struggle:[3]

O! These roaring waves
Unfurling from the sea
Onto the shore
In a tumult of tears and ruptures,
And spattering![4]

All of Sanetomo's ancestors had been famous warriors whose heroic exploits were sung in the "battle accounts" that proliferated in the early Middle Ages, and so the young shogun seemed to have lost his way in this century:

In this low world,
Things reasonable
Or insane
Upon reflection
Are but chimeras.[5]

Because Sanetomo had no successor, he knew that the Minamoto family would die with him. The poet-shogun was murdered at age twenty-seven, in Kamakura on a snowy evening in 1219, in front of the Tsurugaoka Shrine to the war god Hachiman. In an irony of history, the last of the Minamoto fell on the very spot that was dedicated to the departed of his clan. The assassin—Kugyō, his deranged nephew—was quickly executed. The sources for this affair—all of which are favorable to the Hōjō—are very vague on the matter. The question that remains is, who manipulated Kugyō?

Yoshitoki was now master of the game in Kamakura. After having her son and grandson assassinated and putting her father in prison, had Masako plotted to have her younger son murdered? (This affair has inspired novels, plays, and television series.) The rise and fall of the Taira, the usurpation of power by the Minamoto, and their tragic end confirmed their contemporaries' pessimistic view of the world—a world dominated by *inga*, the "fate" that crushed men, taking their pathetic pride and tossing it about like a wisp of straw, "like dust before the wind."[6]

Sanetomo's poems figure in all Japanese poetry anthologies. The late-nineteenth-century haiku master Masaoka Shiki considered him the greatest poet of the Middle Ages. He who had written "this parentless child / Seeking his mother in vain"[7] was no doubt the victim of Masako's unwavering political logic. A kimono-clad Lady Macbeth, she placed the warriors' dominance and values over those of the court, and the triumph of her clan before any other consideration. In fact, throughout the Middle Ages, Masako was held up as an ideal woman, the warrior's wife who defended the supreme interests of the clan.

Following Sanetomo's murder, relations between Kyoto and Kamakura deteriorated. Finally, in 1221, Go Toba declared the regent Hōjō Yoshitoki an outlaw, hoping that the warriors of Kanto would not follow a simple vassal. Again,

Masako played a decisive role. In a speech to the vassals gathered in Kamakura, she recalled the miseries and humiliations suffered by warriors before Yoritomo and swept aside their hesitations by presenting herself as the incarnation of the founder of the regime's thought. Galvanized, the warriors rallied to the Hōjō and crushed Go Toba's troops in a one-month campaign. This war, called the Jōkyū disturbance, was the last episode in the installation of the Kamakura regime, and afterward, institutions and power relations remained stable for more than a century.

THE BAKUFU AND THE VASSALS

Although the Jōkyū disturbance was brief, it had far-reaching political, institutional, and social consequences. For the first time, the imperial forces had been defeated, and the "enemies of the court" had imposed their will. The precarious political balance between Kyoto and Kamakura had been tipped in favor of the latter. In Kyoto, the nobility hostile to the bakufu had been routed and the bakufu's supporters, led by the Kujō and Saionji families (related to the Fujiwara) prevailed. For about a century, until the final years of the Kamakura regime, no real conflict disrupted the harmonious relations between the court and the bakufu. The notion of an indolent and frivolous nobility, impotent and hedonistic, content with drawing on the dividends of its past glory without causing any problems for the leaders in Kamakura, is more a stereotypical image created after the fact than a real explanation. Kuroda Toshio, for example, emphasizes the complementary nature of this dualistic state and terms the coalition of the court nobility, the high clergy, and the great Kamakura retainers a political system characterized by the dominance of the powerful (*kenmon taisei*).[8] This political union of the governing classes in a stable, cooperative system exemplified the medieval state. Although it seemed to be contradictory because of its two centers of power, it also was a time of social stabilization, much as the regime of codes had structured political power in the ancient period and the organizational combination of the Tokugawa bakufu and the fiefdoms of daimyo typified the organization of power in the Edo period.

The crisis in the regime that began in 1156–59 and continued more or less openly until 1221 marked the painful birth of this new medieval state in which the great warriors of Kanto made the greatest gains. The nobility was forced to share authority with the feudal powers in the provinces. Succeeding the cold-war spirit that reigned between Go Shirakawa and Yoritomo and between Go Toba and the Hōjō was the détente between the Kamakura regents and the dominant factions in the court.

Immediately after the Jōkyū disturbance, three former emperors who had taken part in the conspiracy were exiled; among them, Go Toba was sent to his death on the island of Oki.[9] Three thousand estates were confiscated and reassigned,[10] and the household of the retired emperors, which had dominated the court since the late eleventh century, lost much of its influence as well as many of its estates—the economic base of its power. Even the imperial succession began to slip out of its grasp.[11] The shogun had traditionally been chosen from the aristocratic Kujō family (a branch of the Fujiwara clan), but starting in 1252, he was chosen from the imperial family. The way for the Hōjō regents to assume real power thus was clear.

After 1221, the Hōjō were the saviors of the regime in the eyes of the *gokenin* warriors, a victory that strengthened their legitimacy. Paradoxically, the fact that three emperors had been exiled empowered the Hōjō regents to lead the bakufu, and they created the appropriate institutions to control the regime.

The chief of the Hōjō household held the position of *shikken*, the shogun's regent, who indirectly controlled the Kamakura government. He was assisted by a deputy regent, usually an uncle—the chief of a junior branch of the Hōjō family line—who cosigned his petitions (*rensho*). After 1221, the office of the so-called Rokuhara *tandai* was created in the Rokuhara Palace in Kyoto, the former residence of the Taira. The *tandai*, a deputy of the shogun, had the mission of supervising for the bakufu the political, military, and judicial affairs of the central and western provinces. He was appointed by the regent and was usually his oldest son or younger brother—at any rate, always a Hōjō. The close ties between the regent and the *tandai* enabled Kamakura to discourage any ideas that the shogunal administrator in Kyoto might have of taking matters into his own hands. Yoshitoki's son, Yasutoki, was *tandai* before becoming regent when his father died, and then his younger brother, Shigetoki, replaced him. Yasutoki and Shigetoki controlled the shogunal institutions until Yasutoki died, at which time his son, the young regent Tokiyori, was supported by his uncle Shigetoki in Kyoto.[12]

In 1225, Hōjō Yasutoki created a thirteen-member state council, the *hyōjōshū*, which made important decisions and appointments and served as a court of appeal. The regent and deputy regent were de facto members of the council, in which the Hōjō and allied families (such as the Adachi) formed the majority. Members of younger branches of the Hōjō clan, who were jealous of the privileges of the older branch, and descendants of retainers formerly close to Yoritomo were excluded from the most important offices and decision-making functions. Throughout the century, certain powerful vassal families periodically rebelled against the excessive monopolization of functions by the Hōjō clique. They were crushed ruthlessly. This was the case for the Nagoe, a junior branch of the Hōjō clan, in 1246, and the Mura, "historical" retainers, in 1247. With Yasutoki and then Tokiyori, the Hōjō chiefs changed their political style from the despotic bakufu of Yoritomo and Masako to a more conciliatory one with a government by vote, in which important discussions were discussed—a system no doubt better suited to a period of political stability. Nevertheless, as soon as real opposition reared its head, it was quickly quashed.[13]

The shogun's major vassals, peers of the Hōjō, excluded from the path to power in the capital, contented themselves with helping shore up the family's authority by assuming the function of *shugo*, "military governor," in the provinces. At first appointed by the shogun and then by the state council, they maintained order in the districts under their jurisdiction. In a way, they took over the military and judiciary powers of the former provincial governors appointed by the court, for they had the power to arrest criminals, bandits, pirates, and conspirators, and in the event of war or disorder, they could mobilize their province's retainers.

These retainers, *higokenin* (nonvassals), formed a sort of warrior aristocracy within the samurai class, distinct from ordinary warriors serving the court nobility and monasteries. A nonvassal was a man who possessed a deed confirming his estate signed by the shogun or the chief of the Bureau of Samurai. That is, his rights to his estate were recognized and guaranteed by Kamakura. These rights were inalienable, and receiving them meant receiving a good turn (or pension, *onkyū*). Symbolized by a deed of confirmation, the *onkyū* was granted for services rendered for participating in war. Conversely, a warrior who became a vassal owed obligations to his suzerain, including being ready to go to war for his lord, the shogun, under the orders of the provincial military governor, the *shugo*. In peacetime, a vassal had to maintain his guard at his own cost, either in Kamakura near the shogun or at the Rokuhara Palace in Kyoto. The governor had to ensure that each vassal properly acquitted his obligations. During the Mongol invasions of 1274 and 1281, these warriors, at their own expense, patrolled the coasts of Kyushu and fought the foreign troops when they landed.

In exchange for a fief—which, in Japan, meant an office that granted the right to landownership—the vassal owed service to the shogun: guard duties in peacetime, blood in war. This is why Japanese historians see the relationship among the suzerain, the shogun, and the *gokenin* vassals as feudal and why it is possible to see in the Kamakura period the beginnings of the Japanese feudal system.[14]

GOVERNORS AND STEWARDS

The office of governor (*shugo*) was an essential cog in the bakufu's machinery, for the governor controlled the vassals. In the thirteenth century, the governor was simply the shogun's representative in the province. In the fourteenth and fifteenth centuries, he became the suzerain of the vassals in the province, which was transformed into a true fiefdom. But under the Hōjō, his appointment was still temporary, and his position was not hereditary.

Could we say that the military governor had completely replaced the provincial government, which until then was run by the local lords? Although the sources on this point are contradictory, it was certainly the case in the east. From the beginning, the military governor was authorized to appoint low-level local bureaucrats and control the provincial archives, in which the privileges, rights, and exemptions for the estates were recorded. He was thus the chief of the state administration at the provincial level. But during the Kamakura period, his position, though important, did not yet have the feudal character that it acquired in the following century. Even though the governor did not yet have the means to consolidate his hold on the vassals in his region, however, he at least controlled the local bureaucracy.[15]

Lower-ranking retainers who distinguished themselves in service to the ba-kufu were appointed to the position of military estate steward (*jitō*). In 1185, on the pretext of improving the collection of rents for public and private estates, Yoritomo obtained from the court the right to appoint his warriors as stewards. Most of them were local warriors loyal to the Minamoto, who already had administrative positions in estates. But these men also performed a new function for the shogun on estates that he did not own. In other words, through the intermediary of the stewards, the shogun controlled a space—the estate—to which, in principle, his authority did not extend. For example, an estate steward who was a vassal of Yoritomo and who had been appointed to an estate belong-ing to a high-ranking noble complied in principle with the noble's orders in regard to land management but also obeyed the shogun to whom he was a vassal. In addition, as a retainer of Kamakura, if a complaint was made against him, he had the right to be judged before the shogunal courts.[16]

As long as the steward was only a local warrior acting as a traditional admin-istrator, the shogun's right to appoint military stewards did not greatly affect the situation that had prevailed before 1185. In 1221, however, the bakufu began to appoint its retainers to the confiscated estates in the western provinces. The warriors of the east who already owned a guaranteed estate in their part of the country now obtained a new reward in the west for the services they had ren-dered during the war.

Thus, after the Jōkyū disturbance, there was a sort of invasion—on a modest scale—of western Japan by the warriors from Kanto, who settled with their entourages on the estates in the west for which they had received administrative responsibility from the bakufu. In the years following 1221, the eastern warriors who moved to the western part of the country faced a more or less hostile environment, but they were determined to profit from the new situation. Their arrival had both cultural and economic consequences. In this intermingling of populations, one of the largest in the country's history, the new stewards found domestic, dietary, linguistic, cultural, and other habits different from their own,[17] and they also introduced land-development techniques known in Kanto but not yet mastered in the western provinces. Under their influence, the low-lands in the west were planted, land was cleared, and agricultural production generally improved. But the intrusion of the newcomers also caused tension, mainly over the division of peasant rents, the right to manage nonarable land, and the right to appoint lower-ranking estate administrators.[18]

What exactly were these estate stewards' responsibilities? The office of *jitō* was an official hereditary position within the estate. The steward ensured order within the borders of the estate and had the right to investigate, arrest, and even impose sentences for minor infractions. He was allowed to keep for himself half the inheritances confiscated from delinquents; the confiscation of goods was a common penalty, and it enabled the steward to recoup the costs of dispensing justice. In addition, as administrator, the steward collected rents for the land-owner, a task for which he also was compensated. He had the right to rice paddies and fields for his own use on the estate at the rate of one *chō* for every eleven *chō* under cultivation, and he could force the estate's laborers to work on his lands. He also had the right to collect an extra tax of five *shō* per *tan* of cultivated rice paddies (about nine liters of rice per ten ares of land). He shared with the landowner half of the rents collected in various goods on fallow land, forests, and rivers.[19] In sum, the steward collected taxes, appointed lower-ranking managers, policed the region and dispensed sentences for minor crimes, supervised public works, and had irrigation systems maintained and new lands cleared.

By appointing his vassals as estate stewards, Yoritomo acquired considerable power for the bakufu. The shogun's warriors were now located throughout the country, administering the land and slowly encroaching on the privileges of the eminent landlords of the old nobility. Not surprisingly, therefore, after the Jōkyū disturbance, conflicts between the old-time landowners and the newcomers multiplied. The shogunal judges in Kamakura and at the Rokuhara Palace in Kyoto were flooded with complaints of all kinds concerning the stewards' illegally occupying the land, keeping rents for themselves, and committing various abuses. In short, the stewards were usurping the landowners' rights and ignoring the peasants' customs.[20]

THE LAW AND JUSTICE

In response, the leaders of the bakufu tried to make Yoritomo's old judicial institutions more efficient. The creation of a court of appeals in 1225 was one such attempt, and in 1249, examining magistrates replaced the Board of Inquiry that Yoritomo had created in 1184, which was overwhelmed with the number of new cases. But society had undergone a great upheaval in the preceding half century, and judicial practices had changed as well. The regent Yasutoki decided to publish a collection of the judicial practices, customs, and judgments handed down by Yoritomo, which would thereafter clarify and define jurisprudence. This text, the Goseibai shikimoku (literally, a list of rules for distinguishing good from evil in the shogunal household), also known as the Jōei shikimoku, was published in the first year of the Jōei era (1232).

This work was not only a collection of legal documents but also the basic legal code of the Hōjō regime and, beyond that, of the warrior regime. It was consulted throughout the Middle Ages and was still being studied and annotated in the Edo period. It contains fifty-one articles (three times seventeen, the most sacred number), and its content was interpreted, and sometimes modified, by many later additions.

In a letter to his younger brother Shigetoki, then *tandai* in Kyoto, Yasutoki laid out his objectives.[21] His main concern was "a clear distinction between good and evil in order to render proper justice." Judges were to hold an inquiry, hear all sides' arguments, cross-examine witnesses, and establish the facts before making their decision. Yasutoki emphasized that reason was to guide judges when they held their inquiry and that their verdict must be impartial. This instruction was one of the key aspects of the new justice that he was trying to institute.

Good justice, according to Yasutoki, was based on good sense and equity. These notions were behind the ideology of the new government, which was no longer satisfied with ruling by force. The leaders of the bakufu around 1230 were not the provincial warriors who had been Yoritomo's companions around 1180. Instead, they had been educated in Confucian principles in the innermost circles of the Kamakura government, and they were familiar with the Chinese classics. They knew both court law and the warrior customs of Kanto. With a passionate interest in the theological debates that divided the Buddhist monks of their times, they never missed an opportunity to converse with famous monks, Japanese or Chinese, passing through Kamakura. Yasutoki, Shigetoki, Shigetoki's son Tokiyori, his cousin Kanazawa Sanetoki, and Sanetoki's son Akitoki (the founders of the famous Kanazawa library, one of the main centers of scholarship in the Middle Ages) were "intellectuals" in their time, as cultivated and brilliant as the best scholars of the Kyoto court. As a good student of the Chinese classics, Yasutoki held that the principle of good government, a precondition for legitimate power, could be realized only in the context of a just administration based on equitable judicial practice. Good justice did not mean equality of individuals before the law, an idea completely unheard-of at the time — indeed, penalties varied in accordance with the social status of the guilty party — but meant, rather, a clear distinction between the innocent and the criminal.[22]

Yasutoki's other main concern, discernible in the Shikimoku, was to police and pacify warrior society so that order would prevail. The court had ceded part of its power to Yoritomo because he claimed to be the only one capable of keeping order, and so the Hōjō regents therefore also had to show themselves capable of taming the unruly warriors. Thus, severe penalties were imposed on those who were abusive and started fights. Article 12 reads:

Murders are sometimes committed following verbal abuse. If the abuse is serious, he who commits it will be sentenced to exile. If the abuse is light, he will be imprisoned. Whoever makes insults in the court will lose his trial. If the plaintiff is dismissed and insulted by his adversary, part of the estates that belong to him will be confiscated. If he does not own an estate, he will be exiled.

Here the state was interfering in relations between individuals to maintain public order. Warriors had an acute sense of honor, and exchanges of insults were apt to escalate into often fatal brawls, the reason for "a samurai convicted of starting a brawl shall be deprived of his estates."[23]

The bakufu thus sought to make social relations more civil. It was no longer acceptable for a jealous and deceived husband to commit a crime—behavior that had previously been considered normal. Such behavior, once considered private, now fell into the public domain, with the government stepping in to limit vendettas and private wars.[24]

The Shikimoku also granted more rights to warriors' wives. They now could inherit an estate, just as a man could,[25] and even join a vassal organization. When a father died, the mother often became the head of the clan, and a widow could even become a steward when her husband died.[26] In 1327, a provincial *shugo* in Kyushu intervened in an inheritance concerning the position of the *jitō* in an estate in his province:

The daughter of Sagara Saburō, known by the monastic name Renbutsu, has the nun's name Myōha. She has been recognized to possess the office of *jitō* at Toraoka, in the southern part of the Hitoyoshi estate, Higo Province. She received an official order in this regard on the twenty-third day of the eleventh month of the past year (cf. attached letter). She must obey this order immediately. I do not know whether she in fact intends to do so and to hold the fief. I order you to make an inquiry on this subject.

Tenth day of the fifth moon of year 2 of Karyaku
Kamon no suke [seal]
To the attention of Sagara Rokurō Saburō, who has taken Buddhist vows.[27]

In the case of divorce, unless the wife had committed a serious offense (such as adultery), the husband had to give her the estates that he had bequeathed to her before the separation.[28]

Among the punishments prescribed by the law, the confiscation of estates, whether or not accompanied by exile, was an especially heavy penalty for warriors, who, as we have seen, fiercely defended their property. Detention (*mi o meshikin*), a rarity in ancient society, was also a punishment, although it was considered less severe than exile (for retainers, it often consisted of house arrest). Corporal punishment was common. More than the suffering caused, the goal was to shame the guilty party. A brand on the face, an indelible mark borne for life, was a frequent punishment for common criminals. For some crimes considered minor—the rape of an unaccompanied woman, for example (!) —one-half the criminal's head was shaved, making him look ridiculous and disreputable until the hair grew back.[29] The steward of the Ategawa estate, a particularly cruel man, threatened peasants who did not pay their rent with cutting off their noses and parts of their wives' and children's ears.[30]

In the view of the Hōjō, whose Confucianism provided the ideological basis for their power, order depended on the legitimacy of their new power, and the fair administration of justice was a central role of their government. The bakufu was no longer simply the political organ of the retainers, but an authority that, as such, could be used for arbitration. Verdicts could not systematically favor vassals. Thus, if a retainer in Kamakura was proved to have committed an illegal or brutal act against a court noble, a monastery, or even a peasant community, he would be found guilty. The Hōjō regents wanted to preserve the status quo—cooperation with the Kyoto court and the great monasteries—and not to create confrontation. Their power, unlike imperial power, had nothing to do with sacred tradition, nor was it the outcome of a heroic epic such as that of the Minamoto. Rather, they had to prove their ability to rule, and the victory of 1221 did not necessarily suffice. Confucianism, however truncated and adapted to Japanese realities, was to serve as their justification. In the Edo period, the Hōjō regime was still in favor among Neo-Confucianist ideologues close to the Tokugawa rulers.[31]

With the establishment of a written body of shogunal law, medieval society found itself governed by several types of legislation, for the Shikimoku did not supersede the other bodies of law in force. Instead, it was applicable only to vassals of the shogun and those who lived in estates owned by the shogunal household, most of which were located in Kanto. Imperial law continued to apply to public estates and to inhabitants of private estates owned by nobles and monasteries who lived under their respective lords' judicial regimes. This juridical complexity, similar to that of the governing regime, exemplified the decentralized nature of medieval authority.[32] The multiplicity of power centers, seeming to border on anarchy, tended to encourage professional litigation. One court of justice could always be found to issue a judgment reversing another, and the parties had to debate complicated texts and procedures. Whether it was in Kyoto, Kamakura, or the lords' courts of justice, trials were long and impeded by taboos. For example, courts did not sit on unlucky days, and their work would be interrupted if one of the investigators or parties fell ill. If a death occurred, all activity stopped for fifty days. In Kamakura, it could take several years for a sentence to be pronounced. And if the defendant appealed, the plaintiff might wait a decade before justice was rendered.[33]

Conflicts between stewards and the managers sent by estate owners to stop invasions and illegal activities could not always be settled by lawsuits, which generally were long and costly. To remedy this, in the mid-thirteenth century, a system of arrangements between stewards and estate owners began to take shape. This system was encouraged by the bakufu, which preferred to have conflicts settled amicably rather than in a trial that would displease the loser. Furthermore, it was not always easy, given the complexity of the cases and the seriousness of the conflicts, to determine who was right under the law.[34]

Around 1280, in the Ishiguro estate, in Etchū Province on the Japan Sea, the steward and the estate manager were at loggerheads because the steward was no longer playing the annual rents to the estate owner, a Kyoto temple. The steward seemed to be in the wrong, since he was illegally appropriating part of the annual rents. But he argued that for many years, his ancestors and he had cultivated the land once left fallow in the lower part of the valley, which was prone to flooding. The poorest peasants in the region had been recruited for labor, and they lived on the estate, bound to the soil. Once-abandoned lands were now being farmed, and a local market had been created. Under these conditions, it seemed just for the steward to retain a larger part of the rents than before and to have the right to administer what had not existed before his initiative.[35] Thus, agricultural and commercial growth in the thirteenth century brought with it the beginnings of a struggle by the leadership to appropriate the surplus produced.[36]

When compromise seemed to be the best way to resolve a conflict, the parties tried to come to an agreement by making a list of the points on which they were opposed and discussing them. In 1294, in the Tara estate in Wakasa, the steward won on two points under litigation, and the landowner's delegate won on eight others. In this case, the owner of the estate—the Tōji Shingon monastery in Kyoto—had leaned hard on the steward, who had little support from the bakufu.[37] Usually, however, the landowner turned over the management of his estate to his steward in exchange for a tax to be paid. In 1308, in Bingo Province, near today's Hiroshima, responsibility for the entire property went to the steward, and the lord no longer had the right to send an agent to the estate. The steward agreed to pay forty-five *kanmon* in goods per year; if there was a poor harvest, he would meet with an envoy of the estate's owner to evaluate the extent of the damage and reach a temporary arrangement. In the Ōyama estate in Tanba, north of today's Kobe, the steward reached a similar arrangement with the landowner, again the Tōji, in 1241. But between 1276 and 1279, workers at the Ōyama estate came to blows with those at the neighboring Miyata estate over repairs to the irrigation system. Fights between the two ended in the death of a man, and fields were destroyed. The steward then used the situation as an excuse to stop paying rent to the Tōji, which complained to the court in Roku-hara that it was owed 560 *koku* of rice. The affair dragged on, and finally, in 1295, the Tōji and the steward decided to divide the estate into two independent parts. The monastery obtained three adjacent valleys that extended to the river, and the steward kept the rest—about one-third of the territory of the former estate—as its exclusive owner.[38] Based on the fact that the steward had begun with the right to only one *chō* of cultivated land out of eleven, we can calculate exactly how much land the warrior vassals of Kamakura gained during the century at the expense of the old nobility.

All the cases of estates being divided were in western Japan, mainly after the 1270s. In Kinai, however, the practice of abandoning the land under the threat of taxing administration rights seemed to have been in force since the first years of the bakufu. The stewards in that part of the country were not able to gain a foothold, for the court nobles and monasteries were too powerful. During the century, warrior landownership therefore expanded mainly in the western prov-inces, where the Kamakura military stewards managed to carve out entire fiefs. Eastern warriors invaded estates in the central regions around Kyoto only spo-radically and, later, after 1336, but it took a war for this to happen.[39]

THE MONGOL INVASIONS AND THE CULMINATION OF THE KAMAKURA REGIME

During the rule of Tokimune (1268–84), the last of the great Hōjō regents, the threat of an invasion by the Mongols became a reality. In the thirteenth century, all of eastern Asia, from Sakhalin to Java, was affected by Mongol aggression. After northern China, Korea was invaded, starting in 1231, despite the Koreans' heroic resistance that lasted almost half a century. In 1266, Kublai Khan set his sights on Japan and sent, via the Koreans, official letters requesting the com-mencement of friendly relations, accompanied by the following threatening statement: "It would displease us to have to use force." But the Kamakura leaders did not budge, and Kublai grew impatient.[40]

Backed by Korean and Chinese auxiliaries, the Mongols landed on the coast of Kyushu in 1274. Although the combat lasted for only one day, it was unusually brutal. The invaders used poisoned arrows and all sorts of deafening explosive devices. Surprised by these new techniques, in the early battles the Japanese warriors became disoriented. The Mongols gained the advantage, but a storm arose in the evening and they were forced to return to their ships.

Preoccupied with the conquest of southern China (the Southern Song dynasty fell in 1279), the Mongols delayed their second campaign against Japan until 1281. This time, however, their attack was much larger, consisting of a fleet of tens of thousands of men (140,000, according to some sources). Meanwhile, the Japanese had fortified the northwest coasts of Kyushu. As they did in 1274, the Mongols ravaged the Japanese islands off the coast; Tsushima, in particular, paid a heavy toll in human lives. Then they landed on Kyushu. But this time, the Japanese warriors knew their enemy. Thanks to stone walls and battle expertise, the samurai kept the formidable Mongol cavalry from deploying and pinned it to the coast. After a week of fierce combat, the Mongols managed to establish a small beachhead, but they later had to abandon it and withdraw to the already conquered small islands to regroup. Then a second storm arose, coming to the rescue of the defenders. The Mongol armada was dispersed, sunk, broken. Thirty thousand Mongol, Chinese, and Korean survivors, unable to leave the islands, fell to Japanese swords.

In this test, the bakufu's leaders showed their resolve and levelheadedness, and the victory over the Mongols belonged to them above all. It was also a victory for the warriors, both vassals and others, most of them from the western provinces. It was a victory as well for the Kyoto court, which had ordered prayers for the prosperity of the country, and for the shrines, which had twice prevailed on the country's gods to intervene in the form of divine winds (*kamikaze*) against the enemy. Not only had the Hōjō, led by the regent Tokimune, been able to mobilize the fighting spirit of Japan's warriors, but they had also been able to handle an emergency.

The Mongol wars enabled Kamakura to extend its authority in the western part of the country. The bakufu ordered the governors in Shikoku and Kyushu to mobilize all warriors in their provinces, including those who were not direct vassals of the shogun. In 1275, Tokimune appointed nine new governors in the west, six of them from the Hōjō family or allied clans. The Rokuhara administration in Kyoto was reinforced by men sent from Kamakura, and Kyushu was placed under a special administration, based in Hakata and led by Kanazawa Sanemasa, of the Hōjō clan. In 1286, a special court of justice for the island, of the Rokuhara type, was installed. And in 1293, while the Japanese awaited a third Mongol invasion (which never came), the island was supervised by the commanding military general, the *chinzei tandai*. After the Mongol invasions, western Japan was a bit neglected by the distant bakufu and fell directly under the control of Kamakura, which from then on was no longer concerned only with Kanto and its relations with the court but aspired to extend its authority to the entire country. Some historians feel that the bakufu became a truly national power only after this period of war.[41]

After the war came the rewards. This time, there were no estates to redistribute. Yoritomo had confiscated about five hundred Taira estates after the wars of 1185, and the Hōjō had confiscated three thousand estates after the war of 1221. Instead, the depleted bakufu promulgated edicts of "virtuous government" (*tokusei*) for the Shinto shrines, authorizing them to recover the estates that they had ceded, sold, or mortgaged or that had been snatched away from them in the previous twenty years without any compensation. For the many warriors in Kyushu who were not vassals of the shogun, Kamakura confirmed their rights to their estates—estates, of course, that did not belong to the bakufu. In other words, the warriors who up to then were not vassals of the shogun received from the shogunal administration letters of confirmation and guarantee assuring them of ownership of the estates in which they lived, and in turn, the *higokenin* became retainers. The social foundation of the bakufu spread in the western provinces. For warriors who were already retainers who had fought or been watchmen on the coasts (it was believed as late as the early fourteenth century that there would be another Mongol invasion), the bakufu promulgated more edicts of "beneficent government," under which some of the vassals who had been indebted by the war recovered part of their lost property.[42] The issue of rewards for the retainers, however, remained a source of discontent among the warriors. Poorly resolved by the bakufu, it somewhat tarnished the Hōjō's victory.

Despite some bitterness among the retainers in the late 1280s, the Kamakura regime was at its zenith. Its prestige had risen further when the imperial family was divided into two rival factions in 1272. In effect, the court was not able to agree on the imperial succession when the retired emperor Go Saga died, and two of his sons ascended the throne in succession, each claiming leadership of the government of retired emperors. Go Fukakusa and his brother Kameyama retired to the Jimyōin and Daikakuji, respectively, and quarreled. Incapable of resolving the conflict, the court asked Kamakura to decide between the two

Mongol Invasion in 1281

factions. Under duress, the Hōjō proposed an amicable settlement in 1275: the emperors would be chosen alternately from the two branches, and the estates of the household of the retired emperors would be shared. Of course, this was a temporary solution, for it could only result in further conflicts. In the following century, these two branches of the imperial family caused a division of the dynasty into the Northern Court (Jimyōin family) and the Southern Court (Daikakuji family). In the meantime, the Kamakura bakufu, the main crafter of the victory against fierce aggressors, held manifestly indisputable power.

Chapter 5

KAMAKURA: A SOCIETY OF QUESTIONS

The Kamakura period was a great time in Japan's intellectual history, sometimes leaning more to abstract thought than to the building of different ways of life. Those who asked questions in the thirteenth century were thinkers from the leading classes: nobles in the capital, monks, and provincial warriors. For the first time, these men tried to consider all society in their philosophical concepts. They addressed everyone, and they often found a response among the commoners, who were to be included in the different approaches of medieval Buddhism. The texts by the period's great intellectual figures, such as Shinran and Dōgen, also contained a general metaphysical questioning of history and its meaning, of fate, and of humanity as such.

As the historian of literature Tsuda Sōkichi noted around 1920, the Kamakura century was also a time when cultural forms were disseminated throughout society and, more precisely, when popular sensibilities joined more intellectual forms of thought.[1] The huge gap that had separated court culture from the rest of society in the preceding period was slowly closing, and the first wave of cultural homogenization was under way. Hara Katsurō saw in this phenomenon the birth of the "true Japan." Although the historical reflections of a Jien or the theoretical writings of a Dōgen were generally inaccessible and not widely known, the sermons of Hōnen and his disciples and the proselytism of reformers of the Ritsu and Nichiren schools drew crowds who came to listen, look, and share emotions. Society seemed receptive to the new discourses, which reflected a fundamental movement sweeping through medieval society. The emergence of active village communities, economic progress, the awakening of the provinces, and the growth of urban populations resulted in the blossoming of an oral literature in the commoner tradition, of which the *Heike monogatari* is the most striking example.

THE NOBILITY IN TURMOIL

The court nobility had been in power for 350 years, rarely having to resort to armed violence. Conflicts were subdued and limited to factional struggles.[2] And although the ruling class's cultural domination had been nearly absolute as well, in only one or two generations the old order was challenged. For nobles in the late twelfth and early thirteenth centuries, times were hard. They saw their world stagnating, even shrinking, and they were powerless to do anything about it. These illustrious and cultured men, many of them revered poets, could not play a political role worthy of their stature. Even though they occupied high offices, they sensed that the power was elsewhere, that court honors and wealth were worth little. One of them, Kamo no Chōmei, questioned the meaning of the temporal world and the significance of humanity; another, Jien, began to reflect on history.

CHŌMEI

Born around 1155, Kamo no Chōmei felt deep within his soul the degeneration of the world, a manifestation of the impermanence at the heart of humankind and the fundamental instability of the world. Born into a family of priests at the Kamo Shrine, Chōmei was a member of the middle-rank court nobility. He had several disappointments in the course of his career: he did not succeed his father, and then the position he coveted was denied him. When he was about fifty, he retired to a monastery, and around 1210, he went to Kamakura, where he was received by the young shogun Sanetomo. He then returned to Kinai, withdrawing to an even more remote site, a small cabin measuring one *jō* per side (a little more than nine square meters), near Mount Hino. There, around 1212, he wrote the *Hōjōki*,[3] a very short piece in which he describes the various residences he has lived in, as a pretext for his portrayal of his unhappy times and the misfortunes of the people and for his thoughts on the life of someone who had abandoned everything.

> The flow of the water is ceaseless and its water is never the same. The bubbles that float in the pools, now vanishing, now forming, are not of long duration; so in the world are man and his dwellings. . . . Which will be the first to go, the master or his dwelling? One might just as well ask

this of the dew on the morning-glory. . . . The flower may fade before the dew evaporates, but though it does not evaporate, it waits not the evening.[4]

Chōmei had burned his bridges with a futile career in the court, pursuing power and honors. In fact, he was not the first to decide to renounce the temporal world, for many great nobles and warriors retired in later life to a comfortable monastery to enjoy relative tranquillity. Chōmei, though, went further, following a more ascetic path by transforming himself into a mendicant monk. A quarter century earlier, Saigyō, a poet-monk from a good family serving the retired emperors, and the personal master of poetry to the great Teika, had been adored at court—at the time dominated by the Taira—at which young nobles appreciated the exquisite sensitivity of his poems. Then suddenly, Saigyō abandoned everything, including the honors, and went to preach the doctrines of the Buddha in the countryside. For the important personalities of the time, spiritual and physical well-being was an ideal that was difficult to attain without renunciation. Chōmei explained why:

For over thirty years, I had tormented myself by putting up with all the things of this unhappy world. . . . I became a priest and turned my back on the world. . . . Ever since I fled the world and became a priest, I have known neither hatred nor fear. I leave my span of days for Heaven to determine. . . . My body is like a drifting cloud.[5]

Saigyō, Chōmei, and others aspired to transcend the exigencies of the temporal world. Withdrawing to lead a hermit's life, preaching, and performing the duties of charity were ways to ease the terrible anguish gripping the court nobles, who were searching for salvation by fleeing from society. "All human enterprises are stupid and vain," Chōmei declared.

Not everyone chose the solitude of a hermit's life. In the ninth and tenth centuries (and still today), monasteries were a peaceful refuge for aristocrats fleeing responsibility, a position of power, or court intrigues to live out their lives in peace and quiet. Monasteries, where challenging texts were studied and foreign—Indian, Tibetan, and Chinese—ceremonies were conducted, were appropriated by wealthy, cultivated people. The aesthetic sensibility of the Heian aristocracy pervaded monastic life: many of the nobles' gardens were reproduced and often improved, at the monasteries, where they became representations of the world of the Pure Land.

The men who sought solace in renunciation had come to detest the ritualized world of the court, with its power struggles and underhanded cliques. This world, the only one they knew, seemed doomed, and violence was a commonplace. Under these circumstances, flight could well mean reacquiring one's freedom, regaining control over one's fate through total detachment from the material world. "I naturally feel ashamed when I go to the capital and must beg," Chōmei wrote, "but when I return and sit here I feel pity for those still attached to the world of dust."[6]

JIEN

Jien recognized the deterioration of the world as well. But whereas Chōmei saw this decadence as a sign of impermanence, Jien sought the reasons for the phenomenon in history. Historical events had traumatized Jien more than they had Chōmei, but he tried to find a principle, some logic, in the brutality of the facts. In 1220, he wrote *Gukanshō* (My views of history), a work dealing with the conflict between the retired emperor Go Toba and Kamakura, in which he warns Go Toba about the risks of following too aggressive a policy toward the bakufu.

Jien was from the high aristocracy of Kyoto. Born in 1155, the same year as Chōmei, he was a son of the imperial regent and grand chancellor Fujiwara no Tadamichi. Although his older brothers attempted to follow in their father's footsteps, the times had changed. Jien's older half brother based his career on an alliance with Kiyomori, the chief of the Taira, and in 1183, Jien's second half brother joined Yoshinaka, Yoritomo's cousin. Kanezane, Jien's full older brother and founder of the Kujō family, chose the winner, becoming Yoritomo's main ally at court. Born too late for a political career, Jien entered the Enryakuji, the large Tendai monastery on Mount Hiei. He eventually became the abbot, a powerful position, since the monastery, with its many estates, was quick to use its warrior-monks to make its interests known at court. Like many other younger nobles, Jien entered the clergy. He was responsible for praying for the prosperity of the emperor and the state, which put him in close contact with the retired emperor. Appreciated for his poetic talent, which was still a valuable asset at court, Jien was one of the great dignitaries of Kyoto.

In 1196, the anti-Kujō party seized power in the court, and Kanezane fell, taking down Jien with him. Kanezane, now the "leader of the opposition," was impatient, and Jien remained convinced that the cornerstone of his brother's policy, an alliance between the court and the lord of Kamakura, was the right one, that a connection between the nobles and the warriors was essential. Jien was convinced that only the bakufu would be able to maintain the prestige of the court. Many of the warrior leaders seemed to be politically adept—which the court nobles no longer were—and they also knew how to keep order. In fact, the disturbances had resulted from the nobility's blindness to the changing times.

These times—a period of unrest and the rise of the bakufu—had begun with the Hōgen uprisings in 1156. The warriors were now paramount, and their "historic mission" was to bring back peace and order to the country. For Jien, the events of 1156, about which he had been told in his childhood, were truly a family affair: among the defeated were his grandfather and uncle, and among the victors was his father. But above all, blood had flowed in the capital, and the feeling had persisted since then that the nobility's customs and political practices were in upheaval.

Jien began, as a historian, to record the events of this time. He verified events, analyzed the deeds and actions of the protagonists, questioned the survivors, and recorded their testimony. The concept of *dōri* (reason) showed that such acts followed a logic that was discernible only from a distance and that what seemed to cause weakness in the short term might build strength over the long term. But because Jien's contemporaries did not agree, they acted against his conclusions and provoked unrest.

As a monk of the Tendai school, Jien was influenced by the Buddhist doctrine of *mappō*, "the latter days of Buddhist Law," in which history was marching toward decline and "dark days." For Jien, although *dōri* was clearly established for the first emperors, later, it was forgotten. At that time, the Fujiwara held the fate of the country firmly in hand until chaos erupted in 1156, when reason was lost. Jien developed an original line of thought, founded on syncretism; that is, this Buddhist pessimist was an early Confucianist. According to Jien, in Japan, unlike China, the ruler was always chosen from a single dynasty, and all the ministers were from the same family line, his, the Fujiwara. These ministers had been retained because they had a mandate from heaven, but they were unable to maintain order once the warriors arrived on the scene. Jien used an allegory for power: in the beginning, Amaterasu, the Sun Goddess, made an agreement with the god Amagatsuya to ensure government, but the gradual decline of history kept this alliance and the agreement from being respected. The strength of the god Hachiman, protector of the capital, was needed, and above all, the Buddhist Law was indispensable. Jien sketched a picture of a political coalition "of vows." The agreement between Amaterasu and Amenokoyane (protective god of the Fujiwara) was reinforced by the god Hachiman (protective god of the Minamoto) and the Buddhist Law taught by the Tendai sect, whose political influence, we know, was important to Jien. This inexorable decline was arrested as long as this coalition was maintained. Jien had outlined precisely the terms of the alliance that formed the medieval state of Kamakura. His fundamental pessimism—the pessimism of a weakening nobility?—was tempered by a relative confidence in the warriors (although Hachiman protected the Minamoto, he was also the god of war), who now held the future in their hands and perhaps would be able to slow the inevitable degradation.[7]

Chōmei's agony and Jien's pessimism convey the decline of a social class that felt both dispossessed of its power and deprived of a future. But this malaise extended beyond the small world of the capital and affected as a whole in times of great turmoil.[8] The nobles expressed their discontent in literary and historical works.

One calm dawning, as I thought over the reasons for this weakness of mine, I told myself that I had fled the world to live in a mountain forest in order to discipline my mind and practice the Way. "And yet . . . your heart is stained with impurity." . . . To these questions my mind could offer no reply. All I could do was to use my tongue to recite two or three times the *nembutsu*, however unacceptable from a defiled heart.[9]

Because they were searching not for excuses but for a way to soothe the people's anxiety, some Buddhist monks tried to make their thinking more metaphysical. Some found comfort in a new faith in salvation, and others sought enlightenment within themselves.

THE NEW BUDDHISTS

New times, uncertainty, and anxiety combined to push mystical and speculative minds toward broader horizons. Buddhism was the matrix within which the thoughts of founders of different schools of teachings matured.

PRACTICE OR FAITH?

In the eleventh and twelfth centuries, increasing numbers of monks and laymen were pondering the real meaning of the doctrines as they were officially taught. The great sects, centered in wealthy monasteries, seemed too involved with worldly concerns. Busy with managing vast properties, benefiting from the court's support, and maintaining troops, the high-ranking clergy no longer responded to their followers' anxious questions. Many monks were living dissolute, corrupt lives. Some laymen and intellectuals chose to escape their torment by becoming hermits, living in poverty deep in the forest. Increasing numbers of them turned toward the teachings of the Pure Land.

Despite their differences, the various trends in traditional Buddhism shared certain principles, first among them the duty—even the vocation—to protect the country and the emperor. The monks were expected to calm political tensions and protect dignitaries from evil spirits. General salvation depended on teaching the Law. The construction of places of prayer and study, temples and monasteries, hermitages and pagodas, was a means of linking people to Buddha and maintaining the prestige of the religion.

In the Kamakura period, Japanese Buddhism began to diverge into various streams. In opposition to ancient Buddhism, which soon defended itself and counterattacked, appeared the two principal ideas, relying on another's powers (*tariki*) or relying on one's own powers (*jiriki*) to attain enlightenment.

For some religious thinkers of the time, Buddhism's main significance was that it was a faith. Internal divergences were based primarily on the interpretation of texts and the types of practices that would provide access to the hereafter. Faith in a divine hereafter following death transformed the old doctrines into a religion of personal salvation. Despite the obvious differences, the doctrines of the Pure Land and those taught by Nichiren had one thing in common: they were addressed to all human beings, no matter what their social status or sex. Faith was what was essential; people had to throw themselves on Buddha's infinite mercy.

For others, Buddhism meant finding something divine within themselves and reaching a state that eliminated pain and suffering through study or prayer, reflection or meditation, asceticism, the observance of rules, or charity. These divergences pertained to the practices that granted access to this state and the significance accorded to the search. But the solution was sought within the individual's own power.

Practice or faith? Zen of the Sōto school or the True Pure Land sect? Dōgen or Shinran? The two deepest minds of the century opposed each other, but they shared a desire for the absolute. Each subscribed to a theoretical discourse that offered no compromise. Between these two trends other, less revolutionary streams leaned toward compromise with the authorities or other religious trends, unlike the ancient Buddhist sects that undertook internal reforms that took account of the new concerns in an effort to regain their prestige.[10]

Belief in the Western Paradise—the Pure Land—was not new but became more popular at the end of the Heian period, when it was taught in Tendai Buddhism. Whereas Paradise could not be described in concrete terms, only in abstract allegories, Hell, the other side of Paradise, could be portrayed in frightening vividness. On screens set up for ceremonies, images of Hell complete with flames, monsters, and tortured people, inspired fear and encouraged followers to seek salvation.[11] How could passage to the Pure Land be assured? No one really had an answer. In 1027, Fujiwara no Michinaga, the most powerful figure of his century, died. Turning toward the west on his deathbed, he held in his hand nine cords tied to nine statues of Amida Buddha in hopes that Amida would welcome him to his Pure Land.[12]

This relative tranquillity was not, however, for everyone. Following the wars between the Taira and the Minamoto, Kenreimon'in, Taira no Kiyomori's daughter, who had been married to Emperor Takakura and was Emperor Antoku's mother, was forced to leave society at the age of thirty, a victim of the power struggles. She "let her hair fall away" and retired to the Jakkōin, in Ōhara, knowing that she would never leave its walls again until she died.

Perhaps because the road led through the mountains, the twilight shadows began to gather as she journeyed, her eyes lingering on the colored foliage of the surrounding trees. A lonely sunset bell boomed from a temple in the fields, the thick dew on the wayside plants added fresh moisture to her tear-dampened sleeves, a violent wind sent leaves scurrying in every direction, and a sudden shower descended from the cloud-blackened sky, accompanied by the faint belling of a deer and the almost inaudible plaints of insect voices. The melancholy effect of so many depressing sights and sounds was quite beyond comparison. "Even when we were going from bay to bay and island to island, nothing was as bad as this," she thought piteously.![13]

HŌNEN

In 1175, Hōnen, a monk at Mount Hiei, felt that he had discovered the truth. He preached in Kyoto that salvation was possible for all thanks to the infinite mercy of Amida Buddha, who saves humans and welcomes them to the Pure Land. Hōnen believed was that one could be reborn in Amida's paradise if one had faith, expressed in recitation of the formula "Namu Amida butsu." His message spread quickly, and some powerful men rushed to hear the master. The grand chancellor Kujō Kanezane, Jien's brother, was among Hōnen's new disciples.

Hōnen was the first to proclaim that Buddhism was not a discipline of study but, above all, was a faith, and he also spoke of the Buddha as an absolute being and not a model for or an ideal of a man. Indeed, it was the absoluteness of Amida—more precisely, his divine nature—that enabled him to save human beings. Knowledge, study, and ascetic practices were no longer useful, since there was nothing to expect in this world. Only faith counted, according to Hōnen (as reported in the *Heike*):

There are various ways of escaping from the world of illusion, but in these unclean, tumultuous latter days of the Law, the best one is to recite the name of Amida Buddha. . . . The necessary pious acts have been compressed into six syllables [Namu Amida butsu], which even the most slow-witted person can chant. . . . Nor must you lose hope because you think you have performed few meritorious acts: Amida will come to meet anyone who has it in his heart to intone the sacred name one time or ten times. . . . But belief is the key to rebirth. You must believe with all your heart: never, never entertain a doubt.[14]

Hōnen gradually distanced himself from the Tendai school's teachings. His disciples began to disseminate his ideas, and their success angered the monks of Nara and Mount Hiei. Although he had always sought to avoid confrontation, Hōnen was finally expelled from Kyoto in 1207 and moved to Shikoku. His fame was such that he was accompanied to the city gate by commoners, and pleasure girls from the small port of Kanzaki came by boat to escort the ship of the exiled master.[15] Those in power had made a big mistake, for now Hōnen and his disciples could expand their preaching and proselytizing to the provinces. Previously little known outside of Kyoto, Hōnen's teachings now spread very rapidly. Shinran, one of his most devoted disciples, went to Echigo Province, then to Kanto, and preached before low-ranking warriors, peasants, and marginal and itinerant people. The Amidist doctrines were as successful in the provinces as they had been in the capital, so Buddhism now turned to preaching to the lower classes.

For Hōnen, whose own disciples founded the sect of the Pure Land (Jōdo-shū) after his death, and for Shinran, the ancient ways of thinking of Buddhism founded on the study of texts, respect for monastic rules, spiritual and ascetic exercises, and donations for constructing or repairing religious buildings, had been appropriate in the distant past. But in these times of the end of the Law and decline, the Law could no longer be taught correctly, and faith in the absolute beneficence of the Amida Buddha was the only means of access to a better hereafter. The temporal world was hopeless, and nothing could be expected of it. Counting on one's knowledge of texts, fortune, or personal power was a sign of pathetic pride at a time when the world was in decline. Giving oneself over completely to the mercy of Amida, whose "principal vow" was the salvation of all people, was the only Way.

SHINRAN

After Hōnen's death, in 1212, Shinran continued his search and radicalized his thought. After 1231, a dream led him to develop his idea of absolute *tariki*, giving oneself completely to Amida. Shinran had doubts, for wasn't repeating Amida's name proof of a lack of confidence and faith in this Buddha and thus a form of *jiriki*? Since Amida saved all people in the same way, wouldn't it be enough to pronounce his name just once? And wouldn't the person who did so be saved, no matter what his later conduct? Shinran refined his faith through a search for the truth and developed theses that were both provocative and attractive. Hostile to monasticism, since study and prayer were useless, he became interested in the poor, the disinherited, and criminals. Salvation was for everyone, even deaf-mutes incapable of reciting Amida's name, said Shinran: "Even the good will go to Paradise; therefore, for stronger reasons, so will the bad." The true meaning of Amida's original vow was that in his absolute mercy, he saved the humble and the evil who had neither the time to discover the truth by devoting themselves to study or asceticism nor the means to buy off their transgressions by making donations to monasteries. Shinran did not want a sect of his own, although his children—he was married—and disciples somewhat betrayed his philosophy by founding the True Pure Land sect (Jōdo shinshū).

The political and religious authorities rejected the radicalism of Hōnen, Shinran, and their disciples. However, their persecution of these "heretics" was mild in comparison to the heretics' being burned at the stake in the West: they were, at worst, banned from traveling to the capital or were placed under house arrest. Sometimes more obscure and more zealous disciples were condemned to death, but this was very much the exception. In Japan, Buddhism was not unified around a dogma. Rather, from the beginning, it had been divided into trends, sects, and schools that interpreted certain texts in various ways but were linked by common principles. Japanese Buddhism did not have the objective of controlling minds, as did Western religions, and it was thus more tolerant and open than medieval Christianity.

THE REACTION OF ORTHODOX BUDDHISM

Faced with the rapid growth of Amidist movements in the first half of the thirteenth century, the traditional sects felt threatened, and some of them launched reform movements. The laicization of the leaders of some monasteries, corruption, homosexuality, and the luxury in which the high-ranking clergy lived incited the reformers to return to monastic rules. Obedience to the commandments was to turn the monks back into respected and exemplary figures who would be pure, show the way, and save the people.[16] In the mid-thirteenth century, Eison attempted to join the Shingon and Ritsu sects. Personally invited to Kamakura by the regent Hōjō Tokiyori, he publicly announced that salvation was possible for those who followed the precepts of Buddhist life, notably by respecting the bans on killing animals, eating meat, and so on. It is said that Eison converted thousands of commoners by having them repeat the magical formulas that ensured prosperity in this world and salvation in the next and kept evil influences at bay. For the wealthy, Eison advocated charity, and he provided an example by dispensing alms to the ill and the beggars who lived outside the monasteries in Nara.

Eison perpetuated the tradition of the builder-monks by having roads, bridges, and hospices constructed. One of his disciples, Ninshō, founded the first leper colony in Japan and transformed the Gokurakuji, which he had built in Kamakura in 1267, into a hospice. Monks of the Ritsu sect traveled the countryside raising funds for charity. In doing this, they contributed to commercial expansion and encouraged trade. They quickly accumulated fortunes, which they "invested" by offering interest-bearing loans to those who needed money. They built bridges but charged tolls on them. They gave charity but amassed fortunes. To redistribute wealth to the poor, they allied themselves with the wealthy, and they ended up resembling the detested usurers.

NICHIREN

The son of a fishing-boat owner in Awa Province in Kanto, Nichiren called himself a mendicant. He understood the contradictions that tormented the founders of the Amidist movements and the Ritsu reformers. All the preachers from the nobility wanted—through contrition, no doubt—to draw closer to a people about whom they in fact knew nothing. Amidists believed in individual salvation and mistrusted the people of the temporal world, from whom they said they could expect nothing. But people in the temporal world still wanted wealth and protection against bad luck. Nichiren believed that he had a mission to reform the state in order to ensure the well-being of the people and the nation. Having studied the main Buddhist schools, he taught a new faith, which, unlike other teachings, owed little to foreign influences. Until then, Nichiren said, Buddhism had ensured the prosperity of the state, and thus of the people, through the monks' prayers. That is, the religion protected the state.

Nichiren reversed this perspective. Instead, it was up to the state to protect the religion—that is, the doctrine of faith in the Lotus Sutra that Nichiren was preaching. He wanted Buddhism, as he conceived of it, to be the state religion, and he violently attacked the other doctrines. From one point of view, Nichiren was even more radical than the Amidists.[17] Whereas they felt that the teachings of ancient Buddhism were not false but useless, Nichiren felt that the teachings were fundamentally evil and wrong and were driving the country to ruin. He railed against the Amidist doctrines, which led to delusion; he mocked the monk Ninshō, who was accumulating a fortune under the pretext of charity; and he attacked the Zen monks. Nichiren warned of the danger of a Mongol invasion, and he implored the leaders of the bakufu to ban "heretical" sects and support him or else face Japan's destruction. Nichiren was exiled to Sado Island in 1271 because of his intolerance and violent attacks against competing sects. But during his exile, his faith only deepened, and when he was freed, he continued to preach the doctrine of the Lotus Sutra (Hokke sect) among the lower classes.

IPPEN

From a family that led a small group of seafaring warriors in Shikoku, Ippen felt the same frustration as Nichiren had about the Amidist doctrines of Hōnen and Shinran. *Tariki* teachings were an esoteric doctrine that went over the heads of the commoners whom the founders of the doctrines of the Pure Land were trying to reach. Ippen was a disciple of Hōnen, although he was too young to have known him personally (he was born in 1239). Ippen began to

preach the original doctrines in 1274, going first to the Kumano Shrine, a pilgrimage site, for a hundred-day retreat. Then, reaffirmed in his faith, he left
to preach a new version of Amidism around the country. According to Ippen,
one could be reborn in the Pure Land by merely reciting Amida's name,
whether or not one believed in salvation, had committed sins, or was soiled
by impure activities. Ippen distributed Amidist amulets in Kyushu, Shikoku,
the eastern part of the country, and Hiraizumi in distant Tōhoku. In 1279, he
revalued and systematized the Amidist dances. It was an extraordinary success:
commoners danced with him and recited Namu Amida butsu. Ippen gave to
Amidist dances the rhythms of the peasant dances that punctuated the work
in the fields. As the dancers approached a state of ecstasy, their movements
took on a magical aspect. They were said to purify the body and give it the
power both to resist the evil spirits of the dead who returned to persecute the
living and to expel disease. Throughout the country, Ippen's disciples sold
amulets and led followers in dances—whether or not they believed did not
matter. Ippen preached in Kanto and appeared at the gate to Kamakura. The
bakufu banned him from entering the city for fear that his enraptured dancers
would cause disruptions. So they danced on the edges of a city that was prac-
tically in a state of siege. Ippen preached and danced, surrounded by beggars,
lepers, and people of good society disguised so that they would not be
recognized.

Ippen died in 1288, after traveling around the country for eighteen years. He
had been successful because he combined faith in Amida Buddha with the
commoner traditions that he knew so well. Not making the error of neglecting
the latter, he retained his connection to the commoners' devotion sites linked
to ancient Shinto worship. Monks, beggars, and sellers of amulets swept through
the country in his wake. But these itinerant preachers, sometimes surrounded
by laymen, founded no monastery,[18] and this variety of Amidism was never
encouraged by the authorities.[19]

The Amidist sects, as well as Nichiren's Hokke sect, were addressed to all
people and were popular among commoners because of their simple practices.
But the authorities did not trust these new forms of Buddhism, which seemed
unstable and often radical. Although some members of the leading warrior
classes, such as Hōjō Shigetoki and Kanazawa Sanetoki, were attracted by the
doctrines of the Pure Land, they were exceptions.

ZEN

Zen, however, did benefit from the support of the powerful. The success of Zen
in the Kamakura period was linked with that of the Rinzai school. Thanks to
certain political leaders, such as Kujō Michiie at the imperial court and Hōjō
Tokiyori and his son Tokimune in Kamakura, the movement obtained appre-

ciable advantages. Aside from the charm of its doctrine, Zen seemed solid, encouraged the monastic life, supported the social status quo, was not necessarily hostile toward other doctrines, and offered an opening to the new Chinese culture. In short, it seduced the leaders of the bakufu.

After two study trips to Song-dynasty China, Eisai, a monk from Mount Hiei, returned to Japan in 1191 to teach the Zen doctrines of the Rinzai school that he had learned on Mount Tiantai. But Eisai wanted more to return to the true teachings of the Tendai than to found a new religious movement. Persecuted as Hōnen was by the monks of the Mountain, Eisai fled Kyoto for Kamakura, where he obtained Masako's support. She asked him to preside over the ceremonies on the first anniversary of Yoritomo's death, in 1200, and allowed him to construct a temple in Kamakura, the Jufukuji. Then, the second shogun, Yoriie, offered him land in Kyoto to establish the Kenninji, where the Tendai, Shingon, and Zen doctrines all would be taught. Eisai seemed more to be a master of prayers and ceremonies, attentive to the leaders of Mount Hiei, than the founder of a new sect.

Eisai taught that meditation leads to awakening (*satori*), the source of inner enlightenment, and the Rinzai school advocated exercises to attain this goal. Disciples were to meditate in a sitting position and reflect on absurd questions and puzzles that provided the conditions for *satori*.

Dōgen, from the high court nobility, studied Tendai on Mount Hiei, and then, when he discovered Eisai's Rinzai school, he decided to go to China in 1223 in search of *satori*. He returned to Japan in 1227 after achieving enlightenment in the sitting position (*zazen*). Dōgen was much more radical than Eisai, who was given to compromise. For Dōgen, all beings have hidden within them, under the layers of emotion, the essence of Buddha. To reveal this essence, disciples had to achieve *satori*, and Dōgen believed that *zazen* was the only means of doing so. "You need neither incense, prayers, invocation of the Buddha's name, confession, nor sacred writings," he wrote in *Bendōwa* in 1231. "Sit down and meditate." Dōgen recognized that Zen required strict discipline, but he was not attempting to expand a sect. Each individual was to practice *zazen*, which would lead to *satori*. Those who reached this stage had to continue with the exercises. To Japanese warriors seeking spiritual discipline, Zen, which rejected prayer, study, and complex ceremonial rituals, was fascinating for its very simplicity. Although most of the protectors of the Zen sects were warriors, however, not all medieval Japanese warriors practiced Zen. Dōgen, who detested the court society into which he had been born, was persecuted by practitioners of traditional Buddhism, and eventually he was taken in by one of his disciples, an estate steward in Echizen Province, who offered to found a site of practice for him, the Eiheiji. This temple, run by Dōgen's disciples, is now the center of the Sōtō sect.[20]

Despite immense differences in doctrinal interpretation, Dōgen, Shinran, and Nichiren were conducting a similar search for absolute truth that could reside only in a single type of practice. The Amidists invoked the sacred name of Amida; Nichiren recited the Lotus Sutra; and Dōgen conceived of medita-tion in a sitting position and categorically rejected the idea of decadence at the end of the Law, an idea central to Amidist concepts: "Invoking the name of Amida Buddha by simply opening one's mouth is to be like the frogs that croak day and night in the fields in springtime."[21]

Dōgen defined his form of Zen between his return from China and his death in 1252. It was radical, austere, and no doubt too intellectual to be resoundingly successful. Eisai's Zen, on the other hand, was too eclectic and not open to Tendai influences. In the mid-thirteenth century, Hōjō Tokiyori invited the great religious figures of his time to Kamakura: Eison of the Ritsu sect, Enni of the Rinzai school, and Dōgen, who made the journey from the Eiheiji in 1247–48. But Zen began to grow only when the Chinese masters arrived in Japan.

THE FIVE MOUNTAINS

Lanxi (Rankei Doryū in Japanese) landed in Hakata in 1246 with the mission of taking control of the Japanese Rinzai school. He quickly made his way to Kamakura, where Tokiyori received him and offered to build him a monastery, the Kenchōji. This temple, built in the Zen style of Song-dynasty China and based on the rules in force in Chinese monasteries, was the first Zen temple in Japan. Tokiyori, and later Tokimune, practiced *zazen*, but political expedi-ency required them to consider other trends as well. When Lanxi died in 1274, Tokimune looked for another master in China. Wuxue (Mugaku Sogen) arrived in Kamakura in 1279, the year that the Southern Song empire fell to the Mon-gols. In 1282, Wuxue inaugurated the Engakuji in Kamakura. After that, Zen monasteries were built all over Japan. The reasons for their success can be found in the alliance forged between the Zen masters and the leaders of the bakufu. The latter, independent of their real interest in the doctrines that had come from China, wanted Zen to play the role for the bakufu that Tendai and Shingon had played for the court nobility: Zen monasteries offered openings and career opportunities to younger members of warrior families, who often gave up their share of their inheritance when they entered them. A complex of Zen monasteries, protected by military governors and hierarchically linked to the most powerful monasteries in Kamakura and Kyoto, was woven throughout the country. The masters from China had the Chinese Five Mountains (Gozan) administrative and organizational system adopted in Japan in the early four-teenth century, and it operated as a cultural and communications network in close association with the warriors' shogunal state. Zen monks, unlike monks of other sects, refused to arm themselves and so never became a military threat.[22]

The Zen Five Mountains organization made a very clear division of roles within the monastic communities, with some monks performing purely administrative duties while others meditated. The Zen monks' managerial abilities were quickly recognized, and increasing numbers of lords, court nobles, and warriors—starting with the Hōjō—asked them to manage their estates. The Zen monasteries never owned estates—that is, they were never landowners of estates—but they did acquire the administrative rights to the lands that they operated.

The success of Zen in the late Kamakura period was also due to its links with the brilliant Song Chinese culture, which fascinated the Japanese, although it was not yet well known. The Japanese Zen monks who studied in China—there were several hundred of them in the early fourteenth century— provided high-quality information on Song and then Yuan China. The Chinese who had come to Japan were generally hostile to the Mongols and counseled the Hōjō regents on dealing with the invaders. Kamakura welcomed with open arms those from the Chinese intellectual elite who fled the mainland after the Mongol invasion of southern China. By the end of the Kamakura period, more than two hundred Chinese monks were living in Japan.

These Chinese Zen masters, schooled in classical culture, were also open to other doctrines. They became intermediaries for Neo-Confucianism, which thus infiltrated the leading warrior classes in Japan and later played a decisive role in the creation of the Tokugawa regime. The last Hōjō regents, Sadatoki and Tadatoki, were interested in Zen for its artistic and cultural aspects. In the warrior elite, the passion for Chinese objects was in full swing. Ships from the mainland arrived at Kamakura with their cargoes of porcelain—the famous blue vases of the Song period—books, paintings, calligraphies, and lacquered objects. A new style was emerging, in which Kamakura was taking the lead and Kyoto was only following, as Song culture broadened the cultural horizons of the warrior class. Zen enabled the leaders of the bakufu to present themselves as bearers of a new cultural legitimacy that rivaled that of the court nobility. In a single century, the formerly uncultured warriors of Kanto had become the promoters and followers of a culture that was both elegant and spare, combining the Chinese cultural contributions with the local culture to produce a new sensibility. Thus, for example, from the use of tea imported by the Zen monks, the Japanese created a unique aesthetic that reached its peak in the fifteenth and sixteenth centuries.

Buddhism's diverse denominational options gave rise to new schools, some of which mutated into sects, and each of which claimed to be the Truth. But their very juxtaposition—none was in a truly hegemonic position—forced the political powers to be conciliatory and careful. Only the most heterodox—even heretical—trends were suppressed, even though they were the least popular. This plurality reflected a form of religiosity specific to Japan, which tended more toward syncretism and ecumenism than toward the jealous preservation of a particular orthodoxy. Practicing *zazen* in no way impeded recitation of the invocation to Amida Buddha after making a pilgrimage to a shrine dedicated to a Shinto deity.

"All roads lead to the summit of Mount Fuji," according to Mujū in the thirteenth century. This Zen monk, a great connoisseur of esoteric Buddhism, was also interested in Confucianism and the worship of Shinto spirits:

> We should not destroy with our obstinate rejection the efficacy of the Great Vehicle and denigrate the benefits of other doctrines by slandering them. Similarly, we should not go so far as to stupidly criticize other practices and make light of other buddhas, bodhisattvas, and *kami*, using as a pretext an authentic faith in the Original Way [of Amida] and basing ourselves fervently on the merits of the *nembutsu* [invocation of Amida Buddha].[23]

Hōnen, himself beset with doubt, pointed out, "If you are certain you will go to heaven, you certainly will; if you are uncertain, it is uncertain." Around 1330, the author of *Tsurezuregusa* found this remark "inspiring."[24]

THE *HEIKE*: EVOKING THE DEPARTED

The trend toward syncretism was expressed in a monumental work of Japanese medieval literature, the *Heike monogatari*. Although there is a written version of this work, it is mainly the version that was recited and sung in public that I shall discuss here, as it was more significant. In the Middle Ages, more than a literary work, the *Heike* was a "recited story." It told of the exploits of the Taira, the history of the grandeur and decadence of the household of the Hei (Hei is the Sino-Japanese reading of the character for Taira), memorializing those who had died during the uprisings and describing their triumphs and failures. A little like the *Iliad* and *Odyssey* in ancient Greece, the *Heike* was recited and sung by bards—in this case, blind men dressed as monks who accompanied themselves on the *biwa*, a sort of lute. They made their way along the roads, wearing high wooden clogs and preceded by young monks who served as their guides.

These blind men sang the acts of Buddha's glory. Starting from the respective temples with which they were affiliated, they traveled through the countryside reciting edifying or extraordinary tales and performing rites of purification, and they were always respectfully received and offered lodging. These men were organized in regional brotherhoods in Kyushu, Yamato, Kyoto, and elsewhere. In the thirteenth century, the Kyoto brotherhood specialized in the art of reciting the *Heike* and formed a guild, choosing as their protective divinity San'ō, venerated at the Hie Shrine, linked to the Enryakuji temple (on Mount Hiei). This guild nevertheless accepted the favor of other gods, those of the Kamo and

Gion Shrines, as well as the protection of certain powerful families in the court, such as the Nakano and the Koga. Finally, in the fourteenth century, Kakuichi set down a written version of the *Heike* and created a school of recitation.

The *Heike* made audiences both laugh and cry. The action of the tale was lively and extended throughout Japan. Its characters were from almost all social groups: the heroes, of course, were members of the higher ranks of the warrior class and court dignitaries, including the emperors themselves, but there were also people from the lower classes—low-ranking provincial warriors, dancers, courtesans, and even uneducated people. Crowds of all classes and statuses rushed to hear the recitations of the blind "monks" punctuated by plucked *biwa* strings. Nothing is known for certain about the origins of this work. The most likely hypothesis attributes its authorship to a certain Yukinaga, a low-ranking court noble and a client of the powerful Kujō family. He likely used fairly reliable historical sources, perhaps supplied by Jien himself, and consulted the court nobles' daily diaries for the facts. Recitation of the text was entrusted to a blind monk from the eastern provinces, Shōbutsu, an expert on the practices and customs of the Kanto warriors, who would have added some details to the early version. The final version was probably written between 1210 and 1220.[25]

In fact, the *Heike* bears the mark of this double origin. It is not simply a warrior tale full of exploits. It contains stories and anecdotes about various characters, some of which are tales within tales. Some passages are related to the genre of edifying accounts that created legends about the foundation of monasteries. Thus, it is a true synthesis of the literary genres of the time. In describing the rise and fall of the Taira family, the *Heike* takes a position on events, thereby supplying a framework for interpretation. The influence of the Kujō family on the authors of the account is obvious: the *Heike* more or less follows Jien's arguments. The end of the Law, "the degenerate world," men rushing about with no apparent purpose other than their passions but in reality rushing toward their fate, the impermanence of things in this world—these are the classic themes of belief in the Pure Land, which, as we know, greatly influenced Jien and his brother Kanezane. Kanezane was also a disciple of Hōnen, one of the characters in the tale. A prominent place is given to the exploits of a low-ranking warrior, Kumagai Naozane, who converted to Hōnen's doctrines near the end of his life and was one of his most faithful disciples. Finally, the "Initiates' Chapter," the last chapter in the *Heike*, ends on a note of infinite nostalgia, heightened by the words that end the work: the "goal of rebirth in the Pure Land."

To the basic version of the *Heike*, of which no written version exists, accounts, anecdotes, and embellishments have been added. In each generation of storytellers, the tale was enriched until Kakuichi wrote it down. The first version probably had only three books, whereas the most complete versions in existence today have twelve. It is thought, for example, that the chapter devoted to Gio, the courtesan whom Kiyomori loved and left, was added by nuns from the lower classes of society, who traveled through Japan preaching faith in Amida and teaching his virtues.

At the end of the ancient era and the beginning of the Middle Ages, people were convinced that the declaiming of the names of dead people would pacify their souls and bring them back to life. At the end of the chapter devoted to Gio at the beginning of the *Heike*, the monk-emperor Go Shirakawa inscribes the names of dead courtesans in the register of the deceased kept in a temple dedicated to recitation of the Lotus Sutra. In Japan at the time, the voice had a magical evocative power, and talking in a loud voice was a sign of lack of restraint, an infringement of the rules of civility. People whispered more than they shouted, and they certainly did not raise their voices when they wanted to communicate with the dead. The text where the names of the dead were written was thus read out loud to attract the attention of the souls of those whose names were invoked.[26]

Thus, *The Tale of the Heike* was not just a story, it was also a call to the dead, an invocation to the souls of those mown down, many of them gloriously in battle. Above all, it was meant to pacify the spirits of the defeated Taira, and its recitation drew crowds to listen raptly. The blind storytellers had such presence that the listeners covered their faces, a typical gesture of surprise or emotion in the Middle Ages. Illustrated scrolls show people hiding their faces behind kimono sleeves or fans, or wearing wide-brimmed rice-straw hats to hide their emotions.[27] In the fourteenth century, spectators went to hear Kakuichi recite the *Heike* wearing full-face masks (to hide their emotions?), which gave them a "strange appearance" (*igyō*).[28]

In Kyoto, storytellers recited the *Heike* in shrines, temples, and places of worship—rooms devoted to prayer, spiritual exercises, and offerings to the deceased. Elsewhere, the blind monks simply stood at a crossroads under an open oiled parasol, whose shadow symbolized a sacred space, to tell their tale, rapidly drawing crowds. To invoke the soul of the deceased, a place was needed that was, if not exactly sacred, at least an intermediate place between the real daily world and the hereafter. The suggestive effect was stronger if the *Heike* was recited in a temple, because this was where funeral services were celebrated, where devotees told stories about hell and heaven, where people prayed, and because it was a place of passage to the kingdom of the dead. Recitation of the *Heike* in this type of space revealed the importance of the tale to the sensitivities of the times. Listening was an intense experience in which audiences had the illusion of being suspended between life and death.[29]

The storyteller's voice, accentuated by the strings of his lute, resonated in unusual spaces such as these, reinforcing the sense of a special moment. Gio and her rival, Hotoki, and Kiyomori and his son, Shigemori, were reborn in these dramatic performances. The *Heike* became a means of reappropriating the past, identifying with known and loved people. For the enthralled audience, the heroes of the *Heike* were there before them as the storyteller spoke their names. The tale acted as an extraordinary time machine, reproducing history and evoking the past. Thus, the art of storytelling involved a particular vocal technique. For their audiences, the blind monks revived a poignant and glorious time using a voice from beyond the grave. They had to transport the audience from this world into the hereafter, and this extreme illusion was possible only through the voice. The power of the one who was able to pronounce and evoke in a society in which most people did not know how to read was measured by his performance. With regard to the *Heike*, some historians even refer to "spoken literature" (*onsei bungaku*). Some remarks by Roger Chartier about reading practices in France of the *ancien régime* could easily apply to the Japanese Middle Ages. More than reading, recitation, song, and dance were the primary medieval arts. Rather than invoking calm and solitude, the arts of the Middle Ages brought people together.

Itinerant monks, preachers, storytellers, and reciters of the *Heike* were characters typical of an apprehensive and mobile society, fascinated by ever-present death, peopled by a cortege of ghosts who returned to torment the living. Gods and monsters always lurked in the fertile commoners' imagination, which was haunted by the infernal and terrifying images, spread by the monks, that rivaled in horror the macabre representations of hell in the West. Fear and pessimism dominated the early Japanese Middle Ages, although Amidism calmed anxieties by promising the Pure Land to believers. People of the Middle Ages perceived of their world as drowning in decadence. Only the followers of Zen, familiar with Chinese culture, were optimistic, with a faith in humankind that counterbalanced the sentiments of those times. In fact, Japanese society of the Kamakura period was not in crisis, threatened with implosion, prey to irremediable decadence. On the contrary, it was engaged in a fundamental structural transformation, whose social and economic consequences were already being felt.

In the fourteenth century, the visions of hell dissipated and then disappeared. From then on, preferences turned to more tranquil portrayals of famous landscapes, still lifes, and animals. Japanese society seemed to be slowly extricating itself from its fear of the gods, death, and the hereafter.

Chapter 6

KAMAKURA: A SOCIETY IN TRANSFORMATION

THOSE WHO LIVED OFF THE LAND . . .

With the beginning of the medieval period, marked by the uprising of the
warriors of Kanto in the late twelfth century and the emergence of a new political center in the east, Japanese society began a phase of economic expansion
and increasing trade. Because there are no quantifiable sources, it is impossible
to measure the exact scope of this phenomenon, but the few surviving documents attest to a society that seemed to be awakening from a long period of
inertia following the brilliant progress of the regime of codes. This ascent began
with the great land-clearing movements in the eleventh and twelfth centuries,
and by the thirteenth century, the countryside had been reshaped by the new
social order. Although the clearing of land for rice paddies had slowed, except
perhaps in the western provinces, previously free land was now becoming part
of the estate economy. The Kamakura period was a time of growth of domestic
trade, and the introduction of Chinese coins as a major trade instrument dates
from this century. It was also in the thirteenth century that the peasants, especially in Kinai and neighboring regions, began to free themselves from their
position of servitude, a movement that expanded in the following two centuries.
Economic and commercial progress helped create a rural middle class, which
sought to gain control over its affairs and, eventually, to shake off the grip of
the lords. The improved economy was not enough, however, to avoid some-

times violent food crises, such as those in 1259 and 1271. But overall, the Middle Ages seems to have been a time of growth—slow in the thirteenth century, more rapid after the Mongol invasions, chaotic in the fourteenth century, and then more structured in the fifteenth century, especially in Kinai and around the Inland Sea.

THE RURAL ECONOMY

Agricultural production was organized within the framework of the estate economy. Whatever these private estates of the civil and religious nobility were called locally[1] and whatever their economic mode (wetland rice cultivation, dryland farming, exploitation of forests, horse pastures, the harvest of seaweed and seafood and salt production on the beaches), their internal organization was more or less similar. The land was cultivated by wealthy peasants (*myōshu*) or sometimes low-ranking warriors—heads of agricultural operations who were responsible for rent payments and corvées. The *myōshu* formed the middle class in the countryside and was the leading class of village society. They had at their disposal the labor supplied by tenant farmers to whom they rented land, and by servants, farmhands, and various dependents whom they fed and lodged in return for their work. Twentieth-century historians do not agree on their status: were they slaves, serfs, or economically dependent "freemen"? Did they own any land?[2] The written sources mention them only in passing, and so they remain the great silent mystery of Japanese medieval history.

In the Kamakura period, 50 to 60 percent of the country's cultivated land was on the private estates. The rest was under public administration[3] and was overseen by provincial administrators appointed by the court, some of whose prerogatives, as we have seen, were awarded to military governors by the Kamakura bakufu. The exploitation of public lands came to resemble that of private estates. The annual rents charged varied as a function of the status—private or public—of the land and the local power relationships, the greed of the lord, the degree of the peasant community's organization, and the abundance of agricultural labor.

The estates varied in size, and not all were owned by individuals. They were very large in the east and in Kyushu, where they might cover an entire district and surround several villages. In Kinai, they were much more modest—the smallest ones only a few hectares in area—and some peasants cultivated land that belonged to several estates, on each of which they had a different status and lord. Indeed, it was not unusual for peasants to live in one estate and have their fields in another.[4] The multiplicity of feudal authorities created by this situation helped strengthen the rural communities, which were able to play the lords off one another when they were at odds.

Cultivated fields accounted for only half the total area of an estate; the rest was fallow and uncultivated land, woods, marshes, flooded sections, and the like. These areas were indispensable, however, to the villagers, who counted on them as sources for heating wood and the fish, edible ferns, and various tubers that were essential supplements to their diet. Control of the uncultivated parts of the estate thus gave rise to increasingly bitter conflicts between lords and peasants, sometimes involving entire villages.

THE VILLAGE

The village in the Middle Ages was different from that of today, as it was rarely a small group of buildings. The modern vision of peasants bound to the soil, living peacefully in a village, was far from the reality. The folklorist Yanagida Kunio has shown that more than two-thirds of today's Japanese villages were created after the fifteenth century, during the Edo period. Before then, people lived scattered about.[5] Humble peasant cabins dotted the valleys, generally at the foot of a mountain, overlooking the rice paddies, away from marshy land that might flood during a heavy rain. A village was thus equivalent to a community of rural dwellers living off a piece of land.[6] In the western part of the country, the landowner's residence was often located at a distance; in the eastern provinces, it was located on the heights, with an administration building nearby. The lords' manors, with their warehouses and administrative buildings surrounded by ditches and hedges, were a great contrast to the peasants' small, uncomfortable, and dark cabins. A pot, some bowls, a few spades, hoes, and sickles were the only possessions of the poorest peasants. *Myōshu* had a few cows, perhaps a horse, and a greater number of agricultural tools, many of them made of iron. Some of the larger houses had thickly thatched roofs and several rooms. Rice-straw mats were laid on the ground, as *tatami* were still reserved for the wealthier classes and became widespread in their current form only after the fifteenth century. The better-off *myōshu* owned swords and a few chests in which ceremonial clothing was stored.

Village life was regulated by seasonal agricultural work. In the thirteenth century, feasts and Shinto ceremonies were organized by the assembly of well-off peasants grouped in a shrine brotherhood, or *miyaza*. Although poorer peasants, servants, and serfs were excluded from organizing these ceremonies, they were allowed to take part in the festivities. Because the lords were not included, the ceremonies served to bring the village community together. This assembly of villagers offered a place for open discussion where decisions regarding worship (repairs to the local shrine, chapels, preparation of ceremonies, etc.) were made and internal conflicts and various community problems were solved. Meetings took place at the local shrine or sometimes at the home of one of the wealthier peasants, and their sacred nature reinforced the importance of the decisions. Although they were made in a relatively democratic way, the participants were forced to honor their obligations and were expected to uphold the village's sense of community in the case of outside aggression.[7]

The evolution of the estate system was measured mainly by the increase in production and the expansion of trade. Sources of this period supply two decisive indices: the rise of intensive agriculture based on two annual harvests and the institution of rural markets on fixed dates.

THE RISE OF AGRICULTURAL PRODUCTION

Annual double cropping began in the mid-thirteenth century on the shores of the Inland Sea, where the climate was particularly favorable. In 1264, Kamakura recommended to the governor of Bizen and Bingo Provinces (the regions around today's Himeji and Okayama) that he not charge rent on the "wheat" seeded in the rice paddies when the fields were dried out in the fall.[8] The double cropping started when the peasants learned how to combine wetland rice cultivation and grain cultivation. The fields were flooded in late May or early June to plant rice, which was harvested in October. Then the land was drained quickly so that grain could be sowed. Far from exhausting the soil, the rice enriched it and made it available for a second crop. The "wheat" (it was usually barley) matured under the strong spring sun and was harvested at the end of May, and then the land was flooded. On land that could not be flooded, peasants planted legumes such as soybeans, peas, string beans, and broad beans after harvesting the grain. This ingenious arrangement, which drew the admiration of Korean travelers in the fifteenth century,[9] was no doubt aimed at circumventing the rigorous rent-collection system. The landlords were very demanding about rents on rice and frequently checked yields and field sizes, but they were much more lenient on the dry land where the peasants grew crops for their personal consumption. The peasants paid special attention to these small parcels of land. The double cropping could be carried out only on dry lands that could be irrigated artificially, and it could not be done every year.

The wider use of fertilizer—usually decomposed animal and plant waste—made possible these agricultural advances. The increase in production due to the cultivation of new lands, and especially to technical improvements, provided the peasants with surpluses. This, in turn, led to a rural commerce in which produce could be traded at market and to a general rise in the peasants' quality of life, with major social consequences: the appearance of a middle class in the countryside and the emancipation of the lowest class of peasants.

TRADE IN THE COUNTRYSIDE

In the early thirteenth century, the rural estate economy was still almost self-sufficient. There was little trade, and all consumer products, except iron and salt, were produced on the estate. By midcentury, however, local markets had sprung up from Kanto to Kyushu. This phenomenon, noted in historical sources, expanded further in the early fourteenth century. Local markets usually were held three times a month. Some came to have evocative names: Yokkaichi (the market took place on the fourth, fourteenth, and twenty-fourth days of the month), Itsukaichi (the market took place on the fifth, fifteenth, and twenty-fifth days of the month), and so on. Markets were set up near the local lord's manor, at the gate to a temple, at a crossroads, or near a bridge. Poor peasants brought their meager foodstuffs to sell: soybeans, sesame seeds, string beans, and sometimes hemp. The wealthier peasants traded in rice and barley. Traveling merchants came to sell lamp oil, paper, knives, iron hoes, fresh fish, salt, and sometimes fabrics. If the market was held on a thoroughfare or in a small seaport, it might even acquire regionwide importance and draw both landowners and wealthy peasants from the surrounding area. The goods traded at these markets were more valuable: weapons, armor, silk, and luxury craft items made in Kyoto, Nara, Kamakura, or even China. Even small, purely local markets helped increase trade and circulate merchandise and introduced a rudimentary cash economy to even the most remote regions. Peasants began to use Chinese copper coins, even though barter was the most widespread means of exchange.[10]

Increased production and the development of trade were part of an overall social movement that was marked by the emancipation of the lowest class of peasants. Their social condition has not been clearly established, but the following is a description of what we do know.

EMANCIPATION OF THE SERFS

Peasant society was divided into two main social groups: the myōshu, who were relatively wealthy and responsible for taking care of the rice paddies and paying taxes, and peasants in servitude. Historians are divided over the latter. Although it seems certain that there still were slaves in the Japanese countryside in the thirteenth century, does this mean that all serfs were slaves? Was there an intermediate class between the slaves and the myōshu, and were they independent farmers with their own small fields or simply farmworkers?

In the monk Mujū's collection of stories and anecdotes written in 1283 and titled Shasekishū[11] is one that takes place around 1270–71, following a drought, when the provinces along the Tōkaidō were in dire straits. A slave merchant on his way to the eastern provinces stopped for the night in an inn in Mikawa Province (east of Nagoya) with his slaves. Among them was a young man, silently crying bitter tears. When questioned, he said that he was from Mino (Gifu region) and that to save his mother, who was starving, he had decided to sell himself as a slave to a merchant heading east. To comfort him, his mother had told him that as long he was alive, she would hope to see him again. At present, he was going to an unfamiliar land, and he did not know where he would die. Thus, destitute people, starving and incapable of paying their land-owner's rent, were selling themselves to slave traders, who sold them in regions where strong arms were needed. The Japanese texts, however, use the expression "selling one's body" and "trafficking in human beings" without referring explic-itly to slavery. Could these "sold" people buy their freedom back? If so, their slavery would have been temporary.

The Kamakura bakufu issued bans on the trade in human beings several times during the century (proof that the traffic was marginal?), and traffickers in human beings were threatened with being branded on the forehead. Some edifying tales (sekkyō) of that period, such as the story of the steward Sanshō, and nō plays from the end of the following century featured horrifying plots in which women and children were kidnapped by professional slave traders.

In 1276, Nejime Kiyotsuna, a retainer-warrior, had a position in the admin-istration of Ōsumi Province, in southern Kyushu, and he distributed his ninety-four "serfs," or shojū ("those who obey"), among his sixteen children. The ref-erence document clearly indicates that the shojū were grouped in small families.[12] According to the Goseibai Shikimoku, when an estate was divided after its owner's death and the serfs were separated, the boys went with their father and the girls with their mother.[13] In the case of the Nejime family, it seems that the shojū were not slaves in the strict sense of the word, for their master gave them parcels of land to farm, and they lived in cabins that they owned. The shojū men followed their masters to war, serving as porters or grooms. But many of them did not have any family, and the land that they farmed remained entirely under the lord's control, and he could change its assignment at will. Those labeled yatsubara or yatsuko in the documents owned nothing but their own lives.

Were there many serfs and slaves? It is difficult to know. In a society in which only the upper classes could write, documents concerned essentially real-estate law, because land was the only asset considered truly valuable. It was passed down through generations, so landowning families were careful to keep the deeds, real-estate rolls, and land cadastres that indicated how much tax was to be paid and also offered proof of ownership. The abundance of these documents may explain historians' overestimation of the role of land in Japanese society. Conversely, few documents attest to the existence of serfs, who had few posses-sions and led uneventful lives but were responsible for production.

The discovery of some rather unusual documents has given us an opportu-nity to reevaluate the question about slaves and serfs. Most of these documents were preserved because they were sacred texts (sutras, for example), but on their backs, for lack of something else to write on, people took notes on various things that were not worth keeping—drafts of one sort or another (ura monjo). One of the most frequently cited documents in this regard is kept in Nakayama, near

Chiba, in a temple of the Nichiren sect, the Hokkekyōji, where many religious texts, some by Nichiren himself, are preserved. These documents were kept because they had religious value, but a perusal of the "miscellaneous things" written on their backs reveals a world that was not recorded in official medieval writings. One lord accuses the administrator of a neighboring estate of hiding two serfs that belong to him. Another document relates the complaint of one of these serfs, who had "sold his body" to secure a loan of rice to his father and who, once the loan was repaid, was refused his freedom by his master. This indicates that there were perhaps more serfs than the official documents indicated.[14]

Another revelation is that the warriors were not the only ones to use laborers whose status was similar to that of slaves. The *myōshu*, as well, had their lands farmed by serfs whose lives they controlled. In fact, the lands owned by *myōshu* could be described as agricultural operations run by a labor pool in servitude.

In the early Middle Ages, independent peasants had very small farms, whereas the *myōshu* operated estates based on patriarchal and slavery relationships. At least that is the version proposed by some historians.[15] For others, even if *myōshu* peasants did use slave labor, they were still radically different from the landowners. First, they worked in the fields alongside their "slaves," and second, they were exploited by the lords, as they paid stiff rents and took part in corvées. In fact, the *myōshu* did not use many "slaves"; their agricultural labor was composed mainly of peasants with small farms (*kosakunin*), who worked the fields leased to them by the *myōshu* and also did seasonal agricultural work on their own land. Thus, they were not slaves but small independent landowners.[16] Their holdings were extremely small, rarely over twenty to thirty ares (2,000 to 3,000 square meters; a hectare, 10,000 square meters, is considered the minimum area for the subsistence of a nuclear family), and they remained bound to the *myōshu*, who were registered as being responsible for payment of land rents on the landownership documents and were the only interlocutors with the lords or their stewards.

After 1300, especially in Kinai, the names of small peasants were noted in the registers because they paid rents to the lord.[17] Their names also appeared on documents written in common by the village peasants, a sign that they took part in making decisions that affected the community.[18] There is evidence that they exerted pressure in the second half of the Kamakura period. What had changed in regard to social relations in the late thirteenth and early fourteenth centuries? The answer is that these peasants had acquired a new position in the peasant community and now had a right to speak. By the early fourteenth century, they were sitting on the councils of the shrine fraternities alongside the wealthy peasants.

How had the serfs freed themselves? The burgeoning economy enabled the poorest peasants to accumulate a bit of surplus that they could take to market, which led to a general improvement in their quality of life. But the key was dryland farming: because they could grow the grain and vegetables that they needed for daily sustenance, the poorer peasants had become independent of their masters.

Although the agricultural economy was dominated by wetland rice cultivation, its importance has no doubt been overestimated.[19] Here, too, historians may have been led astray by written documents. Because the state and landowners paid greater attention to rice paddies and kept a written record of everything pertaining to this type of land, it might seem that other agricultural production was insignificant. Somewhat beyond the master's purview, however, dry fields in which vegetables, hemp, and grains were grown were carefully tended by the poorest peasants. These fields were the basis of their subsistence, just as the rice paddies were the source of the master's living because they were responsible for most of the rents he collected. At the time, rice was almost a luxury product. The importance accorded to rice paddies arose from the fact that it was difficult for the lord to clear such land. The peasant knew that although he could farm a rice paddy, he could not create it by himself, that the master was able to do so because he could supply the iron tools and requisition the labor to build the irrigation works. Nonetheless, a peasant who was willing could clear a field in the off season, assisted by one or two sons or a couple of neighbors.

The rise in agricultural production was linked to the labor of former serfs, who took over cleared parcels of land where they could grow food for themselves. A number of factors led to the overall expansion of agricultural society: the diffusion of certain agricultural techniques, such as double cropping and the use of fertilizer; the cultivation of dry fields, parcels to which the small-scale peasants were even more attentive, since they owned them; the intensive work of these farmers on their new holdings; and the sale of products in local markets. In medieval Japan, land had a sure, tangible value. Every year, as long as it was not neglected, it supplied a harvest. Accordingly, "possession" meant, first and foremost, the possession of land rights: for the lord, the right to administer an estate and collect rents; for the myōshu peasant, the right to cultivate a series of paddies; and for the small farmer, the right—a new right—to exploit his holding. The affirmation of these rights was a central issue at the time.

. . . AND THOSE WHO DID NOT LIVE
OFF THE LAND

Since the end of Word War II, Japanese historians have been particularly interested in land, estates, landownership, and relations between lords and peasants. Most of the medieval rural archives address these questions. But like those written sources, historians talk more about myōshu peasants than about slaves, more about wetland rice paddies than about patches of land cleared by impoverished peasants, and more about landowners and peasants than about the people whose livelihoods were activities other than farming. Recent research by scholars such as Amino Yoshihiko deals with people who were less marginal than might have been thought. Woodsmen and hunters in the mountains, fishermen along the rivers and coasts who caught fish in nets and weirs or with cormorants, and itinerant artisans and traders all contributed to the general increase in production. These groups, which Amino Yoshihiko classifies as "nonfarmers," were diverse, and through them we have discovered a society markedly different from that of the peasantry.[20]

Agriculture was not the only productive activity in the Middle Ages, and it did not yet hold the dominant position in production that it attained in the Edo period. The sea, waterways, forests, and mountains were "open" spaces where hunting and gathering were still widespread: saltwater and freshwater fish, fowl, grasses, wild vegetables, fruits, and mountain berries provided high-quality foods for the emperor and the court nobility. These products also played an important role in worship of the gods, the *kami*. Foods from the sea were placed on altars as offerings to them. Even at shrines built deep in the mountains, the offerings included fish and seaweed, proof that they were sold by peddlers throughout the country. In the prewar period, the ethnologist Shibusawa Keizō criticized the idea that Shinto was a religion of rice-growing peasants and showed that the *kami* were very often linked to the sea.

During the ancient period, nonagricultural foodstuffs were used as a form of tribute. People living in the mountains and along the coasts had to deliver fresh products from the forest or sea to the court or the shrines. But these tributary populations changed status between the eleventh and thirteenth centuries, when they came under the direct protection of the emperor, the shrines, and the court nobility. By filling the storehouses of the private imperial chancellery that supplied the palace kitchens, the groups called "those who supply the imperial court" (*kugonin*) obtained various privileges: exemption from paying the trade taxes that impeded transactions, safe-conducts ensuring freedom of travel, and the right to tax-free rice paddies. In one sense, these suppliers became the emperor's protégés, and he their patron. Their numbers grew when the retired emperors took power in the court at the end of the eleventh century.

A similar phenomenon took place at the shrines at Kamo, Ise, Kasuga, Hie, and elsewhere, which established client relations with the social classes that subsisted on products from the sea and the mountains. These people of humble status specializing in nonagricultural activities and the supply of tributes were known by a variety of terms. Because they were protected by the shrines that they supplied, they made up fancy titles for themselves—"suppliers of offerings to the gods" (*gusainin*), "people belonging to the gods" (*jinin*)—that left no doubt as to their status: they submitted to their gods, and the gods protected them and made them virtually untouchable. Assaulting these servants of the gods was tantamount to assaulting the gods themselves.

Several conclusions could be made about the existence of these social categories. First, people who made a living by hunting or fishing, offering their products to the court or a patron shrine, and then selling the surplus to other social groups (peasants, warriors) had to confine their activities to uncultivated areas (sea, beach, lake, river, mountain, forest, plain). Although they made their living from trade (and, as a corollary, from transport), they were not really merchants, for the division of labor had not yet taken place. In sum, they caught small game and fish, which they then sold; in other words, they made a living from killing animals.

But Buddhist bans on the slaughter of animals and the consumption of meat were spreading at this time among the Japanese peasantry. There was growing opposition between the peasant populations who were bound to the soil, fed themselves mainly from the plant products that they grew, and were dependent on the warrior class, and the nonpeasant populations, who consumed meat and fish and were protected by the emperor, the nobility, and the shrines.

Second, these populations of "nonfarmers," which, in the thirteenth century, included itinerant artisans such as potmakers, were attached to and protected by the old ruling class (the court and shrines) but had little to do directly with the warriors. Whence an attractive theory: not only was there a geographic and political division of authority during the Kamakura period, but also there was a social and professional division among the dominated classes. By invading the estates of the nobility, the warriors took control of agriculture and the peasantry, and the traditional elites forged ties with the nonpeasant groups who provided the basis of trade, transport, and craft activities and made use of nonarable areas.

Was the polarization of the Kamakura regime rooted in this division of authority over the dominated classes? Why didn't the warriors have absolute power; why did they let the old ruling class continue to exist? I have already partly answered this question in preceding chapters, but it is possible that the existence of privileged links among the emperor, the shrines, and the nonpeasant groups offers yet another reason: in the thirteenth century, the warriors did not yet have control over "nonfarmers," who were completely dependent on the old aristocracy.

Since a detailed description of the complex world of the "nonfarmers" is beyond the scope of this book, I will limit myself to a few regional and social examples.

THE "PEOPLE OF THE SEA"

Wakasa Bay, north of Kyoto, on the other side of Lake Biwa and bordering the Japan Sea, has a very rugged coast. Its many inlets and coves favored the growth of small fishing ports—still active today—near a sea with a plentiful supply of fish. The "people of the sea" had lived on these coasts since ancient times, and they paid the court or the emperor a tribute in salt and fresh sea products. In the twelfth century, these groups were still nomadic, settling along a beach at the end of a cove for a time and then moving on. Wherever they settled, they cleared a few fields behind the beach, made salt, and set nets for their fish. They also used their boats to transport rents along the coast from Hokuriku to the capital. In the thirteenth century, the boats of Takarasu, a small port in the region, could be spotted as far as Izumo to the west and Tōhoku to the north. Starting in the Kamakura period, the "people of the sea" began to settle more permanently in the coves, where they built houses bunched tightly together facing the sea. These fishermen's villages were configured differently from the peasant villages inland, which were still quite dispersed, as they were concentrated and resembled small towns. Sugaura on Lake Biwa, for example, still looks like this today. The comings and goings of boats gave the impression of intense activity. Inns were built to house merchants and itinerant performers; markets sprang up and traders opened shops; and then dancers and prostitutes came to liven up the small ports, which grew into towns. The first of these port towns appeared in the late thirteenth and early fourteenth centuries: Tsuruga in Echizen, Obama in Wakasa, and others. A century earlier, the population in the region was not yet sedentary.

The "people of the sea" organized into communities (*tone*) led by a designated chief called the elder (*osa*). All members had the same rights: in Tsurube, in Wakasa Province, the community worked in an egalitarian and coherent way. Twenty-five family heads shared use of the salt-making oven. Contracts were made between members of the community for setting the nets, and the fishing zones were distributed in such a way that no one person's interest would be overlooked. The community also included the heads of relatively well-off families that had once been members. In a document dating from the early fourteenth century, a member leaves to his daughter a ship (a small boat?), seventy-one *kanmon* (coins), 150 *koku* of rice, a tree-covered mountain, six kimono, and five slaves, including three women. The wealth of the "people of the sea" seems to have been much greater than that of the *myōshu* who lived inland.

Lords and public authorities tried to organize the fishermen's communities, which were still quite independent in the early thirteenth century. Local officials in provincial administrations tried to take control of the beaches, which were considered public land. In 1265, eleven "beaches" in Wakasa Province were transformed into rent-paying public estates. But the nobles and religious institutions also were interested in these people and where they lived. Six "beaches" in the province came under the sway of monasteries or shrines, with the monastery of Mount Hiei even going so far as to obtain ownership of a deserted coast and then inviting the "people of the sea" on neighboring coasts to move there.[21]

Allegiance to public authorities or an estate owner had its advantages. True, the communities living on the coast now had to pay rents, but in exchange, they had the support of an institution that would protect them if they got into trouble with a neighboring community. Above all, they obtained privileges. The "people of the sea" attached to Mount Hiei, for example, were able to sell the products they had fished, gathered, or made (salt) in all estates belonging to that monastery, without paying taxes.

But not all "people of the sea" were organized in this way. Many had formed direct ties with the imperial household or a shrine. In Ise Bay, some fishers supplied the emperor with seafood for his table and received his protection. Others had ties to the Ise Shrine and obtained safe-conducts enabling them to take their boats down the coast along the Tōkaidō. In the Inland Sea, groups of seamen under the protection of the Kamo Shrine received exemptions from toll payments and charges in the ports of the region, where the shrine had many estates.

There was a division of roles in the communities. While the men sailed the boats and made salt on the beaches, the women sold the fresh produce inland as far as Kyoto. All the fish vendors in Kyoto were women from the coast or from fishing communities on Lake Biwa. Women representing the Yamashiro suppliers specializing in cormorant fishing wrapped their heads in white cloths and carried tubs of water filled with trout. In 1248, a conflict over fishing sites broke out between two communities, those living downstream and upstream in the Katsura valley. The people downstream had the support of the Konoe family (of the Fujiwara clan) and won the quarrel. The women of the upstream community, furious over an outcome that they considered a gross injustice, went together to the retired emperor's residence, where they happened to meet the imperial regent Konoe Kanetsune on his way home in his palanquin. They provided an angry escort, shouting and heaping abuse on him![22]

A similar division in roles was found among people who made their living making charcoal in the mountains north of Kyoto. While the men made the charcoal, their wives went down to the capital to sell to the court and the urban population the fuel they needed for cooking and heating.

ARTISANS

The people of the sea, rivers, and mountains were not the only groups in the thirteenth century to benefit from protection from on high that ensured them of relative freedom to travel. Some groups of artisans whose activities were essential to society, such as ironmongers, were also classified as "suppliers to the imperial court." Like fishermen and hunters, ironmongers, blacksmiths, and potmakers were attached to the imperial kitchens, to which they delivered, as tribute, various objects made of iron. The potmakers and ironmongers of Kawachi Province supplied the court with lanterns in exchange for exemptions from corvées and tolls. Ironmongers traveled along the rivers and coasts in boats to sell their products. Those who made gongs for the temples went wherever the demand existed. Makers and sellers of oil, mats, and saké, merchants selling chestnuts and cucumbers, and many others traveled under the freedom accorded to them as "suppliers to the imperial court."[23]

DANCERS AND COURTESANS

Dancer-prostitutes also formed associations to obtain protection and the right to move around. These women were not discriminated against; in fact, they had a somewhat elevated status. Unlike the prostitutes who resided in the "plea-sure quarters" starting in the Edo period, medieval dancers were free to travel.[24]

Prostitution was rarely their main activity; first and foremost, they were danc-ers and musicians. In the Middle Ages, though, roles and activities were not clearly defined, and the worlds of acrobats, actors, and prostitutes were blurred. Although the "arts" were often invented by men, it was women who made them popular and entertained the nobility. Some women moved in powerful circles and even had some political influence. These women often formed an impor-tant liaison between the elite and popular culture, helping transmit court man-ners to the provinces and commoner traditions to the court. They also launched songs and represented the period's "style."

These women belonged to three main groups. First were the *asobime*, who performed "on the water." Notes in journals kept by nobles of the period and illustrated scrolls describe them performing on the Kamo River in Kyoto, at small river ports on the Yodo River, and at ports on the Inland Sea. By boat, they approached travelers on ships entering port and enticed them with their songs and their colorful clothes. Their clothing was comparable, it was said, to that of young women of the aristocracy. As hostesses at inns on beaches and riverbanks, they entertained and encouraged customers to eat and drink. The wealthiest clients sometimes asked them to attend receptions in their villages, and some were invited to the court. The Yodo River basin between Kyoto and the sea seemed to be their favorite place to work, and they took advantage of their freedom of movement in the area.

Kugutsu, or *kugutsume*, played a role analogous to the *asobime*, but they frequented the inns along the major roads. (The word *kugutsu* later was used to refer to puppeteers, who were more often men than women, but in the late thirteenth century, it referred to women whose activity had little to do with puppets.) Those on the Tōkaidō became very popular when Kamakura became an important center and traffic between Kinai and southern Kanto increased. Like the *asobime*, they sang and danced in the inns. Some traveled from one inn to another, while others stayed in one place. Along with artisans and traders, they benefited from the protection of the public authorities, who sometimes even guaranteed them free land to farm.[25] Like the *asobime*, the *kugutsu* were not primarily prostitutes. In medieval Japan, they were considered to have a knowledge of proper etiquette and enjoyed a relatively high social status.

Shirabyōshi were high-class courtesans who specialized in dancing. Dressed in boys' clothes—a concession to warrior fashion?—they performed men's dances. They went to the nobles' manors to sing and dance, and some of them lived there. At the end of the ancient period, some *shirabyōshi* seemed to have been attached to the imperial administration as regular employees. In the thirteenth century, the highest notables in Kamakura sometimes sent for famous *shirabyōshi*.

Some courtesans were the lovers of the most prominent men of the time. Yoshitsune, Yoritomo's brother, had a famous liaison with Shizuka Gozen, and the retired emperor Go Toba loved the beautiful Kamekiku. Many high-ranking nobles, abbots, and famous warriors were the sons of *asobime* or *shirabyōshi*. Yoshitsune, Prime Minister Tokudaiji Sanemoto, and Grand Minister Saionji Sanefu were children of courtesans, a fact that never handicapped their careers. The retired emperor Go Shirakawa was a son of the famous Tango no Tsubone, whose influence on court politics was considerable in the last years of the twelfth century, to the point that Yoritomo himself sought her favors. She was an *asobime* from Eguchi, a small port at the mouth of the Yodo River (where Osaka is today). Her father was the chief of the "imperial suppliers" in the delta and headed communities of fishermen, net layers, and cormorant breeders. Everyone who worked on the water belonged to the "imperial supplier" organization, including the *asobime*, who worked on the rivers.[26]

There is no evidence that these women were treated with contempt or rejected. Because the *shirabyōshi* of Kyoto belonged to associations led by women, they were able to defend their own interests in court. For example, in 1249, *kugutsu* from Suruga won a trial in Kamakura against a lord who claimed that they should pay more rent.[27]

THE PARIAHS

The village inn (*shuku*) was usually located at the center and was a world unto itself. Twenty-two families lived at the Kanazu Inn in Echizen to make sure that it ran smoothly.[28] Of course, the inns accommodated wealthy travelers, but they were also places where locals gathered to eat, drink, and hear the stories and information provided by those passing through. Starting in the fourteenth century, baths were also offered. The inn was run by a chief (*chōri*) who was also responsible for maintaining the local shrine.[29] Many of the people who lived around the inn—the *kugutsu* singers, waitresses, cooks, grooms, valets, and other servants—were known as *hinin*, literally "nonhuman" or "unhuman," an expression for pariahs.[30]

Most *hinin* were employed in subordinate jobs at Buddhist temples or Shinto shrines. Some had a physical handicap or an incurable disease, often leprosy.[31] Although they were not monks, they assumed the title of "sacred man"—Chikuzen hōshi (Brother Chikuzen) or Amida hōshi (Brother Amida)—and were thus false monks, as were most of the blind reciters of the *Heike*. Many of them were beggars, but not all of them were marginal, as evidenced by those who were attached to inns.

In general, the *hinin* performed unrewarding tasks, particularly those that were considered unclean. They collected trash, swept the temples and shrines, cleaned ponds and wells, and tended gardens. The *hinin* also were associated with work having to do with death: they washed corpses, slaughtered sick cattle, and buried or burned the cadavers of animals after skinning them for their leather. Among the female *hinin* were low-ranking prostitutes who worked in alleys at night. The Kiyomizu Temple took a cut of the activities of these women and on those of other *hinin* in exchange for its protection.

The status of these categories of *hinin* is the subject of debate among modern historians.[32] The discrimination against them was real, as revealed in the epithet "nonhuman." Nevertheless, *hinin* in the Middle Ages were not discriminated against as much as were their descendants in the Edo period, whose complaints, which have survived to the present, convey the misery of people encumbered by an extremely low status. In the Kamakura period, the *hinin* had a sense of independence. They performed tasks that gained them special protection and favors similar to those for suppliers to the imperial court. Some were recruited by warriors responsible for policing the capital to serve as armed guards responsible for menial chores deemed degrading by the samurai: guarding prisoners, branding criminals, and even executing them. In an awkwardly written complaint[33] by the *hinin* of Nara against the chief of the *hinin* of the Kiyomizu (proof that some of them knew how to write), is the following sentence: "Although he is a *hinin*, the chief of the people of the Kiyomizu likes to do evil." Amino Yoshihiko explains that the notion of evil appears here as a concept completely foreign to *hinin* society: the plaintiffs were accusing the defendants of acting contrary to their shared sense of morality.

The Japanese of the Middle Ages were repelled by anything associated with death, blood, and, later, meat. Although those people who worked with the dead were permanently impure and thus no longer exactly human, they were not inherently contemptible.[34] For example, to offer a bath to such people was a particularly charitable act. Accordingly, the inns run by *hinin* not only were highly sociable places, they were also places where people could bathe. The Japanese love of bathing goes back to this period; to purify the body with hot water was an idea that became widespread between the tenth and thirteenth centuries. Likewise, acts of charity toward the poor had also been performed for a long time: they were given rice, salt, and clothing, and offered baths. Eison and Ninshō encouraged these acts of charity in the Kamakura period.

Monks had the first public baths built in the monasteries in the thirteenth century. Anyone could bathe there: nobles, warriors, and commoners, pure and impure, men and women, adults and children. Wealthy laymen also had baths built at their own expense, with the prospect of salvation in mind. The baths built in the temples were not simply sites of ablution; they were also meeting places for groups who went to purify themselves and bathe together. Baths in the inns along the roads served a similar purpose for travelers. Sometimes inns were opened near the baths (many used hot springs). At the time of the civil wars in the fourteenth century, baths even became places of peace and asylum. During truces, warriors and foot soldiers of enemy armies often found themselves together, naked and unarmed, in public baths washing themselves![35]

KAMAKURA AND KYOTO

The rivalry between the two powers that constituted the medieval state inevitably created competition between the two capitals, especially because they were the only fairly large cities in the country at the time. The urbanization of Japan began, hesitantly, only in the fifteenth century.

The notions of *kōsho* and *zushi* symbolize the medieval city. *Kōsho* refers to empty areas within the ancient imperial capital, a space theoretically composed of avenues and streets crossing at right angles. The growth of Heian (later Kyoto) did not exactly follow the designs of the city planners in the late eighth century. Both beyond and between inhabited neighborhoods were empty zones, unoccupied land, and avenues converted into cultivated fields. Thus, the city was a checkerboard not of houses and streets but of inhabited sectors and areas without buildings, some of them turned into fields or rice paddies. Heian was thus, in fact, a "city" riddled with fields.

Zushi refers to the roads and crossroads that developed beyond those in the initial checkerboard plan; these places were where the medieval city prospered. *Kōsho*—spaces, cultivated or not, on the site of the ancient city—abounded, as did *zushi*—new streets, crossroads, and routes. These were lively places, where traders in cheap goods, peasants from the surrounding areas, nobles' domestics, passersby, and thieves mixed. They usually were situated on the edge of the city, away from the centrally located nobles' residences and the buildings of the imperial administration.[36]

Kamakura developed rapidly and rather anarchically. Around 1180, it was just a small town, but by the early fourteenth century, the shogunal capital had perhaps 50,000 residents. The area was narrow, and the city's growth was blocked by mountains that surrounded the main avenue, Wakamiya. The arrival in 1252 of a young shogun, the imperial prince, provoked a flurry of urban regulation. At the time, Kamakura was still a pale imitation of the imperial capital: cows wandered through the streets, and rotting horse cadavers were left to foul the air. Shops on trestles, set up haphazardly, narrowed the streets and made circulation difficult.

The shogunal administration took draconian measures.[37] Retail shops were confined to seven neighborhoods; allowing animals to roam free was forbidden; commoners were not allowed to carry swords inside the city; and beggars were expelled. Although there was a lack of space, the construction of shanties over canal ditches was banned. Night curfews were decreed. This new legislation ended up pushing toward the urban periphery the bustling neighborhoods where shopkeepers, street entertainers, peasants from the surrounding countryside, preaching mendicant monks, and prostitutes gathered. The city was surrounded by sloping roads leading to passes that formed natural defenses, and it was on these slopes that marginal society, banished from the city center, settled.[38]

In medieval society, limits, borders, and frontier areas always had a rather sacred connotation. Temples dedicated to spirits, cemeteries, and sometimes the shrine were built on the edges of villages. Thus, sacred sites and populations of wanderers, marginal people, and pariahs often coexisted at the periphery of inhabited places. In Kamakura, this trend was evident: with the exception of the Tsurugaoka Shrine, surrounded by the residences of the shogun and the warrior aristocracy and the administrative and ceremonial buildings, almost all temples were built at the edges of the city.

In Japan, borders and margins were the domain of the itinerant and the sacred—restless travelers, protected by the authorities and yet rejected from the center, forced to live in areas partly beyond societal control—the mountains, the sea, and the slopes on the edges of cities. The riverbanks, which belonged to no one, could not be cultivated, and flooded with the slightest rain, became home to itinerant squatters. The "people of the riverbanks" in Kyoto were *hinin* with a status analogous to those who lived on the hillsides.

This society of marginal people defended themselves by multiplying what protections they could secure, inventing special ties to the gods, and associating themselves with impurity and death. They had the grudging respect of social classes that occupied a more central place in the production process. In the fourteenth century, however, this diffuse anxiety mutated into an increasingly confirmed contempt. By the early seventeenth century, artisans and merchants—not to mention "impure people" and "nonhumans"—were relegated to the bottom of the hierarchy of social values and orders. In the meantime, the traditional protectors of these groups—the emperor, court nobility, shrines, and monasteries—managed to lose all their political and military influence to the warrior class, which, over the centuries, confirmed its hegemony over the peasantry.

Chapter 7

THE SECOND MIDDLE AGES: THE TURNING POINT
OF THE FOURTEENTH CENTURY

The "fourteenth century" was not a clear chronological entity. The Kamakura period continued until 1333, and the Muromachi period began in 1378 or 1392, depending on the source. Although it was a time of transition, this century was significant, as instability and insubordination swept through all sectors of society. The Japan of Shogun Yoshimitsu (1368–1407) was very different from that of the Hōjō regents: a half century of civil war had wrought transformations in power structures, social relations, and cultural life.

These were troubled times. In Kamakura, the Hōjō regime dissolved in 1333 after two years of crisis and was followed by an imperial restoration called the Kenmu era, which lasted barely three years. From 1336 to 1392, Japan was split into two warring states, each of which claimed that it was the legitimate government of the entire country, in a period known as the era of the Southern and Northern Courts (Nambokuchō *jidai*). The courts were based not on control of geographic zones with precise borders but on systems of vassal allegiance. The Southern Court, established in Yoshino south of Nara, sought to maintain the restoration regime, but with its limited influence, at no time was it truly capable of doing so. The Northern Court, by far the more powerful, remained in the capital in Kyoto. There, the emperor reigned, but the real power was in the hands of the new Ashikaga shoguns, who had moved there from Kamakura. The Northern Court accepted the legitimacy of the shogunal dynasty, which its adversary, the Southern Court, refused to do. The intermittent civil war, interspersed with long truces, was not waged simultaneously throughout the country but was at its most violent in the second third of the century. In 1378, the shogun moved into the "palace of flowers" in the Muromachi district of Kyoto, symbolically marking the moment when the new bakufu took almost complete control of the country. With the reunification of the two courts in 1392, the civil war officially ended. The victory of the Ashikaga shogun over the Southern imperial dynasty was total: exhausted, the latter renounced its claim to legitimacy.

This period was also a time of social upheaval. The extension of power by the warrior classes over other social groups indicated the war's true importance. The political and economic collapse of the court nobility was manifested by the loss of many estates, which were taken over by increasingly aggressive warriors. The invasion of western estates by eastern warriors was accompanied by the outbreak of open violence among social classes. For their part, the peasant communities strengthened their local autonomy. Once dominated by the myōshu, the peasants began to acquire land of their own and continued the emancipation movement begun in the second half of the thirteenth century.

Some postwar historians feel that this emancipation movement constituted a "feudal revolution." In their view, slavery, which had up to then characterized production in the Japanese countryside, disappeared during the fourteenth century. The political victory of the feudal warrior class in the late twelfth century thus was reflected a century and a half later in the social victory of the lower peasant classes over the estate system during the civil war. The old landownership system fell apart under the combined blows of warriors amassing their fiefs and village communities successfully resisting the landowners' demands.[1] Although many historians today are not so tied to particular events, the fact remains that the civil war was a major turning point in the history of the Middle Ages, as recent psychohistorical studies have confirmed.[2] Between 1050 and 1280, a sort of psychological and cultural unity marked a change from "traditional" chronological politics, a sort of first Middle Ages or late ancient period. Then from 1280 to 1350, customs, attitudes, economics, and intellectual concepts underwent a transition from which a second Middle Ages emerged that lasted until the mid-sixteenth century.

In the fourteenth century, Zen Buddhism finally triumphed, not because Zen became the dominant religion, but because its cultural hold was such that it eclipsed other trends once the Zen Five Mountains religious organization (see chapter 5) was formed. Although the period of the civil war did not produce major intellectual structures equivalent to those of the Kamakura century, it was a time of ferment for new forms of expression—the nō theater, gardens— that reached their apex in the following century.

As we have seen, although the disturbances of the late twelfth century were traumatic for those who lived through them, the laws were not fundamentally challenged. That is, the ideas that a judgment could settle a dispute between two litigants and that justice was important were not contested. The Kamakura regime of the Hōjō regents perpetuated peace and justice, whereas with the new century, violence among social groups erupted. In *Tsurezuregusa*, written around 1330, Yoshida Kenkō relates an anecdote that typified the times:

> A man went to court over ownership of another man's rice field. He lost his suit and was so disappointed that he sent some laborers to harvest the crop in the field and bring it up to him. The men first of all went about harvesting some other fields on the way. Somebody objected, "This isn't the disputed field. What are you doing here?" The reapers answered, "There is no reason to harvest the crop on that field either. As long as we have come to do a senseless thing, what difference does it make which field we reap?"[3]

This change in attitudes toward state justice was both the bearer of chaos and the vector of a social restructuring on new foundations. The burgeoning of perceptible violence at the end of the Kamakura period culminated in war. Whereas Yoritomo had taken five years to gain victory, it took the Ashikaga shogun almost half a century.

THE RISE OF VIOLENCE AND TENSIONS IN THE REGIME

In the late Kamakura period—the last years of the thirteenth century and the first third of the fourteenth century—the stability of the political institutions established by the Hōjō regents could no longer conceal the growing social tensions and contradictions. A bloody coup d'état was carried out in Kamakura in 1285. The retainers (*gokenin*) had become increasingly discontent with the growing despotism of the Hōjō. Illegal, "savage," and violent appropriations of estates proliferated, as did the looting and pillaging, which the authorities blamed on thugs and bandits. What until then had been considered good customs seemed to have been forgotten, and the provocative behavior and styles of some eminent people was an indication that society was indeed in grave crisis and that the shogun in Kamakura was having more and more difficulty controlling the situation.

The second Mongol invasion, in 1281, and the death of the great regents—Hōjō Tokimune in 1284, and his adviser and father-in-law Adachi Yasumori in 1285—marked a turning point in the political history of the bakufu. Although the regime was at a high point, the first cracks were beginning to show. The half century between the death of Tokimune and the collapse of the regime in 1333 was characterized by a bolstering of the personal power of the head of the Hōjō family over the shogunal institutions; by the rise of private vassals of the

Hōjō line, the *miuchibito*, over the retainers; and by the growing discontent of the latter, who were being pushed further and further from the center of power.

The political regime established by Hōjō Yasutoki after the Jōkyū disturbance of 1221 was a government by council, in which the shogunal regent played a prominent, but not despotic, role. But this system of government was reassessed after Tokimune's death. The regent's Privy Council gained importance at the expense of the State Council. In 1293, the Chambers of Justice were eliminated, and the regent Hōjō Sadatoki claimed the right to be the sole judge of appeal. As the regent's control over the regime grew, the Hōjō family expanded its power in the provinces, especially in Kyushu, by seizing the governorships. At the same time, the private vassals of the Hōjō clan took over key positions in the bakufu, exerted influence on the regent through the Privy Council, and assumed leadership of the central institutions, including the Bureau of Samurai, which controlled the vassals.

After Tokimune's early death in 1284, his father-in-law, the powerful retainer Adachi Yasumori, took over the government, but he was thrown out the following year by the personal secretary of Tokimune's young son. With this particularly bloody coup d'état in 1285, the Adachi clan was destroyed, along with many retainers who had supported them. Five hundred vassals saw their estates confiscated or reduced in size. All the warrior vassals of northern Kanto stopped actively supporting the Hōjō,[4] including the powerful retainers of the region, such as the Ashikaga and Nitta, who betrayed the regime in 1333 and were the architects of its fall. Taira Yoritsuna, who plotted the coup, was the leader of the Hōjō private vassals. Although the confrontation between the shogun's and the regent's vassals was won by the latter, the regent Sadatoki eliminated the meddling secretary in 1293 and took things into his own hands.

A "VIRTUOUS GOVERNMENT"

Thrown back into the opposition—humiliated by the Hōjō vassals, who had seized positions in the shogunal administration, and bullied by the Hōjō clan, which held all the power—the retainer-vassals who had fought against the Mongols and guarded the coasts were still waiting for their reward, and they were becoming impatient. In fact, these warriors were in an increasingly precarious position. Even more than the despotism of the Hōjō, the inheritance system of warrior households was coming under increasing scrutiny. In each generation, younger brothers and sisters consumed part of the inheritance. Although the head of the household still prevailed over the junior families and kept the title of retainer, it became more difficult for him to maintain his prestige, for the Mongol invasions had cost him dearly. If a warrior family did not expand its holdings, its base would erode over two or three generations. The only way to prevent this was to take over neighboring estates through war. In wars in 1185, against the Taira, and 1221, against Go Toba's followers, the victorious warrior clans considerably expanded their properties. Their estate steward positions enabled them to solidify their hold during the thirteenth century, at the expense of the nobles' estates. But the status quo was not in their favor, and not all of them were able to usurp the rights of the nobles in their estates or to amass small fiefs. In 1240, the chronicle *Azuma kagami* reported (on the twenty-fifth day of the fifth lunar month of year 1 of the Enji era) on interdictions by the bakufu that prevented impoverished retainers from selling their land or assets to commoners or to warriors who were not vassals of the shogun and from letting their property be administered by monks.

In an attempt to rectify the situation, the bakufu proclaimed an edict of "virtuous government" (*tokusei rei*) in 1297. This edict, the Einin edict, had a major effect and a constant influence on medieval society and attitudes[5] throughout the fourteenth, fifteenth, and sixteenth centuries. It was a sort of amnesty accorded by the government—in this case, the bakufu—to those who had incurred debts and had had to mortgage or sell their property. The estates of vassal retainers that had been sold or mortgaged over the preceding twenty years (after 1278) were to be returned to their former owners, and the sale of estates and their use as security by the shogun's vassals was forbidden.

This measure might seem extraordinary, since it was retroactive, offered no compensation, and therefore legitimized interclass violence. Although it was correctly applied—many estates were returned to their former owners—it had "perverse effects" that the leaders of the bakufu had not considered, the first being that it was understood to be general, not limited, and thus applicable to the entire country. In Shikoku, the people living in an estate belonging to the Gion Shrine backed with violence their demand that the land they had sold fifty, sixty, or even a hundred years earlier be returned to them.[6] Conflicts between the new owners hurt by the edict and the vassal retainers benefiting from it multiplied. To whom did the lands cleared in the interval belong? To whom did the harvest under way belong?

The edict conveyed a notion inconceivable under modern law, for today the return of property to the seller without compensation to the purchaser would seem totally unjust. But the edict was based on a fundamental idea, that land that had always belonged to someone must be returned to him. In this medieval notion of property, land was not a possession like others. Rather, it had been cleared, developed, and farmed each year by the ancestors of its rightful owner, and some of his forebears might even have been buried there. Therefore, to sell an estate or piece of land was to cut the link that tied an individual to his ancestors. The return to the old order—the restoration of original ownership— was part of the customary logic in the Middle Ages, and it was the intent of the edict. Thus, the *tokusei* decreed by the government was more than a forgiveness of debts; it was the return to a forgotten virtue that had once prevailed—the meaning of the character *toku* of *tokusei*.[7] The "return to virtue" was declared to avoid natural misfortune resulting in greater catastrophes, such as a comet passing overhead being followed by an earthquake. In addition, the Mongol invasions had created resentment that the government wanted to mollify by returning things to their "natural" order.

The edict of 1297, which was followed by similar edicts on a more local level issued by both the bakufu and the court, ultimately sharpened the conflicts instead of blunting them. First, the *tokusei* edicts created injured parties and disappointed people: those who were hoping for an edict that did not come. Finally, and most important, they did not settle the issue for the impoverished retainers, who continued to grow poorer with each generation. By around 1320 to 1330, therefore, nothing had been resolved.

Despite this discontent, the Hōjō reacted by ignoring the problem. They increased their despotic power, exiled opponents, and reduced the margin of maneuver of those who were not their trusted supporters. In doing this, however, they dangerously narrowed their social base.

BANDITS AND PEOPLE WITH STRANGE CUSTOMS

THE EVIL PARTIES

Although the vassal retainers of Kanto, defeated and powerless, barely restrained themselves, more and more people in the western provinces and Kinai resorted to illegal and violent action, creating a climate of unease in the countryside. These people were called *akutō* (literally, "evil parties," "groups of evil men") by the victims of their misdeeds, real or imagined, and by the authorities who pursued them.[8] In the late thirteenth and early fourteenth centuries, the Kamakura bakufu issued more and more decrees to quash the bands, which it likened to pirates and thieves, but they had little success. In the late thirteenth century, these bands usually consisted of ten or twenty marginal people, but by the 1320s, in the last years of the Kamakura bakufu, the gangs numbered fifty to a hundred horsemen armed with swords, armor, and packhorses to transport their food. The bandits had become a national disgrace, and some were threatening the military governors in their provinces.

The activities of these bandits are known to us through the many complaints made against them and through the *Mineaiki*, a chronicle written by an anonymous monk around 1348 that describes in detail their depredations in Harima Province. Between 1299 and 1303, the province was awash in blood and fire and abounding in violence, assaults, piracy, robberies, and manhunts. Even though they were armed, the bandits bore no resemblance to samurai. They were unkempt and carried bamboo spears and long, rusty swords slung on their backs. They didn't bother to wear *eboshi*, the hats worn by everyone except women, children, and *hinin*. Instead, they wore six-sided caps, sleeveless war kimono, and yellow scarves over their faces, making them look "strange" (igyō). This costume was the badge of nonconformity: the sleeveless kimono and six-sided cap were women's garb, and the yellow scarf was the signature of the hinin and the yamabushi, "mountain priests," said by some to be sorcerers, who inhabited the mountains. The bandits sought to differentiate themselves from the rest of the population by presenting their marginality in the form of a challenge.[9]

All the groups of bandits were different. Some hired themselves out as mercenaries and fled with the money; they behaved unscrupulously, committed petty larceny, and often cheated at dice. Some cut hay in the fields in the spring and harvested the rice along with the peasants. They set fire to houses, pillaged, hunted game, fished in the rivers, and laughed at taxes and rents. Although the first akutō were rejects from various social classes, they were not simply marginal people who had become outlaws. In time, it became clear that their leaders were from local ruling classes and that they were the warriors and estate managers fighting for control of their land whom landowners had denounced to the authorities. In addition, some warriors, retainers and others, formed armed groups to force their will on landowners. These local warriors were not at all marginal—although they sometimes acted like marauding bandits—but they were arrested and prosecuted as such. In the Kuroda estate in Iga, which belonged to the Tōdaiji in Nara, the local lord who managed the estate committed violent acts and directly battled with the monastery administration. He was accused of having held back by force the peasants' annual rents to the Tōdaiji.[10] Between 1288 and 1292, crimes were committed by akutō who were local functionaries in the Arakawa estate, which belonged to the monastery of Mount Kōya, and they were supported by low-ranking local warriors and wealthy peasants in their attempt to challenge the hold of the absentee owners.[11] Soon, all of northern Kii Province was in a state of near rebellion. Between 1312 and 1316, bandits burst through the gate to the port of Hyōgo (Kobe) a number of times to steal the rents that had been collected. A monk from Mount Hiei led this group of a hundred bandits, who did battle with the governor's troops.[12] Bandits also targeted toll barriers, gates, markets, and sites linked to trade activities.

As their assets grew and their scope of activities expanded, the akutō became better organized and changed their battle techniques, frequently winning victories over the shogunal warriors sent to defeat them. They built fortified arms depots in impenetrable secret sites, sometimes on rocky peaks. In these "forts," they stored weapons, food, and logs and rocks to hurl at aggressors. They became experts in ambushes using bows and arrows, catapults, and rocks.[13] Rapid and elusive, they knew the land well and had many accomplices. One of the akutō's leaders, Kusunoki Masashige, held off the shogun's troops in the mountains of Kawachi Province from 1331 to 1333 and was thus one of the main architects of the victory of Emperor Go Daigo against the Hōjō leaders of Kamakura in 1333.[14]

Although the *akutō* bandits declared themselves outlaws by espousing violence, they were symptomatic of the profound malaise in Japanese society. They fit into the general context of the dissolution of traditional customs and the development of those characteristic of the turn of the fourteenth century.

STONE THROWING

One of the *akutō*'s favorite forms of combat was slingshot battles, or "stone throwing." Fights involving stone throwing (*tsubute*) first broke out in Kyoto in the eleventh century, often on festival days in the shrines.[15] There is no convincing explanation for this bizarre and deadly phenomenon. It seems to have been limited mainly to the capital, where bands of young men, often servants, waged battles in the streets.[16] In the early fourteenth century, the brawls became more frequent, with restless young men, mendicant monks, inhabitants of riverbanks, and bandits taking part. On the fourth day of the fifth month of 1355, unruly teenagers in Kyoto had a fierce fight with stone throwing, causing great tumult. The parents got involved. Some samurai entered the fray, annoyed that they were being hit. When the injured and dead were taken away, some of them were found to have been killed by sword blows![17]

Stone-throwing brawls were unknown in Kanto until the twenty-first day of the fourth lunar month of 1266, when chronicles reported a memorable skirmish in Kamakura. "We have never seen anything like this in Kanto," reported the *Azuma kagami*. Dozens of commoners assembled in the Hikigayatsu valley for a bout of "stone throwing" that turned into a serious battle, to the point that the "forces of order," disturbed by the new activity, had to intervene.[18] A half century later, residents of Kamakura had become big fans of stone-throwing bouts. Helmeted, with knives or short swords in their belts, they went to confront bands of young men, many of them from the lower classes.[19] These skirmishes were both a magical event and a dangerous game. In the early fourteenth century, the participants were joined by ordinary citizens and sometimes even by samurai.[20] The attacks were made with murderous intent, and the "games" plunged the city into a wave of mass hysteria that could not be explained by the presence of skilled provocateurs. By the end of the fifteenth century, stone throwers were being brought before courts that treated them as seriously as arsonists. They were stopped only in the sixteenth century when they were strictly repressed.[21]

BASARA

The rise of stone throwing in the early fourteenth century and its expansion into Kanto must be associated with the new challenges to the authorities that showed in the attitude of the *akutō* bandits and an increase in protests, anti-conformism, and deliberately violent behavior. This change was symbolized by the appearance of new styles, especially in clothing.

Disguises and masks became common. Travelers often wore wide-brimmed rice-straw hats that both protected them from the sun and rain and concealed their faces. When women went into town, they often hid behind veils and hats so that they would not be recognized. Some people even wore masks to conceal their emotions when they went to hear the *Heike*. But others used disguises to inspire fear. Many texts pointed out that the warrior-monks were masked when they paraded through Kyoto to protest against whatever judicial decision did not favor them: they wrapped their faces in shawls, sometimes even covering their faces completely and cutting out two holes for their eyes. When they demonstrated, they spoke with disguised voices or acted demented to terrorize people and give the impression that they were not of this world, succeeding in inspiring great fear.[22]

Masks, strange clothes, veils, and shawls in *hinin* colors created a furor in the early fourteenth century. Wearing clothing on which characters had been written indicated a position of subordination, even discrimination. In the thirteenth century, dice players and various marginal people wore such garments, which were regarded as taboo, and in the fourteenth century, domestics accompanying their lords proudly wore clothes with a crest or *mon* at ceremonies and festivals. In 1333, when the shogunal regime in Kyoto collapsed, these attitudes led to the appearance of the *basara* style. This term, whose origin is unknown, means "strange, ostentatious, extravagant, extraordinary behavior." *Basara* songs, hairstyles, and clothing became popular[23] and were portrayed in illustrated scrolls. Many *akutō* chiefs adopted the fashion in 1333. Nawa Nagatoshi, a warrior who was the leader of the sardine fishermen's communities that were crucial in 1333 when Emperor Go Daigo was exiled by the Hōjō to the island of Oki, wore a strange hat of a type that became common in the capital during the Kenmu restoration. After 1336, when the Ashikaga banned such clothes, *hinin* fashions, combining men's and women's clothing and hairstyles, became popular.

The model for this "look" was Sasaki Dōyo (1306–73), a high-ranking warrior, military governor of several provinces, and aesthete, who was exiled for his dissolute behavior. He led an unconventional life, consorting with notorious prostitutes, attending tea-drinking gatherings, and studying flower arranging and perfume sniffing. He also hosted actors—still *hinin*—from the incipient nō theater, wrote poems, and went to "linked"-verse (*renga*) parties. This so-called *basara* lord was in the vanguard of new sensibilities and art forms that became part of the cultural explosion of the Muromachi period.[24]

WAR AGAIN: THE FALL OF THE HŌJŌ REGIME

Social tensions, rising violence, disturbances involving retainers, and the growing despotism of the Hōjō chiefs—everything pointed to an explosion. All that
was needed was a leader for the various opposition groups.

The temporary division of the imperial household into two branches ordered
by the regent Hōjō Tokimune, which forced the two family lines to reign alternately, provided the pretext for a new political crisis between the court and
Kamakura. In 1318, Go Daigo, of the Daikakuji branch, ascended the throne.
In 1321, when the retired emperor Go Uda died, Go Daigo assumed power in
the court without abdicating—breaking with an old Japanese tradition that the
emperor ruled without governing. He also surrounded himself with talented
men of modest backgrounds, whom he had met at informal gatherings. Go
Daigo's innovative actions fit well with the "strange" times. Like his predecessors
from the Daikakuji, Go Daigo was influenced by the esoteric Shingon doctrines. The Tōji, the large Shingon monastery near Kyoto, considerably
expanded its economic influence in the early fourteenth century owing to its
links with the Daikakuji branch of the imperial family. Go Daigo permitted
the rise of the monk Monkan,[25] but he was also impressed by the political
doctrines that had come from China. Was he dreaming of a return to the
ancient regime or of a Chinese-style empire on the Song model?

In any case, having abolished the system of retired emperors, Go Daigo
wanted to designate his successor without consulting Kamakura, to the detriment of the interests of the Jimyōin family. In 1324, however, his relations with
the leaders of the bakufu soured when they discovered a plot hatched by Go
Daigo's close associates.

> In the vapors of incense smoke,
> Exposed to the swirling flames,
> The emperor, immobile and demonic,
> Prays for the fall of the bakufu.[26]

Kamakura then decreed unilaterally that Go Daigo's successor would be an
imperial prince of the Jimyōin line. Relations between the court and the Rokuhara shogunal administration became extremely tense.

In 1331, the Hōjō discovered a new imperial plot to destroy the bakufu. Go
Daigo's close relatives were arrested, and some were executed. The emperor
fled to the mountains in southern Kinai and took refuge in a fortress on Mount
Kasagi, where his allies in the region rallied to defend him against the shogunal
troops pursuing him. These allies were low-ranking warriors who were not vassals of the bakufu but suppliers to the imperial court linked directly to the
emperor (*kugonin*), and various bands who formed an underground—hired

hands and warriors ready to seize the opportunity to distinguish themselves. They were led by a brilliant military leader, Kusunoki Masashige, who provided effective resistance. Nonetheless, the emperor was finally captured, after six months as a fugitive, and sent into exile on Oki. Dispersed, exiled, or dead, his supporters at court could do nothing when, in 1332, the bakufu placed its favorite, Emperor Kōgon of the Jimyōin branch, on the throne.

Far from discouraging the bakufu's enemies, Go Daigo's second failure only spurred them on. Bands of *akutō* became increasingly bold. Kusunoki Masashige held off the shogunal troops from Kyoto in a spectacular manner. He lured them into ambushes, using war techniques "invented" by the *akutō*, and threw stones and logs at assailants from his fortifications in Akasaka and Chihaya. All the mountainous regions in southern Kinai were in turmoil.

Finally, in 1333, with the help of seamen loyal to the emperor, half of them pirates, Go Daigo escaped and was received in Hoki Province by Nawa Nagatoshi, the leader of a small group of seafaring warriors. Everywhere in the west, local warriors, such as the Akamatsu in Bizen and the Kōno in Shikoku, joined the battle, building forts and mobilizing their men. In Kyushu, the local warriors threatened the island's military administrators.

Held in check in southern Kinai for two years by Masashige's supporters, the harried shogunal troops had to deal with the beginnings of rebellion in the provinces. Go Daigo had accomplices everywhere, and western Japan was ready to defy Kamakura.[27]

The Hōjō leaders decided to send a new army from the east, led by one of the most powerful retainers of northern Kanto, Ashikaga Takauji. Distant descendants of a junior branch of the Minamoto, the Ashikaga had not been fierce supporters of the Hōjō regents after the coup d'état of 1285, but nothing indicated that Takauji would betray them. He had been very circumspect since becoming leader of his troops in Kinai and had in fact held secret talks with Go Daigo. When Takauji finally led his army into Kyoto at the beginning of the fifth month of 1333, it was to seize the Rokuhara shogunal administration for the ex-emperor. The *tandai* (military governor) of Kyoto, Hōjō Nagatoki, fled eastward with Emperor Kōgon, but then, surrounded at an inn by a band of *akutō* bandits and armed peasants, he and four hundred of his men committed suicide.

At the same time, another great retainer lord of northern Kanto, Nitta Yoshisada, was mobilizing his men to march on Kamakura. He fought several battles on the Musashi Plain with troops sent by the Hōjō to block his progress. Warriors from all over Kanto joined Yoshisada's army, which surrounded the shogunal capital on the eighteenth day of the fifth lunar month of 1333. The battle lasted for five days. The Hōjō and their warriors fought valiantly, and dignitaries of the bakufu and defeated loyal generals committed suicide, one after another. The regent, Hōjō Takatoki, committed *seppuku* on the tomb of his ancestors in a Kamakura temple, followed by 280 of his vassals. On the twenty-third day of the fifth lunar month (July 5), Kamakura fell to the retainer-warriors of Kanto, who were now serving the emperor. The Kamakura regime had breathed its last. Two days later, the warriors of Kyushu captured the local seat of the shogunal administration. In the *Jinnō shōtoki*, Kitabatake Chikafusa comments on the events:

> There was no overall strategy, and yet the country—from Kyushu to the remote Mutsu and Dewa Provinces—was pacified in less than one month. That a simultaneous uprising should take place 6,000 to 7,000 *ri* away is surprising, for it shows both that the time was ripe for reunification of the country by the court and that the fate of the bakufu was sealed.[28]

THE KENMU RESTORATION

The Kamakura regime collapsed because of the success of a temporary coalition of social classes and interest groups. First, the court nobles, always hostile to the bakufu and subdued since the defeat of the imperial party in 1221, rose up in support of Emperor Go Daigo, hoping for a return to the situation that had prevailed in the Heian period. They received military assistance from the warrior-monks of the main temples, including Mount Hiei. Second, the many low-ranking descendants of warriors defeated in 1221, some of them *akutō*, and warriors who were not vassals of the shogun in the provinces of Kinai were linked to the imperial household or the Shinto shrines. Third, the descendants of the great warrior clans of retainers, such as the Ashikaga and the Nitta, opposed the Hōjō after 1285. Finally, the low-ranking retainers impoverished by the financial crisis, especially since the Mongol invasions, were unhappy with the Kamakura regime.

The victory of forces hostile to the Hōjō was possible because the uprising of low-ranking warriors and *akutō* of Kinai in the name of the imperial cause was successful. These forces, traditionally hostile to the bakufu, dealt a severe blow to the enemy troops and made possible the escape and return of their leader, Go Daigo. At first, in 1331, confined to southern Kinai, the rebellion had expanded to all of the western provinces by 1333. Although the shogun's troops had taken some losses, they were far from defeated. Rather, it was the defection of Takauji in Kyoto and the uprising of Nitta Yoshisada in Kanto that were the direct causes of the fall of the Hōjō regime. Yoshisada and Takauji managed to rally the great lords of the east to their cause, but they were not out to destroy the bakufu as a political system. On the contrary, they wanted to preserve the institutions of Kamakura after expelling the Hōjō and their vassals.

This conflict of interest among the victors of 1333 led to the rapid collapse of the restored imperial regime. Go Daigo returned to Kyoto in the sixth lunar month of 1333 and was expelled by Ashikaga Takauji in the fifth lunar month of 1336. The Kenmu restoration lasted only three years.

The measures taken by Go Daigo in Kyoto helped sketch out the terms of new political alliances. Mistrusting the traditions of the court nobility, the emperor deliberately sought out the low-ranking western warriors, competent but of humble birth, who had defended his cause and were his principal military supporters. In doing this, he alienated part of the conservative nobility and angered the warriors of Kanto, whose support had been decisive. In fact, Go Daigo was attempting to divide the eastern generals through the rivalry between Nitta Yoshisada and Ashikaga Takauji. Meanwhile, low-ranking warriors from Kinai underwent a dazzling social ascent. Kusunoki Masashige, a warrior of obscure origins from Kawachi Province, was propelled to high offices: head of police and governor of two provinces in southern Kinai, several positions in the Chambers of Justice created by the new regime, and close adviser to the emperor. Nawa Nagatoshi, a low-ranking *basara* warrior and leader of fishermen on the Japan Sea coast, was appointed administrator of his home province, and he too sat in the Chambers of Justice. The monk Monkan, who had Go Daigo's support, quickly rose to abbot in monasteries as important as the Tōji in Kyoto.

In fact, Go Daigo's political sense was not good, and the new regime immediately made mistakes that alienated some of its supporters. Once reestablished in Kyoto, after forcing Emperor Kōgon to abdicate and taking over the imperial functions, Go Daigo revealed that he wanted to be in control of everything, to both reign and govern. In an attempt to restore the former imperial splendors, he made two seriously flawed decisions. First, for the warriors who had supported him and expected rewards, he decreed that properties would be guaranteed only after careful examination of titles and deeds in the warriors' possession and that new attributions would be handled case by case. Second, he decreed that the imperial palace would be reconstructed and the work paid for by the estate stewards, who would have to donate one-twentieth of their annual revenues.

These two decrees, signed in the first months of the new regime, caused a furor. Warriors from all over Japan rushed to the capital, armed with their precious documents, to obtain official confirmation either through a trial or by pleading their cause. Estate stewards were forced to have their lands surveyed to calculate exactly—and strictly—one-twentieth of their revenues. Kyoto was invaded by unemployed warriors waiting for the new and overburdened administration to settle their claims. They lined up in the streets, and individuals carrying parasols and wearing masks or veils with "strange features" created an uproar with their *basara* behavior. The provincial warriors, some of whom were in the capital for the first time, were curious at first but soon became impatient and exasperated, and the city residents became more and more impatient with the arrogant and deliberately threatening visitors. Trash piled up, the chronicles reported, and the streets were choked with neighing horses. The government finally withdrew and canceled its decrees—a reversal that only caused more discontent for both the city residents and the warriors.

In early 1334, an anonymous text, the *Nijōgawara no rakusho*, no doubt written by a commoner, was posted on the shores of the river at Second Avenue. Through the use of irony, it criticized the regime and the new political practices that were overturning traditions and introducing "arbitrary violence" (*jiyū rōzeki*).

At this time in the capital, among the things in fashion:
assaults in the night, armed robberies, falsified documents,
easy women, galloping through the town, panics for no reason,
chopped-off heads, monks who defrock themselves and laymen who shave their heads,
self-infatuated daimyo with letters of confirmation, rewards, and imaginary armies;
litigants far from their estates of birth, with fine boxes full of documents and deeds,
flatterers, slanderers, Zen and Ritsu monks,
parvenus who are turning the world upside down . . .
. . . acting haughty
with a pathetic animal on their fist with a tail and feathers, vaguely resembling a falcon, that is incapable of catching the tiniest fowl,
with a long saber made of lead, much longer than a long dagger, which they hold by the thumb with the point in the air,
with an extravagant five-branch fan,
with too-large palanquins, emaciated horses, kimono with fine sleeves with old breastplates rented by the day.
Warriors from Kanto bring out their sedan chairs,
High-born and low-born people with no distinction,
wearing beautifully worked undergarments
never taking off their breastplate or clothing,
playing at shooting at dogs without ever having touched a bow,
falling more frequently from their horses than they have bows in their quivers.[29]

By creating more and more decrees and laws, attempting to control everything, and placing inexperienced men in important positions, Go Daigo revealed both his despotism and his incompetence. In 1338, one of his most faithful young generals, the brilliant Kitabatake Akiie, wrote him a letter in which he did not mince words: "People must be made to obey the laws. But the laws must not be constantly changed, or people will no longer know what they are. When one constantly decrees new laws, there are no longer any laws at all."[30]

Kyoto residents, court nobles, and eastern warriors felt cheated. Even the peasants seemed unhappy with the regime. A few of their complaints have survived, such as one by the peasants of the Tara estate in Wakasa in 1334:

Our land had become the direct domain of the Hōjō lords since the Shōan era (1299–1302). Rents and corvées were oppressive, and we had an increasingly hard time making our living. When Kanto [i.e., the Kama-kura regime] was defeated, the estate went to the Tōji monastery and everyone expected the rents to be lowered. Then, would life not become more pleasant? But the rents are now even heavier than before and life is even harder.[31]

As the government's errors, blunders, and unpopular measures multiplied, Ashikaga Takauji's star seemed to be on the rise. He, too, was disappointed by the rewards handed out and jealous of those conferred on his rival, Nitta Yoshi-sada, and he slowly gathered like-minded men around him. Over a number of years, he assembled a personal vassalage. Immediately after his betrayal of the Hōjō in 1333—a few days after entering Kyoto—Takauji agreed to recognize the personal loyalty of a number of his warriors:

I am Iehira, seventh son of Nakano Gorō, religious name Teishin. My father holds the office of jitō on a part of the Yuyama estate, Shinano Province. As for me, I proved my greatest loyalty to your lordship on the eighth day of the fifth lunar month, and I am available to do the same at all of the battles in the future by obeying you and acting always with loyalty to you. With this document, I present myself to you with all of my respect.

(signature on the back of the document)
year 3 of Genkō, fifth moon, fourteenth day
Fujiwara Iehira
Countersigned and approved: Ashikaga Takauji (seal)[32]

In 1335, followers of the Hōjō attempted an audacious strike on Kanto and managed to capture Kamakura for a time. Takauji demanded that the emperor appoint him shogun with the power of subjugation in the east comparable to what Yoritomo had had. Go Daigo refused. But Takauji ignored him and, with-out imperial authorization, went to Kanto to quell the revolt. There he acted as if he were a shogun, distributing rewards to the loyal and building a military vassalage. At the end of 1335, he led an army against Go Daigo, declaring himself a rebel.

In early 1336, Go Daigo was forced to flee Kyoto, and he took refuge on Mount Hiei. Takauji occupied the capital for a time, but he was soon expelled by the emperor's followers, who battled their way back, proving Kyoto's reputation for being easy to attack and difficult to defend. Takauji made his way to the western provinces to assemble the warriors who were estate stewards and those who had risen up in 1333 but had been disappointed by their belated rewards. He rallied the Akamatsu in Bizen and many of the warriors in Kyushu. In the early summer of 1336, he returned with his forces to Kinai.

Go Daigo wanted to confront Takauji personally in battle. Kusunoki Masashige, certain of defeat, wanted to evacuate and attack later when the forces of the Ashikaga had been weakened—that is, at harvest time, when the warriors wanted to return to their fields. But the emperor would not hear of it. The battle took place at Minatogawa (near today's Kobe), and as Masashige had predicted, the imperial forces were crushed. Masashige committed suicide the evening after the battle. In the *bushidō* code of honor written in the Edo period, he was held up as a symbol of loyalty to both the suzerain and the emperor at the same time. Imperial propaganda of the early twentieth century made him a national hero as well, to be used as an example in history and in textbooks for schoolchildren.

After Takauji's victory, the situation was grave for the emperor, who was once again a fugitive on Mount Hiei. New battles took place in Kyoto, and part of the city was burned down. The Ashikaga warriors were victorious, and Go Daigo attempted a compromise, agreeing to abdicate in favor of a prince from the Jimyōin clan, Emperor Kōmyō. In the end, however, Ashikaga Takauji had won little. Many men still opposed him, especially the low-ranking warriors of Kinai. At the end of 1336, Go Daigo fled yet again with the imperial seals—the symbols of his legitimacy—to the mountainous regions of southern Kinai and established a court in exile in the town of Yoshino. Now, two imperial courts, one in Yoshino to the south, the other in Kyoto to the north, fought for predominance and imperial legitimacy. The attempts of Go Daigo's followers to retake Kyoto and hold it failed, as did the expeditions launched by the Ashikaga generals against the warriors who had remained faithful to the Southern Court. The country plunged into civil war.

CIVIL WAR

Starting in late 1336, the military situation became extremely confused. Sporadic battles broke out around the capital and in the provinces from Kyushu in the south to those in the northeast. The Ashikaga generals and the Southern Court led marches across the country, often with no tangible result but the destruction of the provinces that they passed through. Each political center adopted its own calendar and a titular leader who made appointments to official positions and encouraged uprisings, disputes, and various pillages. Private wars were declared in the name of various parties, and there were countless betrayals and changes of alliance.

With the support of the Northern Court, Ashikaga Takauji controlled its political centers, Kyoto and Kamakura. In 1336, in a document entitled Kenmu shikimoku (Articles of the Kenmu era), he laid out his political intentions and established a Kamakura type of regime, with two small but essential differences. First, the capital was established in Kyoto—all that remained in Kamakura was the administration offices for Kanto. Second, Takauji obtained his official appointment as shogun in 1338—the position of shogun's regent that the Hōjō had held was abolished. For a century, the Ashikaga dynasty exercised the real power of the bakufu.

The choice of Kyoto as the shogun's new capital—a decision that was apparently the subject of fierce debate—was explained by a number of connected military factors, essentially that the strongholds of the southern resistance were located in Kinai and it was important to have control near Kyoto. But there were other reasons for the choice. In the fourteenth century, the growing success of the national economy could no longer be ignored, and it was centered in Kinai. A truly national government could not be established without real control over these regions, which, in the second part of the Middle Ages, were constantly being disputed by political forces. The Kamakura bakufu, which had been powerful in the east but was weaker in the west, had "shared" state authority with a still prestigious imperial court. In contrast, the Ashikaga bakufu now sought to present itself as a national monarchy, drawing its legitimacy from a powerless imperial authority.

At first, the new shogunal regime seemed to be a dual power, as expressed in Ashikaga Takauji's collaboration with his younger brother, Tadayoshi. Shogun Takauji was at the head of a vassal and military organization. Like Minamoto no Yoritomo before him, he was the suzerain of warriors, whom he controlled through traditional shogunal institutions: in Kyoto, the Bureau of Samurai, which was responsible for rewards, and in the provinces, the governors (shugo), who controlled the local vassals. Takauji's most important vassals were linked to him by personal oaths of loyalty.

Tadayoshi was more a politician than a warlord and controlled the old Kamakura administration, part of which had been transferred to Kyoto, and the judiciary bodies inherited from the old system. The Ashikaga bakufu was somewhat divided between a feudal and vassal system and a bureaucratic and judicial system and lasted for about ten years after 1335. But the partnership between Takauji and Tadayoshi became increasingly strained.

Tadayoshi based his authority on the shogunal administration established more than a century earlier by the Hōjō, and he had the support of retainer-warriors who were satisfied with the new regime, especially those who had reached agreement with the owners of the estates that they administered. Although Tadayoshi wanted to return to the peaceful power system established by the Hōjō in Yasutoki's time, he was opposed by the "secretary-general" of the shogun (shitsuji), Kō no Moronao, a vassal of the Ashikaga family. Moronao was supported by the provincial warriors, who wanted to take advantage of the disturbances both to take over new functions in the estates that would ensure them of real local power and to seize the properties of defeated landowners. While Tadayoshi was more in favor of an accommodation with the Southern Court, Moronao wanted war. Moronao is often described as a brutal, crude boor: "If you want to build yourself a fief, take the neighboring estate," he is reported to have declared.[33] He is also credited with having made a remark that speaks volumes about the respect of fourteenth-century warriors for the imperial institution: "If the emperor dies, we will build one of wood or of gold. Let the flesh-and-blood emperors go to the devil!"[34]

For a time, Takauji was able to control Tadayoshi and Moronao. However, the conflict between the Ashikaga bakufu and the Southern Court became more complicated between 1349 and 1352 because of a war between Tadayoshi's and Moronao's followers, and the country was split into not two antagonistic factions but three.[35] After hesitating, the shogun himself went over to the camp of the most radical warriors. Following many twists and turns and battles, the war turned in favor of the shogun. Moronao was killed in combat, and Tadayoshi, defeated, was poisoned. For a few years, Japan remained divided in three, with all the compromises and changes of alliance that that implied. The discord between the Ashikaga brothers gave new hope to the supporters of the Southern Court, who even managed to occupy Kyoto for a short period while Kyushu fell into military anarchy. Takauji's eventual victory was solidified by a success for the low-ranking warriors of the central and western provinces, who established fiefs within the estates of the nobility and the monasteries.

With the wars of the mid-fourteenth century, Japan's feudalization intensified. The former akutō, many of whom were lower-class warriors struggling against estate owners, were victorious. "Bandits" a generation earlier, they were now part of the support system as vassals of Takauji or the governors. Having sought to seize lands illegally at the beginning of the century, they were now able to take possession of the estates because of the war. The warriors' strengthened control over the land at the expense of the court nobility and monasteries was possible only in the context of a type of state other than the Kamakura administration, which had too much invested in the social status quo. Tadayoshi and those who, like him, wanted to reconstruct a political alliance among the old nobility, the great temples, and the existing warrior leaders failed because they underestimated the new power relations, especially in Kinai. In the late twelfth century, although the warriors of Kanto had seized local power in their region, they ultimately agreed to share power with the representatives of the old order in the other regions. In the fourteenth century, it was the turn of the warriors of Kinai and the west to take local power over the land. The warriors' victory was harder won in these regions, since the imperial state and the old nobility had greater authority and social support in the nonpeasant classes, which no doubt explains why the civil war lasted so long.

The conflicts within the imperial family and then within the bakufu also affected the people's attitude toward the political authorities. The fall of the Hōjō regime in 1333, the collapse of the Kenmu restoration regime in 1336, and the subsequent division of the court were traumatic. The central authority lost all the prestige that it had accumulated since its inception. The people's confidence was gone as well. The vassal's loyalty to the lord disappeared in the turmoil of civil war. Warriors considered first their own interests and not those of their suzerain. The most dangerous enemy was the neighbor who had his eye on one's land or the cousin who rejected the superiority of the leader of the senior branch over the entire clan.

In 1374, the shogunal deputy, or *kanrei*, Hosokawa Yoriyuki, the highest authority in the shogunal state, sent the following missive to Imagawa Sadayo, then the *shugo* of Bingo Province:

> It is reported to me that the tonsured monk-lord Miyoshi Shikibu has entered the estate of Harumi, Bingo Province, the lord of which is the Yamanouchi family, to make war there. Waging war with another is a very serious act, an offense against the highest justice. Justice must be applied very quickly, and the above-mentioned monk-lord must cease his plotting. Take all necessary measures so that he does so.
>
> Ōei year 7, eighth month, third day, governor of Musashi[36]
> To the attention of monk-lord Imagawa Iyo.

This document shows that civil war between the two courts had almost stopped at this time and that it was mainly the local gentry who were attempting to improve their position in the regions, in spite of the central government's obvious hostility.

Perhaps even more important, the peasantry was no longer sitting by and watching these fruitless confrontations between the leading classes. That is, the wars were not being waged by armies simply trying to seize the enemy's estates or properties or to reconstruct a state. Faced with armies in the countryside and with overwhelming misfortune, the peasants tried to gain an advantage from the shifting situations. Both the emancipation movement by the lower classes of the agricultural communities and the local authority over these communities were strengthened by the civil war. Swept up in the storm, the peasants organized, demanded reparations for the damages caused, deserted, and no longer accepted without question the lords' whims. The state had lost its prestige; the dominant classes as a whole had suffered accordingly; and the peasants had lost faith in their lords. For the lord, getting rid of the neighbor by seizing his land by force was one objective, but control of the land after victory was also necessary. The lord therefore also had to impose control over the communities that farmed the land. If he tried to make farming conditions more difficult, the communities were likely to call on the former lord or a member of his family to support them against the new lord. The power struggle in the fourteenth century was thus paralleled by a social struggle, whose objective was control of the land and the emancipation of the peasants.

Chapter 8

WARRIORS, PIRATES, PEASANTS, AND PRIESTS

NEW GOVERNORS AND LANDOWNER LEAGUES

WAR IN THE PROVINCES AND THE EMERGENCE OF GOVERNORS

To consolidate his authority and keep his most loyal vassals happy—especially the private vassals of the Ashikaga household, such as the Shiba, the Hatakeyama, and the Hosokawa—the shogun appointed them *shugo* (literally, constable) and sent them to the provinces where they were to restore order and take power. The collection of customs of the Kenmu era (Kenmu shikimoku) of 1336 reiterated the functions of the military governors as previously defined by the Kamakura shogunal regime, without major modifications. The shogun retained the right to appoint *shugo* and to revoke the power of traitors and those who were militarily incompetent. Reality, however, quickly forced the new bakufu to change the job description for the *shugo*.

Local warriors who supported the Southern Court were the main enemies of the newly appointed governors, whose first task was to capture "criminals" and "conspirators" and bring them to justice. The *shugo* had military command of the warriors who were vassals of the shogun. But to maintain these warriors on a war footing over the longer term, he had to have more extensive powers. The warriors had to be compensated, and quickly, for if their rewards were delayed, there was every possibility that they would go over to the other side.

Unlike the military governors of the Kamakura period, those of the mid-fourteenth century had to do more than just administer their provinces; they also had to make war against local warriors supporting the Southern forces. Most of the *shugo* were Ashikaga generals from among the shogun's personal vassals—that is, military men from the eastern provinces. Even when most of the local warriors in a province were loyal to the bakufu, they were not always happy to see an unknown governor arrive. To gain control, the *shugo* had to earn the support of these warriors through material rewards. In fact, the *shugo* had gone to war for the Ashikaga in hopes of finally securing some property in the province to which they had been appointed. Thus, they wanted to have the means to reward their loyal warriors by obtaining the right to confiscate and redistribute the lands taken from "conspirators."

In 1359, Hosokawa Yoriyuki, governor of Awa Province in Shikoku, asked the shogun, Ashikaga Yoshiakira—before a battle—for the right to use his judgment to give his men the revenues from the estates confiscated from defeated landowners. The shogun refused: it was he who would compensate the retainers through the Bureau of Samurai and no one else. The reasoning was that if the governors gained this right, the local vassals would switch their allegiance to them, and the shogun would become the pawn of the *shugo*. Judging that he did not have the means necessary to start a campaign, Yoriyuki withdrew to his estate.[1]

The long duration of the war, however, forced the bakufu to back down on one important point. It gave the governors the right, within their provinces, to charge and redistribute a "military" tax and to decide which estates would have to pay it. This temporary prerogative was intended to enable the *shugo* to maintain and feed their armies when they were campaigning, and it was institutionalized under the name *hyōrōmai*. This tax was levied on estates owned by absentee landowners, which was the case for most of the *shōen*, and half the rents (*hanzei*) collected now would go to maintaining the armies controlled by the *shugo*.

Until then, vassals had had to pay the costs of war themselves. Whenever battles took them far from home, the warriors lived off the land, plundering the countryside along the roads. The mounted march of the Southern Court–supporting general Kitabatake Akiie in 1338 had left a bitter memory with the populations in the regions that he had crossed. Houses were sacked and then burned, and nothing was left standing after Akiie's Ebisu[2] passed through: "There remained neither grass nor tree," lamented the *Taiheiki*. In the fifth lunar month of the first year of the Engen era (1336), the peasants on the Akanabe estate in Mino Province complained to their landlord, the Tōdaiji monastery:

During the war, the armies of both Kyoto and Kamakura invaded the estate and took everything from the houses. We do not know how to express our misfortune. The war started last winter, but this year the violence was such that nothing remains on the estate. Everything has been taken. In particular, while they were waiting to take the ferry, the soldiers from both armies destroyed everything, and no one came to help us. To make things worse, all the wheat crops were destroyed because of the snowfalls. Our distress is so great that no complaint can do it justice.[3]

The new tax was thus conceived as a way to alleviate the miseries of war, and it did not increase the peasants' burden, since it affected only the estate owners. It was also meant to be temporary. The tax of 1352 was collected only in that year: half the rents remitted to the lords in estates in Ōmi, Mino, and Owari Provinces were redistributed by the governors of those provinces to supply their armies. But although these taxes were at first temporary and decreed by the shogun, they later became permanent and were levied directly by the governors, and the nobles saw their coffers emptying as their rents were siphoned into the hands of the *shugo*.

For the *shugo*, this tax quickly became a means of building local vassalages among retainers, low-ranking estate administrators, and wealthier peasants. A *shugo* allocated half the rents from such estates to worthy warriors—after he had first expanded his own estate by invading, legally or illegally, those of his adversaries. Weary of various acts of violence and excessive tolls on their income, some landowners turned over the management of their estates to the governor in exchange for an annual payment of part of the rents, the amount of which was specified in a contract. The governor, in turn, sent his own vassals to manage part or all of these estates. In this way, some *shugo* gradually became local potentates in their provinces, with private estates, armies, and financial means, as well as official policing and tax-collecting powers.[4] With his province as his domain, the *shugo* became a lord, a daimyo—or *taimai*, as it apparently was pronounced in the fourteenth century. Historians today call these new types of governors who arose at the end of the civil war of the fourteenth century *shugo-daimyō*, to distinguish them from the less powerful *shugo* of the Kamakura period.

As the *shugo* strengthened their hold on their provinces, it became difficult to dislodge or transfer them. Between 1360 and 1370, the merry-go-round of appointments of governors slowed, and under the third shogun, Ashikaga Yoshimitsu, the position of *shugo* became hereditary. This stability reflected the gradual victory of the Ashikaga over opposing forces and the consolidation of the new bakufu in the last third of the fourteenth century.

But not all *shugo* found it so easy to wield their new powers in the provinces, since the local warrior classes were turbulent, difficult to subdue, and not always willing to recognize the authority of a governor imposed from without by the shogun. Unlike the retainers of the Kamakura period, the warriors of the four-teenth and fifteenth centuries were not so pliable. The authority of the state, as we have seen, was subject to challenge, as was the authority of the Ashikaga, since the new shogun did not have the same influence that the Minamoto had had.

There were various reasons for the instability of the warrior class in the fourteenth century. First, political disturbances and wars enabled victorious provincial warriors to consolidate their properties. Unlike the estate stewards, whose responsibilities could be revoked by the bakufu, many warriors were now owners of a single property, which, though small in size, they controlled. These men were bound to their land—"men of the land," or *kokujin*, as opposed to the governors, who came from elsewhere with their vassals—and could not be expelled from their property simply by an administrative decision. Because their land had been won by war, it could be taken from them only by war. The *kokujin* were always uneasy when a new governor arrived, as he might challenge their right to the property that they had acquired through great struggle, by decreeing that they were hostile to him—"conspirators" or "assassins." In such an event, some local warriors resisted the governor, whereas others relented and became his vassals.

Second, the internal family structure of the warrior class was transformed in the fourteenth and fifteenth centuries. The system of overall control of the family by the clan chief was breaking down, and the position of chief of the senior branch was increasingly being contested. Constant divisions of inheri-tances diluted the income of the junior branches of the family (*bunke*), some of whom took advantage of uprisings to free themselves from the grasp of the senior branch or even to go to war with it. Thus, warriors clans began to lean toward the principle of undivided succession, which had two consequences. It reinforced the absolute power of the heir over his brothers and thus strength-ened the unity of the estate, but it could also lead to violent conflicts among the other branches that wanted one of their members to be named heir. Because the principle of seniority was not used, factions within small vassal organizations sprang up to support the different claimants to the inheritance. Once an heir was designated, the conflict would end only if he was able to exert his influence over the other family members, who were unhappy about being relegated to the position of landless vassals of the heir.

LANDOWNER LEAGUES

Withdrawal to the fief, mistrust of neighboring landowners' maneuvers, and the rise of hostile factions within warrior clans all led to a climate of tension that was extreme to the point of being intolerable. To defuse this dangerous situa-tion, which required everyone to be constantly on guard, the *kokujin* created local alliances of landowners based on sacred vows. The warrior groupings of the twelfth and thirteenth centuries, which had united warriors in a hierarchical structure based on vassalage under a suzerain, were thus replaced by egalitarian federations of warriors (*ikki*) united by vows. These regional leagues brought together men free of vassalage ties who wanted to restore peace, and thus landowner control, and impose the status quo. Members of the league vowed mutual assistance in the case of any outside aggression; that is, any lord whose land was contested by a member of his clan could ask the league for military support. The league tried to settle problems common to other local landowners who had formed organizations and to resolve potential conflicts among their members with regard to estate borders and other issues.[5] In fact, the local warriors were already used to meeting in assemblies for maintaining shrines and paying the costs of ceremonies and festivals. During these meetings, the warriors began to feel bound by common interests in the face of the demands of the governors, who were seeking to make them vassals, and the peasants' claims. The warriors met in a shrine or temple, discussed the issues, and wrote out a pact that was signed by all members of the *ikki*. The league had internal rules to ensure that it functioned smoothly and peacefully. If two members had a dispute, they were not to seek justice on their own but instead were to go before the league's council, which had the right to punish the guilty party. Created to defend the local lords' rights, these leagues soon began to view themselves as autonomous regional powers in the absence of a stable state.[6]

The governors were forced to acknowledge the existence of the *ikki*, whose power quickly became indisputable. The most skillful governors were able to form alliances with the leagues, which became their "shock troops." Accordingly, the League of the Yellow Banner in Settsu Province supported governor Sasaki Dōyo around 1355, and the League of the Bellflower, composed of low-ranking warriors in Mino Province, worked for the governors of the Toki clan in the 1360s. This mode of organization spread among low-ranking warriors in Kanto and seafaring warriors along the northern coast of Kyushu, who formed a league, the Matsura Party, that lasted for several centuries.

These organizations remained autonomous and never allied with a military governor for long. Indeed, an *ikki* might quickly turn against the governor whom it had been supporting if its members' interests began to diverge from his. Despite their best efforts, the governors were never able to integrate the leagues fully into their vassal organizations.

The leagues formed particularly cohesive and formidable military structures. Their members knew one another well and were used to fighting together on the battlefield, helping one another and performing maneuvers together. And they were easily recognizable, since they flew a single banner.

The *ikki* fulfilled three main functions. First, they provided their members with a means of resistance to foreign intrusions. If a governor tried to impose his authority by breaking the power of lords who refused to become vassals, the league would defend the local warriors against him. In 1400, the governor, Ogasawara Nagahide, was forced to flee suddenly after being defeated by a league formed of most of the low-ranking warriors of Shinano Province.[7]

Second, the *ikki* helped ensure peace in their regions. They arbitrated disputes and sometimes served as mutual-aid organizations. Their members swore to assist one another in battle and to help raise the children of those warriors who died for the common cause.[8]

Finally, the *ikki* helped the lords suppress peasant uprisings. Some pacts referred expressly to the need to pursue peasants who were unable to pay their rent and had fled their estate to seek refuge on other land. Landowners who were members of the league had to arrest such peasants and send them back to their original landlord.[9]

Some Japanese Marxist historians have defined the warrior leagues as organizations of low-ranking warriors[10] who united in order to resist pressure from military governors who wanted to transform their provinces into fiefs and from those peasant communities that were increasingly well structured and interdependent.

THE GROWTH OF INTERNATIONAL PIRACY

As many sources have reported, the Japanese seas were infested with pirates from antiquity to the beginning of the Edo period. In the fourteenth century, with civil war and the absence of authority, piracy grew to an unprecedented extent. Japanese pirates, *wakō*, even ventured across the high seas to plunder the Korean and Chinese coasts. They sowed terror throughout eastern Asia.

In the Inland Sea, along the coast of Ise Bay, on the Tōkaidō near Wakasa Bay, and in the seas around Kyushu, groups of seafaring warriors worked as fishermen and shippers. One of their activities was to collect duties and taxes from ships, in a way similar to how landowners charged taxes on markets at certain crossroads, fords, and bridges. When a ship refused to pay this duty, these "men of the sea" felt that they had the right to take it by force. The "pirates" of Kumano were attached to the Kumano Shrine, and their main activity was shipping. Their territory extended from the coasts of the Kii peninsula to Kyushu in the west and to the seas around Kanto in the east. In 1185, the shrine's administrator put a fleet of two hundred ships at the disposal of the Minamoto, whose crews became, according to the need, pirates or warriors.

In the fourteenth century, the pirate-warriors of Kumano supported the Southern Court and ensured communication between southern Kinai and the Southern Court–supporting warriors of Kanto, and several thousand of them launched a raid on southern Kyushu. Armed groups such as the Matsura in northern Kyushu, the Kōno in Shikoku, and the Kuki near Ise were socially recognized as warrior groups. They had maritime privileges that gave them the right to tax passing ships in their position as servants of the sea gods, whose territory they defended against foreigners. At first, the taxes collected were intended for offerings to these gods.[11]

Nevertheless, since ancient times, the public authorities had tried to control the brigands who robbed travelers and mountain convoys. According to the Kamakura legislation, the Goseibai Shikimoku, piracy was a crime—a crime that was also a right typical of the plurality in medieval Japan, in which each group and piece of land constituted a closed society under the authority of a number of jurisdictions reflecting different attitudes. Not everyone saw piracy as reprehensible. To sailors, it was a normal activity, whereas to the Kamakura government it was tantamount to theft.

Then the piracy expanded suddenly in the mid-fourteenth century, perhaps in response to civil war, anxious times, and the growing number of marginal and uprooted people. The sailors of the northern coast of Kyushu and the many sea islands launched expeditions on the other coast of the sea, in Korea. Korean chronicles such as the *Kōraishi (History of Koryŏ)*, compiled in 1451 and considered a fairly reliable document, signaled the new dimensions of the raids in 1350. One hundred ships of Japanese *wakō* attacked the southern coast of the peninsula in the fourth month and then returned the following month and four more times that year. "That is when the *wakō* invasions truly began," the *Kōraishi* continued.[12] From then on, the raids became constant: 130 ships in 1351, 213 ships in 1363, 350 ships in 1374, and so on.[13] The *wakō* ships held between twenty and forty men, and fleets comprised 2,000 to 5,000 men. One Korean source mentions three hundred captured pirates,[14] but the documents dwell more on the larger and more impressive raids than on small one- or two-ship expeditions that ravaged a village.

The main goal of these expeditions was to loot the granaries and harvests on the coasts of Korea, and it is believed that the first raids were made by starving sailors who took by force what they needed. But the incredible ease with which the pirates attacked the Korean granaries attracted the attention of various adventurers and warriors, who were only too happy to plunder with impunity. On the open sea, pirates attacked Korean ships loaded with peasants' rents. They also kidnapped local populations and took them back to Japan or to the Ryukyu Islands to sell as slaves or hold for ransom. The people living on the islands of Tsushima, Oki, and Gotō and along the coves of northern Kyushu could not absorb the abundance of stolen goods and wealth, which flowed through Hakata to inland markets.

The raids became increasingly bold. Like the Vikings in the West in earlier times, the *wakō* sailed farther and farther up the rivers, operating as far inland as the Kaesong region near Seoul. After the southern coasts and islands of the peninsula were completely devastated, their residents left, and the pirates were forced to turn to full-scale military operations, transporting horses on their ships so that they could raid the interior of the country. In 1379, there was a raid by

700 horsemen and 2,000 foot soldiers.[15] The Korean general Li Songgye, founder of the Li dynasty, repelled the pirates a number of times, and in 1380, he captured more than 1,600 horses. But Korea was in a sorry state. Some Koreans joined the Japanese pirates, becoming members of their bands or forming their own pirate bands. In 1392, the reigning Korean dynasty collapsed when it could not defeat the Japanese pirates. In the fifteenth century, the inhabitants of the island of Cheju, in southern Korea, "dressed like the Japanese" and, like their Japanese counterparts on Tsushima, became pirates.[16] In 1446, according to a Korean document, 10 to 20 percent of the *wakō* were Korean.[17]

The Li dynasty wanted to resolve the *wakō* problem as quickly as possible and so started negotiations with the pirate leaders, offering them land and riches, sometimes even official positions in the Korean court, in exchange for stopping their devastating raids. Korea even authorized official trade with them. Consequently, some pirate chiefs became peaceful merchants, and others became liaisons between the new Korean court and Shogun Ashikaga Yoshimitsu. But other pirate chiefs, unwilling to "convert," turned their eyes to the riches of Ming China. After Korea, it was China's turn, in the fifteenth century, to suffer the bloody raids of the Vikings of the Far East.

THE RISE OF THE PEASANTRY

The difficulty that local landowners had in maintaining control over their land was due in part to the better organization of the Japanese peasantry, whose fierce desire for autonomy was one of that period's main features. The peasants were more anxious to form a common front against the armies that were sweeping through the countryside and creating misery. Improvements in agricultural production, the creation of independent village organizations (*sō*), and collective resistance by estate inhabitants against the lords were the three new elements in this troubled time.

Historians have no more quantifiable sources for this period than for the Kamakura period to measure the growth in agricultural production, but indications are that the rise that began in the second half of the thirteenth century continued throughout the fourteenth century. It seems that there was less clearing of land and that instead the intensification of peasant labor in the fields was the main reason for the increase, along with an annual double harvest of rice and barley, the systematic use of fertilizer, and the use of horses and oxen in the fields. The fragmentation of peasant landholdings as the lower peasant classes were awarded the ownership of land parcels kept pace with the intensification of labor. In the late fourteenth century, peasants began to cultivate truck farms on tiny lots of land, rarely larger than one *chōbu* (barely one hectare), on the outskirts of Kyoto. Some sources, however, do mention land clearing. In the Hine estate, belonging to the Kūjo noble family, twelve *chō* of land were being farmed and two *chō* were lying fallow in 1234. In 1316, on the same estate, the cultivated land amounted to thirty-three *chō*. One century later, in 1417, more than fifty-three *chō* were being farmed.[18] Thus, cultivation at Hine increased constantly throughout the Middle Ages, although it may have been an exception.[19] Land was cleared mainly in the bottoms of valleys with streams so that it did not require irrigation and could meet the needs of small village communities. Compared with the land-clearing policies in the great Asian river basins, those in Japan did not involve a greater degree of organization based on the state bureaucracy of an agrarian empire or on an irrigation system.[20] This may be one of the keys to the process of feudalization and the crumbling of state authority in traditional Japanese society.

More than the expansion of land under cultivation, increased yield was characteristic of Japanese agriculture in the fourteenth century. One way to calculate yields is to examine the taxation rate on the estates. In the Kamakura period, many estates were taxed at an annual rate of three *to* (one *to* was equal to approximately eighteen liters) per *tan* (about ten ares) of land, corresponding to between 20 and 30 percent of the harvest. In the fourteenth century, taxation rates of five *to* were common.[21] Other sources attest to the relative enrichment of the peasants. The rise in land-based revenue combined with the overall improvement in quality of life in the countryside can be explained only by an increase in the peasants' productivity.

The ascent of the lower peasant classes—former domestics, serfs, and even slaves who had become small-scale farmers—was an essential aspect of the internal transformation of peasant society, as it led to changes to the real-estate revenue system. Before the fourteenth century, the harvest was divided into two parts: one for the peasant-*myōshu*, who farmed the land with his servants, and one for the annual rents shared by the landowner or public administration and the local warrior-administrators or stewards. In the fourteenth and fifteenth centuries, another tax was added, collected by the *myōshu* on the land cultivated by the lower-level peasants. The *myōshu*, many of whom were now heads of large farms, were gradually transformed within the village communities into small-scale landowners who collected a rent from the peasants with small farms. Those *myōshu* who were armed and owned horses claimed the status of *jiza-murai*, a term for the lowest class of samurai. The collection of rents from the small-scale peasant farmers became a transferable right, and trafficking in that right quickly developed. Because of the strong peasant resistance, the landowners' tax rate was regularly assessed, even though the revenues of landowning peasants were rising. Sometimes the amount collected in farm rents was higher than that collected in landowners' rents. For example, in a document dated 1407 regarding a piece of land belonging to Kanshūji in Yamashina, near Kyoto, the annual landowners' rents were set at three *to*, and the land rent was as high as eight *to*![22] Rather than buying or selling land, the practice of transferring or purchasing the right to collect land rents began to spread. This right had nothing to do with any landowning or administrative functions on the estate. It did not permit its holder to displace the small peasant who was farming the land. Anyone could acquire the right to charge land rent, including estate owners, many of whom recovered in this manner part of the revenues that they could no longer collect otherwise.

The overall rise in agricultural production could not, however, hide the peasants' problems. We have seen how the populations that lived near the main roads were particularly affected by the ravages of campaigning armies. The peasants were not, however, always amenable to dying quietly. Instead, they organized to find solutions to their problems, and some negotiated with the generals of the passing armies to supply food and horses on condition that the troops would not destroy their property. Some warrior chiefs only laughed at them, but others honored their commitments, and armed peasants guarded the entrances to villages to keep out the soldiers. These peasant associations, at first temporary, were maintained after the armies passed through if their actions had been successful. They were called *sō*, a term expressing the notion of a general gathering, a sort of rural commune on the scale of a village or estate.

THE SŌ

Sō villages were based on a high degree of community cohesion. The first sō mentioned in the archives were formed in the mid-thirteenth century, but their numbers grew considerably during the wars of the fourteenth century, and by the fifteenth and sixteenth centuries, they were the basic units of the social system. They drew up their own rules, independent of all lords' authority—and, in fact, in reaction against this authority. Throughout Japan, documents carefully preserved by the villagers themselves, hidden so that they would not fall into the lords' hands, attested to the existence of the "communes" that administered and maintained order in villages.

The oldest written piece about a sō is a "secret document" (*kakushikibumi*) kept in a shrine in the Lake Biwa region and dated 1262.[23] It concerned the people of Okitsushima, who were embroiled in a conflict with the estate administrator over fishing on the lake. The villagers' "secret document" called for a clandestine alliance of all inhabitants against the lord and included the notion of a "community of spirits," or "unanimous solidarity" (*ichimi dōshin*), involving the willing participation of all, as desired by the gods. The vows and meetings took place within the context of the shrine's brotherhood, a village council (*miyaza*) that controlled worship of the Shinto spirits. Those who joined had their convictions reinforced by divine approval. They formed a league, *ikki*, which organized the "community of spirits." "Those who break this agreement will be expelled from their land," warned the vow that the villagers took. Thus, in response to leagues formed by local landowners, similar organizations in the villages were formed, the *sō*, or village communities.

No structured messianic or millenarian ideology supplied a conceptual justification for these peasant movements. The fact that resistance and administration organizations were created in the context of assemblies of worship of the *kami* implies that the sacred was put to use (manipulated?) for the cause, as certain types of opposition to the lords attested. Again in Okitsushima, where the documents were well preserved, there was mention in 1342 of a general meeting of the estate inhabitants, after which they formed a procession and shook the "sacred tree trunk" venerated at the local shrine.[24] The protesters were calling on the spirits to bring their wrath to bear on the noble who was responsible for their unhappiness. The worried noble presented himself before the procession, made honorable amends, and admitted the errors of his ways.

THE ESTATES IN REVOLT: SHŌKE NO IKKI

From the Kamakura period to the beginning of the fifteenth century, the forms of peasant resistance broadened into various types of increasingly radical practices and the appearance of real political autonomy among the rural classes.

Type 1. The peasant communities were by nature hostile to changes in customs, and many of the stewards sent by Kamakura, sometimes men from other regions, tried to impose their will by force. The peasants then appealed to the estate owner—monastery or court noble—to persuade the vassals from Kamakura to tone down their demands. Such alliances between the traditional nobility and the peasantry against upstart warriors were common. The peasants might lodge a complaint about an steward's abuses, but they would never act on it unless their communities were supported by the lord, who was happy to take down the retainer-warrior a peg or two. Some peasants decided to leave the land temporarily and take refuge in the forest, and others abandoned their fields for good and went elsewhere, where a lord needed labor and working conditions seemed better. Most went to another estate belonging to their lord to escape the demands of the local steward.

Historians use the term "leagues of men of the estate" (*shōke no ikki*) to describe the groups that took part in the frequent peasant conflicts within the estates in the fourteenth and fifteenth centuries. These leagues were formed by agreements between peasants or by coalitions, sometimes involving vows. The peasants submitted a document to the lord stating their grievances and complaints or demanding a lowering of or exemption from the annual rents, a corvée, or a tax, and citing the source of their anger—the ravages of war or bad weather. They sometimes asked that a certain functionary who had broken laws or customs resign, and they even threatened to leave the land if the lord refused to cooperate.

In a 1428 document, the peasants of the Kami Kuze estate, property of the Tōji monastery and located a few kilometers south of Kyoto, complained about the new administrator sent by the monastery. This lord, Maita Keitei, had just been appointed to the position of *kumon* (administrator) on the estate by the owners, the monks of the Tōji. He was obliged to promise to conduct himself well:

> With regard to the position of archives administrator (*kumon*) on the Kami Kuze estate, Yamashiro Province, property of the Hachiman Shrine attached to the Tōji monastery:
>
> • The administrator shall serve the monks faithfully without betraying them.
> • The administrator shall collect the annual rents before the tenth lunar month and make sure that all that is due is paid and that the corvées are completed. He shall receive no orders from a third party and shall make note of everything that is not normal.
> • The administrator shall make no special contracts with either the peasants on the estate or other powerful parties.
> • He shall oversee transportation of the rents.
> • He shall not ally himself with the peasants if there are disturbances.
> • If he does not respect these commitments, the administrator will agree in advance to be removed from this position.

Very pleased with his promotion, Maita began his term by going to the Kami Kuze estate with some companions and having a party. Five days later, the inhabitants complained to the landowner:

> The lord Maita has just been appointed to the estate. It is agreed that we must supply him with food and cook meals for him and his entourage. However, the lord had people come from outside the estate and invited them to eat with him. This was not agreed to as part of the corvées. We ask you to have him cease doing this or else to pay for the food that he consumes. If not, we will make it known that the peasants will flee the estate.[25]

This document is typical of the swift reaction by the peasants, who accepted not the slightest departure from custom. Fleeing and moving away were brandished as threats against the lords, who were not authorized to pursue them to other estates. In most cases, the lords had to give in to the peasant union.

Type 2. In the late fourteenth and early fifteenth centuries, peasants in Kinai expressed their demands independently, without going to the estate administrator. In the Kamakura period, the peasants were still appealing to one estate jurisdiction, as opposed to another. After the first half of the fourteenth century, however, they felt that their communities had become strong enough that they could confront the landowners directly, and they began to agitate for reductions to or elimination of the annual rents charged by the lords or their stewards. The example of the Yano estate in Settsu Province is typical. In 1359, the peasants asked the owner of the estate, the Tōji, for an exemption amounting to 50 percent of the rent. The monastery was forced to accept. In 1361, the Tōji agreed to accord a rollback of twenty *koku* of rice on the annual rent. In 1362, the peasants obtained an exemption on one-third of the product of the rice paddies and a total exemption on dry fields. In 1363, they again demanded an exemption and obtained a reduction of seventeen *koku*. In 1364, they received an exemption of fifteen *koku*, which continued for the following three years.[26]

Type 3. The peasants no longer restricted their demands to petitions respectfully submitted to the lord but now engaged in demonstrations of force at the seat of the landowner's administration. The entire village went in a procession to the lord; in effect, the peasants went on strike! In the spring of 1437, because of heavy rains, the Kuze estate belonging to the Tōji was flooded. That fall, during the ninth lunar month, the peasants demanded that the monastery lower their rents considerably. The monks turned a deaf ear. The villagers then wrote a document in which they demanded a one-time reduction of one hundred *koku* on the annual rents, estimated at about two hundred *koku*—a decrease of 50 percent. The monks of the Tōji agreed to a reduction of only ten *koku*. Furious, the inhabitants of Kuze went en masse to the monastery. What happened next was recorded in a document:

> With regard to the damages done to the Kuze estate, the peasants and *myōshu* of this estate came en masse to bring their complaints to the temple. There were about sixty of them,[27] and they spent the night there, sleeping in the granaries. We first agreed to accord them a discount of ten *koku* on the rents, but because they were demanding even more, we finally awarded them ten more, for a total of twenty *koku*.[28]

A few days later, the peasants returned. Finally, the monks had to give them a discount of fifty *koku*. Through their demonstrations, the peasants had obtained a 25 percent reduction in the rents!

These conflicts involved *myōshu* and small-scale tenant peasants united in *sō*. In the late fourteenth century, the peasants' league on the Yano estate was well organized and certainly was one of the most turbulent. In 1369, the *sō* held regular meetings on the estate on the thirteenth day of each month, and its council issued decisions that everyone had to abide by strictly.[29] Peasant communities drew their strength from their ability to resist the feudal authorities and their exceptional degree of cohesion. The smallest defection from the association would spell the end of the sō. During a general meeting held in a consecrated place, members swore that they would obey the rules, so to disobey was to break a sacred vow. Behind the acts of resistance of a peasant democracy stood authoritarian—even totalitarian—practices. The fight against the authorities and the leading classes required iron-fisted discipline and unquestioned unity. Woe to those who did not submit to the common need. People who refused to bend to the law of the sō were "excommunicated": they were no longer helped with their agricultural work; their fields were no longer flooded; they were no longer spoken to. There was nothing for them to do but leave the village:

Decision regarding the unanimous solidarity of the leaders of the two shrines [those in Ōshima and Okitsushima] and the villagers.

We are registering our strong resentment of taking the oath to respect this decision, given the fact that the inhabitants and administrators of the Nakano estate have destroyed the wattles that we had placed in the lake [Lake Biwa] to catch fish for the religious festival, and we are now taking action. If there has been treachery, malicious gossip, or a criminal act against the village association, the offender shall be expelled from the estate and condemned. If someone has perjured himself, he will be doomed to divine curses, including that of the venerated god of the temple, in a form known or unknown. So be it.

Eini year 6, sixth lunar month, fourth day [1298]

Appendix
On this subject, if there were other developments, the association of the two estates would have to make a new decision.

This is a good illustration of the tight cohesion of a rural community that formed a common front on the day of a trial to manifest its unanimity. The threats evoked the gods' anger in a known form, *shimbatsu* (illness, accidents, paralysis, etc.), or an unknown form, *meibatsu* (appearance of monsters, ghosts, etc.).[30]

During the second half of the Middle Ages, peasant resistance to the landowners was based on a combination of religious and folk beliefs—an alliance between the divine and the collectivity. Medieval rebels could call on the gods to justify their struggle against the disdain of traditional values, which had led to oppression and discrimination. The peasants marched in procession dressed in yellow orange garments, the color of lepers and pariahs but also a sacred color symbolic of their contempt for taboos and determination to struggle—a challenge thrown in the faces of the powerful. Communal oaths were sworn in temples or shrines, where water from a sacred spring was drunk. Folk religion came to the aid of peasant defense organizations: Shinto beliefs were used to strengthen the union and the community, and those who acted against the common will risked divine punishment.

THOUGHTS AND ATTITUDES: FROM THEORISTS TO ORGANIZERS

The period of civil war between the two courts, unlike the Kamakura century, produced few eminent intellectuals capable of constructing new systems of thought. The only truly original thinker in the period was the main ideologue of the Southern Court, Kitabatake Chikafusa, who referred to the ancient imperial chronicles to support his legitimist philosophy, which was hostile to the Ashikaga bakufu. After the great turmoil of the thirteenth century, Buddhism sought to organize communities of followers. Although the culture of the Muromachi period was beginning to blossom, it took a respite during the hostilities for the culture called Kitayama to come into full flower.

HISTORY AS SEEN BY KITABATAKE CHIKAFUSA

Three years after the conflict between the Southern Court and the new shogun began, a court noble, Kitabatake Chikafusa (1293–1354) wrote the *Jinnō shōtoki* (History of the correct succession of the gods and emperors). Although the text fell into obscurity, it was rediscovered during the Edo period and had a considerable influence on nationalist thinkers up to World War II. A work of propaganda supporting the legitimacy of the Southern Court, the *Jinnō shōtoki* was intended to convince warriors in Kanto who had not yet made up their minds to join Go Daigo's followers against Ashikaga Takauji.

Like most nobles, Chikafusa was a literate man familiar with Chinese culture, Buddhism, and Confucianism, but he was also influenced by the thought of Watarai Ieyuki, one of the great priests of the shrine in Ise, a region where the Kitabatake family had many estates.[31] The Shinto doctrine of Ise was developed during the last years of the Kamakura era. In the late thirteenth century, the idea spread in aristocratic circles that the storms that had destroyed the fleets of the Mongol invaders had been sent by the *kami*.

The *Jinnō shōtoki* began with the famous sentence "Greater Japan is the land of the gods"—a sentence assigned to schoolchildren before World War II as a handwriting exercise. Chikafusa related the history of Japan from its divine origins to the reign of Emperor Go Daigo and offered a political discourse based on three convictions: Japan was superior to other countries; the social hierarchy had to be respected; and the principles of good government had to be duly applied. The seed of nationalism discernible in Chikafusa's thought was the reason for his work's popularity in later centuries.

According to Chikafusa, Japan was superior to other countries because it was the land of the gods. This was so because there was a link between the gods and the emperors, for the Sun Goddess Amaterasu was the ancestor of the first emperor of Japan, Emperor Jinmu (who supposedly founded the empire in 660 B.C.). Not only was Japan the land of the gods, it also benefited from the gods' protection. In other countries, such as India and China, order was often swept away and imperial dynasties crumbled. But in Japan, the existence of a single imperial dynasty since the beginning was proof of Japan's divine favor, which gave the Land of the Rising Sun its "particular essence," *kokutai*. This term from Chikafusa's work was widely used in ultranationalist circles in Japan before 1945. Chikafusa defined the three principles that, along with the transcendental wisdom of the emperors, would ensure good government: the emperor had to choose his ministers from among the wisest men, reward his subjects according to their rank, and render fair justice. Once he had done this, the sovereign had no need to entangle himself in political affairs. In fact, the government's legitimacy was the main imperial objective. Chikafusa also distinguished between the imperial family—the transcendental source of virtue, above all criticism—and the behavior of individual emperors, who could be the recipients of criticism. In the regime that Chikafusa advocated, the emperor would rule as absolute sovereign but let his ministers govern political affairs and, with their clan, be responsible for good public management. If they failed in their task, they would legitimately lose their power. This idea reveals the influence of Confucianism on the Shinto underpinnings of Chikafusa's thought. Indeed, like Jien, Chikafusa was a high court aristocrat who justified his existence by his ability to direct the affairs of state based on the correct interpretation of past facts. He who could forge a coherent historical discourse would legitimize his privileged position.

According to Chikafusa, Japan's ideal epoch had been the middle of the Heian period, when emperors occupied the throne without governing and political affairs were directed by an aristocratic oligarchy composed of several households, such as the Fujiwara and the Murakami Genji, his own ancestors. It was important to him that each individual in society remain in his given rank and not claim higher functions. Thus, under the threat of himself sinking to the rank of a simple functionary, the emperor was not to intervene personally in political affairs and compete with the aristocratic families responsible for administration.

Although the warriors had reestablished order, this did not give them any particular rights. Their social standing was below that of the court nobles. The first shogun, Yoritomo, had deluded himself by claiming titles and positions to which his birthright did not give him the right, which might explain the extinction of his family. For Chikafusa, the ideal warrior was Hōjō Yasutoki, who had been able to install a regime of peace and prosperity in the first half of the thirteenth century, after the Jōkyū disturbance, while contenting himself with the modest official title of *shikken*, regent of the shogun. Although they had kept the court from playing an important political role, the Hōjō regents had been able to keep order, and this reinforced, according to Chikafusa, the definitive character of the principle he was expounding.

The warriors, however, had been too eager for compensation beyond their worth. The appointment of stewards and military governors by the Kamakura regime upset the traditional state of affairs. The art of good government was lost, and consequently, the Hōjō regime was destroyed. Therefore, the warriors were required to ensure order and had to be content with staying in their place. To halt the disorder, Chikafusa recommended the militarization of the civil aristocracy, citing the example of his son Akiie, a court noble who deliberately became a general to serve the cause of Emperor Go Daigo.

Chikafusa did not understand why the warriors of his time were simply opting for the best offer. The "Way of the Warrior," he thought, resided in loyalty to the suzerain and not in a frenzied rush to profit, which was mercenary behavior unworthy of faithful and devoted subjects. Obviously, in the society of his times, torn apart by civil war, Chikafusa lacked a sense of tactics, and by accusing them outright of basing their support for the Southern Court on rewards, he pushed the warriors into the arms of his enemies.

Nevertheless, Chikafusa expressed the opinions of the nobles of his time. For him, the not negligible influences of Buddhism and Confucianism were balanced by an unswerving faith in the justice of good principles of government, based on the need to defend order and the social hierarchy. He was very hostile to the historical pessimism of those who, like Jien, believed in the doctrine of *mappō* decadence and attributed the collapse of the Hōjō in 1333 not to the uprising of the highest-ranking generals but to the will of the gods. For Chikafusa, who believed in Japan's uniqueness, the age of the warriors was only a step toward the return to the ideal regime desired by the gods.

This notion of the gods' desire for a return to the ideal regime was a constant in the medieval mind, which could not be expressed in simple theoretical constructs. The edicts of "virtuous government" were juridical practices both authorizing and justified by a return to the ancient order. Chikafusa took up this idea with a view to restoring the nobility to its political function, and he used the imperial chronicles based on Shinto to claim legitimacy for the Southern Court. The peasants acted similarly when they opposed the demands of a lord: they recalled ancestral customs, defended their ways, placed their resistance within a backward-looking context, and demanded a return to the old order that had been overturned by the lords. Because their anger was divine in nature, they claimed, they could rightly appropriate the sacred.

Whether used by members of a nobility headed for political marginalization or, on the contrary, by lower-level communities struggling against the existing powers, Shinto chronicles, myths, and practices played a central role in the political and social disputes of the Middle Ages. Until the nineteenth century, the ideas of turning back and restoration were associated in Japanese minds with liberation and amelioration. The radical movement in the late Edo period was based on a return to the sources of national tradition, and it was not by chance that the Meiji regime was designed above all as a restoration.

RETURN TO CONSERVATISM
IN THE NEW BUDDHISM

Hōnen and Shinran taught salvation through absolute faith in Amida Buddha and proclaimed the total equality of human beings in the light of divine mercy. They denied the traditional distinction between master and disciple and thus logically rejected the gathering of followers in sanctuaries or sects. The negation of the separation between master and disciple was a thirteenth-century innovation of radical Amidist thought. Nonetheless, organizations were beginning to form around both Hōnen and Shinran, as disciples, popularizers, auxiliaries, and preachers tried to rally the faithful. In fact, even though the founders of sects were not trying to attract large followings, few of them impeded the organizational efforts of their disciples, many of whom had known the master and wanted to assemble his few teachings with a legitimate desire to make them universal.[32]

In the second half of the thirteenth century, Yuien, a disciple of Shinran, compiled the *Tannishō*, a collection of Shinran's speeches and Yuien's complaints about the heterodoxy of the other followers. Bitter disputes soon broke out regarding the interpretation of their master's thought, poisoning the relations among Hōnen's five main disciples. The most persuasive established their own schools and became masters. Discord came even more easily among Nichiren's followers because the master's thought was volatile and changed with the times, and his six disciples fought over who would succeed him.

Organizations of followers gradually formed to put their masters' teachings into practice or even to worship the masters themselves. At the end of the Kamakura period, Hōnen's and Shinran's disciples celebrated the anniversaries of their masters' deaths,[33] and the divinization of the ancient masters began. Scrolls were painted to recount the lives of the holy men. Their stories were idealized and inflated with edifying anecdotes and legends. In Shinran's case, a family line descended from the master led the sect.[34] The divinization of the founder strengthened his family's position, and they organized a cult around relics and objects that had belonged to him. Kakushin'ni, Shinran's daughter, built a mausoleum, the Ōtani byōdo, in Kyoto, in which a picture of her father was venerated. In the 1320s, Kakunyo, Shinran's grandson, gathered followers in a religious community organized around a temple, the Honganji, and gave himself the title of high priest (*hossu*) of the Amidist sect.

Followers gathered to worship in halls which became temples, whose management sometimes became a source of conflict. Nichiren's followers were opposed to the management of the Kuonji, and Dōgen's followers disputed that of the Eiheiji. Little by little, the leaders refined the rituals and defined the practices. Shinran maintained that he himself was neither monk nor layman, but the next generation of his followers saw themselves as religious professionals. The manager of the hall gradually became the sect leader, the representative of the assembly of followers, and an expert in organizing believers; the followers evolved into disciples. The creation of the Honganji in the early fourteenth century and of a sect around the temple solidified the new state of affairs.

In other sects, the faithful organized around temples, and those who played an important role in the construction of these buildings became their representatives. In Jōdo Amidism and the Rinzai Zen sect, supporters who were powerful nobles and warriors had a great influence on the sects' internal organization. They specified rites and ceremonies and excluded ordinary followers, who had less and less right to speak. Most of the new sects founded in the thirteenth century returned in the fourteenth century to the traditional Buddhist practices that had been so heavily criticized. Sects were "privatized" by a family or a group of disciples assembled into a faction. The trend toward conservatism had begun.

ZEN OF THE FIVE MOUNTAINS

Zen Buddhism of the Rinzai school had been popular among the military elites in the late Kamakura period and throughout the fourteenth and fifteenth centuries under the Ashikaga while the Five Mountains system slowly built an administrative organization. In both Zen Buddhism and the Amidist currents, the fourteenth century was dedicated more to organization than to reflection.

The Five Mountains (Gozan) system corresponded to the administrative organization of Zen temples under state control developed in Song-dynasty China, which the Chinese monks who went to Japan sought to re-create there. Closely associated with the Hōjō regime and then with the Ashikaga bakufu, the Zen monasteries were protected by the state. The prestige of Zen at the time was linked to its capacity to ally itself with those in power by training an intellectual elite of monks who became diplomats, political advisers, writers, and artists and who played an important behind-the-scenes role in the government. The political and economic power of the Zen monasteries never seemed to pose a threat. As training schools, they produced an elite that advised those in power. The success of the Zen monks was somewhat analogous to that of the Jesuits in some European monarchies. But because it was so closely associated with the state, the Five Mountains system nearly fell with the Ashikaga bakufu in the sixteenth century.[35]

At first, the Five Mountains entailed only temples linked to Kamakura. But with the geographic shift of power in 1333 and the construction of large Zen temples such as the Nanzenji and the Tenryūji in Kyoto, the Five Mountains system spread into Kinai. In 1341, the Ashikaga decided to extend the system from Kamakura to Kyoto, and it was stabilized in 1386 during the rule of the third shogun, Ashikaga Yoshimitsu.

At the top of the hierarchy was the Nanzenji in Kyoto. Under it were five major monasteries, the "five mountains," in Kamakura and five in Kyoto. The last monastery, the Shōkokuji, was erected between 1382 and 1385 and was the personal place of worship of the shogun Yoshimitsu. Its seven-story pagoda, built in 1399, was nine hundred meters high. Although it towered over the capital, the pagoda was fragile and collapsed when it was hit by lightning in 1403. Hierarchically under the Five Mountains were the Ten Monasteries, or *jissatsu*. In 1386, there were in fact twenty-two of them, and by the end of the Muromachi period, there were about sixty. Below the Ten Monasteries were temples of lesser importance whose numbers slowly grew (there were 230 at the beginning of the Edo period). It is this entire Zen monastic organization that is designated by Gozan, the Five Mountains.

In the early years of the Ashikaga bakufu, the monk Musō Soseki played a decisive role in the establishment of the Gozan and its extension to Kyoto, the seat of the new government. He founded the Tenryūji and was a brilliant organizer and diplomat. A disciple of great Chinese monks such as Yishan Yining (Issan Ichinei), who taught in Kamakura in the early fourteenth century, he knew the regent Hōjō Takatoki and the emperor Go Daigo, as well as the shogun Ashikaga Takauji and his brother Tadayoshi. Musō was responsible for several confidential missions to negotiate agreements between the shogun's followers and the Southern Court. He was also a very talented garden designer, and he planned the extraordinary moss garden at the Saihōji, near Kyoto. His nephew and disciple, Shuruoku Myōha, the "converted" shogun Yoshimitsu, who appointed him *sōroku*, or director of the organization.

The Zen organization had considerable economic power throughout the fourteenth century. During an era of disturbances and the disintegration of nobles' estates, the Zen monks, because of their reputation as administrators, were entrusted with the management of many estates belonging to nobles in difficulty, through which they built huge fortunes. They then began to lend money and became experts in speculation. The bakufu protected, and even encouraged, the economic activities of the major Zen temples and, under various pretexts, forced them to pay taxes. The Zen monks continued to be indispensable intermediaries with China and were behind the dissemination in Japan, in the fourteenth and fifteenth centuries, of "Five Mountains literature," consisting of Chinese-inspired poetry,[36] treatises by Buddhist monks, and Neo-Confucian writings. The Zen monks also spread the Song style of ink painting (*sumi-e*), introduced to Japan by Mokuan—an art that Sesshū, another Zen monk, brought to perfection in the sixteenth century.

Chapter 9

THE SPLENDOR AND MISERY

OF THE MUROMACHI CENTURY:

THE CULMINATION OF THE ASHIKAGA

AND THE DEVELOPMENT OF TRADE

Unlike the Kamakura period, the Muromachi period had no well-defined boundaries. It started with Shogun Ashikaga Yoshimitsu's reign, from 1378 to 1392, and ended somewhere between the end of the terrible Ōnin War (1467–77) and the coup d'état led by Hosokawa Masamoto, the great lord *shugo* who was prime minister, *kanrei*, in 1493.

The Muromachi period was one of contrasts. There was a strong shogunal government until 1441, when Shogun Yoshinori was assassinated, followed by political anarchy in the second half of the fifteenth century as the Ashikaga shogun, whose authority had melted away in the provinces, retreated to Kinai and power passed into the hands of the great vassals, the *shugo*. Another contrast was between this political anarchy, which some historians of the past too hastily associated with a decline, and the strength of the Japanese economy, which was diversifying and becoming international. Furthermore, there was a contrast in the social and cultural arenas between the decline of the traditional nobility of the imperial court and the massive burgeoning of the working classes. This phenomenon of "the lower commanding the upper" (*gekokujō*) gave rise to social struggles of an often surprising radicalism and to a brilliant culture unencumbered by forms inherited from tradition, freer in expression and liberated from the exclusive circles of the leading classes. A growing economy, the partial emancipation of commoners, and a new culture shaped the new values: the cult of money, protocapitalist attitudes, and a universalist, but sometimes

already rationalist, spirit went hand in hand with an aesthetic sense that transformed the difficult concepts of *yūgen* (the depths of mystery), *sabi* (elegant
simplicity through the patina of time), and *kanjaku* (serenity) into the basis for
an art of living.

THE POLITICAL CADRES: STABILITY AND THEN
FAILURE IN THE ASHIKAGA SHOGUNAL REGIME

The Ashikaga regime reached its peak during the reigns of the shoguns Yoshimitsu (1368–1408), Yoshimochi (1408–28), and Yoshinori (1429–41). Of the three,
Yoshimitsu was the most important. He reestablished peace and reunified the
two rival imperial courts in 1392, and he presented himself as symbolic of the
merger that he was trying to effect between the court nobles and the warriors.
In addition, he was recognized by the Chinese emperor (Ming dynasty), who
conferred on him the title of "king of Japan."

After a difficult beginning under the first shogun, Takauji, the Ashikaga
regime was consolidated in the 1360s and 1370s. While retaining most of the
main institutions of the Kamakura regime, it introduced two decisive innova-
tions: a regional bakufu in Kamakura (Kantō *kubō*) and a deputy (*kanrei*) to the
shogun in Kyoto.

In 1336, Takauji decided to transfer the bakufu's headquarters from Kanto to
Kyoto. Control of the east—the traditional base of the warrior regime—was
essential. The Hōjō regents, confronted with a similar division in the state, had
created an administration of oversight at the Rokuhara Palace in Kyoto. The
head of this administration, the *tandai*, was related to the regent in Kamakura
and usually succeeded him. But while the Kamakura regents and the Kyoto
tandai had cooperated without major difficulties, the political tandem developed by the Ashikaga was destined for conflict. Takauji passed on his position
to his older son, Yoshiakira, while the regional bakufu, the Kantō *fu* in Kamakura, went to his younger son, Motouji. The shogunal dynasty was thus divided
from the beginning between a senior branch, which reigned with the title of
shogun in Kyoto, and a junior branch, which held the office of deputy shogun
in Kamakura. The younger branch, ruling over the eight provinces of Kanto
(plus Izu and Kai Provinces) had a great degree of autonomy, and this ultimately
threatened the balance of power.

Kyoto had prerogatives that would normally enable the senior shogunal
branch to maintain control over the regional bakufu, including assigning all
important positions in the Kamakura administration. In 1353, however, the
regional bakufu obtained the right to allow warriors to transform into fiefs those
estates within their sphere of power. Thus a network of vassalages loyal to the
junior branch of the Ashikaga clan was created. Kamakura then obtained judicial autonomy with a system inspired by the justice system that had functioned

under the Hōjō. These concessions, necessary for better control of the provincial vassals during the civil war, were risky when peace was reestablished, for they could only push the deputy shogun toward greater independence of Kyoto. In 1392, the deputy shogun also gained authority over the northeastern provinces.

Relations between the two Ashikaga branches became increasingly strained. The junior branch was rife with plots and sought support among those opposed to Kyoto for an attempt to oust the senior branch, which turned to the high-ranking vassals of Kanto who were opposed to the deputy shogun's policies. Skirmishes repeatedly broke out, and the only reason they did not explode into all-out war was that the weakening of central authority that affected the Ashikaga regime after 1441 had started earlier in Kamakura. The deputy shogun of Kanto were preoccupied with the opposition of local warriors, who formed defense leagues (*ikki*) or supported various of the deputy shogun's ministers. The ministers of the Uesugi clan tried to take power several times. To the difficulties that the deputy shogun was facing with his vassals and ministers were added succession struggles that completely paralyzed the regional bakufu, and in the second half of the fifteenth century, it finally split into two equally impotent branches.

In Kyoto, the shogun abolished the hereditary element of the positions of regent (*shikken*) and chief of the Board of Retainers (Samurai dokoro no bettō) and spread these important responsibilities among several families of *shugo* who were vassals of the Ashikaga. When war broke out between Shogun Takauji and his brother Tadayoshi in 1350, it became evident that the new regime lacked coherence. And indeed, the Ashikaga dynasty might very well have lost power in 1367, when the second shogun, Yoshiakira, died in the midst of civil war, leaving his ten-year-old son Yoshimitsu as his successor. On his deathbed, Yoshiakira named as *kanrei* (prime minister) a very high-ranking vassal of the Ashikaga, Hosokawa Yoriyuki. With regard to the Ashikaga, the Hosokawa were in a position analogous to that once held by the Hōjō with regard to the Minamoto. But Yoriyuki did not have the ambitions for his clan that the Hōjō had had for theirs, and the military situation was more precarious. As soon as he reached adulthood, Yoshimitsu got rid of Yoriyuki, and three vassal families of the Ashikaga—the Hosokawa, the Shiba, and the Hatakeyama—shared the position of *kanrei*, as the shogun exploited the rivalry among those eligible in order to stay in power. Until 1441, rather than threaten the authority of the shogun, the *kanrei* ran the council composed of the main *shugo* lords in the capital on his behalf.

In fact, the Ashikaga shogun's main problem was maintaining a balance among these different forces. The deputy shoguns were neutralized by their vassals, who were manipulated by Kyoto. The powers of the *kanrei* were limited by the ambitions of the other high-ranking lords. To transform his relative authority into absolute control, Yoshimitsu had to solidify his position as suzerain of the warriors, but he also had to find support outside the warrior classes.

He was able to play off these contradictions brilliantly by flattering the old court nobility, dissuading his vassals from treason by letting them go to war, and diverting others by summoning them to the capital to play a role in the central administration of the bakufu and to benefit from the Kitayama culture. He tried to create a kingdom by absorbing the Southern Court and having himself declared king—as the official subject of the Ming, of course, and favored interlocutor of the Middle Kingdom. As long as the Ashikaga shogun, at the top of the social pyramid, maintained this precarious balance, they were the true masters of the country. It is easy to understand why Ashikaga Yoshimitsu was tempted to establish absolute rule.[1]

Between 1378, when Yoshimitsu took power as an adult, and his death in 1408, the bakufu underwent major changes. To overcome the traditional difficulties of the shogunal dynasty, Yoshimitsu tried to change the foundations of his government. He inaugurated a new policy of reconciling the civilian nobles of the imperial court and the warrior aristocracy.[2] Unlike the shogun who had preceded him, Yoshimitsu accumulated titles at the imperial court, where his career had a meteoric rise. He was an auditor in 1373, third minister in 1381, then minister of the left, and finally prime minister in 1394. Among the honors bestowed on him was that of "treatment in the manner of empresses," long reserved for regents from the Fujiwara household. Later, Yoshimitsu celebrated the entrance to adulthood of one of his sons using the protocol for imperial princes, which some Fujiwara had also dared to do, and he married a woman from the Hino family, the most powerful noble clan in Kyoto. He charmed the court nobility, of which he had become a member, but at the same time, he weakened it by every means possible. Under him, invasions of nobles' estates by warriors multiplied, and governors obtained the right to appropriate half of the real-estate tax (*hanzei*) collected on nobles' estates. In the late fourteenth century, the real-estate revenues of the warrior classes rose above those of the nobility for the first time.

So that he would not become a pawn of the most powerful lords, Yoshimitsu inaugurated a policy of constantly alternating alliances among his main vassals. He systematically undermined the *kanrei*—if he seemed to be accumulating too much power—and supported an opposing faction. In 1379, he removed Hosokawa Yoriyuki and replaced him with the head of the Shiba household, and in 1391, he recalled the now elderly Yoriyuki to counter the Yamana household, which had become too powerful. On the pretext of visiting the famous landscapes and architectural marvels of the countryside, Yoshimitsu made a number of trips to the provinces, which gave him an opportunity to visit the governors and make a show of force. Finally, he quickly subdued or did battle with lords who had become powerful enough to contest his authority: the Toki, in 1379; the Yamana, defeated in a military campaign in 1391; and the Ōuchi, in 1399.

In 1394, Yoshimitsu resigned from the position of shogun, which he left to his son and heir, Yoshimochi. He gave up his court responsibilities, withdrew from the lay world, and took the religious name Dōgi, becoming a sort of "retired shogun," just as there once had been retired emperors. Although Yoshimitsu continued to run political affairs from his Muromachi palace, his new position enabled him to sidestep social ranks and status and avoid the cumbersome ceremonial routine. In 1397, he moved to the Golden Pavilion, which he had had built in Kitayama, near Kyoto, and he made use of the same apparatus as had the cloistered emperors.

In the last part of his life, Yoshimitsu was primarily interested in trade with Ming-dynasty China, and he sent Japan's first mission to the Chinese court in 1397. An official exchange of letters took place between the "retired shogun" and the Ming emperor, who offered Yoshimitsu the title of "king of Japan"—a title that he accepted. Although this placed Yoshimitsu, according to the diplomatic rules of the Far East, in the position of tributary vassal to the Chinese emperor, it meant that the Chinese recognized him as a privileged interlocutor and the sovereign of Japan, and they agreed to open official trade relations, a source of enormous profits for the Japanese in general and the shogun in particular. Far from weakening his position, the new title strengthened Yoshimitsu's hold on government. Now he was the only real sovereign in Kyoto, eclipsing the emperor. As for the lords, they were simply respectful vassals of the monarch—for Yoshimitsu was more than an emperor or a shogun; he was the ruler of both nobles and warriors.

Under Ashikaga Yoshimochi, there was a return to the traditional bakufu. Yoshimochi succeeded his father in 1408. He detested Yoshimitsu and thus tried to undo his work. In this, he had the support of his *kanrei*, Shiba Yoshimasa, who had been very skeptical of Yoshimitsu's overall policy and urged Yoshimochi to return to more orthodox policies. The shogun turned back to the major vassal households for his power, ending the policy of catering to the nobility, and set up a council of *shugo* to govern. He also ended all official relations with China.

Yoshimochi died in 1428 without choosing an heir, so this task fell to the council of *shugo*, led by the *kanrei*. The deputy shogun of Kamakura made known his claim to the position, but on the advice of the monk Mansai, a skillful politician, the successor was chosen by lot from among the possible heirs. In the end, it was Yoshimochi's fourth-youngest brother, Yoshinori, who was designated shogun "by the will of the god Hachiman," the guardian god of shogunal dynasties. Yoshinori officially became shogun in 1429.

Ashikaga Yoshinori turned the regime toward despotism. Because he had been chosen by lot, he was in a weak position vis-à-vis the lords. He tended toward authoritarianism, and all his measures were aimed at reducing the powers of the council of *shugo* and the *kanrei* and increasing his personal power over the shogunal institutions. Yoshinori instituted a judiciary reform intended to place the commissioners responsible for military training under his direct

authority, previously a prerogative of the *kanrei*. By intervening in every important matter and making decisions personally, he increased his power considerably. So that he could fend off attacks without depending on his vassals' armies,
Yoshinori assembled a personal guard made up of young vassals from estates
held directly by the shogunal household, the *hōkōshū*. This special guard, with
no attachments to the *shugo*, was 2,000 to 3,000 horsemen strong, and its members swore their personal loyalty to the shogun.[3]

Yoshinori also restored a policy dear to Yoshimitsu—he reestablished trade
with the Ming dynasty—but the warriors and court nobles opposed returning
to any of the terms of Yoshimitsu's reign. Although Yoshinori was forced to cede
on this point, he continued to become more autocratic. He intervened successfully in affairs in Kanto, where he crushed an attempted revolt by the deputy
shogun, dispatched the monks of Mount Hiei, and meddled more and more
frequently in the internal affairs of the *shugo* lords, especially in successions.
Using any means necessary to weaken vassals who were becoming too powerful,
he confiscated estates, exiled or condemned his adversaries, and drove them to
reveal their intentions so that he could undermine them. He sowed terror
among the lords, promoted his favorites, and went so far as to interfere in the
love affairs of courtesans. The atmosphere in Kyoto became very tense.[4]

In 1441, Akamatsu Mitsusuke invited Yoshinori to a banquet with a *sarugaku*
(a genre of early medieval theater) performance in his villa in Kyoto. Surrounded by dignitaries, Yoshinori was relaxing and enjoying the performance
when suddenly warriors commanded by Mitsusuke surrounded the house. Yoshinori was assassinated by a sword blow, and several courtesans were killed in
the melee. Quietly, Mitsusuke had his villa set afire, and he then headed for
Harima Province, his fiefdom, with the shogun's head on the end of a spike.
Kyoto was stunned. Imperial Prince Sadafusa commented on the event in his
journal: "No one cut open his stomach [committed suicide] when he saw the
shogun's body. Akamatsu was able to escape, and no one pursued him. Perhaps
some lords were his accomplices. . . . It was said that the shogun was killed like
a dog. It is the first time I have heard such things said."[5]

"Killed like a dog"! The murdered shogun's high-ranking warriors reacted
quickly. Of course, Akamatsu Mitsusuke had to be punished, and he was
betrayed by his barons. On the whole, though, the collapse of Yoshinori's dictatorship was seen as a great relief, and from then on, the power of the Ashikaga
shogun waned, gradually passing into the hands of the lords. The lords, however, were preoccupied with their local barons organized in leagues, who, in
turn, were having a hard time keeping the peasants from exploding with anger.
Japan had entered the epoch of *gekokujō*.

The failure to create a feudal monarchy may be explained, beyond the combination of circumstances, by the absence of a homogeneous Japanese society
in the Muromachi period. The shogun could not rely on a strictly ideological
doctrine, such as that of the Christian Church, to unify the culture. Medieval

Japan was a society of multiple power centers. Although political unification was achieved in response to changes in the bakufu's economic and social foundations, it was too soon to bring the court nobility and warriors together in a single aristocracy under the authority of a ruler-shogun. The income from its own estates and the taxes collected from vassals no longer supplied the main share of the bakufu's finances. Starting in Yoshimitsu's reign, the bakufu gained most of its revenue from trade activities—charging income taxes on the cargoes of ships from abroad, at barriers and gates, and on markets. Add to this its extortion of various financiers and moneylenders, and the bakufu was able to build villas as sumptuous as the Golden Pavilion.

GROWTH IN INTERNATIONAL TRADE

Japan's trade structures evolved considerably during the Muromachi period. The advent of active international trade, the growth of an urban bourgeoisie in Kyoto and in the ports of western Japan, the multiplication of trade routes and means of communication, and the massive influx of Chinese copper coins profoundly changed the mental constructs of the time. Expansionism seemed to be a common phenomenon in the Far East. Japan, awakening from a long period of inertia, was perhaps just one participant, but it was an increasingly active one.

According to Tanaka Takeo, an expert on Asian maritime relations in the late Middle Ages,[6] the attempted Mongol invasions in the late thirteenth century led to a shift in the Japanese concept of the outside world. First, the high seas (yashioji), up to then a subject of unspeakable fear, became less anxiety provoking. In the fourteenth century, ideas about the rest of the world began to change among the elite. The vision inherited from antiquity of a world divided into three parts—Japan (honchō); the Chinese cultural sphere, including Korea (shintan); and the rest, originally India (tenjiku) and later the world outside the Sino-Japanese universe, perceived only very vaguely—was replaced by a more accurate knowledge of geography. The Koreans and Chinese came within the Japanese purview, and vice versa. When official trade between China and Japan began in the first years of the fifteenth century, the Chinese rulers held talks with Japanese emissaries, and their general knowledge of Japan became more accurate. When Marco Polo, visiting the Yuan court in the late thirteenth century, had spoken of "Cipango" as a land of gold, it was because to China, Japan was still a mythical place. A century later, Japan was paying tribute to China and was a very important trade partner.

In 1976, the wreck of an old ship was found on the Korean coast. A series of underwater excavations yielded a great deal of information on the ships involved in international trade in the Far East. Then the discovery of wooden tablets in 1983 enabled part of the ship's history to be reconstructed. This vessel, which

sailed between a Chinese port—no doubt Ningbo—and Japan, had been put
to sea in 1323. It was twenty-eight meters long and almost seven meters wide
and resembled a Chinese junk. Its cargo included 18,600 ceramic pieces, several
tons of Chinese copper coins, and blocks of sandalwood. Part of the merchandise belonged to the Tōfukuji, the Zen temple in Kyoto that had burned down
in 1319, and some of the profits from the merchandise were to be devoted to its
reconstruction. The crew was made up of sailors from all over, but the captain
was Japanese. Most of the kitchen utensils on board were Chinese, with some
Korean ones; Japanese wooden clogs were also found.[7] With a cargo from
China, a Japanese shipowner and captain, and a mixed crew, it would be hard
to draw conclusions about the sailors' nationality: Chinese, Koreans, and Japanese worked side by side on the twenty-eight-meter ship. Even a century later,
the *wakō* pirates had no trouble recruiting Koreans to plunder the Chinese
coasts. Other discoveries made in the sea off Kamakura have supplied much
concrete information on the history of navigation and trade in the Far East.

In the early fourteenth century, ships were assigned by Japanese authorities
to trade with the Chinese, with the profits to be used to construct large Zen
temples. Throughout the century, an unofficial trade developed between
China, Korea, and Japan at the same time as piracy was growing. In fact, this
piracy ultimately changed international relations. After Korea, it was China's
turn to suffer raids by the *wakō* from the coast of Zhejiang to the island of
Hainan. The Chinese coasts were fortified in Fujian, and coast guards were
deployed to fight off the marauders. The Chinese junks that had crossed the
sea to Japan for the past several centuries were now increasingly rare.[8] Trade
between the archipelago and the mainland, which had been conducted mainly
by Chinese merchants, slowed. But although the Chinese were reluctant to
travel to Japan, Japanese traders did go to the mainland in the wake of the Zen
monks and *wakō*. Traffic at the port towns of Hakata, Hyōgo, and Sakai became
more congested, and the towns began to expand. During the fourteenth century,
the Chinese lost their monopoly on navigating the seas of East Asia.

The installation of a new dynasty, the Ming, in 1368, and the policy adopted
by the Chinese rulers regarding international trade had an effect on trade structures in Asia. Some Ming-dynasty emperors saw the traders as threatening the
foundations of their state. To bolster their dynasty's power, they decreed the
closing of China to foreign commerce and tightly controlled all trade. Chinese
subjects could no longer go to foreign ports, and maritime trade became a state
monopoly—that is, it could no longer be conducted officially except between
states. The Ming cost the Chinese their almost total monopoly on international
shipping, and the seas were now filled with ships from Japan, Korea, the Malay
peninsula, and elsewhere. This policy had two indirect consequences: it
encouraged the birth of a small state on Okinawa, and it reinvigorated the *wakō*,
who now concentrated on contraband operations along the coasts of the Middle
Kingdom.

Official trade using "seals" was based on concessions of authorization to enter Chinese ports. After an exchange of diplomatic correspondence in 1401–2 between the emperor of China and the shogun Yoshimitsu, who accepted the Chinese title of "king of Japan" conferred on him, trade between the two countries officially began. To distinguish Japanese merchant ships from *wakō* ships, the Chinese authorities gave them seals.[9] This official trade prospered until 1547. But the number of convoys was limited to seventeen in a century and a half, during which time eighty-five ships furnished with seals made the round trip between the archipelago and the Chinese mainland. Under Yoshimitsu, two ships made the trip each year between 1401 and 1410. Few details are known, except that Japan used this opportunity to acquire a large number of Chinese copper coins. Trade was interrupted under Shogun Yoshimochi and started again under Yoshinori. Three ships with a crew of three hundred men made two trips in 1432 and 1434. The ships were owned by the shogun, the great lords, and some temples, including the Kōfukuji in Nara. Their concerns were purely economic: they wanted to procure luxury products and coins in China.[10]

Two rival clans, the Hosokawa, who had a strong influence on the bakufu and controlled Sakai, and the Ōuchi, who controlled Hakata, began to dominate the trade with China in 1465, and wealthy merchants in those two towns profited greatly. Trade was officially in the form of a tribute made by the Japanese to the Ming emperor, who, in exchange, offered gifts to the visitors. Under this arrangement, the Japanese exported gold, sulfur, and swords to China and were authorized by the Chinese emperor to sell part of their cargo at the trading post in the port of Ningbo or in Beijing for copper coins, with which they purchased cotton and silk to resell in Japan at a colossal profit.

A mixed-blood merchant, Kusaba Sainin, explained how trade with China was conducted to the monk Jinson, who reported on it in his personal diary. Sainin bought copper in Bizen Province for ten *kanmon* and resold it at five times the price in China, where he procured the raw silk. A bolt of silk purchased for 250 *mon* in China was resold for 5,000 *mon* in Japan. Japanese swords, which had an excellent reputation, were sold in China at a profit of 500 percent. The shogun charged a tax of 10 percent on private merchandise brought back. After a trip to China in 1475, Yukawa Sen'a, a merchant from Sakai, paid the shogunal government about 4,000 *kanmon*, which suggests that he brought back 40,000 *kanmon* worth of merchandise. Sasaki Ginya estimated Yukawa's net profit at about 25,000 *kanmon*. By comparison, construction of the new shogunal palace in 1431 cost about 10,000 *kanmon*.[11]

Maritime technology advanced somewhat in the fourteenth century. According to Tanaka Takeo, who studied the evolution of trade ships in the Muromachi period, their tonnage grew constantly. At the end of the Kamakura period, few ships were larger than thirty tons, which obviously limited their freight capacity, but in Yoshimitsu's time, many ships carried 150 tons. In the mid-fifteenth century, the largest junks carried 250 tons, but they were rare. According to the archives of the port of Hyōgo, out of the 1,600 ships that entered the port in 1445, only six carried more than one hundred tons. These relative giants sailed the high seas to reach the mainland, and they held 150 people, including travelers. However, more links with the mainland did not lead to a technological revolution in navigation similar to that achieved by the Portuguese in the fifteenth century. Rather, the Japanese simply improved and enlarged the ships that had been used for coastal shipping in the Inland Sea, but they also learned to use the winds according to the seasons and began to use compasses. Despite this progress, Chinese junks were still the best ships on Asian seas until the sixteenth century, when they were outclassed by Portuguese vessels.[12]

In the fifteenth century, even more ships from Hakata, Hyōgo, and Sakai were plying the maritime routes linking Japan to China and Korea. Hakata was an important port in international maritime trade in the China Sea and quickly became prosperous. Strategically located, it had always played a pivotal role in relations between the mainland and the archipelago. Its international vocation was reinforced after Tsushima, the pirates' island base, was destroyed by the Koreans in 1419, and it became the crossroads of trade between Japan and Korea. In the last years of the fourteenth century, relations were also established with Sumatra. Ships from Java were seen in Hakata, Korea, and elsewhere. Ships from Palembang twice entered Wakasa Bay to unload exotic animals—elephants, parrots, and peacocks. In the early fifteenth century, the Koreans made a "map of the Japanese archipelago," demonstrating their interest in their Japanese neighbors; it is the oldest known map of Japan that includes the Ryukyu Islands and shows the northern island of Hokkaido. Merchants from Hakata also received trade authorizations from the Korean government, and merchant dynasties, such as the one founded by Sōkin, were formed in the town to negotiate directly with the bakufu and receive "licenses" from the Korean kings. Dōan, another Hakata merchant, represented the king of the Ryukyu Islands in the Korean court.[13]

OKINAWA: "A BRIDGE BETWEEN COUNTRIES"

In the late fourteenth and early fifteenth centuries, a new state was formed at the gateway to the Japanese archipelago: the Ryukyu kingdom. After centuries of internal strife, three principalities were created on the main island, Okinawa, in the fourteenth century. Toward the end of the century, the princes of Okinawa agreed to pay a tribute to the emperor of China in exchange for the establishment of official trade between the Ryukyu Islands and the Middle Kingdom. In 1429, the islands were unified under King Sho Hashi (1372–1439). All foreign trade from the islands came under his hegemony, and he presented himself to China officially as a loyal supporter of the Ming emperor. Twice a year, the king's delegates took a tribute to China as a sign of loyalty.[14] In 1401, Yoshimitsu had been forced to do the same thing.

The sailors of Okinawa took over from the Chinese merchants, who had been banned by the Ming regime from maritime trade. The Okinawans brought back Chinese porcelain and silk from Fujian to Naha, their capital, in exchange for their tribute. The tribute was quite small, since the Ryukyus were not very wealthy. The Okinawans had little choice but to sail into the China Sea to find products to sell to the Chinese, and delegations from Okinawa were sent to the bakufu in Kyoto in the fifteenth century. In every Japanese port, Okinawan merchants were seeking art works, swords, and copper to purchase. In 1389, their presence had been recorded in Korean ports. In the fifteenth and sixteenth centuries, ships from the Ryukyu Islands dropped anchor in Malacca, the Sunda Islands, Annam, and as far away as Patani in Siam, where they acquired perfumes, spices, pewter, ivory, and other exotic products to bring back to Naha. According to the chronicle entitled *Rekidai hōan* (written in Chinese), started in 1424 by the sovereigns of the Ryukyu Islands to record relations with foreign countries, at least twenty ships from Okinawa went to Malacca, and eleven went to Patani between 1425 and 1570.[15] The sailors of the Ryukyu Islands became indispensable intermediaries between the ports of Southeast Asia and those of Korea and Japan. Sasaki Ginya has written about a triangular trade among Okinawa, the Japanese archipelago, and the Korean peninsula.[16] The people of the Ryukyu Islands—the Rekio, as the Portuguese called them—thus helped make the East Asian seas an active trade area. In 1458, the king of the Ryukyu Islands, Shō Taikyū, had a bell cast in Naha with the kingdom's motto engraved on it: "By sailing our ships, we shall make Okinawa a bridge between countries."[17] In a just few dozen years, Okinawa became one of the great trade powers of the Far East.

In the fifteenth century, major ports were built in the Asian seas, such as Hakata in Kyushu, Ningbo in China, Naha in Okinawa, Palembang in Sumatra, and Malacca on the Malayan peninsula. The East Asian seas, on which ships bearing precious cargoes sailed, became a space that connected remote areas for the first time and began to function, according to Braudel's concept, as a world economy.[18] In this context, the odyssey of the first meeting of Westerners with Japanese does not seem coincidental: in 1542, a Chinese junk was headed from a Southeast Asian port (perhaps Malacca) to Macao. It probably belonged to Wang Zhi, a pirate chief, who in the sixteenth century had built a maritime empire encompassing Shuang Yu, the Zhushan Islands, and the islands of Gotō and Hirado. Beset by unfavorable winds, the junk, carrying three Portuguese foreign nationals with firearms in their possession, was shipwrecked on Tanegashima. The Portuguese who sailed the Asian seas in these times had heard of Cipango and Rekio from sailors—Japanese and others—who stopped at the ports of Southeast Asia, and the opportunity that this encounter provided was not lost. Although its geographic location was far from ideal, Japan was open to foreign influences and knew how to profit from them. It was in this maritime network, composed of merchants and crews of multiple "nationalities," that the Portuguese meddled so successfully in the second half of the sixteenth century.

DOMESTIC TRADE IN THE ARCHIPELAGO: GUILDS AND MONEYLENDERS

The growth of international trade in Japan corresponded to a time of overall expansion of production in the Far East, in which the Japanese economy was but one element. Nevertheless, the country's commercial dynamism had specific internal causes and an influence on Japan's social evolution.

The usurpation of political power by the warrior classes under the Ashikaga shogun, coupled with their expanding economic role owing to the growing share of the land rents that they were absorbing, sent the court nobility and monasteries sliding into an irreparable decline. By the fifteenth century, the nobility of Kyoto no longer constituted the important political force that it had in ancient times and throughout the Kamakura period. Although their real-estate revenues were in free fall, the social classes linked to the old power structures nonetheless managed to slow their economic collapse by transforming themselves into financial organizations or offering protection to the rising groups of merchants and artisans. The great Enryakuji monastery on Mount Hiei controlled much of the circulation of ships on Lake Biwa, on which Kyoto depended for its supply of rice. The priests of the Hie Shrine, protected by Mount Hiei, accumulated donations—cash and grain—and invested this capital by making usurious loans. The Zen monks of the Five Mountains specialized in managing and collecting taxes on the estates and amassed immense fortunes. Both nobles and monks expanded their patronage and protection of merchant and craft guilds, and they built tollgates and barriers on trade routes to absorb some of their deficits. Such actions provided an essential financial resource for the court nobility and the abbots of the great monasteries in the fifteenth century.

In the Middle Ages, although their markets still were restricted, the merchants and artisans feared future competition in regard to the manufacture and sale of their products. In a move typical of precapitalist merchant societies, they decided to form trade guilds called *za* to protect their activities rather than letting the market rule. *Za* brought together traders and artisans with identical occupations. They first were formed in the mid-twelfth century, with their numbers reaching a peak in the fourteenth and fifteenth centuries. With protection from the lords, the *za* defended their monopolies in their respective areas of activity. Their members paid their patron (court noble, monastery, shrine, sometimes the shogun) a tax and obtained two privileges in exchange: a monopoly on sales in a given region and tax exemptions, including the right to circulate freely.

According to the historian Toyoda Takeshi,[19] the birth and proliferation of the *za* in the fourteenth century could be traced to two phenomena. First, "nonfarmers" who had been closely attached to the emperor or a shrine were beginning to loosen their grip, and they became specialized merchants or artisans. Their emancipation was due in part to the expansion of the market, which encouraged people to specialize in the manufacture or distribution of a single product. With this greater division of labor, specialists acquired irreplaceable know-how and techniques, which placed them in a strong position vis-à-vis their former lords. Second, formerly dependent artisans and merchants were swept up in the wave of autonomous and associative social organizations, such as village communes and leagues of low-ranking warriors. The term *za* itself is indicative of this evolution. It means a place to sit—the seat that each member of the guild had a right to use at the meeting of the council where decisions were made that advanced the aims of all members of the association.

Merchants, artisans, and "artists" (*geinōmin*) formed *za*. Those who were not members of a *za* could not practice their craft unless they were given permission. By the mid-fourteenth century, the Kōfukuji temple in Nara controlled more than eighty *za*. Although there were fewer *za* in Kyoto, they usually were more powerful, so each trade began to use this model. The oil merchants' guild, attached to the Iwashimizu Shrine, was typical. The shrine was dedicated to Hachiman, the god of war, and it was located south of Kyoto, near the river port of Yodo, where ships from the Inland Sea unloaded their cargoes. Sesame, from which lamp oil was made, was grown on many estates that the shrine managed on the shores of the Inland Sea. In the thirteenth and fourteenth centuries, the shrine's dependents, who provided the military defense of its assets and made and sold the oil, obtained various privileges of free circulation. They also received from the court—then the bakufu—a monopoly on the sale of oil in Kyoto. Members of the oil merchants' *za* traveled as far as Shikoku to buy oil, which they resold on their way back.[20]

Curiously, the growth of a cash economy in the late thirteenth century was translated not into the issuing of imperial or shogunal coins but into the increasing importation of copper coins struck in China. Emperor Go Daigo had planned to mint coins during the Kenmu restoration (1333–36), but the rapid collapse of his regime forced him to give up this idea. The Ashikaga did not take the initiative in this regard, granting themselves instead a monopoly on the importation of Chinese coins. It was not until the late sixteenth century that coins were struck in Japan, and until then, the Japanese used Chinese coins. Cash began to be used in transactions because of the difficulties involved in transporting the rents in kind and the bartering of estate products. In the early fourteenth century, estate owners often did business with traders who stored rice in warehouses or granaries. These people were usually landlords' officials who lived in a port and were responsible for overseeing the unloading of rents transported by ship from distant provinces. Gradually escaping their lords' employ, they became moneychangers and wholesalers (*toimaru*) who converted rice and other staples into cash (Chinese coins), lent money, and speculated. By the mid-fourteenth century, they had become bankers, though with still modest fortunes. They lived in Hyōgo, on the Inland Sea, or in Yodo, the river port near Kyoto, and maintained regular relations with their associates at most of the markets and ports of western Japan. They also inaugurated "modern" banking practices, such as bills of exchange.[21]

With the increase in agricultural production, the expansion of trade, and the use of cash, new occupations—moneychangers, bankers, and moneylenders (*dosō*) who made cash loans at usurious interest rates—came into existence. Originally, *dosō* were earthen warehouses (as opposed to wood), in which were stored the annual rents and certain valuable objects that needed to be protected from fire. By extension, the term came to designate the people who guarded the warehouses, which were akin to huge safes. Under Shogun Yoshimitsu, the *dosō* enriched themselves considerably, taking in great quantities of coins or rice and becoming masters in the art of making the goods entrusted to them increase in value. In the mid-fifteenth century, most moneylenders and usurers lived in Kinai: more than 350 in Kyoto, about two hundred in Nara, and some thirty in the town of Sakamoto, in Ōmi Province.[22] Similarly, saké brewers and sellers, or *sakaya*, grew rich and lent money against security at exorbitant rates. Most of them had originally been attached to the Hie Shrine. *Sakaya* also lived in the trading cities and towns of Kinai, including Sakamoto and Nishinomiya, in Settsu Province. In the late fifteenth century, there were about two hundred *sakaya* in Nara and probably more than three hundred in Kyoto.[23]

In 1393, Yoshimitsu decided that the moneylenders must pay taxes. Whether or not they were affiliated with and protected by a temple, they would have to share the costs of the bakufu's administration department (the *mandokoro*) by remitting an annual tax of 6,000 *kanmon*, to be paid each month. This direct tax, very high but not out of line with the fortunes accumulated by the lenders, became one of the bakufu's main sources of revenue.[24] Without it, Yoshimitsu would not have been able to build the sumptuous Golden Pavilion or maintain his opulent way of life. Thus, the bakufu, which had previously drawn most of its resources from the land, made a major change in its sources of income to profit from the growth of Japan's cash economy. The historian Sasaki Ginya notes that 1393 was an important year in the history of public finances in Japan, for it showed a political clairvoyance and flexibility typical of a century full of rapid changes in attitudes.

In Kyoto, the largest saké brewery, Yanagizake, fashioned itself a trademark, a shield with six stars. The owner paid a monthly tax of sixty *kanmon* to the shogun, who, for purposes of comparison, made his governors pay an extraordinary annual tax of two hundred *kanmon* so that he could rebuild one of his residences.[25] The wealthiest saké brewers in Kyoto had fortunes bigger than those of provincial warrior governors.

The storied wealth of the moneylenders provoked some contempt among lords, both nobles and warriors, who envied them but were sometimes forced to use their services. Thousands of ordinary people who had been robbed of their possessions, even their land, hated the usurers. Although they lived in towns, the moneylenders reinvested a good portion of their new assets in the land by purchasing farming rights from indebted and impoverished low-ranking warriors and peasants. Thus, during the first half of the fifteenth century a form of "bourgeois" landownership quickly developed in the countryside around the capital.

A new word, *utokunin*,[26] was coined in the early fifteenth century for this new and rapidly rising group. It was applied to all men who were neither warriors nor peasants and had become wealthy by accumulating cash, such as merchants, moneylenders, saké brewers, *dosō*, and monks who skillfully managed monastery properties and became usurers. These individuals were described as stingy and profit minded, but their fortunes were coveted by the authorities. By taxing them, however, the government were both complying with and relying on them. In fact, the *utokunin* saw virtue in what others took for being hard-nosed. They liked to save their money, live frugally, and reinvest their capital quickly, and they patiently accumulated the wealth that they ripped from the hands of those suffering in the countryside.[27] The ambiguity with regard to the activities of the *utokunin* is reflected in the word that defined them, as *toku* can mean both virtue and profit. That is, depending on the character used, *utokunin* can mean either "virtuous people" or "profit makers." An adage coined on this play of words went, "Virtue is profitable, and profit makes virtue."[28]

The *utokunin* knew how to take advantage of a situation to accumulate wealth. This way of thinking blossomed in the following century, and Nichiren's disciples, organized in the Hokke sect, gave it an ideological and religious context. Success in the temporal world was the fruit of perseverance. Handling money, making a profit, and accumulating wealth were seen as positive behaviors. The worship of money in Japan was born at this time, and with it, the country entered an era of mercantile capitalism.

KINAI AT THE HEART
OF A PROSPEROUS ECONOMY

With the increase in agricultural production, the development of transportation of raw materials, and the rise in trade, Kyoto became the heart of a new trade system, concentrated in the two major navigable routes in Kinai, Lake Biwa and the axis formed by the Yodo River basin and the Inland Sea.

LAKE BIWA AND ŌMI PROVINCE

Lake Biwa and the region around it—Ōmi Province—were of fundamental economic importance in supplying the capital. Ōmi was both an advanced agricultural zone and a major center of intermediary trade. All the towns on the banks of the lake were gradually transformed into small ports where merchandise and rents from northern regions were transshipped en route to Kyoto. The fishermen on the lake, who supplied the court with fresh fish, also transported rice that had come from the north. It is estimated that more than half the rice consumed in the capital passed through Ōmi Province. A large portion of the rice surplus was sent to Sakamoto, a small town in the foothills attached to the Enryakuji monastery, which dominated shipping on the lake. Tamon'in Eishun, from Nara, who went to Mount Hiei in 1570 via Sakamoto, wrote, "All of Ōmi Province cannot be taken in at a glance, and everywhere ships are coming and going."[29] Tolls were set up in the ports, with seven in Sakamoto alone! The tolls collected and the transportation fees for the rents were used to pay for maintaining and repairing buildings belonging to the monastery on the mountain.[30] By the fifteenth century, monasteries as large as the Enryakuji were depending on trade for the bulk of their income. Also significantly, the *shugo* governors had no part to play in the region's commerce.

In Sakamoto, where most of the rice convoys converged, teamsters (*bashaku*), who were also shippers, conveyers, and occasionally merchants, formed groups. They served as a military support force to the warrior-monks of Mount Hiei by providing ground transportation of heavy merchandise on packhorses or wagons (*shashaku*). Other *bashaku*, in Kizu south of Kyoto, transported merchandise between Nara and the ports of the Inland Sea.

Like the moneylenders, the rice merchants in Kyoto accumulated fortunes by speculating on their merchandise. In 1330, waves of speculation led to an explosive inflation in prices, despite the good harvest, which threatened to lead to a food shortage in the capital. The authorities then forced the merchants to sell at the official price. In 1431, famine broke out in Kyoto because the merchants were keeping rice from entering the capital, in order to raise the price. The bakufu had to intervene and order that all available rice be sold at 40 percent below the price being charged by the wholesalers, who then bribed the chief of police charged with applying the order. When Yoshinori heard about this, he had six important members of the guild arrested as an example and subjected them to justice "by the gods," an ordeal in which they had to pick up a stone placed at the bottom of a cauldron full of boiling water. Those who did not succeed were executed for having scorned shogunal justice; those who passed the test were pardoned in conformity with the apparent will of the gods.[31] Despite this incident, which did cause the speculation to abate for a while, the rice market in Kyoto continued to be controlled by a handful of monopolists who had formed a guild[32] composed of sixty wholesale merchants. But most of the rice merchants were simple retailers—many of them women—who sat on cushions with sacks of rice and waited for buyers. In the second half of the fifteenth century, the bakufu created two official rice markets in Kyoto, administered by the guild's delegates, but the black market in rice probably continued, to judge by the many decrees denouncing the practice.

FROM KYOTO TO HYŌGO

In the late Middle Ages, traffic was heavy in the Yodo River basin between the capital and today's Osaka Bay. Small ships sailed up the Yodo and its many branches, from the seaports of Hyōgo, Sakai, Amagasaki, and others, to the river port of Yodo at the mouth of the Katsura. Yodo was originally a market for salt fish for Kyoto. It is estimated that it took about twenty-four hours to sail up the river from the sea to this market, where small-scale retailers from the capital came to purchase stock to sell in the city. In the late fourteenth century, six wholesalers held a monopoly on the stock of salt fish. Salt, an important source of rents in the estates near the Inland Sea, was shipped from the sea to Yodo and sold to the merchants from Kyoto. The market in Yodo began to prosper in the fourteenth century. It was run by the noble Saionji family, which in 1460 was earning from it an annual revenue of 170 *kanmon*. The Saionji offered 1 percent of this sum to the nearby Iwashimizu Hachimangū Shrine, which owned the land on which the fish market was located.[33] Certain merchants in Yodo might well have originally been attached to the shrine and might have been responsible for supplying fish for the ritual offering to the god in exchange for authorization to trade. A document from 1444 reveals that the dependents of the shrine and net fishermen in the Yodo River basin had "eleven ships" exempted from tolls on the river and brought fish from the ports at the river's mouth to Yodo. Such authorization of free passage was important, for in 1441, there were 380 tollgates on the Yodo! The dependents of the Hachimangū Shrine had a huge advantage over other merchants, but they were not allowed to make the round trip between Hyōgo and Yodo more than eleven times a month.[34] In 1444, the Kōfukuji temple in Nara, which earned much of its revenue from these tollgates, protested to Minister Madenokōji Tokifusa about the huge drop in revenue that this exorbitant franchise caused.

The ports on the Inland Sea became even more active during this period. In the fifteenth century, the major seaport for Kinai was Hyōgo (Kobe), which was supplanted by Sakai only in the last years of the century, after the Ōnin War. An excellent document on Hyōgo—a register of payments for ships entering the port by the northern barrier in 1445—was discovered by the historian Hayashiya Tatsusaburō in 1964. Found in poor condition, it was restored in 1978 and published in 1981.[35] The oldest document of its type after the Lübeck customs archives for the year 1368–69, it lists the comings and goings of all ships that transited through Hyōgo en route to Kyoto and paid the toll at the gate set up by the Tōdaiji monastery at the entrance to the port. For every day and every ship, it recorded the ship's home port, the merchandise on board, the tonnage, the toll paid, the name of the ship's captain, and the name of the wholesaler— that is, the manager of the warehouse where the unloaded products were stored.

The document gives a good picture of the trade routes used by ships in western Japan in the mid-fifteenth century and of the products and quantities shipped. It also provides indirect information about, for example, what the people of Kyoto ate. About 1,960 ships passed through the tollgate in 1445. If one adds the 350 ships listed as passing through another tollgate, for which a register has also been preserved, this adds up to about 2,300 ships, far more than at Lübeck (about 900). Japanese ships also were smaller than those of the Hanseatic fleets. In Hyōgo, only four ships held more than 1,000 koku, or 180 metric

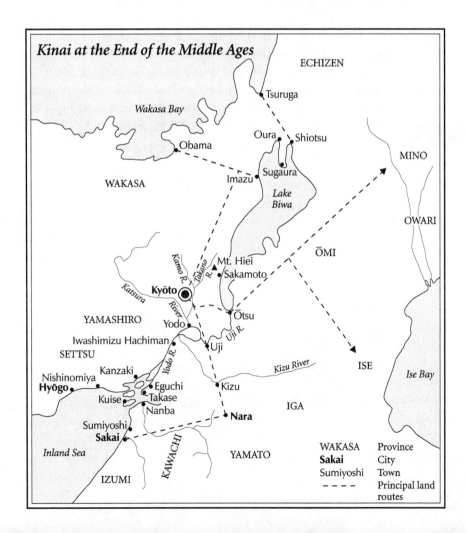

Kinai at the End of the Middle Ages

ECHIZEN

Tsuruga

Wakasa Bay

Oura   Shiotsu

Obama   MINO

WAKASA   Imazu   Sugaura

Lake
Biwa   OWARI

Kamo R.   Takano R.   Mt. Hiei   ŌMI
Katsura   Sakamoto

Kyōto ◉

YAMASHIRO   Yodo   Ōtsu

Iwashimizu Hachiman   Uji R.
SETTSU   Uji
                    Yodo R.   Kizu River   ISE
Kanzaki   Ise Bay
Nishinomiya
Hyōgo   Eguchi   Kizu
Kuise   Takase   IGA
        Nanba
Sumiyoshi   Nara
Sakai
Inland Sea   YAMATO | WAKASA | Province |
                                            | **Sakai** | City |
IZUMI   KAWACHI | Sumiyoshi | Town |
                                            | - - - - | Principal land routes |

tons, and they came from Onomichi, near today's Hiroshima. A wide variety of products were shipped. In addition to rice and salt, cargoes included pottery from Bizen Province, cushions, lamp oil, charcoal, fish (no doubt headed for the capital), and dyes—mainly indigo from Shikoku.

We do not have any documents with information that would allow us to estimate how many workers there were in Hyōgo. Descriptions of the port from the mid-fifteenth century indicate that the permanent population was quite small. Ports were essentially large villages; only Hakata, on Kyushu, probably resembled a true city. But around Hyōgo, the port towns were numerous. According to many sources, Kuise, Kanzaki, Kashōma, Eguchi, Takase, Namba, Sumiyoshi, and Sakai all were active ports. All these towns were located within the borders of today's Osaka, which gives an idea of the population density in a region of, at most, some thirty kilometers in area. The port archives of Hyōgo show that the ships that landed there came from widely scattered ports of origin and indicate that there were many more small ports than large towns.

In the 1960s and 1970s, excavations at Kusado Sengen (today, the area around Fukuyama) uncovered a small port town that was active in the Muromachi period and destroyed by floods in 1673. Many ceramics and coins were excavated, testifying to the scope of medieval trade routes: some pottery came from central China, other pieces from Korea. These discoveries indicate that in a town with a population of only a few hundred or thousand people, objects used in daily life may have been imported from very distant lands, attesting to a relatively affluent level of life in the small ports of the Inland Sea.[36]

Chapter 10

THE SPLENDOR AND MISERY
OF THE MUROMACHI CENTURY:
NEW UPRISINGS, NEW CULTURE

Although the standard of living rose, trade expanded, and social mobility became easier during the Muromachi period, the contradictions linked to such rapid growth quickly became apparent. They were manifested first in strong discontent among rural classes in the more advanced regions of Japan. The accumulation of huge fortunes by the new wealthy merchant class, the *utoku-nin*, had its counterpart in the relative impoverishment of the rural peasants in Kinai, many of whom were hurt by the too-rapid introduction of a cash economy. The slow process of the peasants' emancipation begun in the late thirteenth century was threatened by the formation of wealthy, and usually urban, groups who speculated on prices and created artificial economic tensions.

After the assassination of the shogun in 1441, the inability of the bakufu to reestablish a strong regime incited the *shugo* to form factions, which fought viciously for power. The Ōnin War started in Kyoto in 1467 between supporters of the Hosokawa and Yamana clans. It laid waste to the city, which had been peaceful for more than a century.

THE *DO-IKKI*: CULTIVATOR DISPUTES

In 1428, Shogun Yoshimochi died without designating an heir. In Ise Province in Kinai, supporters of the Southern Court took up arms. Famine stalked the countryside. The teamsters who carried merchandise from Ōmi Province sparked disturbances during the eighth lunar month of the year. Twice before, in 1418 and 1426, several thousand of them, originally from Ōtsu and Sakamoto in the Lake Biwa region, had agitated against rice speculation. This time, however, their movement stretched out behind them like a trail of gunpowder, setting the peasantry alight. The following month, inhabitants of the Daigo region, near the Kyoto gates, began to grow restless. In the eleventh lunar month, the disturbances reached the capital, and riots broke out in Yamato around Nara. Within a few weeks, all of Kinai was swept by the wave of protests. Villagers struck their gongs and met in *ikki*, associations of people sharing a common objective. In armed groups, they attacked the earthen warehouses of the *dosō* and the houses of wealthy saké brewers, tore up their debt notes, and took back the goods that they had given as security. The demonstrations were so large and violent that the bakufu, paralyzed in its succession crisis, was incapable of reacting. Estate owners, moneylenders, and usurers were shaken. Jinson, of the Daijōin in Nara, reported in notes that he compiled, in the ninth month of year 1 of Shōchō (1428), the dumbstruck state of the leading classes:

> The peasants in the country are in revolt. They are demanding a "virtuous government" [an edict abolishing debts] and destroying earthen store-houses, saké brewers' houses, and temples. They are seizing anything they want and taking back the cash they owe in debts. . . . This is the first time that we have heard of peasant revolts in Japan.[1]

Although the Kōfukuji monastery in Nara canceled the debts owed to it, no general official edict was promulgated by the bakufu. In any case, the insurgents obtained through violence what the bakufu was unable to grant them. As they seized the goods that they felt should legitimately be returned to them, the rebels began to understand their own strength. The revolt of 1428, the first of its type, involved a level of military organization and a scope that radically changed the nature of peasant struggles in medieval Japan.[2] The peasants and low-ranking warriors of Kinai, allied with teamsters, rose up against the usurers. In Yagyū, near Nara, the inhabitants engraved a short text testifying to their victory on a stele dedicated to Jizō: "As of year 1 of Shōchō, all debts are canceled in the villages of the region."

From then on, the cultivator disputes (*do-ikki*)[3] were unceasing. In 1431, the new form of revolt expanded into Kyushu. In 1432 and 1433, violence broke out again around Nara and in Ise Province. In 1434, it was again the turn of the teamsters of Ōmi. In 1441, following the assassination of Yoshinori in the sixth month of year 1 of the Kakitsu era, there were clashes throughout Kinai, especially in Nara and Kyoto. The disturbances started on the outskirts of Kyoto and then spread into the city, where the houses of usurers and moneylenders were attacked and burned. Teamsters took part in the revolt alongside peasants and low-ranking warriors from the surrounding countryside: they attacked an inn belonging to Rokkaku Mitsutsuna, the governor of Ōmi Province. Battalions of insurgents—tens of thousands of them—converged on Kyoto. On the fifth day of the ninth lunar month, sixteen camps of rebels were in the capital, with 3,000 settling within the walls of the Tōji monastery and even more at the Kitano Shrine. The capital seemed to be surrounded by crowds of unhappy armed men demanding justice—abolition of their debts and "virtuous government" (*tokusei*). Trained in the art of battle by *jizamurai* warriors, they were able to stand up to their opponents and defeat the shogun's troops. The government then tried to divide them by promising to cancel the debts of the low-ranking warriors. But the *ikki* rejected the offer and demanded a *tokusei* edict that was equal for all. Finally, the authorities became frightened and issued an edict of "virtuous government": land sold over the previous twenty years would be returned to its former owners; cash debts would be eliminated; and goods and lands given as security would be returned.[4]

It was yet another victory for the insurrection. Now the peasants and low-ranking warriors realized that armed struggle could solve some of their problems, but the leading classes still did not know how to respond. Uprisings were reported in no fewer than fifteen of the years between 1441 and 1466—the eve of the Ōnin War—most of them in Kinai, especially on the outskirts of Kyoto and Nara. The historian Nakamura Kichiji counted 144 uprisings over the century that followed the first revolt in 1428. Three-quarters of them took place in Kinai, and most were aimed at eliminating debts and abolishing tolls.[5]

With the introduction of a cash economy in the central regions, the small amounts of capital accumulated by the working classes was forwarded to the great religious institutions of Mount Hiei, the temples in Nara, and the Zen monasteries, which controlled a large number of moneylenders and saké brewers. These newly wealthy institutions began to reinvest the capital that they had amassed through usury, by buying up the land of peasants and low-ranking warriors around the capital. Accordingly, in Kinai, where double and even triple cropping was common, the surplus that should have remained in the hands of the peasants because of their increased productivity went into the pockets of moneylenders and usurers, thereby leading to the impoverishment of the rural dwellers, who then demanded the recovery of what had been taken from them. Direct representatives of the capital became the targets of social violence. In the fourteenth century, peasant uprisings in the estates usually broke out after the lords collected the annual rents, but in the fifteenth century, struggles to obtain a *tokusei* edict were struggles against indebtedness and for a return to an old order that was seen as better.[6]

We have already seen in the *tokusei* edict of 1297, decreed by the Kamakura bakufu to favor its retainers, the logic behind the demands for "politics by virtue." This central notion of returning to the ancient order, the restoration of their original state, laid the foundation for the recovery of land. The purpose of the uprisings was simply to return to a "normal" situation.

The historian Kasamatsu Hiroshi has written that throughout history, the peasants' latent consciousness was manifested through various practices. For example, ethnographers have pointed out that the groundbreaking ceremony after the first day of the new lunar year (generally in mid-February) had great symbolic value, for it made the land "come alive again" in springtime. The term *jiokoshi*, "awakening the land," also has a second meaning, the recovery of a piece of land by its former owner. This notion of renewal was linked to an old order that had been disturbed or degraded through history, and the uprisings were aimed at returning to that order, in which each thing had its place in a harmonious society. These ideas took the place of political thought. One could bring back the past by destroying the real world, just as one could make the land come alive again by breaking the ground with a shovel during a *jiokoshi* ceremony.[7]

Because of such movements, the political authorities sometimes were paralyzed, for one reason or another, creating a power vacuum. This was particularly evident in 1428 and 1441. In 1447, the insurgents in Nishioka, just outside Kyoto, were low-ranking vassals of the Hatakeyama lords, who were themselves in conflict with the shogun's minister, the *kanrei* of the Hosakawa household. Suddenly, the *kanrei* could not take military action against the insurgents for fear that this would lead to open war with the Hatakeyama. All these events help prove that the insurgents knew how to use the government's hesitation — evidence of a very strong political awareness, according to some historians.[8] Kasamatsu Hiroshi, however, sees them as a more common phenomenon linked to the amnesties accompanying a change in rule. The year 1428 corresponded to year 1 of the Shōchō era, and 1441 to year 1 of the Kakitsu era. The change in sovereign had to be accompanied by a change in era, and the peasant leagues thought these times were propitious for demanding — or even imposing — an abolition of debts. This was why most of the major revolts for "virtuous government" followed "catastrophes" such as the death of a shogun or a famine. Populations weakened by hunger and thought to be numbed by their miseries revealed, on the contrary, a stunning capacity for rebellion, as Kasamatsu Hiroshi noted. Famine thus became a reason to hope. This is why the uprisings of 1462 and 1463 were so violent — they broke out just after the worst famine of the century, in 1460–61.[9]

The summer of 1460 was cold, and the rice did not ripen well. The bakufu requisitioned food and auxiliaries in Kinai to fight the seditious lord Hatakeyama Yoshinari. That fall, famine struck. Beggars multiplied in the city. Some peasants refused to pay their rents, and others left the land. The following year, an epidemic broke out. The corpses left to lie in the streets became bloated

THE MUROMACHI CENTURY: NEW UPRISINGS, NEW CULTURE   165

and smelled atrocious. Exasperated by the authorities' incompetence, a monk of the Ji sect, Gan'ami, used his own money to build an asylum, the Rokkakudō, where dying people could be cared for. The name of the era was changed in late 1460, in hopes that the situation would improve. In western Japan, cases of cannibalism were reported. In the Kawaguchi estate in Echizen, which belonged to the Kōfukuji, 9,868 people died and 757 disappeared with no trace in the six months from the end of 1460 to the summer of 1461. The estate was devastated, reported the survivors, who pleaded for elimination of the lords' rents. In Kyoto, the monks of the Kiyomizudera buried up to 1,200 corpses under the Gojō bridge on the third day of the third month of 1461. There were reports of 80,000 dead in Kyoto alone. Practices that were thought forgotten reappeared, with some people selling themselves or their children as slaves.[10]

With a good harvest in 1462, however, things improved. In the fall, *ikki* formed once again and rioters swarmed into Kyoto to demand a moratorium on debts. Their anger ranged far and wide: houses of the wealthy were burned down, and entire neighborhoods were set ablaze. In Nara, insurgents forced their way into usurers' houses. The following year, the peasants' anger exploded once again.

Whereas the peasants' campaigns around the capital were directed mainly at the moneylenders to whom they were indebted, movements in the provinces took a somewhat different form, with the lords, rather than usurers, as the targets. In the Niimi estate in Bingo Province (between Okayama and Hiroshima), following the famine of 1460–61, the peasants formed an *ikki* against the lord Yasutomi, who was managing the estate on behalf of the Tōji monastery, the owner—a task that he was not performing particularly well. In a meeting before the gods of the local shrine, the peasants vowed to unite to expel Yasutomi and return to direct management by the Tōji. Forty-one peasants signed a document addressed to the monastery to demand that it reassume management of the estate. They were very critical of the monks, whom they accused of being unable to maintain order. As often happened in the thirteenth and fourteenth centuries, they turned to the owner of the estate—in this case, the monks of the Tōji—to defend them against the steward Yasutomi, who was a local warrior and vassal of the Hosokawa *shugo*. In 1462, the monastery decided to send a delegate named Yūsei to the estate. Although the monk was well received by the people of Niimi, soon after he arrived, he began to act like a despot. But times had indeed changed, and the peasants would no longer accept such barbaric treatment. Because he did not understand this, Yūsei fell victim to those whom he mistreated. In 1463, the peasants ambushed and killed him, and a crowd surrounded the lord's residence and set it on fire. In less than two years, the people of Niimi had eliminated two stewards who had displeased them.[11]

A few years later, the Niimi estate was confiscated by the *kanrei* Hosokawa

Katsumoto, under the pretext that its owner, the Tōji monastery, was conspiring with the Yamana, Katsumoto's enemies. The estate was annexed to the direct domain of the shogun and managed by a delegate of the *shugo*. The estate's peasants, who were not consulted, met and organized an *ikki* to keep the *shugo's* new delegate from entering the estate. The only lord they would accept was the Tōji monastery. The alert was given, the gong was struck, and the estate was patrolled by armed peasants who had decided to stand and fight. Hosokawa Katsumoto, who had other things on his mind in this period of civil war, retracted the confiscation of the estate. The peasants of Niimi had won again!

There is an explanation for the peasants' successive victories and the authorities' inability to resist. The rural insurgents made intelligent use of the government's internal conflicts and organized their leagues efficiently. The *ikki* were difficult to dissolve because they were united by vows sworn before the gods, and they were effective militarily because they formed quickly and always acted on a local level on known terrain. Furthermore, they always had specific objectives—the abolition of debts, the elimination of a toll, the ruin of an steward— they never represented a political threat to the leading classes as a whole. The bakufu was forced to defend the usurers because it depended on them for its revenues, but it could just as quickly withdraw its support, since it did not feel its link with them was unbreakable. Once they had obtained satisfaction, the insurgents returned to their affairs.

The uprisings certainly had an effect on the capital, which was controlled by Buddhist temples and was home to many usurers. For example, the formation of a landowning bourgeoisie around Kyoto was impeded by the resistance in the countryside. Moneylenders began to sign contracts with their debtors that contained "anti-*tokusei*" clauses, but this measure had limited success. For their part, many of the warriors, themselves victims of the moneylenders' greed, stood by while the rioters did their work; after all, they, too, would profit from the abolition of their debts. Some leagues were in fact formed by low-ranking warriors leading discontented peasants. These armed *ikki* were imposing military forces, impossible to defeat in battle without large numbers of troops. The bakufu had a small police force in Kyoto, but it was quickly overwhelmed by even a minor uprising and the *shugo's* troops had to be called in from the provinces. However, the long duration of the mobilization and the rapidity with which the violence spread made the armies of the provincial governors ineffective. In fact, the armies were reluctant to intervene: what reward could a warrior expect who made war on peasants who were rebelling?

THE TERRIBLE ŌNIN WAR (1467–77)

The balance of power that Yoshimitsu had patiently built in the late fourteenth century was upset by Yoshinori's authoritarian policies based on the shogunal bureaucracy, corps of private troops, and promotion of his favorites and family members. After he was murdered in 1441, these groups were able to keep the most powerful *shugo* divided for almost a quarter of a century.

The murder of the shogun symbolized the crisis regarding the vassals' relations within the warrior class. Until the civil war of the fourteenth century, the "global control" (*sōryōsei*) system ruled inheritances. It called for estates to be divided among all sons and daughters, thus reducing the warriors' wealth by diluting it in each generation. This was the principle used by Shogun Takauji when he made his younger son deputy shogun in Kamakura and his older son shogun in Kyoto. The older son became the leader of the Ashikaga household, and the younger son in Kamakura, in theory, owed him obedience. It was to avoid the danger that this type of inheritance represented for succession that the warriors adopted the principle of indivisibility in the fourteenth century. Because the principle of seniority was not used, indivisibility meant that the leader of the household could choose a single heir from among his children. If that person was deemed able to fulfill his duties, the brothers who had been denied acquiesced and had to live off his largesse. They might receive positions on the family estate, but they could no longer pass them on to their own children. This system of succession had the advantage of preserving the patrimony, but it also created frustration. During times of civil war, those not happy with their lot went to try their fortunes elsewhere, and the Zen monasteries attracted young, skilled people from warrior families who had been deprived of an inheritance. But with the return of political—if not social—peace in the fifteenth century, the issue of successions in large families took on new proportions. Cliques formed within landowning clans in favor of a particular claimant, while wives and concubines maneuvered to promote their offspring. Because of the adoption system common in the Middle Ages, legitimate sons were not alone in the competition; they also had to keep an eye on their half brothers and nephews and on strangers adopted by their father—who might also be named heir.

As suzerain of the vassals, Shogun Yoshinori was able to give advice with regard to difficult succession problems in landowning households. But given his authoritarian desire to weaken the *shugo*, he intervened brutally on behalf of his favorites, in the process sowing discord within families. He had managed to weaken the powerful Shiba clan and was preparing to do the same with the Akamatsu, which is why the leader of the Akamatsu clan had him assassinated.

Clan quarrels—groups and factions battling for power and control of successions—dominated the politics of the bakufu. This infighting weakened the great lords and left the field open to other social groups. Those close to Yoshinori, the "three demons"—the head of his personal guard, a skillful court noble who was one of his favorites, and the nurse of the young heir, Yoshimasa, born in 1436[12]—took over the bakufu but then were gradually pushed out by Hino Shigeko, Yoshimasa's mother. She held an important position even in the council of *shugo*, chaired by the *kanrei*, and her opinion often held sway. Shigeko promoted the tutor of her child, Ise Sadachika, appointing him head of the shogunal administration and leader of the government. In the 1460s, Shigeko and Sadachika were joined by the official wife of the shogun, Hino Tomiko, who played an even greater role because Yoshimasa was totally uninterested in political affairs. All these figures—the "three demons," then the wives of the Hino family and the former tutor of the young shogun—were former favorites or close associates of Yoshinori or of his young successor. They managed to keep most of the great lords away from power.

One by one, the great warrior families fell victim to fights over succession. The Shiba were divided into two factions, which favored the rise of their vassals. The Asakura took over one of the two cliques and became more powerful than their suzerain. To place their candidate at the head of the Shiba family, the Asakura, who had taken control of the wealthy Echizen Province, formed an alliance with the head of the shogunal administration, Ise Sadachika, and Sōzen, the powerful head of the Yamana household. A schism also opened within the Hatakeyama family: Masanaga, an adoptive son and the designated heir, had to do battle with Yoshinari, a legitimate son who felt wronged and took up arms. The stakes were high. Not only was the head of the Hatakeyama household in line for the position of *kanrei*, but he also was *shugo* of Yamashiro Province, where Kyoto was located. In the provinces of southern Kinai, the Hatakeyama vassals split into two hostile factions. Masanaga pressed his claim with the *kanrei* Hosokawa Katsumoto, who intervened on his behalf. But Hatakeyama Yoshinari refused to acquiesce and went to make war in southern Kinai in 1460, on the eve of the great famine.

The only noble family to profit from the murder of Shogun Yoshinori was the Yamana. In 1391, these lords of western Japan had had their pride deeply wounded by Yoshimitsu, who could not bear the fact that the great lords were so powerful around the Inland Sea and in a position to threaten relations between Kyoto and the mainland. The Yamana saw in Yoshinori's assassination by the Akamatsu lords an opportunity to rebuild their strength. In the name of the council of *shugo*, the Yamana led an energetic campaign to eliminate the Akamatsu and received in return some of the fiefs confiscated from them, which happened to be located near their own. Thus, the fall of the Akamatsu led to the rise of the Yamana, who now controlled a number of estates on the shores of the Inland Sea. The Kyushu–Kyoto axis was now dominated by two major noble clans, the Hosokawa and the Yamana. Confrontation seemed inevitable.

The *kanrei* Hosokawa Katsumoto was the leader of the most powerful household of *shugo* governors, who were private vassals of the Ashikaga. The Hosokawa clan was one of the few not to be affected by internal conflicts over succession. Although Katsumoto's hold on his clan was firm, he was aiming for more, control of the bakufu. However, the political scene became more complicated after 1464. Shogun Yoshimasa, thirty years old and tired of power, wanted to abdicate. Because he had no children, he adopted his younger brother, Yoshimi, and named him his successor. The following year, however, his ambitious wife, Hino Tomiko, gave birth to a son, Yoshihisa. Quickly, cliques formed and alliances were created. Tomiko and Ise Sadachika wanted to eliminate Yoshimasa's brother, who had suddenly become an encumbrance, and so they planned a coup d'état. But the coup failed, because the *shugo* saw in the affair an opportunity finally to rid themselves of the group of favorites who ran the government. The Hosokawa and Yamana, united for the occasion, eliminated Ise Sadachika. Now Hosokawa Katsumoto and Yamana Sōzen were face to face.

The confrontation between Katsumoto and Sōzen began in early 1467 (year 1 of the Ōnin era) in Kyoto.[13] The city was soon split into two camps. Sōzen, at the head of the Western Army, lost ground. Katsumoto, leading the Eastern Army, established his headquarters at the Muromachi palace in the company of the shogun Yoshimasa, his son, and the emperor. Fierce battles were fought in the city, and barricades went up in the streets between the two armies. Neither side, however, seemed able to score a victory. More than a war of great maneuvers, the Ōnin War consisted mainly of skirmishes. Fighting took place everywhere: in houses, palaces, gardens, and temples. Enemy camps in adjacent streets were raided. Many areas of Kyoto burned. A large part of the population fled to Sakai and other towns. Most of the *shugo* in the provinces of central and western Japan rushed with their vassals to join one or the other army. With the arrival of reinforcement troops sent by the Ōuchi lords, who controlled the market town of Hakata, the Yamana were able to drive out their adversaries from the capital in the fall of 1467, but Katsumoto soon returned in force. The war dragged on, moving to the provinces. In 1473, the coincidental deaths of both Katsumoto and Sōzen cooled the ardor of the troops on both sides, although the battles continued sporadically, stimulated by the fierce hatred between the two Hatakeyama rivals, Masanaga and Yoshinari. In 1477, their energy dissipated, they ended the war with a compromise with no winners or losers.

The Yamana family emerged exhausted from the war and lost its dominance in the west to its erstwhile allies, the Ōuchi. Most of the *shugo* who had gone to Kyoto to fight had left deputy *shugo*, *shugo-dai*, in their provinces to keep order. Once in place, many of the *shugo-dai* were difficult to dislodge, and many of warrior clans lost local power to their vassals. The world had turned upside down—everywhere the "lower commanded the upper." The only ones who did not stop fighting were the two Hatakeyama rivals. Yoshinari, deprived of victory, built himself an estate in Kawachi Province without bothering to get permission from the official authorities, or what remained of them.

The Ōnin War did not raise much passion, either while it was in progress or afterward. The confused sequence of events, absence of clear objectives, lack of heroic or tragic characters, mediocrity of the leaders, and waste of lives and resources, especially in Kyoto, did not inspire great epic tales such as the *Heike monogatari* or even the *Taiheiki*. The war was also different in another way. The number of troops mobilized was huge, and the pride of their leaders was inordinate: Katsumoto led 160,000 soldiers; Sōzen, 90,000. It is possible that these figures are exaggerated, but the fact remains that the armies were incomparably larger than they had once been. Warriors commanded squadrons of foot soldiers (*ashigaru*), who were recruited from the lower classes and were armed with long lances and went bare-legged so that they could run more easily. This rough infantry of uprooted men, former peasants or ruffians hoping for booty, requisitioned cattle and food and pillaged and burned houses and temples in Kyoto. They were the ones mainly responsible for the destruction of the city.

In the midst of this tragedy, Shogun Yoshimasa wanted nothing more to do with useless confrontations and became besotted with luxury and elegance. In late 1467, soldiers of the Yamana launched a surprise attack and burned down the Shōkokuji. The fire threatened to spread to the Muromachi palace, where Yoshimasa was holding a banquet. His feast was interrupted, and he was urged to flee. Unperturbed, Yoshimasa declared that he was going to finish his meal, "as usual," and is said to have remarked, "If the empire must collapse, oh well, let it collapse!"[14]

Yoshimasa is traditionally described as a weak character—the pawn of battling warlords, prey to the ambitions of his wife, Hino Tomiko, and indifferent to the suffering of his people. In fact, Yoshimasa had chosen to leave behind the world of plots and power to enjoy the pleasures of life. He was interested in artists and became the great patron of his times.

NEW FORMS OF SOCIABILITY AND ART

In the last years of the fourteenth century, Ashikaga Yoshimitsu retired to the Golden Pavilion in Kitayama in the hills north of Kyoto to spend most of his time supervising political affairs and sponsoring artists. Historians have labeled the cultural blossoming of the first part of the Muromachi period (late fourteenth to early fifteenth century) the Kitayama culture. Yoshimasa, Yoshimitsu's grandson, also retired, soon after the Ōnin War, in a time that was certainly more troubled, to a villa called the Silver Pavilion in Higashiyama in the hills east of Kyoto. The Higashiyama culture (late fifteenth century) was one of the high points of Japanese civilization. From nō theater to the art of sand gardens, from architecture to the tea ceremony and the art of flower arranging, this magnificent culture changed the foundation of Japanese society. Like the upheavals of the previous century, the cultural developments in the fifteenth century reflected the phenomenon of *gekokujō*—the reversal of traditional hierarchies and the emergence of new values.

The court nobility lost its cultural preeminence, whereas the shogun and great *shugo* lords sponsored brilliant artists, most of whom were from humble backgrounds and often faced discrimination. The new *utokunin* bourgeoisie also played a growing role in cultural fashions of the century. An urban culture blossomed in the fertile ground of Kyoto, and the Kitayama and Higashiyama cultures reflected the capital's predominance over the rest of the country. In the mid-fifteenth century, Kyoto had perhaps 150,000 inhabitants, including 10,000 court nobles with their families and servants, and probably some 40,000 warriors who had settled in the city since the Kenmu restoration (1333–36). Although he forced the great *shugo* warriors to live near him, Yoshimitsu flattered them by letting them participate in the inspired civilization of his times and treated them as courtiers. These warriors, bearers of provincial cultures, injected new blood into the aristocratic society of the capital—so much so that representatives of the warrior classes dominated Kyoto in the fourteenth and fifteenth centuries. With nobles, warriors, and *utokunin* but also peddlers, artisans, servants, and *hinin* living side by side, the capital constituted a unique society in Japan and was the cradle of the stunning culture that arose after the Ōnin War in spite of the troubled times.[15]

Different social classes mingled in Kyoto, and the very notion of such encounters was central to medieval art forms. The overturning of hierarchies, a phenomenon specific to this era, originated in the desire of people in the Middle Ages to form groups. At these meetings, people ate and drank together, held discussions, developed strong communal bonds, and strengthened their ties of solidarity. Such bonds created a climate favorable to revolts, of course, but they also created a strong sociability. People gathered to attend performances, sat on councils where decisions were discussed and made, and joined leagues, which became armed forces ready to do battle for a common cause.[16] The medieval term *ichimi dōshin* designated the "community of minds" that the group needed to carry out a project. Although some groups were formed for the purpose of protest—the abolition of debts, for example—others were much more peaceful and dedicated to pleasure rather than anger. If the Muromachi period could be defined as an era of *ikki*, horizontally organized and egalitarian social associations created for a common objective, it could also be defined as the time when the arts became appreciated by groups.

Although the literary forms of poems and novels originated during the ancient period, the Middle Ages was definitely the high point for "linked" (*renga*) poems, which were composed in groups. It was also a time when people got together to listen to the *Heike*, were fascinated by *sarugaku* theater, laughed together at *kyōgen* (a type of theater), and forgot their anxieties in Amidist dances. Rather than appreciating the arts in calm and solitude, people preferred to enjoy them in groups and not as silent audiences. Accordingly, everyone became a performer, especially during *renga* poetry meetings and the tea ceremony. Even in the theater or during public recitations of the *Heike*, spectators sought aesthetic sensations that they could share and that justified the reason for meeting. More than literature (the number of accomplished readers remained very small and reproduction processes too limited), storytelling, singing, and dancing formed the core of the medieval arts. Aesthetic pleasure came through music and rhythm, via spoken or sung storytelling—and was always enjoyed in a group.[17]

The Kenmu shimimoku, the founding text of the Ashikaga shogunal regime, written in 1336, forbade meeting for the purpose of drinking and entertainment. In truth, although some meetings were held simply for the purpose of composing poems or serving tea, others were opportunities for rowdy basara behavior, with much gambling and some plotting. In these years of political crisis, the warriors in Kyoto created new forms of sociability, and meeting sites sprang up in great numbers. The Taiheiki mentions that some took place in inns in Kyoto. "Meetings" had previously been held in other contexts: in the eleventh century, monks and laymen held informal gatherings to study sutras and religious commentaries. Around 1320, Emperor Go Daigo, in step with his times, brought followers and friends together in meetings devoid of protocol. In the Muromachi period, meetings and encounters for pleasure, outside any ceremonial activity, multiplied. In the late fourteenth century, wealthy warriors had independent meeting places built in their residences, sometimes separated from the main house. The reception hall of the traditional aristocratic residence was abandoned in favor of a small, detached pavilion to which the lord could invite a few friends for a "party" for no particular reason.

Renga became popular in many circles starting in the fourteenth century.[18] Poetry meetings were often held outside under blossoming cherry trees. Their organizers were often Amidist hermits from Ippen's Ji sect—or sometimes monks of the Ritsu sect—who invoked the souls of the departed. The canopy of the weeping cherry tree, like the oiled parasol of the reciter of the Heike, defined a space of shadow, midway between this world and the next. After the invocations, the participants wrote renga poems. Each in turn composed a verse on a given theme, which was continued by the next in line until all present had made up a verse. The quality of the poem reflected the degree of the participants' closeness. Anyone could come to these renga sessions "under the blossoms." Attendees had to hide their identities under loose-fitting clothes and broad-brimmed rice-straw hats that covered their faces. In the complete anonymity that guaranteed equality to each, everyone participated in the collective creation of a poem in the shadow of a tree, a space made sacred for a time by the invocation of the dead and the implicit agreement of the participants. Thus, because renga meetings eliminated both status and sex barriers, a highly placed court noble or lady could draw pleasure from these meetings side by side with the lowest hinin.[19]

In the fifteenth century, the low-ranking samurai of Muroo, near Nara, got into the habit of meeting each year for *renga* parties at the local shrine at Someda dedicated to Tenjin. The meeting was organized by the *kō*, or brotherhood—the group of followers who made their devotions at the shrine. This type of parish went beyond the context of the estates to bring together all the low-ranking samurai in the region. The *kō* ultimately metamorphosed into a combat league composed of low-ranking warriors, and they presented themselves in 1434 as an autonomous regional power beyond the traditional administrators and estate managers. There thus was a relationship between the process of composing a *renga* poem and forming a league, according to the medievalist Katsumata Shizuo.[20] To write a "linked poem," all the people involved had to reveal their individuality and personality. This was the very condition of producing a poem line by line. But at the same time, these people had to become a group, a unity that was developed and harmonized by the autonomous activity of each individual at the meeting. The same conditions were required for the formation of a league: a meeting of motivated people in a sacred space—unless the meeting itself made the space sacred—equality of the members, autonomy of the individuals in the group, and solidarity of the group until the common objective was achieved. The social activity of revolt and the artistic activity of making poetry were tied together in the search for new modes of sociability.

People in the Middle Ages liked plays on words, puzzles, and jokes (*share*). *Renga* poems made as "private jokes" reinforced the sense of complicity between participants and the feeling of belonging to a group, outside of hierarchical social relations, even if it was only for the fleeting moments of the meeting. Following the civil war of the fourteenth century, traditional family or clan solidarity was replaced by new links based on identification with a piece of land or a place. Words admitted the existence of different types of people and created a bond no longer assumed by blood ties.

Various forms of shows—sung, recited, and danced performances—developed during the fourteenth century. There were a number of styles: more or less improvised comic dialogues that led to *kyōgen*; *dengaku* theater linked to peasant folklore of the past but now adopted by the court; *sarugaku*, with acrobatics performed in the middle of the show; *imayo* songs; and the dances of the *shirabyōshi* courtesans. In the second half of the fourteenth century, these forms became intermingled, giving birth to a new type of theater that integrated many scenic and thematic elements. This theatrical form, called *sarugaku nō*, was stunningly successful in a Kyoto in the midst of civil war. The actors began to specialize in genres and organized, like artisans and merchants, into *za* guilds, forming theater troupes with a monopoly on a type of show in a given region. The theater company that gave rise to the Kanze school operated in the southern Nara basin and another troupe that was very famous in its time played in Ōmi Province.

During the sixth lunar month of 1349, on the banks of the Kamo River near the Shijō bridge in Kyoto, a performance was given in the *dengaku* style, a theatrical genre about which, unfortunately, little is known but from which nō is in part derived. An enormous crowd went to see the show, including imperial princes, the imperial regent, and a sixteen-year-old boy, the adoptive son of a leader of the troupe, the future Kan'ami. Monks took a collection among the spectators. People who arrived late went onto the bridge where they could catch a glimpse of the performance. Suddenly, the bridge collapsed under the weight of the spectators, and several hundred people were killed. In the ensuing panic, thieves tried to grab the actors' costumes, and the actors gave chase, still wearing their demon masks, which frightened the crowd even more. This unhappy incident was attributed to the untimely action of a *tengu*, or demon, that had descended from the mountain to spread disorder among humans.[21]

When he became leader of the troupe, Kan'ami introduced music and rhythm into its repertoire of *sarugaku* plays. He began to perform around 1368 and immediately attracted the attention of Sasaki Dōyo, a famous *basara* lord.[22] Kan'ami was an extraordinary actor, equally brilliant playing an old man, a ghost, or a young woman. The young shogun Yoshimitsu heard about him and wanted to see his work. Kan'ami and his young son, Zeami, performed at the court. Moved by the dramatic power of the *sarugaku-nō* show produced by Kan'ami (who played under the actor's name Kanze), the shogun decided to help the troupe. This enabled Kan'ami to write many plays, which Zeami refined, and Zeami later enriched the repertoire.

Because of his father's success, Zeami, who was of the same generation as Yoshimitsu, had access to the highest-ranking officials of the state. In addition to youth and beauty, Zeami was very talented, and Yoshimitsu made him his favorite. Zeami was unbeatable in *kemari* (a ball game); he was a good poet; and above all, he had inherited his father's gifts as an actor. He was influenced by the great minds of his time, those of his own father, the artist lord Sasaki Dōyo, and the former regent Nijō Yoshimoto, a *renga* master who became fond of him. Zeami received gifts from wealthy warriors on behalf of whom he intervened with various highly placed nobles.

Zeami was twenty-two in 1384 when he inherited his father's position and became Kanze II. His reputation was still growing, and Yoshimitsu's support was as strong as ever. Between 1395 and 1400, however, he fell into some disgrace, and during this time, he wrote theoretical reflections on the nō theater. For his troupe to win competitions against other theater troupes, he posited, both its repertoire and its staging had to offer dramatic situations of such intensity that audience would be motionless in their seats and overcome with emotion. He called this "the flower" that would captivate audiences. Just as the blind man reciting the *Heike* was able to sway his audiences, nō theater had to create an atmosphere that seemed to bring the dead back to life. With nō, Zeami devised both the apparition of ghosts during dreams and a vision for his drama. The action took shape in the dream of a character, and the performance offered a privileged "communion of minds" between the actors and the audience. Kan'ami's and Zeami's theater manifested an aesthetic of mystery (*yūgen*) to ignite the public's imagination.

After Yoshimitsu died, Zeami lost his influence in the court, for Yoshimochi preferred the *dengaku* genre of the master Zō'ami. Zeami retired, and his life took a turn for the worse: he lost his prodigal son Motomasa, and he died in exile, the reasons for which are not clear. His turn of fortunes in the court no doubt gave him an understanding of the precariousness of his lot and the fragility of his theater and perhaps inspired him to write the plays and reflections on directing that enabled the Kanze troupe to survive its leader's disgrace. Independent of the intrinsic talents of Zeami and Motomasa, the troupe's performances gave rise to "communication" between this world and the next. The founders of nō introduced their audiences to a world in which ghosts held court. They thus multiplied the effect that the reciters of the *Heike* already knew how to produce, and they demonstrated an unequaled capacity to match the art of drama with the sensibilities of an era.

By the late fifteenth century, *sarugaku nō* had eclipsed all other forms of *sarugaku* and *dengaku* theater. In 1464, Yoshimasa had the Kanze troupe perform a series of nō dramas alternating with comical *kyōgen* plays. Bleachers for audiences were built on the riverbanks at the confluence of the Kamo and Takano Rivers, and the performance lasted for three days. All the great figures of the regime attended, and the leader of the troupe, the elderly On'ami, Zeami's nephew, personally received from the shogun the sum of one hundred *kanmon* for his troupe's performance.[23] Official recognition of the Kanze-za, which had been in disgrace for many long years, by the highest personages of the time marked the true consecration of the Kanze school of nō theater.

CONDITIONS FOR ART PRODUCTION: SPONSORSHIP AND DISCRIMINATION

"COMPANIONS" AND JI MONKS

The ties between the shogun and the playwright Zeami indicate how important the role of sponsorship was to production of art in the Muromachi period. The shogun Yoshimitsu and his successors surrounded themselves with connoisseurs, specialists, and Zen monks and also with artists, both monks and laymen, forming a coterie of artists and aesthetes (*dōbōshū*). The greatest artists of the period were favorites of those in power and lived off their patronage, among them Nōami, a tea master; Taiami, an expert in flower arrangement; Kan'ami and Zeami, *sarugaku* actors; Zōami, a *dengaku* actor; Zen'ami, a great garden designer; and So'ami, a painter and master of decorative arts. Not only did these artists create works, they also were advisers and, on the eve of ships' departure for China, gave the authorities a list of objects to bring back to Japan.

All *dōbōshū* had names with the suffix "ami," an abbreviation of Amida, similar to the names that pilgrim monks of the Amidist Ji sect, founded in the late thirteenth century by Ippen, had taken. These monks had made a vow to be with dying warriors on the night after the battle to help them invoke Amida as they were about to pass into the next world. Assured of being welcomed by Amida in the Paradise of the Pure Land, the warriors would die in peace. Monks of the Ji sect lived near their lords to aid them in both combat and death. They were noted for their obedience and loyalty to their lords, virtues that were in themselves commendable in these times of treason. However, their conduct was motivated not by respect for their vassal links or the precepts of the warrior class but by religious considerations. These men, most of them of common origin, gained respect, and some warriors began including several of these monks in their entourages. In times of peace, they spent most of their time writing *waka* poems, organizing *renga* poetry parties, arranging tea parties in lords' residences, and practicing various arts, at which many of them excelled. They shaved their heads, carried swords, and favored rather gaudy clothes.[24]

Not all the artists who lived under Shogun Yoshimitsu's patronage were members of the Ji sect; many, like Kan'ami and Zeami, had their name conferred on them by their protector. Why did these artists use a name ending with "ami"? There were two reasons. First was imitation: because many famous artists, originally members of the Ji sect, were known by their "ami" name, those adopting a similar name might be able to pass for a master. But pride was not the only explanation. Most artists in the late Middle Ages were from humble backgrounds and had suffered discrimination. Held in contempt because they were itinerant and not settled in one place, they perhaps wanted to take a name that differentiated them and reflected their disadvantaged condition. In a sort of reversal, they trumpeted their social origin as commoners by using these names. As Zeami's story shows, artists were in a precarious position because they were not nobles or warriors or landowners. Rather, they were intruders into court society. At the mercy of the prince's whims, they were in turn powerful and vulnerable—feared for their proximity to power, envied for their brilliance, but reviled for their weakness. In the late Heian period, some imperial princes had been sons of courtesans. But under Yoshimitsu, no powerful figure thought to link himself to a *dōbōshū* family through marriage.

KAWARA SOCIETY

Not only were many artists from nonaristocratic backgrounds, but many came from the *kawaramono* social group. This term was used in Kyoto to designate *hinin*, "nonhumans," who lived on the banks of the Kamo River.

In the Middle Ages, riverbanks and beaches were desolate, untamed places, constantly flooded by rivers or tides. They were, however, rich sites from a sociocultural point of view—a discriminated-against yet creative world.[25]

In Kyoto, the riverbanks were used as cemeteries, where *hinin* disposed of corpses. They were permanently "soiled" by their handling of cadavers, which were neither buried nor cremated except when there were many deaths and the living were to be spared the sight of mass graves. Impurity was tolerable in these places because the tide swept away the decomposing bodies. The river water was a purifier. The riverbanks were also where the condemned were executed. In the medieval imagination, these spaces became a natural frontier between one shore, the symbol of this world, and the other shore, the hereafter. In the nō theater, many ghosts appeared on desolate beaches or the banks of a river near a ford or bridge. *Kawara* were natural border areas, places near to death and the hereafter, and thus haunted.[26] Fox demons often lived at the foot of bridges, which were highly symbolic because they physically linked one shore to the other. Riverbanks and beaches were also favorite places for stone-throwing battles. Whereas bridges and fords were always strategic spots, riverbanks offered open spaces where troops could perform maneuvers.

As impure and haunted places—places without a lord, that is, not required to pay rent—riverbanks were intermediary spaces with a particular status, where people suffering from terrible diseases such as leprosy,[27] those who had renounced the world, and those who had severed all links with traditional society took refuge. Peddlers' and artisans' markets sprang up at meeting places near bridges. Trade was not conducted according to the traditional mode of social giving and reciprocating. Rather, buying and selling in the context of a market implied the end of this social connection, as these acts constituted a purely commercial activity, with the relations between those concerned ending when the transaction was completed. Such commerce was possible only on the riverbanks, places devoid of social ties.

In the Middle Ages, markets also meant entertainment. In the fourteenth century, traveling artists came to the riverbanks to perform, and the *kawara* also served as theaters. *Hinin*, peddlers, rejects, and artists learned to live side by side on the riverbanks, in a special world where legend was intermingled with reality. Some deliberately chose this world because it allowed them a measure of freedom. But that freedom was costly, for it meant joining the world of the "nonhumans," the *hinin*.[28]

Those who lived on the riverbanks were constantly confronted with impurity. They were responsible for processing and cutting up animals, recovering the skins and tanning them for leather, and making saddles for warriors' horses and quivers and strings for their bows. The *hinin* were also hired to construct terraces and whitewash walls for village aristocrats. As well diggers, they knew how to make the water that slept beneath the earth spring up, thus manifesting in yet another way their unusual links with the other world. Because the *hinin* also cleaned shrines and temples, they knew how to sweep, maintain, and even design gardens. Gardens were another border space—one between the indoors and the outdoors, and thus between this world and the next, because most gardens were symbols of the Pure Land. As they became indispensable to the art of building and arranging such gardens, the people of the *kawara* came into contact with the powerful figures of society.[29] Despite the repugnance they provoked, some of them had talents that were sought out by the aristocrats. This was the case for Zen'ami, the creator of the garden at the Shōkokuji (which was destroyed during the Ōnin War) and the Daijōin in Nara; he also designed, with his son and grandson, the gardens for the shogun's villa in Higashiyama.[30]

Admired by the shogun for his expertise, Zen'ami was from the world of the riverbanks, where his father had been a renderer. It was said that he escaped that miserable environment by creating the dream landscapes that were the gardens of the time and, with them, a school of landscaping. This career path was not so exceptional. Although Zen'ami was an extraordinary artist and most *kawaramono* did not escape their world, almost all of Kyoto's gardeners came from the society of the "people of the riverbanks."

The world of sand and river pebbles was projected—symbolically or sub-consciously—into temples and aristocratic residences in the form of gardens made of sand and stones. Just as nothing grew on the riverbanks except stunted bushes, the dry gardens, or *kare sansui*, contained no plants. The gardens were thought to have been influenced by Zen symbolism and Chinese-style mono-chrome painting. Although this may be true, they may also have been simply following the aesthetic of those from the strange *kawara* world who actually designed them.

Thus in the Muromachi period, the world of the arts was dominated by these "companions" of the powerful—most of them from humble origins and serving the aristocracy. The *dōbōshū* were peculiar to the culture of late medi-eval times, for they had not existed in the Heian and Kamakura periods, when art was produced by the aristocracy. The numbers of these "professional" artists continued to grow in the fifteenth century. Their activities diversified and spe-cialized, and some became experts in "things Chinese" (*karamono*). Nōami and Gen'ami, for instance, recognized the price and value of the small pieces of furniture and paintings imported from China, as well as the conservation and cloth-backing techniques for the works that were so dear to Yoshimitsu and the great men of his time who collected them.[31]

A NEW ART OF LIVING: THE CHINESE STYLE
AND THE CREATION OF A "JAPANESE" STYLE

In the early fourteenth century, the monk Gen'e, a connoisseur of the Chinese classics, wrote a work, *Kissa ōrai*, that describes the ambience of the first tea parties. According to Gen'e, the tea party had three parts. First, refreshments were served to welcome the guests. Then they strolled in the garden, and finally they returned to the place where the tea was served. This was almost exactly the same tea ceremony as that performed in the sixteenth century. But the rooms where it took place were nothing like contemporary Japanese interior spaces.[32]

The rooms were decorated in the Chinese style, with chairs, cabinets, and other furniture imported from the mainland. These furnishings, arranged in the Chinese manner, must have seemed exotic for a Japanese in the fourteenth century. Everything was in the best of taste and in the latest style. Red and black, the colors of the lacquered objects and pieces of furniture, dominated the room. Although there were neither mats nor an alcove (*tokonoma*), sometimes there were a few screens painted by Chinese masters. Bronze or porcelain vases held flowers, which added a lighter note; the Japanese art of flower arranging, *ikebana*, had not yet been invented.

In the fourteenth century, the art of these meetings was in the process of being formulated, but it was not yet established, and Chinese-style décor played an important role.[33] Chinese styles had been emulated since the ancient period, but the expansion of trade and the presence in Japan of a large contingent of Chinese Zen monks encouraged even further the taste for "things Chinese." This fashion reached its peak in the imitation—even counterfeiting—of Chinese paintings, not because the Japanese were fraud artists or imitators by nature, but because there were too few Chinese paintings available to satisfy the demand. Rather, the copies reflected the degree of infatuation of the Japanese elite with Chinese art, and particularly the paintings of the Southern Song dynasty (thirteenth century). As they copied their models, however, Japanese artists acquired techniques and skills that set the stage for the birth of a new and original style of Japanese painting in the late fifteenth and sixteenth centuries.

The fashion for "things Chinese" that culminated under Yoshimitsu began to subside in the era of Shogun Yoshinori, when the interest in techniques of decorating and arranging rooms was increasing. The master Nōami and his grandson, Soami, developed and set down in writing several of the original rules. Their evolution from the Chinese style of the previous century is apparent. We have an accurate description of this style in the interior decoration of the Kitayama villa, the Golden Pavilion, in 1408, when Yoshimitsu hosted the emperor for a twenty-day "vacation,"[34] and of the Muromachi palace in 1437, when Yoshinori hosted the emperor there. The style invented by Nōami reflected a sense of social grace and distinction that influenced the Japanese way of life in later centuries. It differed from previous forms of interior design in its systematic use of mats and a new form of internal space in the house.

In the early fifteenth century, the aristocracy began to use *tatami* (straw mats) throughout their rooms and not just for seating. The way in which they were placed indicated their use: first used as a seat or bed, they became a general floor covering. As their use became widespread in the houses of wealthy warriors, bamboo blinds and hangings were gradually replaced by movable partitions covered with white paper, or *shoji*, which let the light filter through. Distribution of the space became freer, and rooms were organized to suit personal preferences. This relative autonomy, transparency, and light in the house won over members of the Kyoto aristocracy—nobles and especially warriors—as well as the upper middle class. It was not until the late sixteenth century, however, that the new interior style reached the wealthier classes in the provinces.

In the warrior aristocracy's residences, the increased use of *tatami* was accompanied by the introduction of a new architectural form, the *shoin zukuri*—a space used as a reading room or small meeting room with chests of drawers and shelves for storing scrolls.[35] An alcove (*tokonoma*) was built into one corner. This interior style, which evolved into the "Japanese house," became popular during the era of Shogun Yoshimasa and the Ōnin War.[36]

The new types of spaces invented by the interior designers gave rise to an art of living created from the new aesthetic awareness that came of age in the mid-fifteenth century and was firmly established by the Higashiyama era in the 1480s. First, people were more interested in local art production, especially pottery for use in the tea ceremony. Second, the size of objects had to be reduced in order to fit into the *shoin zukuri*, and small rooms, 4.5 *tatami* in area, became fashionable among the bourgeoisie of Kyoto and Sakai after the Ōnin War.

A great master of the late fifteenth century, Murata Jukō, assistant to Noami, Yoshimasa's tea master, passed on to one of his disciples several recommendations that summarizing the standards of the new aesthetic in terms of both moral conduct and the art of living. For example, one should always consider oneself an imperfect being, never brag—the epitome of poor taste—and be able to recognize the essential, to distinguish the Chinese from the Japanese.[37] Shinkei, the great *renga* master, who had considerable influence on the masters of the tea ceremony, invented the aesthetic notion of *kotan*: those who possessed a mastery and sense of art should express themselves with the greatest simplicity and elegance, never scorning the beginning disciple.[38] From simplicity came beauty. From the concept of *kotan* was derived, in the last years of the fifteenth century, that of *wabi*, cultivated by the urban middle classes, who had rustic pavilions built in which they could appreciate humility, melancholy, and the ravages of time.

Chapter 11

THE SENGOKU PERIOD:

COMMUNES, RELIGIOUS LEAGUES,

AND NEIGHBORHOOD ASSOCIATIONS

OVERVIEW OF THE YEARS 1480–1570

After the Ōnin War, Japan entered a new period called the Sengoku, literally "country at war." This word, coined during the Tokugawa period, alluded to what sinologists call "the era of warring states" in Chinese antiquity. The final epoch of the Middle Ages—a short century that lasted from the 1480s to the 1570s—the Sengoku period was dominated by a number of apparently contradictory trends.

First, the inversion of hierarchies called *gekokujō*, which started in the Muromachi period, continued with even more vigor. A product of the emancipation of the working classes, *gekokujō* was also a source of political anarchy. During the sixteenth century, however, feudal lords began to build principalities, and historians have dubbed this new type of lord *sengoku daimyō*—literally, "lord of the age of warring states." As sovereigns over their lands, the warlords battled with one another to maintain and expand their fiefs and, after the mid-sixteenth century, for hegemony over the entire country.

The contradiction between the aspiration to political autonomy by the masses and the process of centralization of power initiated by the warlords was not solely the result of class oppositions. It also reflected an inequality in development between central Japan, around Kyoto, Lake Biwa, and the Inland Sea, which was economically prosperous, engaged in urbanization, and formed the

core of the new Japanese culture, and a peripheral Japan, more backward economically, with less social agitation but ruled by feudal lords who were capable
of unifying a region and transforming it into an integrated space—the first step
in unification of the Japanese market, and of the country.

For the warlords, the battle for hegemony would be won by the conquest of
Kyoto and control of the advanced regions of Japan, where social and political
autonomy and religious specificities impeded the building of a strong state. War
was the logic of the times. It alone could resolve the contradiction between
gekokujō, which affected mainly central Japan but, in a certain sense, paralyzed
the country, and the formation of embryonic but strong regional states in the
periphery.

Gekokujō, a vivid expression that means "the lower commanding the upper,"
portrays the point to which people at the time sensed the acceleration of social
mobility, already perceptible in the Muromachi period. Deplored by the powerful figures of the time, *gekokujō* was the result of the lords' inability to stabilize
their control when the rise of economic forces was combined with a high degree
of organization by the local working classes. Starting with Shogun Yoshimasa,
the government slipped beyond the control of the shogun and into the hands
of the *shugo* who opposed him. Most of the great warrior clans dispersed, victims
of their inability to resolve the succession quarrels. All major lords—except the
Hosokawa—emerged from the Ōnin War weakened, and their power over the
provinces was stolen by their vassals, who, in the absence of the *shugo* who
were away fighting in Kyoto, provided the real provincial authority. These vassals, delegated by *shugo* to exercise their authority, were called *shugo-dai*, governor's deputies. They were hard put to keep the local barons (*kokujin, kinishū*)
and low-ranking warriors (*jizamurai*) from forming *ikki* whose purpose was to
take over local power and expel them or the *shugo*. The *ikki*, in their turn, had
to be careful of the "village communes" (*sōson*) and, later, the "urban communes" (*machishū*).

The Ōnin War thus signaled the obsolescence of the old estate system. Society in the sixteenth century was no longer organized around *shōen* but around
villages and towns, and the country was rapidly being urbanized. As the estates
disappeared, the court nobles' social position became increasingly precarious.
In the early sixteenth century, it was said, in order to survive, Emperor Go Nara
had to sell poems that he had written by hand. Whether true or false, this
anecdote is revealing of the difficulties of the old nobility. The former grand
chancellor Kujō Masamoto left the capital in 1501 to live in one of his remaining
estates, the Hine estate in Izumi. He wanted to ensure that the rents due him
were paid.[1]

In the eastern provinces, which were feeling some effects of economic
growth, hostilities among local lords had been unabating since the mid-fifteenth
century. All real state authority had disappeared. Locked in conflict, the two
deputy shogun left the city of Kamakura, which then reverted to a simple town.

Between the mid-fifteenth century and the first quarter of the sixteenth century, eastern Japan was entangled in a web of feudal struggles.

The warlords, who built and consolidated regional principalities and ran them as small states, ensured a minimum of social stability in the peripheral regions. These new forms of authority were part of the *gekokujō* movement. Although the warlords would soon be fighting one another for complete control of the country, they also created the political and military structures that would end the anarchy. They contributed to the economic awakening of the regions that they dominated by unifying markets and stimulating crafts and trade, and they acquired enough power to break up the local warriors' leagues and integrate them into their military apparatuses. Firearms, which arrived with the Portuguese in 1543, allowed the lords to move even closer to military supremacy. Oda Nobunaga, who emerged around 1570 as the only lord strong enough to establish hegemony over the country, finally triumphed through a brutal war and a decisive victory over the leagues of peasants and low-ranking warriors in central Japan organized by the Amidist *ikkō* league formed by Shinran's disciples.

Between the end of the fifteenth century and the 1570s, Japanese society was affected by two contradictory movements: the breakup of power and the desire for autonomy by central Japan's working classes, versus the construction of regional states with a view toward hegemony. This period gave rise to the drive toward reunification, from which a new state, that of the Tokugawa, emerged in the early seventeenth century. In the interval before reunification, which became definitive only with the historic victory of Tokugawa Ieyasu in 1600, the country gave the impression of being "a world without a center," to use Barry's expression.[2]

THE QUEST FOR AUTONOMY: VILLAGE "COMMUNES"

From social instability was born a process of fracturing power and decentralizing authority that explains the gradual waning of the Ashikaga shogunal regime in the Sengoku period. The basic social units signaled their autonomy by creating egalitarian structures—leagues whose participants worked toward a common goal. But these organizations dissolved when their members felt that their objective had been attained. Accordingly, the rise in commoner autonomy was marked by the emergence, on the local level, of long-standing community organizations called *sō*. The term *sō* refers to "ensembles" of inhabitants of a village or region, and most Japanese historians compare them with the West's medieval communes. *Sō*, which provided local government, multiplied in central Japan between the fourteenth and sixteenth centuries. Soon after the Ōnin War, regional "communes" were formed that also somewhat resembled the Swiss cantons of the fourteenth and fifteenth centuries. In the early sixteenth century, similar organizations began to appear in Kyoto and in most merchant towns.

The "village commune," or *sōson*, attested to the rise of traditional rural communities. In the late Middle Ages, the system based on estates gradually evolved into one based on villages. The growing autonomy of communities that evolved into *sōson* cost the local lords their administrative, political, and judicial authority. These communities gained legal recognition and became tax-collecting units, took over the right to manage their water (previously the lord's privilege), oversaw cleared land and forests, and organized to provide self-defense. They also formed protection leagues with other communes in the area, and by reaching beyond the old framework of the estate, these alliances caused the domination of the landowners to disintegrate. Some villages joined with others to manage local resources and valley waters. In several cases, however, bloody conflicts broke out when the *sōson* formed an alliance with a landowner or monastery in order to weaken a neighboring village.

The rural landscape was changing. The pattern of dispersed habitations typical of the ancient and Kamakura periods was giving way to larger groups. As towns grew, the hamlets sprinkled across the estates were abandoned during the Muromachi and Sengoku periods. In Yamato, for example, people built their houses behind earth levees and surrounded them with ditches and ponds. In Kinai and other regions, peasants seemed to have construction fever in the fifteenth and sixteenth centuries: they hauled mud, dug ditches, and erected embankments. The village of Kami Koma in southern Yamashiro, where the great revolt of 1485 started, is typical: around a group of houses were long moats and ditches that formed a defensive complex whose military function was obvious. Most communal villages were organized because of the inhabitants' desire to block invasions by outside armies. The peasants seemed to have withdrawn to their villages, which they intended to both defend and govern. This phenomenon, apparent in Kinai, spread to regions where feudal war was almost incessant, such as Kanto and even Tōhoku. Villagers deserted the insecure countryside, leaving it to outlaws and the armies that roamed the area, and banded together behind fortified works. With this process of consolidation came a concomitant strengthening of the inhabitants' councils that met at the local shrine. War thus often encouraged peasant solidarity.

The towns that grew around Lake Biwa and on the coast of the Japan Sea were concentrated settlements of fishermen and boatmen. These communities, whose primary activity was not agriculture, had formed *sō*-type collective organizations much earlier, in the thirteenth century. Sugaura, at the northern end of the lake, was a good example of this type of "commune."[3] It is located at the end of a mountainous peninsula that isolates it from the surrounding land, and until as recently as the 1960s, the only means of communication with the outside world was by boat. In the late fifteenth century, the village of Sugaura, composed of about eighty families (perhaps four hundred inhabitants), was made up of houses placed close together facing the lake, with their backs to the mountain. The people of Sugaura, like those of most of the towns around the lake, transported travelers and merchandise, fished, and cultivated a few acres of rice. Around the lake, it was not war that created community solidarity, as each village had fishing and shipping privileges. Instead, the villagers united around the defense and extension of these rights. Among these communities, too, the existence of *sōson* was borne out in the countryside by a highly concentrated habitat.

The emancipation of the lower peasant classes that had started in the Kamakura period expanded in the fifteenth and sixteenth centuries. The clearing of small lots and the greater labor productivity and trade, especially in Kinai and the surrounding regions, encouraged this general movement. The cadastres made by landowners in some estates offer a good picture of this evolution: the number of names of those responsible for the taxes (the *myōshu*) multiplied by an average of five between the beginning and end of the fifteenth century.

The clearest social phenomenon in the countryside between 1450 and 1550 was the appearance of a rural middle class composed of a relatively large number of village notables. These men, who were designated in various ways (*dogō*, *jizamurai*, and others), played a central role in the internal village organization and began to distinguish themselves from the *myōshu* and the peasants.

In the fall of 1459, following violent typhoons in the Nishioka region near the gates to Kyoto, the peasants became restless as the time for paying rents approached, and they demanded a *tokusei* edict. This time, the shogunal government took the lead and required a written vow from the inhabitants that they would not form a league. Those living in the Kuze estate, belonging to the Tōji monastery, decided to sign.[4] In the village of Kami Kuze, eighty-four commoners (*hyakushō*) and twenty-one samurai signed the pact; in Shimo Kuze, fifty peasants and eleven samurai signed. Rural society was clearly divided into two distinct categories: peasants (themselves also socially divided into those responsible for taxes and small-scale tenant farmers and landless dependents, but these differences were not mentioned in this text) and samurai, who accounted for more than 20 percent of those who signed. The enrichment of the upper peasant classes in the Muromachi period gave rise to a new social category, between the wealthy peasants and the local landowners, whose members claimed warrior status by calling themselves samurai. Although they no longer worked in the fields, they still lived in the villages among the peasants, with whom they felt a kinship. But they also differentiated themselves from the peasantry, to whom they rented parcels of land to farm, by showing off their new social position: the samurai carried swords openly and owned horses. These village samurai, or *jizamurai*, formed protective vassal links with the *shugo*. After the Ōnin War, a certain Samukawa was a vassal samurai of the Hosokawa in Kuze. Another, Maita, served the Hatakeyama. Both were competing for the position of *kumon*, estate administrator.[5]

In the Heian period, the term *samurai* applied to armed servants of the emperor and high dignitaries of the court; in the twelfth century, it designated provincial warriors who managed operations on the estates. In the late fifteenth century, the samurai of Kuze were a new "species": wealthy *myōshu* peasants who had ties with estate lords and claimed the status of warrior. Anyone with the means—land, weapons, and a connection with one or several lords—could make this claim.

The *jizamurai*—whose status was so new that in the West it might have been said that they still had mud on their shoes—lent power to local community organizations if they promoted their belonging to a commune, or to lords who wanted to hold onto their land if they emphasized their vassal subordination to the landowners. In the fifteenth century, the *jizamurai* were still close enough to the peasants to feel loyalty to their own kind, and they led rural uprisings for abolishing debts and promoting local autonomy. By the mid-sixteenth century, however, they were sufficiently detached from the peasantry that their material interests had also diverged; they then joined the vassal organizations that the warlords had started to build in their fiefs and help expand the new feudal authority. Relations between the peasants and *jizamurai* were complex. The sense of belonging to the community was strong and cohesive, especially because peasants and low-ranking warriors were often related by blood. Whenever there was a poor harvest, the samurai lent food, money, and seeds to peasants in difficulty, who were then beholden to them. Sometimes the samurai, like the peasants, were victims of exploitation by urban usurers, in which case, they became spokesmen for the entire community with the landlord or bakufu. Therefore, there were links of both solidarity and domination between the samurai and the peasants. As long as the sense of the solidarity was stronger, the *sōson* were almost invincible. But as soon as conflicts arose between samurai and peasants in the community, the village union fell apart.

The rules of the *sō* were discussed and adopted in meetings, and they evolved into administrative rules and legislation. For example, the *sō* needed funds to manage their autonomous units. The village ceremonies had to be held according to tradition. Irrigation systems had to be maintained constantly. Above all, large sums had to be set aside to cover the costs of trials in which the village might become involved. These needs were, in principle, fulfilled by the income from communal lands farmed by everyone and by a tax that the *sō* charged to each house in the village.

Unlike the landowners' taxes, taxes in the *sō* were collected by and used for the village. In the estates, the lords collected a tax called *kuji*, which was supposed to be used to maintain common parts of the estate, but instead they kept it for themselves. The communes brought back the *kuji* in a new and egalitarian form. For example, in Sugaura, the amount charged depended on the wealth of the head of the family or the size of the house. Those who had a large house paid 173 *mon*, while the others paid only 85 *mon*; those who owned only a shack or small cabin were exempt. Owners of the most highly taxed houses were the most important members of the rural community. A 1492 regulation in Oki-tsushima, on Lake Biwa, stipulated, "Those who do not pay this tax will have to leave their house. They will lose their *yana* privilege [the permit to place fish traps in the lake]. Mountain fields and collective possessions of the village that have been lent to them will be confiscated immediately."[6]

The commune also took over the judicial administration of its territory. Peasant society dealt severely with those who broke the unity of the *sō* with a criminal act. The heaviest penalties were reserved for arsonists, thieves, and murderers.[7] While theft was considered a minor crime by the bakufu, it was the most heinous crime for rural populations. Kujō Masamoto, a great dignitary of the imperial court who was visiting his estate in Hine, expressed his indig-nation over the barbarism of village justice in notes that he took during his stay. The death penalty was imposed for the theft of any possession worth more than a pittance. Masamoto described two such incidents. He had invited peasants from one of the villages on his estate to his residence on New Year's Day and prepared a banquet in honor of the new year for the village chiefs. During the banquet, one of the villagers was robbed of a valuable dagger. To catch the thief, Masamoto had the village chiefs meet in the sacred space of the local shrine and "appeal to divine justice" through the test of boiling water. Fright-ened, the guilty party stepped forward. Masamoto quickly exercised his lord's right of justice, depriving the peasant of his rights in the village and ordering that management of his household—that is, his operation—go to his son. But the other peasants saw this theft, committed on New Year's Day in the lord's residence where they were guests, as causing great injury to the community. Humiliated, they decided a few days later to exercise their own brand of justice. A group went to the thief's house, killed him, his wife, and his three sons, and burned down his house. Masamoto was appalled: the peasants had overridden the lord's judgment and applied their own justice, and he had no way to stop them.[8]

The other incident that Masamoto related was a theft committed during a period of famine—aggravating circumstances—in the winter of 1504. The sit-uation in Hine was desperate, and the villagers of Iriyamada were reduced to digging in the dirt to uncover the roots of ferns, which they ground to a powder from which a thin gruel could be made. The powder was distributed to each family according to how many mouths it had to feed. One night, the powder was stolen, but the young villagers standing guard surprised the thief as he fled and killed him on the spot. A judgment then took place: the villagers killed the thief's parents and children. Kujō Masamoto was revolted by such cruelty. But he always had food on his plate when he was hungry, and the examples of barbaric justice that he reported showed that he and the peasants did not share the same values.[9] Because the village association was essential to the group's survival, it could not tolerate the slightest deviation from the common law. Theft earned the contempt of everyone because it betrayed the community spirit. Accordingly, it was punished with an exemplary sentence that was intended to create fear. To avoid any encroachment of the lord's justice on village justice, villagers in disagreement with the community did not have the right to approach any judicial body other than that of their village. There was thus no appeal possible to an external form of justice. In Sugaura, a sign placed at the entrance to the village said, "It is forbidden for *shugo* to enter this place, which is under autonomous judicial administration."[10]

SŌKOKU: REGIONAL COMMUNES

The best-known *sōkoku* was the one created after the great revolt in Yamashiro. In 1485, an unusual uprising broke out in southern Yamashiro, in the countryside south of Kyoto. It was led by the *ikki* of Yamashiro Province, an *ikki* different from those preceding it, as it was aiming not for the abolition of debts or the lowering of rents but for complete control of a region.

THE YAMASHIRO UPRISING

The revolt in Yamashiro was the direct consequence of the Ōnin War and the continued conflict between the two rivals from the Hatakeyama clan for the position of provincial governor, which divided the barons of the province and the *jizamurai* into two hostile camps. After 1477, when the war ended, Hatakeyama Yoshinari built himself a fiefdom in Kawachi, the neighboring province, while his enemy, Masanaga, became more or less master of Yamashiro. But Yoshinari was not ready to quit; he once again tried to invade Yamashiro, where he had solid support. Between 1483 and 1485, the enemies' armies crossed the regions south of Kyoto a number of times in a prolonged battle for control of the road linking Kyoto to Nara and of the large town of Kizu, located on the river of the same name, where merchandise from the Yodo River was unloaded to be transported over land to Nara. Kizu was a place frequented by boatmen and cart drivers. During the summer of 1485, Yoshinari sent his troops to Yamashiro, where they encountered the low-ranking warriors linked to his party. Masanaga hurriedly mobilized his forces and managed to contain Yoshinari's attack. A frontline was established near Kizu. Both armies lived on local estates, requisitioning supplies, plundering, and burning down houses. They were camped face to face for more than three months, to the great displeasure of the population. During the summer of 1485, uprisings followed one after the other throughout the region. Peasants marched on the capital yet again to obtain an edict abolishing their debts. In the Nara region, they threatened to leave the land en masse. The cart drivers also demanded a *tokusei* edict and demonstrated for the removal of all toll barriers on the roads. Armed peasants' leagues throughout southern Yamashiro took advantage of the internal conflicts among the warrior classes, whose armies were confronting one another instead of fighting the insurrectionist movement. The war was even more frustrating because it was blocking part of the traffic between Kyoto and Nara. Although they were committed to one of the two armies, the local warriors could no longer see any advantage in continuing to fight.

On the eleventh day of the twelfth lunar month, the local barons and warriors of the southern districts of Yamashiro formed a council with thirty-six members and went solemnly, bearing torches, to the nearby Iwashimizu Hachiman shrine, where they exchanged bowls of sacred water and held talks. Their curiosity piqued, the peasants of the area went running to the shrine. Soon, a crowd surrounded the sacred site where the council was meeting. It was decided to mobilize the entire population of southern Yamashiro in an *ikki*. An ultimatum was sent to the two armies, demanding their immediate and unconditional withdrawal from the province, and the league threatened violence against those who did not comply. On the seventeenth day of the twelfth lunar month, the local barons and low-ranking warriors, the backbone of both Hatakeyama armies, deserted en masse, and the leaders were forced to retreat.

After that, assemblies of low-ranking warriors and peasants were held all over southern Yamashiro Province. This time, the initiative clearly came from the low-ranking warriors rather than the peasants. On the thirteenth day of the second lunar month of the following year, 1486, the warrior chiefs of Yamashiro met in the Byōdōin temple in Uji and promulgated a provincial constitution called the Rules and Laws of the Province. According to the chronicles of that period,[11] the constitution, now lost, indicated the warriors' clear desire to take over the province's affairs. The league formed an assembly of thirty-six members, most of them provincial barons and low-ranking warriors, and the body leading the insurrection was called *sōkoku*, "provincial commune."

The Yamashiro *sōkoku* provided itself with a financial base by charging a tax—a prerogative reserved, in theory, for the governor. It also dispensed justice, even in criminal matters. In short, it took over all the powers of the *shugo*, but it was nothing like a peasant commune, even though it was supported by the peasantry. Rather, it was led by low-ranking warriors who had organized to expel the armies of the *shugo* from the province and eliminate their rivals so that they could seize power in the province. Initially, the peasants and the warriors formed an alliance to respond to outsiders, but then very quickly, the peasants stopped supporting the new government. To deflect threats and keep the province running, the *sōkoku* was forced to reestablish tolls, which led to a peasant revolt in 1492. The *sōkoku* was now in an awkward position, caught between the bakufu—or, rather, the *shugo*—and the peasantry. Almost all the leaders of the Yamashiro league decided in 1493 to switch their allegiance to the new *shugo* appointed by the bakufu, and the *sōkoku* collapsed. Nevertheless, for eight years it had been a new form of provincial government, nearly within sight of the capital.[12] Although the Yamashiro revolt captured the imagination because of its scope, it ended with the political failure of the local low-ranking warriors, who were not able to find sufficient support among an uncooperative peasantry.[13]

THE IGA COMMUNE

In the sixteenth century, other regional communes, although smaller in scope, managed to last for several decades. One example was Oyamato. In this small region in Ise Province, in the upper Kumozu River basin, the inhabitants signed two documents in 1494. The first, signed by 350 heads of peasant families in the villages, was a five-article constitution laying out principles concerning rural life, such as "You must not rob from others their right to cultivate the land: you must not steal." In the second document, written a month later, forty-six *jiza-murai* of the Oyamato region formed a collective to ensure power in the region: "If anyone acts badly, inside or outside Oyamato, he will be judged and sentenced." The warriors' league seized administrative and judicial control, and its authority was based on the charter signed by the 350 peasants. The two social groups had formed a united front. Although the low-ranking warriors had their own system of cooperation, they had to respect the agreement with the peasants, without which the region's autonomy could be challenged, as it had been in the Yamashiro commune several years earlier. Oyamato, once an estate, now became an autonomous society, independent of outside hierarchical control, with a double structure: the assembly of the forty-six low-ranking warriors and the general peasant assembly. The two groups had a relationship of power and domination, but without either a suzerain or absolute power.[14]

The regional commune in Iga Province seems to have been a sort of geographic extension of Oyamato's political and social structure.[15] Its twelve-article constitution was written around 1560. The communities of the Iga River basin had been defending themselves since around the beginning of the sixteenth century. The neighboring region of Kōga in Ōmi, similarly organized, had no fewer than 230 fortification works. In Iga, local power was exercised by the *jizamurai*, sixty-six of whom had taken vows. Entrenched in their small fortresses, they collectively administered the territory and made laws. Talks were usually held in a Buddhist temple, the Heirakuji, but the basis of the regional commune was a federation of village communes, which wrote a "constitution." The following are some excerpts:

> In keeping with the union sworn by the members of the league, any attempt by foreign troops to invade the province will be repelled.
> If an alert is signaled by the watchmen who are guarding the fortified passes, the inhabitants must sound the alarm in each village and imme-

diately go on alert. In this case, food and arms must be contributed and the fortified positions along the routes defended without a loss of strength.

Men between the ages of seventeen and fifty will be mobilized. If the campaign lasts a long time, the men will work in shifts. In each place, captains will be designated among the warriors, and the people of the communes must obey them. In the temples and monasteries in the region, the older monks will pray for the prosperity of the country while the younger monks will go to fight.

The text of the vows, in which the vassals of the samurai in the communes swore to obey their master and follow him to the end, whatever the fate of the *ikki*, will be posted in all villages. . . .

Those mobilized peasants . . . who are particularly successful and able to seize an enemy position on the border will be rewarded with the status of samurai.

Anyone who is persuaded to enter into secret relations with foreign armies and to help them penetrate the province will be arrested immediately by the league. The inheritance of the traitor in question will be confiscated, his name struck from the registers, and his property consigned to the temple. Revealing the communes' situation to the enemy is considered a similar crime, and the punishment will be the same as that for traitors: death with public exhibition of the head.

. . . The affairs of Iga having been well settled, we now see fit to unite our forces with those of Kōga. Therefore, common assemblies between the two parties will held outside at the border between the two countries.

Thus is it decreed and signed.
The sixteenth day of the intercalary lunar month.[16]

The main concerns of the leaders of the league of communes in Iga were defense and war. The province was at war with the Miyoshi and with small-scale lords in neighboring Yamato Province. In Iga, the fighting had been constant, it seems, since the late thirteenth century. In the Kuroda estate, for example, studied in detail by Ishimoda Shō, banditry was endemic, and *akutō* attacked the Tōdaiji monastery in the late Kamakura period. During the civil war of the fourteenth century, local samurai formed regional alliances (*gunnai ichizoku*), which were transformed into organizations that in the sixteenth century assumed all local powers.

The strength of the regional commune was in the military leadership of the peasants by low-ranking warriors. Although the social difference between the former and the latter was clear, it was not insurmountable, for the Iga commune also promoted heroic fighters.

The Iga league of communes lasted much longer than did the one in neigh-

boring Yamashiro Province. The reason was probably the particular configu-
ration of the area, a mountain basin relatively distant from the major routes.
Oda Nobunaga finally put an end to the league by invading the province with
his troops in 1581. Despite the difficulty of conquering a population that was
completely mobilized for war and had very effective guerrilla fighters, Nobunaga and his artillery crushed the "people of Iga" with cannon fire and dismantled all their small forts. The indomitable survivors kept up a sporadic guerrilla
resistance for several years, but Tokugawa Ieyasu finally was victorious when he
made them specialized auxiliaries in the lower echelons of the bakufu.

The structure of the regional communes in Oyamato, Iga, and Kōga was
apparently both horizontal and vertical. At the local level, *jizamurai* and peasants were organized within the community framework of the village. These
communes were linked to other, similar ones to form a federation. But the
jizamurai also provided hierarchical collective control of the region as a whole.
These forms of organization were reminiscent of the "valley communities" of
the Swiss Waldstetten in the late thirteenth and early fourteenth centuries. The
pact of 1291, considered to be the founding act of Switzerland, was a "peace
charter" among local communes to prevent outside aggression, similar to the
ultimatum made by the Yamashiro rebels to the Hatakeyama armies in 1485
and the twelve-point charter of the Iga commune around 1560.

Regional communes of various sizes existed for different periods of time in
Kinai, Ōmi, Settsu, Izumi, Tanba, and other provinces. The existence of these
federations on the scale of a region or province kept any centralized power from
controlling the provinces of central Japan.

"WE WHO HAVE FAITH": THE IKKŌ LEAGUES

When the low-ranking warriors seized power in Yamashiro in 1485–86, their
movement was not entirely new. Their alliance with the peasants, an essential
condition for creating regional communes, was based on a new element in
Kaga Province: peasants and low-ranking warriors sharing the same faith and
worshiping at the same temple as did members of the Ikkō sect.

In the early 1470s in Hokuriku, especially in Kaga and Echizen Provinces,
unrest of a new type arose. It was led by the Ikkō sect, a name given by its
detractors to the "true school of the Pure Land" (Jōdo shinsū), which claimed
to follow the teachings of Shinran. For about a century, the Ikkō sect played a
historic role by providing a social and religious context for the uprisings by low-
ranking warriors and peasants that historians call Ikkō *ikki*.

Like most medieval Buddhist sects, the Ikkō sect was characterized by the
desire to reform religious morals by purifying the doctrine. It was the main
branch of the Amidist current, which recruited followers from all classes,

including the most humble, in rural areas. Between 1457 and 1499, Rennyo, the eighth leader of the sect, built his religious movement into a sect, with great masses of followers, mostly peasants and low-ranking warriors.

Persecuted by the monks of Mount Hiei, who were not pleased to see that he was recruiting from among the peasants, fishermen, and artisans of the villages around Lake Biwa, Rennyo was forced to flee to Hokuriku, where his sect already had a large following. From a monastery located on the border between Kaga and Echizen Provinces, he sent out written sermons[17] containing the following instructions: organize all classes in the villages, including those below the *myōshu*; teach the law of Buddha in such a way that it is comprehensible to people with no education, and likewise write sermons in simple language (without using Chinese characters); make it known that invoking Amida Buddha will bring happiness in the hereafter; and after they have joined the faith, organize followers around a *dōjō* (practice hall).

Rennyo and his followers taught a simple faith that promised salvation for all. With his sermons, written in plain sentences that everyone, "even women and the most miserable peasants," could understand, he converted the peasants in the more advanced agricultural plains, where the *jizamurai* and *myōshu* had dismantled the estate system and founded communes. In fact, Rennyo's plan was to found a sect that matched the *sō* with the *kō*, a local religious organization, a brotherhood of followers—a type of parish.[18] Meetings of the *kō* dealt more with agrarian issues than with religious ones, although followers talked openly and on an equal footing about issues of faith. The villagers met on the twenty-eighth day of each month at the *dōjō*, which might be in a Buddhist temple that had fallen into the Ikkō sect's hands or in the home of the village's wealthiest peasant.[19] Rural communities became sites for proselytizing the new faith. There were no splendid ceremonies. Although they had adopted religious names, the owners of the *dōjō* were laymen, usually members of the *jizamurai* class. By linking religion and daily life, Rennyo founded a sect that was able to control entire regions, excommunicate infidels, and collect tithes, which quickly replaced the annual rents paid to landlords.

In the wake of the Ōnin War, a conflict broke out within the household of the Togashi, the local governors of Kaga Province. The Ikkō sect intervened in the conflict, helping one of the antagonists get rid of the other in 1474. But the new governor, who owed his power to his alliance with the followers of the Ikkō sect, did not like this obligation and eventually was at odds with the sect. Despite Rennyo's wishes, the sect mobilized its followers, formed a league, and defeated the governor, who committed suicide in 1488.[20] The *jizamurai* in Kaga Province, like those in Yamashiro in the same period, expelled the governor and created a local government controlled by their league. As his followers began to take the initiative, Rennyo called repeatedly for prudence, but the insurgents did not listen. The Ikkō *ikki* was formed out of an alliance between the peasants, who wanted to preserve their autonomy and refused to pay rents to any landlord, and the *jizamurai*, who led them. Followers of the sect freely gave a donation (*konshi*) to their church, which quickly became an obligatory tithe, though less than the lords' taxes that it replaced.

After their decisive victory in 1488, Rennyo and the high clergy of the sect realized that the *jizamurai* were establishing a new and effective social organization, based on new relation of domination over the peasantry—new because they were less onerous than the old ones in the estates or the fiefdoms of powerful warriors. The *jizamurai*, who included the low-ranking clergy in the village, promised to eliminate rents and replace them with lower taxes, and the peasantry, galvanized by their religious discourse, joined the new regime created after the governor was defeated.[21] Having eliminated the *shugo*, the rural middle classes, a sort of gentry, wanted to form a new aristocracy of the land, the "estate of Buddha" (Bupporyō)[22]. In short, the Ikkō sect supplied a millenarian ideological framework for the rural revolution.[23] Rennyo finally realized that he could become the "pope" of this territory, which had been "liberated" by his followers.

In 1496, Rennyo and the senior leaders of the sect built a new temple, the Honganji, in Yamashina, near Kyoto, where they could negotiate from a position of strength (the sect now had a territorial base, armed followers organized in leagues, and revenue) with the other Buddhist sects, in particular the fearsome warrior-monks of Mount Hiei. In the last years of the fifteenth century, Rennyo behaved like a lord. His successors (in fact, his sons, since the Ikkō sect was a family affair—all the leaders of the sect were Rennyo's direct descendants) quickly distanced themselves from the sect's early egalitarian principles. Rennyo even gave one of his daughters in marriage to the head of the Hosokawa household.

Still, the close ties that bound the Ikkō sect and the peasantry were maintained by the support of the peasant community organizations. Although they depended on the hierarchical structures that had transformed them into a new religious aristocracy, the dignitaries could not detach themselves completely from their followers, who were organized in leagues under the leadership of local priests to form the sect's "shock troops." This basic organization remained relatively egalitarian. The contradiction between the newly aristocratic religious hierarchy and the peasant organizations at the base was concealed as long as the people in the countryside refused to pay the lords' rents and agreed to pay a tithe to the Honganji. The land had indeed become "the estate of Buddha." By farming it and defending it with their weapons in hand, the faithful attained salvation.

In the first half of the sixteenth century, the Ikkō sect formed a sort of independent local government in the provinces of Hokuriku, with Kanazawa as its capital. It then spread throughout most of the central provinces, especially the regions where Osaka and Nagoya are today. But the organization was becoming increasingly rigid and distanced from the principles that had won it its initial victories. Excommunications were imposed on those who dared to rebel against the dignitaries of the Honganji. In contradiction to Rennyo's own teachings, his descendants reestablished the death penalty for traitors who collaborated with enemies of the sect. The religious bureaucracy of the Honganji acted as a completely separate protagonist in struggles against the upper classes, sending leagues of followers to fight warlords who were hostile to the sect. The leadership maneuvered among the different lords, always trying to weaken them, and moved to a fortress said to be impenetrable in Ishiyama, very close to the town of Sakai. Alliances and betrayals followed one after the other. In 1532, the 30,000 men of the Ikkō sect ejected the daimyo of southern Kinai, the Hatakeyama and Miyoshi.[24]

Starting in the mid-sixteenth century, the Ikkō leagues of central Japan were swept into the fight against the warlords who had established control in outlying provinces, where the village communes were poorly organized, and who had become strong enough to try to seize central Japan and march on Kyoto. Where the warlords were powerful, they made low-ranking warriors into vassals, but where they seemed to be a distant threat, these independent warriors preferred to organize with the peasants so that they would not find themselves in the position of dependent vassal. Between 1570 and 1580, a bloody battle took place between Oda Nobunaga, a warlord who was later to become all-powerful, and the rural leagues of the Ikkō sect. The leagues organized the resistance to the lords' attempts to integrate them, but they were crushed one after another.

URBAN AUTONOMY AND SELF-DEFENSE

The Ōnin War had a major effect on the capital of Japan. The most violent battles took place between 1467 and 1469, most of them in Kyoto. It is estimated that between a third and a half of the city's buildings were burned down during these years. Many artisans fled to Nara, Hyōgo, and Sakai, which benefited from this inflow of skilled labor to expand from large towns into true cities.[25] It took a full generation for Kyoto to recover from the terrible destruction, and when it did, it was a changed city.

First, Kyoto was no longer really the capital.[26] Although it remained the seat of the imperial court, or what remained of it, and of the bakufu, whose power had become an empty shell, many of the court nobles had left the city, and the lords had returned to the provinces with their warriors. In the sixteenth century, Kyoto was mainly a trade city dominated by crafts and commerce, owing to the growth in productivity that led to the marketing of most agricultural products. During the century, new trade cities sprang up, and provincial markets began to resemble towns: port towns, inn towns, temple towns, and then castle towns.

THE MACHISHŪ

At the dawn of the sixteenth century, Kyoto resembled two neighboring towns (see map 5). In Kamigyō, the upper city, businesses were concentrated alongside most of the buildings that housed the traditional functions of the capital: the imperial palace, the shogun's palace, and the residences of the nobility and some high-ranking warriors. The lower city, Shimogyō, was a dynamic and densely populated trade town. According to Hayashiya Tatsusaburō, the overall population was about 100,000—below the estimates for Kyoto in Yoshimitsu's and Yoshinori's times. Kamigyō and Shimogyō were about two kilometers apart and linked by Muromachi Avenue, which was bordered with residences.

Following the Ōnin War, insecurity ruled the city. Nighttime burglaries in the residences of the wealthy were reported. Court nobles were assaulted. With political crisis, war, and disorder came groups of bandits who took advantage of the absence of strong authority to impose their own nocturnal law. The bakufu seemed completely unable to organize a serious police force. The Hosokawa lords, who controlled the government, tried to use their own forces to replace the shogunal police, but they were not much more effective. Citizens, merchants, artisans, and court nobles, weary of the authorities' obvious inability, began to organize their own defense of the city.

With the self-defense organizations necessitated by the collapse of the state, urban autonomy was born in Kyoto. Like the peasants in village and regional communes, city residents felt the need to protect themselves by taking local control. At the end of the fifteenth century, defensive palisades were built around the city with gates at the entrances so that people entering could be stopped and questioned. Barricades and obstacles closed the streets at night. In the West and China, urban dwellers had long had curfews and closed their gates, and towns were built behind walls, but in Japan, access to the city had still been free. In 1527 and 1528, years of political disturbances, aristocrats such as Sanjō Sanetaka worked alongside ordinary citizens to convert the bamboo palisades into control posts. The noble Yamashina Tokitsugu had bamboo cut at his estate in Yamashina to provide inhabitants with defensive weapons and supplied saké to workers erecting the fortifications.[27] The inhabitants of Kyoto armed themselves and repelled Miyoshi Motonaga's troops, who were trying to force their way into the city.

Each neighborhood surrounded itself with moats and earth levees, and the district, or *machi*, became the basic unit of city life. There were six *machi* in Kamigyō, and five in Shimogyō, each united by a strong sense of solidarity. The Rokuchō *machi* in Kamigyō decided to build fortifications for the imperial

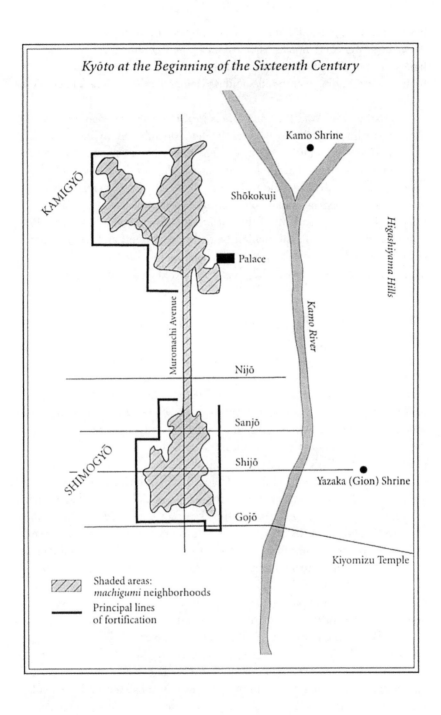

Kyōto at the Beginning of the Sixteenth Century

KAMIGYŌ

Kamo Shrine

Shōkokuji

Palace

Higashiyama Hills

Muromachi Avenue

Kamo River

Nijō

Sanjō

Shijō

Yazaka (Gion) Shrine

SHIMOGYŌ

Gojō

Kiyomizu Temple

Shaded areas:
machigumi neighborhoods

Principal lines
of fortification

palace and obtained substantial tax exemptions in return. Despite the city's social diversity, court nobles, moneylenders, and commoners cooperated to fight fires and repel foreign armies, bandits, and the newest threat, peasants from the surrounding countryside holding violent demonstrations for abolition of debts.

Before the Ōnin War, the commoners in Kyoto had supported the peasant insurgents who flooded into the city. In the sixteenth century, however, the urban residents just wanted some peace. The rural peasants attacked the houses of the monopolists, of course, but their anger spilled over into other neighborhoods. Artisans and small-scale merchants in the city were increasingly exasperated by the peasant bands' plundering and by the bakufu's inability to respond. In 1486, inhabitants of the *machi* armed themselves to fend off the peasants, and the traditional division between commoners and wealthy moneylenders faded. The enemies of urban populations were the lords' armies, bandits, and peasants angry at the usurers who lived in their city.

THE LOTUS LEAGUES

Another important element fueled the antagonism between the city and the countryside. In the early sixteenth century, the Ikkō sect quickly attracted commoners in the countryside of Yamashiro. The peasants, already quick to organize in leagues to eliminate their debts, were now led by the *jizamurai*, who were under the orders of the Honganji. Around the same time, the Hokke sect, the Lotus sect[28] of Nichiren's disciples, was spreading across the urban areas, including Kyoto. This sect advocated the importance of succeeding in this world, an idea that fit well with the ideology of profit held by merchants and artisans.[29] Aside from their fanaticism, the Ikkō and Hokke sects shared their hostility toward feudal lords. While the Ikkō sect developed mainly in the countryside and had as its main aim the rejection of responsibilities, corvées, and rents imposed by the lords, the Hokke sect categorically rejected feudal rents and demanded the abolition of urban taxes, including the *rakuchū jishisen*.[30] These demands coincided with those of districts' inhabitants, the *machishū*, who refused to pay the tax. Followers of the Hokke sect believed that one could profit in this world and that happiness in the here and now was possible for all who persevered in their religious practices. Their proselytism struck a chord with a hardworking, profit-oriented population, and temples affiliated with the sect sprang up all over Kyoto. The twenty-one that existed around 1530 were imposing buildings surrounded by moats and embankments, such as the Honnōji and the Myōkenji, and they served as both meeting places and small fortresses.[31] Just as the Amidist Ikkō sect was giving a religious context to the millenarian aspirations of rural dwellers, the Hokke sect supplied frameworks of belief to match the aspirations of urban populations.[32]

In early 1532, conflicts broke out between the great lords in southern Kinai. Harumoto, the young leader of the Hosokawa clan, asked for support from the Honganji, now led by Shōnyo. He was Rennyo's maternal grandson and had close ties with the Ikkō sect. Shōnyo mobilized rural leagues, composed of some 30,000 soldiers, and defeated Harumoto's enemies. He then pursued Miyoshi Motonaga, Harumoto's traitorous vassal, ran him to ground in a temple of the Hokke sect in Sakai where he had taken refuge, burned down the building, and killed him. Ikkō leagues also marched on Yamato, attacked the Kōfukuji, and devastated the region. In Kyoto, the rumor spread quickly that the leagues had burned down a Hokke temple in Sakai—which was true—and were getting ready to attack Kyoto—which was false. Soon the Hokke followers formed leagues in the capital, and the sect's temples became the vanguard of the resistance movement. Meanwhile, the extent of the Honganji's victory took the lords of Kinai, starting with Hosokawa Harumoto, by surprise. Harumoto thereupon reneged on his alliance and reached an agreement with the Hokke militias of Kyoto, for "poison is cured with poison."[33] At this point, there was a general uprising in Kyoto. Supported by warriors serving the Hosokawa, militias formed of urban residents won several victories over the advance guards of the Ikkō leagues, which retreated. The Hosokawa thought that they had won, but they had underestimated the armed Hokke leagues in Kyoto, which had their own agenda and were not easily manipulated. The Honganji temple in Yamashina, near Kyoto, was burned down in reprisal. More important, authority in the city fell into the hands of the *machishū*, many of them affiliated with the sect. Encouraged by Hokke followers, they stopped paying taxes in 1532.

From 1532 to 1536, the Hokke sect expanded its influence within Kyoto and extended it to the village communes on the city's outskirts, such as Uji and Yamashina. It was trying to bring Kyoto under its total control and make it the "estate of the Lotus." However, the aggressive and not very conciliatory methods used by the sect's followers when they were in a position of strength provoked hostile reactions among more moderate citizens. Members of other religious sects, starting with the monks of Mount Hiei, were not pleased with the proselytism of Nichiren's disciples. The warrior-monks of Mount Hiei were skillful in gaining the assistance or neutrality of other sects, including the Ikkō sect, and the support of the Rokkaku lords of Ōmi. War broke out in 1536, and battles lasted several days in Kyoto. Shimogyō was burned down again, but the Hokke leagues were defeated. As the senior clergy of the Hokke sect fled to Sakai, the bakufu officially banned the sect's activities in Kyoto.

Although the Hokke sect had suffered a serious defeat, the autonomous *machishū* organizations were far from beaten and seemed to prosper by filling the vacuum that the sect had left behind. In 1537, *gumi* (groups) were organized in Shimogyō to carry out the decisions made by the council of *sōdai*,[34] or delegates of Kyoto's municipal management. In the mid-sixteenth century, the sharing of powers between the *sōdai*, most of them wealthy merchants who saw the new urban autonomy as a means of establishing control over the city, and the *machishū* became a source of conflict. The *sōdai* wanted special privileges. Most of them were landlords who rented out the houses in which the *machishū* lived, and they maintained a dominant relationship with them similar to that between the *jizamurai* and the peasant communes. In Kyoto, the movement toward urban autonomy brought political power to those who already had economic power. But the social unit of the districts re-formed quickly if there was danger from outside, such as when Oda Nobunaga threatened in the early 1570s.

SAKAI

For the city of Sakai, too, 1532 was a pivotal year, for it was destroyed by a huge fire.[35] Several hundred people died, and more than 4,000 houses were destroyed. But the reconstruction was rapid. The city, which had been built on an estate cut in two by the border between Settsu and Izumi Provinces, formed a unified urban space with a population of around 40,000 in the mid-sixteenth century. Like Kyoto, Sakai was divided into about ten districts, or *machi*, governed by an oligarchy of powerful merchants. Since the 1470s, Sakai had been managed independently by a three-man council of merchants representing the *egōshū*, the city's wealthy class. The councils served for twelve-month terms.[36] The powerful *egōshū* negotiated directly with the great lords, including the Hosokawa, who exercised theoretical control over the city as the governors of Settsu and Izumi Provinces. About Sakai, a Jesuit wrote, "It is an immense city populated by wealthy merchants and, like Venice, administered by a council."[37] The *egōshū* had one overriding policy: avoiding war, which impeded business and brought unhappiness. In one of his regular reports to Rome, a Jesuit missionary (Gaspar Vilela) wrote,

> Unlike Sakai, Japan in general is not a tranquil country. In the provinces, there are disturbances everywhere. These are unknown in Sakai. Vanquished and victors can come here to live in peace. Here, they talk, instead of fighting. There is no disorder in the city's districts. . . . In each district are lookout towers ready to intervene in case of brawls. . . . The city has a secure position, surrounded by the sea and by moats filled with water.[38]

It is true that Sakai was more peaceful than was the rest of the country.[39] But it was to come under fire for its prosperity, and its resistance as a free city to Nobunaga's hegemonic intentions was to prove fatal. Most of its inhabitants were moved by force to Osaka, several kilometers away, where Hideyoshi was building his citadel.

The mingling of wealthy merchants and court nobles in *machi* society gave rise to a culture that was heir to the Higashiyama culture. The Tenmon culture reached its peak during the Tenmon era (1532–34), which corresponded to the high point of the movement for urban autonomy in both Kyoto and Sakai. Most of its ideas were based on aesthetic concepts originating in the previous period, but they were now brought to a higher degree of refinement—to *wabi*, evoking peace and solitude, and *seijaku*, calm and simplicity.

In the 1530s, the fashion born in the Higashiyama period of small rooms measuring 4.5 or 6 *tatami* in area was at its peak. The nobles had them built in their old residences to emulate small mountain hermitages, such as the one where Kamo no Chōmei had retired in the early thirteenth century to write "An Account of My Hut." Rooms measuring 4.5 *tatami*, which still exist in modern Japanese homes and whose small size is now linked to urban overpopulation, had a completely different function in the sixteenth century. Such rooms were where rich people could go to find a sense of intimacy, escape the world and be alone, or gather their thoughts.[40]

This new fashion was mainly urban at first. In the middle of Shimogyō, the tea master Sōju had a small "hermitage," or pavilion, where he could appreciate the pleasure of simplicity and tranquillity.[41] Wealthy merchants had small pavilions built at their villas, and they were ideal places for intimate tea parties. These pavilions were carefully planned. At the entrance to Master Sōju's pavilion were pines and cryptomerias. In the garden, a few leaves of yellow ivy could be seen on the ground. Sōju, like Takeno Jōō, a Sakai merchant who made a fortune manufacturing saddles for military use and had introduced the concept of *wabi* to the tea ceremony, was seeking uncompleted beauty. Jōō had the idea of celebrating the tea ceremony in a space apart from the everyday world, the urban hermitage, which recalled the rustic atmosphere of the mountain. One of his disciples, Sen no Rikyū, brought the art of tea to its apex, and he became close to Nobunaga and then Hideyoshi, to whom he taught the highly aesthetic pleasures of the tea ceremony and a love for ceramics.[42]

Sen no Rikyū was also a *machishū* in Sakai. Although he is remembered mainly as a master of the tea ceremony, he was also an artist. All the greatest painters of the sixteenth century, including those who founded the Kanō school—Motonobu, Hideyori, Hasegawa Tōhaku, and others—were wealthy *machishū* merchants in Kyoto, fierce supporters of Nichiren's teachings, and followers of the Hokke sect.[43]

A century of war, marked by the emergence of powerful lords in the provinces, the Sengoku period also saw the cultural triumph of the bourgeois oligarchies in Kyoto and Sakai. All artists, whether their art was the tea ceremony, flower arranging, or landscape painting, were part of a new aesthetic. This also was the first lay culture, very much distinct from the topoi of Buddhism. They were the product of a society already largely won over by "disenchantment with the world" and resolutely marching toward modernity.

Chapter 12

THE SENGOKU PERIOD: WARLORDS SEEKING POWER

THE COLLAPSE OF THE SHOGUNAL REGIME

Following the Ōnin War, as we have seen, the bakufu no longer had any control over the capital and surrounding regions. But even though its authority no longer had much meaning, the bakufu still had political legitimacy. Nonetheless, the *kanrei* ministers had become the true leaders of the government, and Hosokawa Katsumoto had managed to eliminate those close to the shogun.

In 1493, the direct rule of the Ashikaga came to an end. With a coup d'état, Hosokawa Masamoto deposed the shogun and replaced him with the son of one of the two deputy shogun who were fighting for power in Kanto. Masamoto gained control of the bakufu by taking over the position of *kanrei* from a Hatakeyama lord. Now he was the master, and the new shogun was his pawn. Masamoto regarded both the shogun and the emperor with contempt. "He who does not hold power should not claim to be sovereign," he declared as the imperial court was desperately trying to find enough money to pay for the enthronement ceremony for Go Kashiwabara. These words were a perfect reflection of the *gekokujō* mentality.[1]

Hosokawa Masamoto stayed in power from 1493 until his death in 1507. Then, succession quarrels, which had touched all the great families of *shugo* lords, broke out in the Hosokawa household, splitting it into two rival branches. The Ōuchi, powerful lords from the west and masters of the city of Hakata, succeeded the Hosokawa at the head of the bakufu for several years. The Ōuchi had taken advantage of the Yamana's weakened position after the Ōnin War to consolidate their power in the west,[2] and when Masamoto took power in 1493, the deposed shogun fled to their territory. From 1508, after Masamoto's death, to 1518, Ōuchi Yoshioki lived in Kyoto and held power. He wanted to obtain a monopoly on official trade with Ming-dynasty China, for which he needed the bakufu's official seal of approval. Taking advantage of the division in the Ashikaga family and then in the Hosokawa family, Yoshioki supported one of the factions, returned Yoshitada, the shogun who had been deposed in 1493 — which left one of the Hosokawa claimants with the title of *kanrei* — and ran the shogunal government himself.

Ōuchi Yoshioki had just returned to his estates in 1518 when the power struggles between warriors started again, even though they were no more than a series of theatrical gestures with no lasting effects. The shogun were the pawns of their vassals, and even the Hosokawa *kanrei* were the pawns of their vassals in the Miyoshi clan, which was fighting one branch of the Hatakeyama household for control of southern Kinai. In 1549, Miyoshi Nagayoshi eliminated his main rivals and became, with the Honganji of the Ikkō sect, the main source of authority in Kinai. It was he who allowed the missionary Gaspar Vilela to preach in Kyoto in 1559. In 1563, the Miyoshi were threatened by the rise of a vassal family, the Matsunaga. But the true political stakes were now elsewhere, far from Kinai.

WARLORDS: TWO EXAMPLES

THE HŌJŌ LORDS

In the late fifteenth century, the political situation was at least as complex in Kanto as it was in Kinai. The junior branch of the Ashikaga, which had governed the region as deputy shogun since the mid-fourteenth century, had split into two rival factions, while the powerful Uesugi lords, who held the title of *kanrei* in the regional bakufu, were also victims of incessant internal quarrels over succession.

An obscure vassal of the Imagawa governors, who controlled the Tōkaidō, struck in 1491. He invaded Izu Province, killed the young Ashikaga Chachamaru, chief heir of one of the two Ashikaga branches, and captured the fortified place of Nirayama. This warrior, later known as Hōjō Sōun, was sixty years old at the time. Four years later, he launched a second surprise attack against a neighboring lord and captured Odawara Castle. Sōun had inaugurated a tactic that later was adopted by most of the warlords: remain vigilant, wait for the right moment, and spring into action. Over the ensuing years, Sōun consolidated the estate that he had built illegally, forming alliances with those who were more powerful than him and absorbing those who were weaker. In 1513, he attacked the Miura, his neighbors in Sagami, who were allied with one of the Uesugi families. Once he defeated them, though not without difficulty, he took over their land in 1517. It had taken him more than twenty-five years to bring Izu and Sagami Provinces under his complete control.

The success of the man who had chosen the name Hōjō—Izu was the homeland of the Hōjō family, which had dominated the Kamakura bakufu[3]— came from both his own military skills and the new way in which he constructed his army and made profitable a territory that had no remarkable economic strength. Sōun had convinced the low-ranking warriors of the regions that he controlled to join his vassal organization: forty-five warrior families of the region served him and formed his bodyguard. There were no plots or revolts in his estates during this period, an extraordinary fact in those times. Since Sōun had no legitimacy, he started by ordering a reduction in rents on the lands he had invaded, for he needed all the goodwill he could muster and the support of the peasant middle classes.

In 1518, when he was eighty-eight, Sōun named his adoptive son, Hōjō Uji-tsuna, as the heir to his estate. He also wrote recommendations for his family (*kakun*), a sort of moral code for his descendants to use:

> Before washing in the morning, you must tour the grounds—the out-houses, stables, gardens, gates—and tell the workers what must be cleaned. Only then, you must wash, and quickly. Water must not be wasted, even when it is abundant. . . . You must bow before heaven and walk softly. . . . You must be of sound mind, make honesty a rule, respect your superiors, and pity your inferiors. Everything must be in its place.[4]

These recommendations may reveal something about Sōun's personality, but they also are indicative of new ways of thinking. Starting with nothing, Sōun had been able to acquire an enormous territory through patience and self-control. But at a time when human ties were especially important, he maintained that a leader with a watchful eye and a sense of moral rectitude were more valuable than prestige, tradition, and family. The new warlords had to depend on their own strengths.

Under Ujitsuna, the Hōjō estates extended into northern Musashi Province. By the time he died, in 1541, the Hōjō controlled southern Kanto and were the main military power in the east. In 1520, Ujitsuna had the lands in Sagami systematically surveyed in order to justify the real-estate tax. This survey was opposed by low-ranking samurai and peasants who preferred the old estate cadastres, which were long out-of-date. Ujitsuna overcame their resistance and became the first warlord to conduct such a survey, and he was quickly imitated by others. He encouraged the merchants of western Japan to settle near his castle in Odawara by offering them various privileges. A town rapidly developed, and by the mid-sixteenth century, Odawara was Kanto's economic and cultural center.

Ujiyasu, the third Hōjō lord, ruled his estates from 1541 to 1571. One of the best military leaders of his time, he waged war in northern Kanto against Uesugi Kenshin, who was installed in Echigo. Ujiyasu quickly learned to use the firearms introduced by the Portuguese after 1543, and he armed his troops with them. His well-organized army performed precise maneuvers to the sound of trumpets. Indeed, the Hōjō were among the most powerful lords of their times, but their remoteness from Kinai excluded them from the direct lines of power.[5]

THE IMAGAWA LORDS

Very different from the Hōjō were the Imagawa, who controlled the land along the Tōkaidō. While the Hōjō rose from rather modest beginnings, the Imagawa

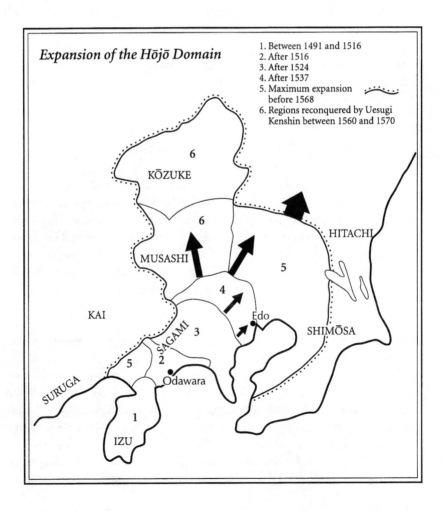

Expansion of the Hōjō Domain

1. Between 1491 and 1516
2. After 1516
3. After 1524
4. After 1537
5. Maximum expansion before 1568
6. Regions reconquered by Uesugi Kenshin between 1560 and 1570

were major vassals of the Ashikaga and had obtained the hereditary position of military governor, *shugo*, in Suruga Province in the fourteenth century. They had demonstrated their loyalty to the shogun by solidly supporting the Kyoto regime in the face of vague attempts at independence by the deputy shogun in Kamakura in the early fifteenth century. But the Imagawa's power structure began to change after the Ōnin War. The head of the family was killed and disturbances broke out in the province, where the local barons split into two factions. Imagawa Ujichika managed to defuse the situation without the help of the bakufu. In 1517, he cut off all relations with Kyoto and seized his neighbor's estates in Tōtōmi Province.

Ujichika controlled only two provinces, but he ran them as if he were the king of a small state. Between 1520 and 1524, he had a collection of laws, the Imagawa kana mokuroku,[6] written. This "constitution" of the Imagawa regime served as a model for other lords' legal codes (*bunkokuhō*). One of Ujichika's sons, Yoshimoto, succeeded him and extended the territory to the west, absorbing the Matsudaira family and negotiating advantageous peace agreements with the Takeda to the north and the Hōjō to the east. Fascinated by Kyoto's urban culture, Yoshimoto constantly dreamed of marching on the capital. In 1560, he invaded the small estates of his neighbor in Owari, Oda Nobunaga, but he died in the battle of Okehazama. The most powerful lords on the Tōkaidō, the Imagawa, thus lost their regional predominance to Nobunaga.

WHAT IS A WARLORD?

Whatever their social origins—obscure, as in the case of Hōjō Sōun, or prominent, as in the case of Imagawa Ujichika—the warlords who emerged in the early sixteenth century had certain characteristics in common. They represented a new development in the social rise of the warrior classes. Their power was independent, unrelated to any traditional form of authority—imperial court or bakufu. The warlord asked no one's permission to act and imposed himself as the supreme authority in the region he controlled, which could more rightly be called a principality than a fiefdom, since he had not been enfeoffed by anyone.

Unlike the *shugo* of the fifteenth century, whose estates were still fundamentally tied to their authority as functionaries for the shogunal state, the daimyo of the sixteenth century had complete suzerainty over their lands. They formed the government on their new estates and gave fiefs to their vassals in the territory they controlled. If their power had not been so precarious—the era of the warlords lasted no more than two or three generations—and the territories they controlled had not been so small (the equivalent of two or three prefectures in today's Japan), their principalities might almost have been called kingdoms. Because they had no legal form of power, they imposed themselves by force and by their ability to keep peace within their territories, and they were accepted because, in the eyes of their vassals and subjects, prosperity depended on their authority. Precisely because they had no legal right to "rule," the daimyo were quick to establish "provincial laws,"[7] feudal constitutions that gave them the legitimacy they needed to run their small states.

Most of the new lords were from the *shugo* class or the families of local barons, *kokujin* or *kunishū*. *Shugo* such as the Imagawa made all local barons in their provinces vassals and transformed themselves into warlords on the spot. But those from the families of local warriors, such as the Amako in Izumo and the Mōri in western Honshu, got rid of the *shugo* and made other warriors vassals under their suzerainty.

The historian Nagahara Keiji adopted the following typology for warlords according to the social origins of their clan:[8]

Type 1. This group was composed of lords from families that held the position of *shugo*. They controlled only one province but did so firmly. They did not represent an important enough power for their political maneuvering in the shogunal court of Kyoto to bother their neighbors or rivals. During the Ōnin War, they returned to their provinces. Taking advantage of the central authority's dissolution, they did their utmost to shape their provinces into separate principalities and gradually to become the suzerain of all the warriors in their territories. Of the *shugo* who transformed themselves into warlords during the Muromachi period, none were from the most powerful warrior clans. All their clans—the Shiba, the Akamatsu, the Yamana, the Hatakeyama—fell from glory in the second half of the fifteenth century, and the Hosokawa followed in the early sixteenth century. This group also included the Imagawa; the Takeda, who had settled in the mountains north of Mount Fuji since the end of the Heian period; and the Shimazu, warriors who had once been Minamoto no Yoritomo's retainers at the southern tip of Kyushu. From the Takeda clan arose the legendary figure of Takeda Shingen (1521–73), a great general and Oda Nobunaga's unlucky rival. The Shimazu ruled the principality of Satsuma, which was too remote geographically from central Japan to play a pivotal role in the sixteenth century but was to be instrumental in the fall of the Tokugawa regime in the mid-nineteenth century.

Type 2. This group was formed of lords who had been governor's agents. In the fifteenth century, some *shugo* living at the shogunal court in Kyoto or at the regional bakufu in Kamakura delegated their local authority to their vassals, granting them the title of *shugo-dai*, "governor's deputy." They were from the families of either the *shugo* or a baron who had long been an ally and vassal. The governors depended on them to run the local administration while they took part in the brilliant culture of the capital and plotted against the bakufu. But the governors lost contact with their estates, thereby leaving them open to the *shugo-dai*, who seized real power during the Ōnin War and managed to eliminate their former masters entirely. In Owari, the Oda disposed of their suzerains, the Shiba. Nagao Kagetora was the government agent for the Uesugi clan in Echigo. The leader of one branch of the family, defeated by the Hōjō in Kanto, took refuge with his vassal in Echigo and adopted him. Thus Nagao Kagetora became the warlord Uesugi Kenshin, perpetual enemy of Takeda Shingen.

Type 3. This group included warlords from the class of local barons. It took them a relatively long time to become warlords, since they had to consolidate their position in the province as local lords against the other barons and then fight to defeat the *shugo* or *shugo-dai*. Typical of this group were the Mōri lords, who dominated western Honshū; they were the masters of the future fiefdom of Chōshū, which, like Satsuma Province, played an important role at the end of the Tokugawa regime. The Mōri were ordinary barons and vassals of the powerful Ōuchi *shugo* in Aki Province. Between 1540 and 1551, through skillful alliances, they managed to become the most powerful barons in their province under Mōri Motonari. In 1551, Ōuchi Yoshitaka was killed by one of his vassals, Sue Harukata. Mōri Motonari rallied all the former Ōuchi vassals who were angered at Sue Harukata's military coup and defeated him in a battle in 1555. The Mōri family thus inherited the Ōuchi's estates and expanded their territories to the west by seizing the Amako family's estates in Izumo in 1566. By 1568, when Oda Nobunaga entered Kyoto, Mōri Motonari ruled a principality comprising ten provinces in western Japan. The Chōsokabe in Shikoku, the Date in Tōhoku, and the Matsudaira (the future Tokugawa) on the Tōkaidō in Mikawa were from this class of local barons who were able to take over provinces.

Type 4. The last group consisted of warlords with obscure origins. The clan founder was usually an adventurer. The Hōjō in southern Kanto are the best-known example. With his audacity and skill at filling the political void in the region, Sōun was able to create an estate independent of his former masters. His power did not derive from position, title, or family ties. Rather, his case is the best illustration of the phenomenon of *gekokujō*, the reversal of the hierarchy in which the lower came to command the upper. Starting with nothing, Sōun managed to take over a part of Japan that had been the estate of the junior branch of the Ashikaga in Kamakura. He also provides an example of the extraordinary social mobility that ruled in those troubled times, when the lower classes were constantly contesting the order that the traditional leading classes were in fact no longer even trying to impose.

In the same group was Saitō Dōsan, lord of Mino, whose career was just as astonishing. This man from a mysterious background entered a Kyoto temple as an apprentice monk when he was eleven and then left to marry the daughter of an oil merchant. He in turn became a merchant and spent his youth traveling through eastern Kinai. Later, he forged an alliance with one of the vassals of the *shugo* of Mino, of the Toki clan. He entered the service of the younger brother of the *shugo*, whom he urged to plot against his brother. In 1533, the plot succeeded, and Dōsan, the former oil merchant, was made a samurai as a reward. He was posted to guard a castle, and in 1538, he took the name of the former *shugo-dai*, Saitō. But in 1542, he suddenly attacked the *shugo*, his old patron, and expelled him from the province. At forty-six, the man whom historians have described as a Machiavellian figure became a warlord. He married his daughter to the young Oda Nobunaga. Like Hōjō Sōun, Saitō Dōsan had stolen into a province like a thief and gained his power by scheming.

For all the warlords, whatever their origin, the end justified the means. What counted most was personal power, which gave the leader charisma and earned him the unconditional loyalty of his vassals. This "ability" (*kiryō no jin*), or leadership skill, became indispensable to gaining and maintaining authority when no supreme order was able to temper passions and curb appetites for power. In the collection of "recommendations" that he left to his descendants, the *Asakura Sōteki waki*, the warlord Asakura Norikage, who ruled in Kaga and Echizen, stated explicitly that those who did not have this "skill" could not hope to stay in power for long.[9]

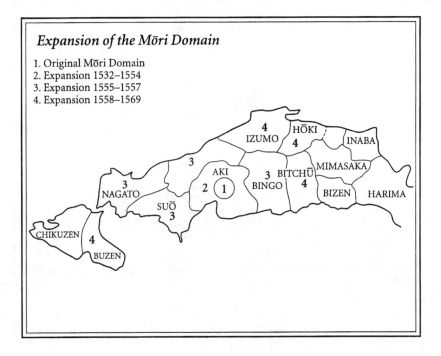

Expansion of the Mōri Domain

1. Original Mōri Domain
2. Expansion 1532–1554
3. Expansion 1555–1557
4. Expansion 1558–1569

THE NEW VASSALAGE: "A STRONG ARMY"

The warlords tightly controlled the lower warrior classes. The vassal organization was divided into several groups, and this structure endured, without major changes, into the Edo period.

The lord's top vassals were divided into three categories.

The *ichimon* were members of the lord's family—"blood princes" and collateral relatives. When undivided succession was instituted, they no longer benefited, as they once had, from part of the inheritance. Instead, they had to be content with forming the top ranks of the leader's vassals, and he allocated them an income in cash or rice. The loyalty of the *ichimon* was not automatic, and if there was difficulty with the succession, they might plot to get their hands on the inheritance.

The *fudai* were generally the most stable and reliable vassals. They were too distantly related to the warlord to claim the inheritance; or they were the lord's companion warriors from provincial warrior families who had agreed very early to become vassals of the daimyo (or their descendants); or they were low-ranking warriors whose estates were located near those of the future lord and who therefore saw an alliance as preferable to confrontation. In the Hōjō clan, for example, a group of twenty-eight *fudai* attended the chief. Takeda Shingen was sur-

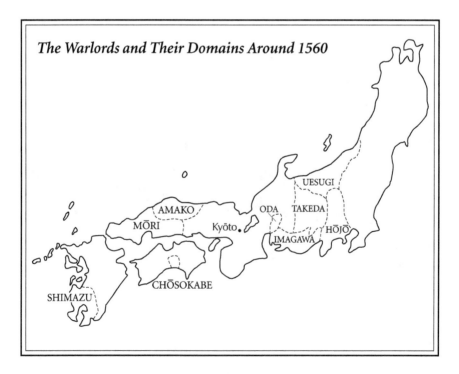

The Warlords and Their Domains Around 1560

rounded by a group of twenty-four generals, all *fudai*. They were confirmed at the head of their estates by the daimyo; sometimes the lord moved them to manage a new estate that was felt to be more important economically or strategically.

The *tozama* were external vassals whose estates had been merged into the daimyo's principality when he expanded his territory through war and annexations. Most were defeated warriors who had perforce become allies, unless they had refused to enter an alliance. The lord made them vassals, of course, but the *tozama* preferred this relationship to a hostile one that might well result in their obliteration. Although they remained masters of their estates, the *tozama* were closely supervised and quickly lost all their autonomy. They nevertheless presented a danger, as they were ready to commit treason at any moment.

Under these three categories of warriors, who formed the upper classes of the vassal hierarchy, was a fourth group of lower-ranking vassals to whom the lord granted land within his own estate. They generally formed the daimyo's personal guard and were divided into specific categories: horse guards, foot soldiers, pages, stable hands, and so on. The *ichimon*, *fudai*, and *tozama* in turn had vassals who were thus the undervassals of the suzerain.[10]

Vassals were forced to perform military service according to a very strict formula. Because of the cadastres that all warlords, following the example of the Hōjō, had conducted in the mid-sixteenth century, lords knew precisely their vassals' income and could demand that they participate in the war effort. In 1581, in the principality of the Hōjō, a warrior named Ikeda Sozaemon, whose estate was estimated at 191.6 *kan*, had to serve along with twenty-six men: six horsemen and twenty foot soldiers. The latter were to be composed of at least one musketeer, twelve men armed with lances, and one archer.[11] *Jizamurai* and wealthy peasants were also made to contribute to their lord's war, either by joining the daimyo's army for the duration of a campaign or by supplying arms, military equipment, or food. This very regimented organization of vassals made the lords' armies formidable war machines.

THE NEW ORGANIZATION: "A RICH COUNTRY"

The lords' system of control over their principalities was very different from former systems. First, the new leaders managed to destroy the social organization of the old estates with its tangled web of land rights, and all land now belonged to the lords. The lord represented the public authority (*kōgi*), and the old nobility lost its ability to collect rents on cultivated lands. The former political forces of the court had no place in the new lords' system, and the court nobles who had survived were forced to live on the patronage of the daimyo. In 1562, for instance, Mōri Motonari decided to pay the costs of the enthrone-

ment ceremonies for Emperor Ogimachi in Kyoto. Warlords who fancied themselves men of culture sometimes extended the hospitality of their capitals to
nobles. The Ōuchi in Yamaguchi, the Hōjō in Odawara, and the Imagawa in
Sunpu (the future Shizuoka) attempted in this way to recreate the atmosphere
of Kyoto in its prime in the main towns of their principalities.

The warlords conducted systematic surveys of the land under their control
based on the *kandaka* system, which estimated in cash the value of the average
harvest of a piece of land (a *kan* was equal to 1,000 copper coins). By applying
this criterion to all fiefs within the principality, the daimyo knew the exact
volume of the agricultural production in his small state (and taxed the peasants
accordingly) and the exact incomes of the warriors. The warlord was, in any
case, the main landowner within his principality and thus the wealthiest man.
Some granted themselves the privilege of issuing money, which enabled them
to tighten their control over their territory even further. Inhabitants on a warlord's estate were thus divided into peasants, subjects required to pay an agrarian
tax, and warriors, those vassals of the lord required to pay a military tax.

By surveying the cultivated land when each new suzerain came to power,
the warlords could raise the amount of land tax collected. In the estate of the
Hōjō, thirteen villages saw their taxes rise anywhere from 13 to 560 percent.[12]
Other estimates show that on average, the peasants' payments doubled. The
new system was thus an aggressive exploitation of the peasantry. And the peasants, even in the estates of the most powerful warlords, reacted in various ways:
through written protests, demonstrations, flight to land where labor was
needed, and a collective refusal to work the land. In fact, the poorest peasants
were so badly off that they were nearly insolvent, and the lords were sometimes
forced to agree to exemptions on taxes and even to promulgate edicts abolishing their debts.[13]

The economic expansion in most regions controlled by the lords in the
sixteenth century was the result of more than simply an increase in peasant
labor. All lords had public works built to stimulate production: dikes were built
along rivers, land was drained and planted, dry fields were converted into rice
paddies that could be flooded. An improved taxation system, based on cadastres
and not on custom, led to larger operations that made large profits, some of
which were reinvested in production. The lords needed to rationalize operations on their estates in order to have the means to carry out their policies. All
the lords wanted to increase the wealth of their small states. Not only did they
promote agriculture, but they also welcomed artisans, especially those who
helped with the "war effort." The lords opened mines and used the ore to strike
coins, brought towns and ports under their direct control, established series of
inns along the roads, inaugurated a postal service, took down the barriers and
tollgates set up by former landowners, created tax-free markets, and unified
weights and measures.

To make his war machine operate efficiently, the lord's finances had to be healthy. The elimination of estates and the change to the *kandaka* system did not necessarily mean the payment of taxes in cash, but this was occurring more and more frequently, as money was becoming an important economic tool and the warlords were seeking any means to obtain it. A growing number of low-ranking vassals and *ichimon* were enfeoffed not through assignments of land but through allocations of rice or cash. This placed them in a position of absolute dependence on their lord and transformed them into salaried officers without any relationship with the land or the peasantry. They went to live in the towns that the warlords had built at the foot of their castles, in the first step toward the bureaucratization of the warrior class that picked up speed in the Edo period.

REFLECTIONS ON JAPANESE FEUDALISM

The system of vassals that characterized relations within the warrior classes seem to have been particularly solid during the period when feudalism was rising to fore in the twelfth and thirteenth centuries. The preeminence of vertical hierarchies led to warrior groupings, *bushidan*, gathered under a charismatic leader who took the title of shogun in 1192. In the sixteenth century, the emergence of new lords who were sovereigns in their land signaled a new wave of feudalism, which reached into a large number of social sectors. Again, vertical hierarchies featuring warrior vassalage, *kashindan*, seemed to be the motivation for this evolution. However, other warrior organizations emerged in the fourteenth and fifteenth centuries, with more horizontal and collective structures. The *ikki*, as we have seen, were able to create locally stable power structures that were efficient and difficult to overthrow. These republican-style microstates, based on the control of a region, were set up primarily to keep the peace and provide self-defense. They were sometimes the last line of opposition to the centralization of power, as they impeded the creation of large regional suzerainties. The march to reunify the country in the late sixteenth century and the birth of a new order, that of the Tokugawa, required the military destruction of these social organizations.

According to historians such as Amino Yoshihiko, the first vertically hierarchical organizations appeared in the peripheral regions of the country—Kanto, the northeast, Kyushu (where the old state's power may have been the weakest)—but they had much more difficulty taking root in central regions such as Kinai, where no fiefdom endured very long. Some popularizers believe that if this is so, then it is only a short step from this to contrasting an anthropological model of a hierarchical, patriarchal, and feudal Kanto (horses, dryland culture, clans) with a model of a more collectivist, horizontally organized, and perhaps Asiatic western region (boats, rice, villages).

The reality, however, is more complex. What emerges from recent historio-

graphic research is evidence of multiple spheres of power coexisting throughout the country—and not always in competition with one another. Another vision
of Japanese society has slowly replaced the image of a court aristocracy gradually
reduced to subsisting on an allowance by conquering warriors whose failure to
abolish the ancient imperial order seems incomprehensible. The "ancient"
leading class of the Heian period (the court, the monasteries) was gradually
stripped of its real-estate revenues by the warrior classes and turned quite early
to other activities, including the protection and control of groups that earned
a living from trade (merchants, artists, etc.). There was thus a sharing of social
functions in the Middle Ages: to the warriors went control of the peasants who
were bound to the land, and to the aristocrats and religious institutions went
increasingly tight control over nonagricultural social classes (through control
of the *za*, for example). The new thrust of the warrior class in the sixteenth
century, and then its final triumph, corresponded to a time of considerable
expansion of the sphere of activities controlled by lords from the warrior classes.
By encouraging craft activities and trade and then concentrating them in castle
towns, the leading warlords wrested from the monasteries and court aristocracy
some of the influence that they had exerted over merchants and artisans through
patronage. Of course, the gradual closing of the country in the early seventeenth
century, inspired by centralizing policies promulgated by the rulers in China
and Korea was a reaction against both what was perceived as a Western threat
and the old leading classes, which were now reduced to subsistence allowances.

A new portrait of medieval Japanese feudalism emerges, that of a system of
control over a perpetually unstable land—a system that was unable to ensure
control of social groups that were not locked away in agricultural production.
Attacked from all sides—as much by the appetites of rival lords as by the resistance of village communities—the feudal lords were ultimately unable to invent
a viable social order before the second half of the sixteenth century. Feudalism
was thus only one element of social domination in medieval Japan, alongside
the clientelism of the old aristocracy, which expanded its domination to entire
social classes. The medieval system described by Kuroda Toshio as an alliance
of necessity between two dominant social groups condemned to supporting
each other, to coexisting in some way, in the end seems quite convincing. But
with the victory of the warriors in the sixteenth century came a reassessment of
this unstable balance just as Japan was beginning to undergo another
transformation.

CREATING A NEW ORDER

In 1543, the Portuguese landed at the small island of Tanegashima, south of
Kyushu, at a time when Japanese society was involved in a great movement of

economic and trade expansion, accompanied by a degree of political instability that was almost too severe to imagine. In the mid-sixteenth century, Japan was a dynamic but fragmented country, divided into very separate spheres of power. While the warlords formed their principalities in the far reaches of the country and went to war with one another to expand their hegemony over the provinces, central Japan was prey to social and religious struggles. Regional communes, the Ikkō sect, and lords with reduced power shared control of the peasantry while the cities were being administered by merchant oligarchies drawing their power from urban populations organized into districts.

As long as the rural and regional communes remained socially united and ideologically structured by the Ikkō sect, their political and military power was considerable. None of the most powerful warlords—except for Nobunaga— penetrated as far as Kinai without being repelled. But the communes were threatened from inside. Built on the basis of a union between peasants and low-ranking *jizamurai* warriors, they were in fact led by the upper classes of rural society (by wealthy merchants in the case of urban communes). Although these contradictions did not necessarily lead to open confrontation, they did contain the seeds of a possible power struggle. In the mid-sixteenth century, fissures began opening within these rural communes. Those peasant villagers who had been promoted to *jizamurai* quickly became wealthy by seizing the surplus no longer within the grasp of the old upper classes.In addition, their relations with the rest of the peasantry became increasingly contentious, as they were seeking to transform these other peasants into tenants on their estates. But they were torn between the village communes—which they led, of course, but which were becoming hostile toward them—and the warlords, who were enticing them by promising them protection and rewards in return for their services. The upper class of the peasantry (or the lower class of warriors) between 1550 and 1570 quickly became vassals. Those *jizamurai* and peasants who had become vassals of the lord then became his agents in the community. This process sometimes halted, however. In 1568, four inhabitants of the autonomous village of Sugaura, on Lake Biwa, who had links with the Asai lords were expelled from the commune. They were forbidden to attend the communal meetings, and they were severely punished.[14] The reason was that the local lords wanted to overthrow the villages' autonomous judicial power, but they did not succeed.

But where the warlords were powerful and able to depend on massive military forces, the *jizamurai* had little choice. Either they ran their territory with the free support of the peasants and led the armed leagues in resistance, or they became vassals of a warlord, which greatly hampered their freedom.

The savagery with which Oda Nobunaga broke the resistance of various communes in Kinai between 1568 and 1582 matched the resistance that he faced. The regional commune of Iga, which Nobunaga finally demolished in 1581, had resisted for more than ten years. Nobunaga's victorious armies set the province awash in fire and blood to forestall any notion of further revolt. For their part, the *machishū* of Kyoto were unceremoniously expelled. The Ikkō leagues of Mikawa were finally defeated, too, and Nobunaga proceeded to massacre the vanquished parties in the early 1580s.

Nobunaga's new military techniques were fearsome. He crushed the armies of lords who conducted war according to the old tactics: the Takeda were routed in the battle of Nagashino in 1575. The arrival of the Portuguese in 1543 had changed the political order. The Japanese lords discovered firearms and then artillery, and war took on a new dimension. Japanese artisans could not make enough of the new weapons, given the enormous demand, and the lords had to be courteous to the "barbarians from the south," who sold them the valuable and costly guns. In regard to Christianity, which at first was considered a curiosity, some warlords, such as Nobunaga, no doubt saw it as a way to compete with the Ikkō sect.

Many Japanese experts feel that these warlords, who acquired their power by destroying the old order, began a process of feudalization (or refeudalization) of Japanese society, a process that culminated with the birth of a "feudal monarchy," the Edo regime. By crushing the peasant communes, the Ikkō sect, and the "free towns," Nobunaga and Hideyoshi brutally put an end to the commoners' autonomy and a final end to the Middle Ages. The new state was forged with terror and intimidation, which helped give the Tokugawa regime its image as a police state. Bruised by a century and a half of "the lower commanding the upper," the leading warrior classes were no longer prepared to face challengers. Some historians even detect a sort of social counterrevolution in the reunification of Japan.[15] In any case, this unification ended the war. It also ended the multiplicity of land regimes and laid the groundwork for a new and unprecedented rise in production and population growth, which continued throughout the seventeenth century.

Although almost all Japanese historians agree that medieval times began with the establishment of a new form of power in Kanto in the late twelfth century, they have a harder time setting a date, even a symbolic one, to mark the end of this period. The Sengoku period is often seen as a transitional interval leading to the emergence of the shogunal monarchy of the Tokugawa. The balance of medieval society was disrupted a number of times in its latter stages, with the rise around 1480 and then the fall around 1580 of varieties of commoner autonomy, the birth in Kyoto around 1530 and then in Sakai of a bourgeois culture that blossomed in Osaka in the late seventeenth century, rapid urbanization, increased production, and Japan's contact with the Western world after 1543.

On a social level, the dreams that motivated the lower classes—Buddha's paradise on earth and a return to an idealized ancient order—resulted only in an extreme compartmentalization of power. This fragmentation hobbled economic progress. Although Kinai was always the most developed area in the archipelago, the peripheral zones quickly caught up, owing to the warlords' systematic economic development. If there was modernity or premodernity in the sixteenth century in Japan, it was evident more in the Machiavellianism of the warlords than in the religious dreams of the low-ranking warriors who had converted to Amidism. Jacques Le Goff's analysis of the millenarian dreams of the medieval lower classes in the West could be applied to the letter to Japan in the late Middle Ages: men in medieval times could not imagine a truly new world. "[Their] golden age was only a return to origins. Their future was behind them. They walked looking backward."[16]

When Nobunaga entered Kyoto in 1568, expelled the last Ashikaga shogun in 1573, repressed communal forms of autonomy established in Kinai in the 1570s, and destroyed the last military forces of the great traditional temples such as the Enryakuji in 1571, he introduced a major political change. In short, he destroyed what remained of the Middle Ages and invented a new social order that was both more brutal and more rational. On the cultural level, however, the rupture between medieval and modern times came much earlier, with the birth of a "Japanese" style that reflected new sensibilities and a new aesthetic. In the 1920s, in a series of lectures on the history of Japanese culture, the sinologist Naitō Konan made a rather provocative statement: "When one does research on the history of Japan to understand today's Japan, there is no need to study ancient Japan. It is enough to know the history of the country after the Ōnin War. Everything that took place before can be thought of almost as the history of another country."[17] For Naitō Konan, there was only one important chronological schism: that between the 1470s and 1480s, which marked the collapse of both the Ashikaga bakufu and the court nobility and the simultaneous advent of Higashiyama culture, the cradle of "traditional" Japanese culture.[18]

More recently, a number of historians have examined the global change of perspective that took place among the Japanese elites around 1550, after the Westerners arrived—the revelation of the immensity of the world and the relative weakness of Japan. The most ambitious warlords—the most "modern"?—understood the need to recreate a strong government encompassing the entire archipelago, consolidate the economic bases of their territory, and forge military forces on a new scale. These forms of thought presaged those of the mid-nineteenth century: *fukoku kyōhei*, "a wealthy nation, a strong army" could have been the order of the day for the most dynamic warlords.[19] It was a long way from the mentality of the country's leaders in the 1470s, when the shogun Yoshimasa watched with indifference as his regime collapsed. In this sense, the Sengoku period was in fact more than the end of a period in Japan's history, a "renaissance" that formed the basis for the creation of a new state—and a new society.

NOTES

1. The Curtain Rises

1. Kasamatsu Hiroshi, "Youchi" (Night attack), in Amino Yoshihiko, Ishii Susumu, Kasamatsu Hiroshi, and Katsumata Shizuo, *Chūsei no tsumi to batsu* (Crime and punishment in the Middle Ages) (Tokyo: Tōkyō daigaku shuppankai, 1983), pp. 91 et seq.
2. This event is described in many sources of the period, including the *Azuma kagami*. Ishii Susumu describes how the incident unfolded, in *Kamakura bakufu*, vol. 7 of *Nihon no rekishi* (History of Japan) (Tokyo: Chūō koron, 1974), pp. 2 et seq.
3. *Musha no yo*. It seems that the expression was used for the first time in *Gukan-sho* (My views of history), a work attributed to Jien, the grand abbot of the Tendai, in the early thirteenth century.
4. The term was used by Arai Hakuseki in the early eighteenth century but did not catch on. See Hara Katsurō, *Nihon chūseishi* (History of the Japanese Middle Ages) (1906; reprint, Tokyo: Kōdansha gakujutsu bunko, 1978).
5. The bakufu was the government of the warrior class headed by a shogun. In contemporary documents, the bakufu was often designated by geographic terms such as Kamakura and Kanto.
6. On the history of the concept of feudalism in Japan, see Pierre F. Souyri, "La Féodalité japonaise" (Japanese feudalism), in E. Bournazel and J.-P. Poly, eds., *Les Féodalités* (Feudalisms) (Paris: Presses universitaires de France, 1998). On the reconstruction of the past with regard to this period, see Jeffrey P. Mass, *Antiquity and Anachronism in Japanese History* (Stanford, Calif.: Stanford University Press, 1992). See also Ishii Susumu, "Nihonshi ni okeru chūsei no hakken

to sono imi" (The discovery of the Middle Ages in Japanese history and its significance), *Sōbun*, no. 93 (February 1971).

7. Again, Hara Katsurō went the furthest in this direction in *Nihon chūseishi*. See
also Katsourō Hara, *Histoire du Japon des origines à nos jours* (History of Japan
from its origins to the present) (Paris: Payot, 1926). This author described the
Kamakura period as a "resurrection of Japan," as did Tsuda Sōkichi in the 1920s.
In his history of Japanese literature, Katō Shū'ichi defended fairly similar
theories.

8. Uchida Ginzō, *Nihon kinseishi* (History of modern Japan) (1903); Fukuda
Tokuzō, *Nihon keizaishi ron* (Essay on the economic history of Japan) (1907).
See also Hattori Yukifusa, *Zettaishugi ron* (Essay on absolutism) (1948). On these
problems, see Nagahara Keiji, *Rekishigaku josetsu* (Interpretations of history)
(Tokyo: Tōkyō daigaku shuppankai, 1978).

9. This is the theory that underlies, for example, the 1938 work by the sociologist
Nakamura Kichiji, *Kinsei shoki nōseishi kenkyū* (Studies of agrarian policies at
the beginning of the modern period), which he addresses again in part in *Buke
no rekishi* (History of the warriors) (Tokyo: Iwanami shinsho, 1967). See also
Amino Yoshihiko, "Le Moyen Âge japonaise et quelques questions qu'il pose aux
historiens aujourd'hui" (The Japanese Middle Ages and some questions it poses
to today's historians), *Cipango, Cahiers d'histoire japonaise*, no. 3 (November
1994): 125–58.

10. On this issue, see in particular Fujiki Hisashi, *Sengoku no sahō: Mura no funsō
kaiketsu* (Constructing the law in the Sengoku era: How regional fights between
villages were resolved) (Tokyo: Heibonsha, 1987). In French, see Fujiki Hisashi,
"Le village et son seigneur (XIVᵉ–XVIᵉ siècles)" (The village and its lord
[fourteenth–sixteenth centuries]), *Annales (Histoire, Sciences Sociales)*, no. 2
(March–April 1995): 395–419.

11. Miura Hiroyuki was the first Japanese historian to draw attention to these social
conflicts, in a course he gave at Osaka University in 1919–20. See Miura Hiroyuki, *Kokushi no shakai mondai* (Social problems in Japanese history) (Tokyo:
Iwanami bunko, 1990).

12. Imatani Akira, *Biwako to Yodo no suikei* (Lake Biwa and the Yodo River basin),
in *Asahi hyakka Nihon no rekishi*, vol. 20 (Tokyo, 1987), p. 258.

13. Excerpt from the missionaries' report on Japan addressed to the Brothers of the
Society of Jesus in India, by Gaspar Vilela, dated August 1561 (*Caras que os padres
e irmaos de la Companhia de Iesus escreuerao dos Reynos de Japao & China aos da
mesma Companhia da India & Europa, des do anno de 1549 ate o de 1580*), often
cited by contemporary Japanese historians. See, for example, Hani Gorō, *Nihon
jinmin no rekishi* (History of the Japanese people) (Tokyo: Iwanami shinsho, 1974),
p. 44; Takao Kazuhiko, "Kyoto, Sakai, Hakata," in *Iwanami kōza Nihon rekishi*, 9,
Kinsei 1 (Tokyo: Iwanami shoten, 1963), p. 127; Hayashiya Tatsusaburō, *Tenka ittō
(Unification of the empire)*, vol. 12 of *Nihon no rekishi* (Tokyo: Chūkō bunko,
1974), pp. 52–53. See, more recently, Wakita Haruko, "Fêtes et communautés
urbaines dans le Japon médiéval: La Fête de Gion à Kyōto" (Festivals and urban
communities in medieval Japan: The Gion festival in Kyoto), *Annales (Histoire,
Sciences Sociales)*, no. 5 (September–October 1997): 1039.

14. This was particularly true in prewar history textbooks, in which the Middle Ages was often described as a period of decadence and the usurpation of power. See Pierre F. Souyri, "Aux racines du consensus: L'Écriture de l'histoire au Japon" (At the roots of consensus: The writing of history in Japan), in Alain Touraine et al., eds., *Japon, le consensus: Mythe et réalités* (Japan, the consensus: Myth and reality) (Paris: Economica, 1984), pp. 67–90.

15. Amino Yoshihiko, Ishii Susumu, and Fukuda Toyohiko, *Chinmoku no chūsei* (The silences of the Middle Ages) (Tokyo: Heibonsha, 1990), esp. ch. 3, "Tetsu: Gijutsu, henreki, higashi to nishi" (Iron: Techniques, travels, east and west).

16. See, for example, Hayashiya, *Tenka ittō*, pp. 16 et seq.

17. On modifications in military strategy as a consequence of the arrival of the Portuguese, see Fujiki Hisashi, ed., *Asahi hyakka rekishi o yominaosu* (Rereading the Asahi encyclopedia of history), vol. 15: *Shiro to kassen: Nagashino no tatakai to Shimabara no ran* (Castles and battles: From the battle of Nagashino to the Shimabara revolt) (Tokyo, 1993). On the battle of Nagashino, see Fujimoto Masayuki, "Nagahino no tatakai," in Fujiki, ed., *Asahi hyakka*, pp. 18–31. See also Abe Takeshi, *Rekishi no mikata, kangaekata* (Visions and analyses of history) (Tokyo: Tōkyōdō shuppan, 1996), pp. 7–12. Abe Takeshi questions this hypothesis by showing that the Takeda also had regiments of harquebusiers and an infantry. Filmmaker Kurosawa Akira made a (perhaps fictional) portrayal of this battle in his movie *Kagemusha*.

18. Sanjay Subrahmanyam, *The Portuguese Empire in Asia 1500–1700: A Political and Economic History* (London: Longman, 1993).

19. See Hiroyuki Ninomiya, "L'Époque moderne" (The modern era), in Francine Hérail, ed., *Histoire du Japon* (Le Coteau: Horvath, 1990).

20. There are a number of introductions to Japanese medieval paleography. See, for example, Satō Shin'ichi, *Shimpan: Komonjogaku nyūmon* (Revised introduction to paleography) (Tokyo: Hōsei daigaku shuppankyoku, 1997). The historical encyclopedia *Asahi hyakka Nihon no rekishi* was published in 1989 in the Rekishi no yomikata series, no. 5, with a section edited by Satō Shin'ichi entitled "Bunken shiryō o yomu: Chūsei" (Reading the historical archives: The Middle Ages). See also Ishii Susumu, *Chūsei o yomitoku: Komonjo nyūmon* (Reading and explaining the Middle Ages: Introduction to the ancient archives) (Tokyo: Tōkyō daigaku shuppankai, 1990).

21. There are English translations: Delmer M. Brown and Ishida Ichirō, *The Future and the Past: A Translation and Study of the* Gukanshō, *an Interpretative History of Japan Written in 1219* (Berkeley and Los Angeles: University of California Press, 1979); H. Paul Varley, trans., *A Chronicle of Gods and Sovereigns Jinnō Shōtoki of Kitabatake Chikafusa* (New York: Columbia University Press, 1980).

22. Takeuchi Rizō, *Kamakura ibun* (Tokyo: Tōkyōdō shoten, 1971–90).

23. Satō Shin'ichi and Ikeuchi Yoshisuke, eds., *Chūsei hōsei shiryōshū*, 3 vols. (Tokyo: Iwanami shoten, 1955–65). The collection *Nihon shisō taikei*, published by Iwanami shoten in the postwar period, comprises sixty-seven volumes, many of which deal with medieval society. In English, see Jeffrey P. Mass, *The Kamakura Bakufu: A Study in Documents* (Stanford, Calif.: Stanford University Press, 1976), which gives a list of written sources for the Kamakura period.

24. French readers can refer to poetry anthologies such as that by Karl Petit, *La Poésie japonaise: Anthologie des origines à nos jours* (Paris: Seghers, 1959); and G. Renondeau, ed., *Anthologie de la poésie japonaise classique* (Paris: Gallimard, 1971). On medieval poetry, see the excellent study by Jacqueline Pigeot, *Michiyuki bun: Poétique de l'itinéraire dans la littérature du Japon ancien* (*Michiyuki bun:* Travel poetry in the literature of ancient Japan) (Paris: Maisonneuve & Larose, 1982).

25. René Sieffert translated some of these into French: *Le Dit de Hōgen, Le Dit de Heiji* (The tale of the Hōgen, The tale of the Heiji) (Paris: Publications orientalistes de France, 1976); *Le Dit des Heiké* (The tale of the Heike) (Paris: Publications orientalistes de France, 1978). In English, see Helen C. McCullough, trans., *The Tale of the Heike* (Stanford, Calif.: Stanford University Press, 1988).

26. The translations into French are Yoshida Kenkō, *Les Heures oisives,* trans. C. Grosbois and T. Yoshida (Paris: Gallimard/UNESCO, 1968); Ichien Mujū, *Collection de sable et de pierres: Shasekishū,* trans. H.-O. Rotermund (Paris: Gallimard/UNESCO, 1979). In English, see Donald Keene, trans., *Essays in Idleness: The Tsurezuregusa of Kenkō* (New York: Columbia University Press, 1998); Robert Morrell, *Sand and Pebbles* (*Shasekishu, the Tales of Mujū Ichien, a Voice for Pluralism in Kamakura Buddhism*) (Albany: State University of New York Press, 1985).

27. See, for example, in French, Dōgen, *La Vision immédiate: Nature, éveil et tradition selon le Shōbōgenzō* (The immediate vision: Nature, enlightenment, and tradition according to the *Shōbōgenzō*), trans. and commentary by Bernard Faure (Paris: Éditions Le Mail, 1987). In English, see Thomas Cleary, trans., *Shōbōgenzō: Zen Essays by Dōgen* (Honolulu: University of Hawaii Press, 1992).

28. Kamo no Chōmei, "Notes de ma cabane de moine," trans. R. P. Sauveur Candau, in Yoshida Kenkō, *Les Heures oisives.* In English, see "Kamo no Chōmei: 'An Account of My Hut,'" in Donald Keene, ed., *Anthology of Japanese Literature: From the Earliest Era to the Mid-Nineteenth Century* (New York: Grove Press, 1999), pp. 197–212. *Towazugatari* is available in English as *Lady Nijō's Own Story: The Candid Diary of a Thirteenth-Century Japanese Imperial Concubine,* trans. W. Whitehouse and E. Yanagisawa (Tokyo: Tuttle, 1974).

29. Some of these works have been translated into French: Zeami, *La Tradition secrète du nō* (The secret tradition of nō), followed by *Une journée de nō* (A day of nō), trans. and commentary by René Sieffert (Paris: Gallimard/UNESCO, 1960); Zeami et al., *La Lande des mortifications: Vingt-cinq pièces de nō* (The land of mortifications: Twenty-five nō plays), trans. from the Japanese with an introduction and annotations by Armen Godel and Koichi Kano. (Paris: Gallimard, 1994). There is also a study by Sakaé Giroux, *Zéami et ses entretiens sur le nō* (Zeami and his discussions on nō) (Paris: Publications orientalistes de France, 1991). In English, see J. Thomas Rimer and Yamazaki Masakazu, *On the Art of the Nō Drama: The Major Treatises of Zeami* (Princeton, N.J.: Princeton University Press, 1983).

30. Brief descriptions of the stele are given, for example, by Sasaki Ginya, *Muromachi bakufu,* vol. 13 of *Nihon no rekishi* (Tokyo: Shogakkan, 1974), pp. 186–87. See also Irumada Nobuo, *Chūsei kokka to ikki* (The medieval state and revolts), in

Ikki, vol. 5 (Tokyo: Tōkyō daigaku shuppankai, 1981), p. 149; and Wakita Haruko, *Muromachi jidai* (The Muromachi period) (Tokyo: Chūkōshinsho, 1985), p. 100. There are also some steles in Kanto in memory of the warrior families who erected them. See Ishii Susumu, *Chūsei bushidan* (Warrior organizations) (Tokyo: Shogakkan, 1990), pp. 228–51. On estate steles, see Suitō Makoto, "Kinsekikubun" (Inscriptions), in *Kōza Nihon shōen shi* (Series on the history of Japanese estates), vol. 1: *Shōen nyūmon* (A primer on estates) (Tokyo: Yoshikawa kōbunkan, 1989), pp. 254–82.

31. See, for example, the series *Nihon no emaki* (Japanese scrolls) (Tokyo: Chūō kōronsha, 1980–90). See also, in the historical encyclopedia *Asahi hyakka Nihon no rekishi*, in the series *Rekishi no yomikata* (Readings in history), vol. 1, the section edited by Kuroda Hideo, "Egashiryō no yomikata" (Reading iconographic historical documents) (1988).

32. On this point of view, there are two exemplary studies: Kuroda Hideo, *Sugata to shigusa no chūseishi: Ezu to emaki no fūkei kara* (Attitudes and behaviors in medieval Japan: From images and illustrated scrolls) (Tokyo: Heibonsha, 1986); and Hotate Michihisa, *Chūsei no ai to jūzoku: Emaki no naka no nikutai* (Love and dependency in the Middle Ages: Flesh in painted scrolls) (Tokyo: Heibonsha, 1986).

33. Some reproductions can be found in Nicolas Fiévé, *L'Architecture et la ville du Japon ancien: Espace architectural de la ville de Kyōto et des résidences shōgunale aux XIVᵉ et XVᵉ siècles* (Architecture and the ancient Japanese city: The architectural space of Kyoto and shogunal residences in the fourteenth and fifteenth centuries) (Paris: Maisonneuve & Larose, 1996). On collections of estate charters, see, for example, Oyama Yasunori and Satō Kazuhiko, *Ezu ni miro shōen no sekai* (The world of estates according to maps) (Tokyo: Tōkyō daigaku shuppankai, 1987). See also Kuroda Hideo, "Shōen ezu no shiryōgaku" (The study of sources from estate maps and reproductions), in Amino Yoshihiko, Ishii Susumu, Inagaki Yasuhiko, and Nagahara Keiji, eds., *Kōza Nihon shōen shi*, 1, *Shōen nyūmon* (Series on the history of estates in Japan, vol. 1: Introduction to shōen) (Tokyo: Yoshikawa kōbunkan, 1989), pp. 148–86.

34. On medieval archaeology and the methodological problems it poses, see, for example, Ishii Susumu, "Chūsei to kōkogaku" (The Middle Ages and archaeology), pp. 3–33, in Ishii Susumu, ed., *Kita no chūsei: Shiseki seibi to rekishi kenkyū* (Northern Japan in the Middle Ages: Preservation of the heritage and historical research) (Tokyo: Nihon editaaru sukuuru shuppanbu, 1992). Sakuma Takashi discusses medieval archaeology and its contributions in "Hakkutsu sareta chūsei no mura to machi" (Excavations of medieval villages and towns), in *Iwanami kōza Nihon tsūshi* (History of Japan) (Tokyo: Iwanami shoten, 1994), vol. 9, *Chūsei* 3, pp. 175–206. See also, on urban archaeology, Kamakura Center for Archaeological Research, ed., "Kamakura kōkogaku kenkyūjo," in *Chūsei toshi Kamakura o horu* (Excavating Kamakura, a medieval town) (Tokyo: Nihon editaaru sukuuru shuppanbu, 1994).

35. Shibusawa Keizō studied the maritime communities that harvested salt and made their living from fishing, in *Shibusawa Keizō chosakushū* (Works by Shibusawa Keizō), 3 vols. (Tokyo: Heibonsha, 1992); Miyamoto Tsune'ichi studied

island populations in, for example, *Wasurareta Nihonjin* (The forgotten Japanese) (Tokyo: Iwanami shoten, 1984); Iwasaka Takeo researched the psychological states revealed by medieval tales in *Sanshō daiyū ko: Chūsei no sekkyō katari* (Administrator Sanshō: The telling of edifying tales in the Middle Ages) (Tokyo: Heibonsha, 1973). Gorai Shigeru looked at medieval popular Buddhism in, for example, *Odōri nenbutsu* (Invoking the Buddha Amida by dancing) (Tokyo: Heibonsha, 1988); and Inoue Toshio studied mountain populations, their way of life, and their beliefs in *Yama no tami, Kawa no tami: Nihon chūsei no seikatsu to shinkō* (Peoples of the mountains and rivers: Daily life and beliefs in medieval Japan) (Tokyo: Heibonsha, 1981). All these authors greatly advanced the work methods of medievalist historians.

36. A collection entitled *Nihon rekishi minzoku ronshū* (Anthology of essays relating to the history and ethno-folklore of Japan), edited by Amino Yoshihiko, Ishii Susumu, and Fukuda Ajio, was published in 1992 in ten volumes by Yoshikawa kōbunkan. See, in particular, the first volume, *Rekishigaku to minzokugaku* (History and ethnofolklore). For a study of medievalist Japanese historiography, see Amino Yoshihiko, "Le Moyen Age japonais." See also the introduction by Ninomiya Hiroyuki and Pierre F. Souyri to "L'Histoire du Japon sous le regard japonais" (The history of Japan in Japanese eyes), *Annales (Histoire, Sciences Sociales)*, special issue (March–April 1995): 227–33.

37. Amino Yoshihiko recently emphasized the fact that the designation of Yamato by the original Chinese term "Nippon" (Japan = Land of the Rising Sun), used by the imperial court starting in the late seventh century, placed the archipelago in a close relationship with China (the Rising Sun is the country east of the Middle Kingdom). He mischievously points out that nationalists did not shout from the rooftops the fact that the very name of their country was borrowed from the Chinese. See Amino Yoshihiko, *Nihonron no shiza: Rettō no shakai to kokka* (A look at theories on Japan: Society and state in the archipelago) (Tokyo: Shogakkan, 1990), pp. 5–20.

38. Relatively speaking, given Europe's population densities in the same period, Japan's population was already quite large. Even today, four-fifths of the territory is uninhabitable. In comparison, the population of the Korean kingdom of Choson in the thirteenth century would have been 2.1 million, an underestimated figure according to new research, which assesses the population of the kingdom of Koryŏ at 5.5 million when it was founded in 1392. See Yi Tae-jin, "The Influence of Neo Confucianism on 14th–16th century Korean Population Growth," *Korea Journal* 37, no. 2 (Summer 1997).

39. These demographic data are drawn from *Nihon rettō ni okeru bumpu no chōjiki keiretsu bunseki* (An analysis of population distribution in the Japanese archipelago) (Tokyo: Shakai kōgaku kenkyūjo, 1974); and Kitō Hiroshi, *Nihon nisennen no jinkōshi* (Two thousand years of history of the population of Japan) (Tokyo: PHP, 1983). Many historians feel that the demographic sources are not sufficient to advance such figures and remain skeptical of data that result from evaluations or even simple projections. Nevertheless, these numbers give a rough idea.

40. Ishii Susumu, *Kamakura bakufu*, pp. 27 et seq.

41. Keene, *Essays in Idleness*, p. 127.

42. See, for example, Amino Yoshihiko, *Higashi to nishi no kataru Nihon no rekishi* (East and west in the history of Japan) (Tokyo: Soshiete bunko, 1982); Oishi Naomasa, "Tōgoku, Tōhoku no jiritsu to 'Nihonkoku'" (The independence of the east and the northeast and "Japan") in *Nihon no shakaishi*, 1, *Rettō naigai no kōtsū to kokka* (Social history of Japan, vol. 1: Trade in the archipelago and the state) (Tokyo: Iwanami shoten, 1987).

43. On medieval roads and the world of travel, see Toda Yoshimi, *Rekishi to kodō* (History and the old roads) (Tokyo: Jinbun shoin, 1992); and Shinjō Tsunezō, *Kamakura jidai no kōtsū* (Communications in the Kamakura period) (Tokyo: Yoshikawa kōbunkan, 1996).

44. On these social classes, see, for example, *Kyōto burakushi kenkyūjo* (Kyoto: Kyoto Research Center for the History of Buraku), Yokoi Kiyoshi, ed., *Chūsei no minshū to geinō* (Folk art in the Middle Ages) (Tokyo: A'unsha, 1986). See also Miyachi Masato, "Geinō to geinōmin" (Art and artists), in *Nihon no shakaishi*, 2, *Kyōkai ryōiki to kōtsū* (Social history of Japan, vol. 2: Early territories and communications) (Tokyo: Iwanami shoten, 1987).

45. Quoted by Amino Yoshihiko, *Asahi hyakka Nihon no rekishi*, vol. 3, "Yūjo, kugutsu, shirabyō-shi" (Pleasure girls, puppeteers, and court dancers) (Tokyo, 1986), p. 70.

46. Amino Yoshihiko, *Nihon chūsei no hinōgyōmin to tennō* (Nonfarmers and the emperor in medieval Japan) (Tokyo: Iwanami shoten, 1984). See, by the same author, *Muen kūkai, raku: Nihon chūsei no jiyū to heiwa* (Absence of links, space without lord, and site of free trade: Freedom and peace in medieval Japan), rev. ed.) (Tokyo: Heibonsha, 1987).

47. In an exceptional show of faith, the emperor-monk Go Shirakawa (1127–92) made the pilgrimage from Kyoto to Kumano no fewer than thirty-four times.

48. Amino Yoshihiko, *Umi to rettō no chūsei* (The sea and the archipelago in the Middle Ages) (Tokyo: Nihon editaaru sukuuru shuppanbu, 1992).

49. See Pierre F. Souyri, "Une forme originale de domination coloniale? Les Japonais et le Hokkaidō avant l'époque Meiji" (An early form of colonial domination? Japan and Hokkaido before the Meiji period), in *De Russie et d'ailleurs: Feux croisés sur l'histoire, Mélanges pour Marc Ferro* (Of Russia and elsewhere: Highlight on history, Miscellanies for Marc Ferro), Institute of Slavic Studies, 1995, pp. 373–88. See also Kaiho Mineo, *Chūsei no Ezochi* (The land of Ezo in the Middle Ages) (Tokyo: Yoshikawa kōbunkan, 1987).

50. Hokama Shuzen, *Okinawa rekishi to bunka* (History and culture of Okinawa) (Tokyo: NHK shimin daigaku, 1984); Takara Kurayoshi, *Ryūkyū ōkoku* (The Ryukyu monarchy) (Tokyo: Iwanami shinsho, 1993).

51. On the period preceding the Middle Ages, see Ivan Morris, *The World of the Shining Prince: Court Life in Ancient Japan* (Tokyo: Kodansha International, 1994); Francine Hérail, *Fonctions et fonctionnaires au début du XIᵉ siècle* (Functions and functionaries in the early eleventh century), 2 vols. (Paris: Publications orientalistes de France, 1977); Francine Hérail, *La cour du Japon à l'époque de Heian aux Xᵉ et XIᵉ siècles* (The court of Japan from the Heian period to the tenth and eleventh centuries) (Paris: Hachette, 1995).

2. Social Dynamics in the Late Heian Period

1. On these questions, see G. Cameron Hurst III, *Insei: Abdicated Sovereigns in the Politics of Late Heian Japan, 1086–1185* (New York: Columbia University Press, 1976). For a more recent view, see Gomi Fumihiko, "Insei to tennō" (The regime of the retired emperors and the emperor), in *Iwanami kōza Nihon tsūshi*, 7, *Chūsei* 1 (Tokyo: Iwanami shoten, 1993), pp. 73–104.

2. See John W. Hall and Jeffrey P. Mass, eds., *Medieval Japan: Essays in Institutional History* (New Haven, Conn.: Yale University Press, 1974).

3. For this entire period, see an excellent analysis by Takeuchi Rizō, *Nihon no rekishi*, vol. 6: *Bushi to tōjō* (The warriors enter the scene) (Tokyo: Chūkōbunko, 1973).

4. In a very interesting book, Thomas Keirstead recently questioned the notion of the *"shōen* system." For Japanese historians, this expression refers to a system of real-estate ownership that started around 1000 or a little before (in the eighth century for "proto-*shōen*") and disappeared completely in the sixteenth century. This idea of a birth, development, culmination, then deterioration and disappearance of a land-use system, all in seven or eight centuries, seems to Keirstead to be an organicistic view of history, and in fact just a construct of historians. See Thomas Keirstead, *The Geography of Power in Medieval Japan* (Princeton, N.J.: Princeton: Princeton University Press, 1992).

5. There is a considerable literature in Japanese on the real-estate system and the rise of the warrior class. See, for example, Inagaki Yasuhiko, "Ritsuseiteki toshiseido no kaitai" (The dissolution of the real-estate system of the regime of codes), in Takeuchi Rizō, ed., *Toshiseidoshi* (History of real-estate systems) (Tokyo: Yamakawa shuppansha, 1973), vol. 1, pp. 139–72. Tabata Yasuko supplies some recent historiography in "Shōen kenkyūshi" (History of research on estates), in Amino Yoshihiko, Ishii Susumu, Inagaki Yasuhiko, and Nagahara Keiji, eds., *Kōza Nihon shōen shi*, 1, *Shōen nyūmon* (Series on the history of estates in Japan, vol. 1: Introduction to *shōen*) (Tokyo: Yoshikawa kōbunkan, 1989), pp. 312–84.

6. "Protect and develop the villages, encourage the cultivation of mulberry bushes and breeding of silkworms," according to the Shikiin rei (Edict regarding holders of responsibilities) in Ryōgige.

7. Takeuchi Rizō, *Heian ibun* (Tokyo: Tōkyōdō shoten, 1963–68), p. 334.

8. On these problems, see chapter 1 of the excellent book by Ishimoda Shō, *Chūseiteki sekai no keisei* (The forms of the medieval world) (1946; reprint, Tokyo: Iwanami bunko, 1985). See also Nagahara Keiji, *Nihon chūsei shakai to kokka* (Society and state in medieval Japan) (Tokyo: Aoki shoten, 1991), esp. pp. 40–68.

9. See Shimizu Mitsuo, *Nihon chūsei no sonraku* (Villages in medieval Japan) (1943; reprint, Tokyo: Iwanami bunko, 1996). See also, for example, Kimura Motoi, *Mura no kataru Nihon no rekishi kodai: Chūsei hen* (History of villages in Japan: Ancient and medieval periods) (Tokyo: Soshiete bunko, 1983), esp. pp. 133–89.

10. See Toyoda Takeshi, *Bushidan to sonraku* (Warrior organizations and villages) (Tokyo: Yoshikawa kōbunkan, 1994).

11. Shimizu Mitsuo, *Nihon chūsei no sonraku*.

12. Toyoda Takeshi, *Bushidan to sonraku*. See also Ishii Susumu, *Nihonshi no shakai shudan*, 3, *Bushidan* (Social organizations in the history of Japan, vol. 3: Warrior organizations) (Tokyo: Shogakkan, 1990).

13. The sequence of events is known essentially through the *Shōmonki* chronicle. A good analysis of this episode is found in Fukuda Toyohiko, *Taira Masakado no ran* (Tokyo: Iwanami shinsho, 1981). Anne Walthall underlines the importance of the veneration of Masakado in the peasant imagination of the eighteenth century in the context of the Sakura Sōgorō affair that took place in the region of Kanto where Masakado's revolt had occurred nine centuries earlier. See Anne Walthall, ed. and trans., *Peasant Uprisings in Japan: A Critical Anthology of Peasant Histories* (Chicago: University of Chicago Press, 1991).

14. On differences in the nature of these disturbances, see Amino Yoshihiko, *Higashi to nishi no kataru Nihon no rekishi*, pp. 87–98.

15. On these wars, the main source is *Mutsu waki*. For a good analysis, see Shōji Hiroshi, *Henkyō no sōran* (The wars on the borders) (Tokyo: Kyōikusha, 1977). On Minamoto no Yoshiie, see the article under his name in *Dictionnaire historique du Japon* (Historical dictionary of Japan), sec. 14 (Tokyo: Publications de la maison franco-japonaise, 1988).

16. It has been posited that this change corresponded to a change in family relations in the Heian aristocracy. Until then, the children had been raised in the mother's family; the mother lived with her father, and her children were thus under the control of their maternal grandfather. Now, the wife was forced to live with her husband, and her children were raised in their father's house. This change in custom (of unknown origin) strengthened the imperial household to the detriment of the Fujiwara's external family relations. On this subject, see Simone Mauclaire, "La Construction du rôle du père à l'apogée de l'aristocratie de cour de Heian (xᵉ–xiᵉ siècles)" (Construction of the father's role at the culmination of the aristocracy of the Heian court [tenth–eleventh centuries]), *L'Homme* 36, no. 140: 26–61.

17. *Chūyuki*, Kanji 4 (1090), 1st lunar month, 16th day.

18. On the internal organization of monasteries, see Hisano Nobuyoshi, "Chūsei ji'in no sōryo shudan" (Monastic organizations in the Middle Ages) in *Nihon no shakai shi*, 6, *Shakaiteki shoshūdan* (History of Japanese society, vol. 6: Social organizations) (Tokyo: Iwanami shoten, 1988), esp. pp. 241 et seq.

19. See, for example, Hayashiya Tatsusaburō, in *Iwanami kōza Nihon no rekishi*, 5, *Chūsei* 1 (History of Japan, vol. 5: The Middle Ages, vol. 1) (Tokyo: Iwanami shoten, 1963), pp. 10 et seq. On the relations between the Taira and the retired emperors, see Takeuchi Rizō, *Bushi to tōjō*, pp. 57–85.

20. Ishimoda Shō, *Chūseiteki sekai no keisei* (The formation of the medieval world) (1946; reprint, Tokyo: Iwanami shoten, 1985), p. 338.

3. The Crisis in the Late Twelfth Century

1. Helen Craig McCullough, trans., *The Tale of the Heike* (Stanford, Calif.: Stanford University Press, 1988), p. 28.

2. Amino Yoshihiko, *Higashi to nishi o kataru Nihon no rekishi* (East and west in the history of Japan) (Tokyo: Soshiete bunko, 1982). Ishii Susumu, "Jūni Jūsan seiki no Nihon, kodai kara chūsei e" (Japan in the twelfth and thirteenth centuries, from the ancient period to the Middle Ages), in *Iwanami kōza Nihon tsūshi*, 7, *Chūsei* 1 (Tokyo: Iwanami shoten, 1993), pp. 44 et seq., shows the importance of maritime trade in the Inland Sea and the growing influence of the community of Chinese merchants in Hakata in the late twelfth century.

3. Ishii Susumu, *Kamakura bakufu*, vol. 7 of *Nihon no rekishi* (Tokyo: Chūō koron, 1974), p. 59.

4. Sieffert, *Dit des Heiké*, p. 236 (trans.).

5. Ibid., p. 244 (trans.).

6. McCullough, *Tale of the Heike*, pp 437–38.

7. See the study by climatologist Arakawa Hidetoshi, *Kikin no rekishi* (History of famines) (Tokyo: Shibundō, 1967).

8. My trans. On this episode, see Kawane Yoshiyasu, *Chūsei hōken shakai no shuto to nōson* (The capital and villages in medieval feudal society) (Tokyo: Tōkyō daigaku shuppankai, 1984), esp. ch. 3, pp. 55–123.

9. See Amino Yoshihiko, *Mōko shūrai* (The Mongol invasions) (Tokyo: Shogakkan, 1974), pp. 16–17.

10. Ibid., pp. 19 et seq.

11. Donald Keene, ed. and trans., "Kamo no Chōmei: An Account of My Hut," in Donald Keene, ed., *Anthology of Japanese Literature from the Earliest Era to the Mid-Nineteenth Century* (New York: Grove Press, 1999), pp. 201–2.

12. Ibid., pp. 202–3.

13. McCullough, *Tale of the Heike*, p. 282.

14. *Azuma kagami* (The mirror of Azuma), quoted in Nakamura Kichiji, *Buke no rekishi* (Tokyo: Iwanami shinsho, 1967), pp. 58–59 (trans.).

15. McCullough, *Tale of the Heike*, pp. 188–90.

16. On feudal manors in the early Middle Ages, see, for example, Gomi Fumihiko, "Chūsei no yakata to toshi, Mikuro no kūkan kara" (Medieval manors and towns: Spaces and microcosm), in *Asahi hyakka, Rekishi o yominaosu*, vol. 7 (Tokyo, 1994). In English, see Ishii Susumu, "The Formation of Bushi Bands," *Acta Asiatica* 49 (special issue, *Studies on Bushi [Samurai]*) (1985).

17. Nakada Kaoru, *Chigyōron* (On the fiefdom) (1907), in *Shōen no kenkyū* (Research on the *shōen*) (Tokyo: Shōkōshoin, 1948). See also Toyoda Takeshi, *Bushidan to sonraku* (Tokyo: Yoshikawa kōbunkan, 1994), pp. 133 et seq.

18. Ishii Susumu, *Kamakura bushi no jitsuzō* (Portraits of the Kamakura warriors) (Tokyo: Heibonsha, 1987), pp. 342–43.

19. Ishii Susumu, *Kamakura bakufu*, pp. 43–44.

20. *Heike monogatari*, quoted by Tanaka Minoru, "Insei to Jijō-Juei no ran" (The regime of the retired emperors and the wars of 1180–85), in *Iwanami kōza Nihon no rekishi*, 4, *Kodai* 4 (Tokyo: Iwanami shoten, 1976), p. 209 (trans.).

21. "[Yoritomo], reduced . . . to seven or eight riders . . . fled to Sugiyama in the Toi region after a desperate stand." McCullough, *Tale of the Heike*, p. 173.

22. Ishii Susumu, *Kamakura bakufu*, pp. 62–63.

23. Kasamatsu Hiroshi, "Chūsei no ando" (Confirmation of land in the Middle Ages), in *Nihon no shakai shi*, 4, *Futan to zōyo* (History of Japanese society, vol. 4: Responsibilities and donations) (Tokyo: Iwanami shoten, 1986).

24. Anecdote reported in the *Gyokuyō*, quoted in Ishii Susumu, *Kamakura bakufu*, p. 82 (trans.).

25. Anecdote reported in *Azuma kagami*, quoted in ibid., p. 144 (trans.).

26. McCullough, *Tale of the Heike*, pp. 306–7.

27. Paul Varley, *Warriors of Japan as Portrayed in the War Tales* (Honolulu: University of Hawaii Press, 1994), pp. 93 et seq.

28. In the original expression, *ikkasho no shoryō ni inochi o kakete*, *sho* was written using the character for *tokoro* (place). But in modern Japanese, in the expression *isshōkenmei*, *sho* is written using the character for *sei*, "life," meaning "desperately." (That is, both characters, though different, can be read *sho*.) See Ishii Susumu, *Kamakura bakufu*, pp. 146 et seq.

29. At least this is the thesis by Amino Yoshihiko in *Higashi to nishi no kataru Nihon no rekishi*.

30. *Gukanshō* 6, quoted by Tanaka Minoru in *Iwanami kōza Nihon no rekishi*, 4, *Kodai* 4, p. 214 (trans.).

31. McCullough, *Tale of the Heike*, p. 282.

32. *Gyokuyō*, Juei 2, 10th month, 22d day (trans.). See also *Hyakurenshō*, Juei 2, 10th month, 14th day. Satō Shin'ichi attaches much importance to this edict and discusses its interpretations in *Nihon no chūsei kokka* (The Japanese medieval state) (Tokyo: Iwanami shoten, 1983), pp. 75 et seq.

33. Satō Shin'ichi, *Nihon no chūsei kokka*, pp. 76–77.

34. *Gyokuyō*, Juei 3, 2d month, 23d day.

35. *Azuma kagami*, Genryaku 1, 8th month, 24th day; 10th month, 20th day.

36. *Azuma kagami*, Bunji 1, 11th month, 22d day.

4. Kamakura: The Warrior Regime

1. A good summary of the political rise of the Hōjō in the early thirteenth century can be found in Yasuda Motohisa, *Kamakura shikken seiji: Sono tenkai to kōzō* (The policy of the Kamakura regents: Its evolution and constants) (Tokyo: Kyōikusha, 1979), pp. 23–86.

2. Ishii Susumu, *Kamakura bushi no jitsuzo* (Portraits of Kamakura warriors) (Tokyo: Heibonsha, 1987), p. 192.

3. Kawazoe Shōji, *Kamakura bunka* (The Kamakura culture) (Tokyo: Kyōikusha, 1978), pp. 65–93.

4. Gaston Renondeau, *Anthologie de la poésie japonaise classique* (Anthology of classic Japanese poetry) (Paris: Gallimard/UNESCO, 1971), p. 181 (trans.).

5. *Kinkai wakashū*, vol. 3 (trans.).

6. Helen Craig McCullough, trans., *The Tale of the Heike* (Stanford, Calif.: Stanford University Press, 1988), p. 23.

7. Renondeau, *Anthologie*, p. 184 (trans.).

8. Kuroda Toshio, "Chūsei no kokka no tennō" (The state and the emperor in the Middle Ages), in *Iwanami kōza Nihon no rekishi*, 6, *Chūsei* 2 (Tokyo: Iwanami shoten, 1963), pp. 263–301. For a discussion of this concept, see Uwayokote Masa-taka, "Kamakura Muromachi bakufu to chōtei" (The Kamakura and Muromachi bakufu and the imperial court), in *Iwanami kōza Nihon no shakai shi*, 3, *Ken'i to shihai* (History of Japanese society, vol. 3: Prestige and domination) (Tokyo: Iwanami shoten, 1987), pp. 84–93.

9. Uwayokote Masataka, "Jōkyū no ran" (The Jōkyū war), in *Iwanami kōza Nihon no rekishi*, 5, *Chūsei* 2 (Tokyo: Iwanami shoten, 1963), pp. 165 et seq. See also Jeffrey P. Mass, "The Kamakura Bakufu," in Kozo Yamamura, ed., *The Cambridge History of Japan*, vol. 3: *Medieval Japan* (Cambridge: Cambridge University Press, 1990), pp. 46–88.

10. More precisely, it was the rights (*shiki*) to the estates that were confiscated.

11. The law of primogeniture did not exist in the imperial dynasty at this time. Emperors had a number of wives and official concubines. The designation of a crown prince was always the subject of bitter debate among pressure groups that were constantly forming and re-forming. In the late eleventh century, the retired emperors were more or less novices at imposing their point of view on the question of succession. After 1221, the factions in the court shifted to try to control the imperial succession, and Kamakura tried hard to stick to its game plan.

12. On Shigetoki, see Carl Steenstrup, *Hōjō Shigetoki (1198–1261) and His Role in the History of Political and Ethical Ideas in Japan* (London: Curzon Press, 1979).

13. Uwayokote Masataka, "Kamakura bakufu to kuge seiken" (The Kamakura bakufu and the power of the court aristocracy), in *Iwanami kōza Nihon no rekishi*, 5, *Chūsei* 1 (Tokyo: Iwanami shoten, 1975), pp. 35–77. Cf. Amino Yoshihiko, *Mokō Shūrai* (Tokyo: Shogakkan, 1974), pp. 32–60; Andrew Goble, "The Kamakura Bakufu and Its Officials," in Jeffrey P. Mass and William B. Hauser, eds., *The Bakufu in Japanese History* (Stanford, Calif.: Stanford University Press, 1985).

14. See Yasuda Motohisa, "History of the Studies of the Formation of the Japanese Hōken System," *Acta Asiatica* 8 (1965): 74–100.

15. Jeffrey P. Mass, *Warrior Government in Early Medieval Japan: A Study of the Kamakura Bakufu, Shugo and Jitō* (New Haven, Conn.: Yale University Press, 1974), pp. 203 et seq.

16. Ibid., pp. 171 et seq. See also Gomi Fumihiko, "Shugo-jitō sei to tenkai to bushi-dan" (Development of the system of *shugo* and *jitō*, and warrior organizations), in *Iwanami kōza Nihon rekishi*, 5, *Chūsei* 1 (Tokyo: Iwanami shoten, 1975), pp. 79–120; Irumada Nobuo, "Shugo-Jitō to ryōshusei" (*Shugo, jitō*, and the feudal system), in *Kōza Nihon rekishi*, 3, *Chūsei* 1 (Tokyo: Tōkyō daigaku shuppan-kai, 1984), pp. 85–126.

17. Ishii Susumu, *Kamakura bakufu*, vol. 7 of *Nihon no rekishi* (Tokyo: Chūō koron, 1974), pp. 382 et seq.

18. Abe Takeshi, in *Nihon shōen shi* (History of Japanese estates) (Tokyo: Shinseisha, 1972), pp. 290 et seq., makes a detailed study of the Ōyama estate in this context.

19. See the Jōō Edict, Jōō 2, 6th month, 15th day. Cf. Ishii Susumu, *Kamakura bushi no jitsuzō*, pp. 340–41.
20. Abe Takeshi, *Nihon shōen shi*, pp. 297–98.
21. Letter from Yasutoki to Shigetoki, Jōen 1, 8th month, 8th day.
22. Katsumata Shizuo, *Ikki* (Tokyo: Iwanami shinsho, 1982), pp. 7–12.
23. Goseibai shikimoku, article 13 (trans.).
24. Ibid., article 34.
25. "Parents, to preserve the love of their children, must consider girls and boys on the same footing with regard to the succession of land." Goseibai shikimoku, article 18 (trans.).
26. Nitta Iwamatsu *monjo*, cited by Jeffrey P. Mass, *The Kamakura Bakufu: A Study in Documents* (Stanford, Calif.: Stanford University Press, 1976), p. 48.
27. Unpublished manuscript, sent to me by Satō Kazuhiko (trans.).
28. Goseibai shikimoku, article 21.
29. Ibid., article 34.
30. Archives of Mount Kōya: Kōyasan *monjo*, 6, Kenji 1, 10th month, 28th day.
31. On the Goseibai shikimoku, see the commentaries by Kasamatsu Hiroshi in *Nihon shisōtaikei*, 21, *Chūsei seiji shakai shisō, jō* (1972), pp. 479–85, and esp. Ishimoda Shō, pp. 565–88. See also Kasamatsu Hiroshi, *Nihon chūsei hōshi ron* (Essays on the history of medieval Japanese law) (Tokyo: Tōkyō daigaku shuppankai, 1979), pp. 25–50.
32. Haga Norihiko, "Ryōshu shihai to hō" (Feudal domination and the law), in *Iwanami kōza Nihon rekishi*, 5, *Chūsei* 1 (Tokyo: Iwanami shoten, 1975), pp. 169–210.
33. On these questions, see Kasamatsu Hiroshi and Katsumata Shizuo, "Tokusei rei: Chūsei no hō to saiban" (Edicts of moratoriums on debts: Law and courts in the Middle Ages) in *Shukan Asahi hyakka Nihon no rekishi* (The Asahi Weekly's encyclopedia of Japanese history), *Chūsei* 8 (Tokyo, 1986); Inaba Nobumichi, "Chūsei no soshō to saiban" (Trials and courts in the Middle Ages), in *Nihon no shakai shi* (History of Japanese society), vol. 5: *Saiban to kihan* (Courts and norms) (Tokyo: Iwanami shoten, 1987), pp. 245–82; Kasamatsu Hiroshi, ed., *Hō to soshō* (Law and trials) (Tokyo: Yoshikawa kōbunkan, 1992).
34. Mass, "The Kamakura Bakufu," pp. 83–87.
35. This affair was cited by Kuroda Toshio in *Mōko shūrai* (The Mongol invasions), vol. 8 of *Nihon no rekishi* (Tokyo: Chūkōbunko, 1974), pp. 294–95.
36. Ōyama Kyōhei, "Shōen sei" (The estate system), in *Iwanami kōza Nihon tsūshi*, vol. 7, *Chūsei* 1 (Tokyo: Iwanami shoten, 1993), pp. 161–77.
37. Amino Yoshihiko, *Chūsei shōen no yōsō* (Aspects of medieval estates) (Tokyo: Kakusensho, 1966), pp. 148 et seq.
38. Abe Takeshi, *Nihon shōen shi*, pp. 290–300.
39. Jeffrey P. Mass, "Jitō Land Possession in the 13th Century: The Case of Shitaji chūbun," in John Whitney Hall and Jeffrey P. Mass, eds., *Medieval Japan: Essays in Institutional History* (New Haven, Conn.: Yale University Press, 1974).
40. Amino Yoshihiko, *Mōko shūrai*, pp. 130–32.
41. Murai Shōsuke, "Jūsan jūyon seiki no Nihon, Kyōto—Kamakura" (Japan in the thirteenth and fourteenth centuries: Kyoto and Kamakura), in *Iwanami kōza Nihon tsūshi* 8, *Chūsei* 2 (Tokyo: Iwanami shoten, 1994), pp. 23–24.

42. Kasamatsu Hiroshi, *Tokusei rei: Chūsei no hō to kanshū* (The edicts of virtuous government: Laws and customs in the Middle Ages) (Tokyo: Iwanami shinsho, 1983), pp. 36 et seq.

5. Kamakura: A Society of Questions

1. Tsuda Sōkichi, *Bungaku ni arawaretaru waga kokumin shisō no kenkyū* (Research on Japanese thought as it was manifested in literature), vol. 3 (Tokyo: Iwanami bunko, 1977), pp. 17–26. Tsuda was taking up an idea expounded by Hara Katsurō.

2. Francine Hérail, *Fonctions et fonctionnaires japonais au début du XIe siècle* (Japanese functions and functionaries in the early eleventh century) (Paris: Publications orientalistes de France, 1977), 2 vols. See also Francine Hérail, *La cour du Japon à l'époque de Heian aux Xe et XIe siècles* (The court of Japan in the Heian period in the tenth and eleventh centuries) (Paris: Hachette, 1995).

3. Donald Keene, "Kamo no Chōmei: An Account of My Hut," in Donald Keene, ed. and trans., *Anthology of Japanese Literature from the Earliest Era to the Mid-Nineteenth Century* (New York: Grove Press, 1999).

4. Ibid., pp. 197–98.

5. Ibid., pp. 206, 211.

6. Ibid., p. 211.

7. Akamatsu Toshihide, "Kamakura bunka" (Kamakura culture), in *Iwanami kōza Nihon no rekishi, 5, Chūsei* 1 (Tokyo: Iwanami shoten, 1963), pp. 327–42. See also Ōsumi Kazuhiko, "Heike monogatari to Gukanshō," in *Asahi hyakka Nihon no rekishi,* 5 (Tokyo, 1986).

8. Ryūfuku Yoshitomo, "Tenkanki no kizoku ishiki" (Aristocratic consciousness in a period of change), in *Iwanami kōza Nihon tsūshi, 7, Chūsei* 1 (Tokyo: Iwanami shoten, 1993), esp. pp. 289–94.

9. Keene, "Kamo no Chōmei," p. 212.

10. Ōsumi Kazuo, "Kamakura bukkyō to sono kakushin undō" (The Buddhism of Kamakura and reform tendencies), in *Iwanami kōza Nihon no rekishi, 5, Chūsei* 1 (Tokyo: Iwanami shoten, 1975), pp. 211–49. See also Ōsumi Kazuo, "Buddhism in the Kamakura Period," in Kozo Yamamura, ed., *The Cambridge History of Japan* (Cambridge: Cambridge University Press, 1990), pp. 544–82.

11. See, for example, the painted scroll *Jigokuzōshi* (Notes on hell), in *Nihon no emaki* 7 (Tokyo: Chūō kōronsha, 1987). See also Takeshi Umehara, *La Philosophie japonaise des enfers* (The Japanese philosophy of hell) (Paris: Méridiens Klincksieck, 1990).

12. *Eiga monogatari,* ch. 30, Manju 4, 12th lunar month, 4th day, cited by Francine Hérail in *Notes journalières de Fujiwara no Michinaga ministre à la cour de Heian (995–1018)* (Daily notes by Fujiwara no Michinaga, minister to the court of Heian [995–1018]) (Geneva: Droz, 1987), p. 25.

13. Helen Craig McCullough, trans., *The Tale of the Heike* (Stanford, Calif.: Stanford University Press, 1988), pp. 428–29.

14. Ibid., pp. 334–35.

15. See *Hōnen shōnin eden* (Illustrated history of the holy man Hōnen), scroll 34, in *Zoku Nihon no emaki* 2 (Tokyo: Chūōkōronsha, 1990).

16. Taira Masayuki, "Chūsei shūkyō no shakai tenkai" (The social development of medieval religion), in *Kōza Nihon rekishi*, 3, *Chūsei* 1 (Tokyo: Tōkyō daigaku shuppankai, 1984), pp. 262 et seq.

17. Kawasaki Tsuneyuki, "Kamakura bukkyō" (The Buddhism of Kamakura), in *Iwanami kōza Nihon no rekishi*, 5, *Chūsei* 1 (Tokyo: Iwanami shoten, 1962), pp. 302 et seq.

18. On Ippen, see *Ippen shōnin eden* (Illustrated history of the holy man Ippen), *Nihon no emaki*, 20 (Tokyo: Chūōkōron, 1988); Ōhashi Shunnō, *Ippen to Jishū kyōdan* (Ippen and his followers in the Ji sect) (Tokyo: Kyōikusha, 1978); Gorai Shigeru, *Odori nembutsu* (Danced invocation of the Buddha Amida) (Tokyo: Heibonsha, 1988). See also Kuroda Hideo, *Asahi hyakka rekishi o yominaosu* 10, *Cūsei o tabi suru hitobito* (People who traveled in the Middle Ages) (Tokyo, 1993). In French, see Satō Kazuhiko, "Des gens étranges à l'allure insolite: Contestation et valeurs nouvelles dans le Japon médiéval" (Strange people of unusual demeanor: Contestations and new values in medieval Japan), *Annales* (*Histoire, Sciences Sociales*), no. 2 (March–April 1995): 307–40.

19. Taira Masayuki, "Kamakura bukkyōron" (Regarding the Buddhism of Kamakura), in *Iwanami kōza Nihon tsūshi*, 8, *Chūsei* 2 (Tokyo: Iwanami shoten, 1994), esp. pp. 257–301.

20. On Zen, see, for example, Yanagita Seizan, *Zen to Nihon bunka* (Zen and Japanese culture) (Tokyo: Kōdansha, 1985).

21. Quoted in Shuichi Kato, *Histoire de la littérature japonaise* (History of Japanese literature), vol. 1 (Paris: Fayard, 1985), p. 272.

22. See the works by Martin Collcutt, including "The Zen Monastery in Kamakura Society," in Jeffrey P. Mass, ed., *Court and Bakufu in Japan: Essays in Kamakura History* (New Haven, Conn.: Yale University Press, 1982); and "Zen and the Gozan," in *The Cambridge History of Japan*, vol. 3.

23. Ichien Mujū, *Collection de sable et de pierres: Shasekishū* (Collection of sand and stones: *Shasekishū*), trans. H.-O. Rotermund (Paris: Gallimard/UNESCO, 1979), vol. 10, pp. 68–69 (trans.).

24. Donald Keene, trans., *Essays in Idleness: The* Tsurezuregusa *of Kenkō* (New York: Columbia University Press, 1998), p. 36.

25. On the Heike, see René Sieffert's introduction to his translation *Dit des Heike* (Paris: Publications orientalistes de France, 1978), pp. 5–28. See also, for a critical history, Gomi Fumihiko, *Heike monogatari, shi to setsuwa* (Heike, story and tale) (Tokyo: Heibonsha, 1987). In English, see H. Paul Varley, *Warriors of Japan, as Portrayed in the War Tales* (Honolulu: University of Hawaii Press, 1994).

26. Amino Yoshihiko, "Kōshō to biin" (Speaking out loud and whispering), in Amino Yoshihiko, Kasamatsu Hiroshi, Katsumata Shizuo, and Satō Shin'ichi, eds., *Kotoba no bunkashi* (Cultural history of words), *Chūsei* 1 (1988), pp. 9–37.

27. Amino Yoshihiko, *Igyō no ōken* (The extravagant monarchy) (Tokyo: Heibonsha, 1986), pp. 81–93.

28. Yamamoto Kichisō, *Heike monogatari to Gukanshō*, in *Asahi hyakka Nihon no rekishi, Chūsei* 5 (Tokyo, 1986), pp. 154, 155.
29. On these aspects, see Sakurai Yoshirō, "Chūsei ni okeru hyōhaku to yūgei" (Wandering and entertainment arts in the Middle Ages), in *Iwanami kōza Nihon no rekishi*, 5, *Chūsei* 1 (Tokyo: Iwanami shoten, 1975), pp. 323–24.

6. Kamakura: A Society in Transformation

1. The general term is *shōen* (estate or manor). Lands cultivated to supply the imperial court or for offerings to gods were called *mikurya* and belonged to the Shinto shrines. Forests used for timber were called *soma*; truck gardens were called *sono*; and cultivated parts of the seashore were called *ura*.
2. In the postwar period, there was a fierce debate among Marxist-oriented historians: Matsumoto Shimpachirō argued that the civil wars of the fourteenth century corresponded to a "feudal revolution" that liberated the peasant classes from slavery. See Matsumoto Shimpachirō, *Chūsei shakai no kenkyū* (Studies of medieval society) (Tokyo, 1955), a collection of essays written after 1942. Araki Moriaki, in "Taikō kenchi no rekishiteki zentei" (The historical origins of the Hideyoshi cadastre), *Rekishigaku kenkyū*, no. 163–64 (Tokyo, 1953), contended that this liberation did not occur until the late sixteenth century. Other historians—the majority today—think the opposite, that slavery was not significant (in terms of share of production) by the beginning of the Middle Ages. The debate was started again in the 1980s, when Amino Yoshihiko wrote a book on the notions of freedom and dependence in medieval societies: *Muen, kūkai, raku, Nihon chūsei to jiyū to heiwa*, rev. ed. (Tokyo: Heibonsha, 1987).
3. Ishii Susumu's estimate in Abe Kin'ya, Amino Yoshihiko, Ishii Susumu, and Kabayama Kōichi, eds., *Chūsei no fūkei* (Medieval landscapes) (Tokyo: Chūkō-shinsho), vol. 1, p. 11.
4. This was the case, for example, in Iga; see Ishimoda Shō, *Chūsei teki sekai no keisei* (The formation of the medieval world) (Tokyo: Iwanami bunko, 1985).
5. Comments taken from Amino Yoshihiko, *Mōko shūrai* (Tokyo: Shogakkan, 1974), p. 76.
6. Abe Takeshi, *Nihon shōen shi* (Tokyo: Shinseisha, 1972), pp. 319 et seq.
7. On this question, see Fujiki Hisashi, "Le Village et son seigneur (14ᵉ–16ᵉ siècles)" (The village and its lord, [14th–16th century]), *Annales (Histoire, Sciences Sociales)* (March–April, 1995): 395–419.
8. *Shinpen tsuika*, Bun'ei 1, 4th lunar month, 26th day.
9. Song Huigyong, *Rōshōdō Nihon kōroku* (Account of a trip to Japan from Nosong-dang), 149, edition developed by Murai Shōsuke (Tokyo: Iwanami bunko, 1987), p. 144.
10. Satō Kazuhiko, *Nambokuchō nairan* (Japan in the era of the civil wars between the two courts) (Tokyo: Shogakkan, 1974), pp. 261 et seq.
11. *Collection de sable et de pierres* (Collection of sand and stones), translated from the Japanese, with a preface and annotations by Hartmut O. Rotermund. The anecdote here is not from Rotermund's work but was reported by Amino Yoshihiko, *Mōko shūrai*, p. 82.

12. Amino Yoshihiko, *Mōko shūrai*, p. 83.

13. Goseibai Shikimoku, article 41.

14. Amino Yoshihiko, *Mōko shūrai*, pp. 86–88.

15. This is Matsumoto Shimpachirō's point of view; see note 2 of this chapter.

16. Ishimoda Shō is among those who defended this point of view after the war in *Chūsei teki sekai no keisei*.

17. For the case of Ōyama, see Abe Takeshi, *Nihon shōen shi*, pp. 315, 318, 321.

18. To produce these texts, the peasants generally appealed to someone nearby who could write. Usually, a monk wrote out the documents as they were dictated by the peasants. On writing procedures in the Middle Ages, see Amino Yoshihiko, *Nihonron no shiza: Rettō no shakai to kokka* (A look at Japanologies: Society and the state in the archipelago) (Tokyo: Shogakkan, 1990), pp. 317–62.

19. Amino Yoshihiko, "Les Japonais et la mer" (The Japanese and the sea), *Annales (Histoire, Sciences Sociales)*, no. 2 (March–April 1995): 235–58.

20. The following was inspired by Amino Yoshihiko, *Nihon chūsei no hinōgyōmin to tennō* (Nonfarmers and the emperor in the Middle Ages) (Tokyo: Iwanami shoten, 1984).

21. Ibid., pp. 282–332.

22. Ibid., pp. 392 et seq., pp. 410–16.

23. Ibid., pp. 432 et seq.

24. On dancers and prostitutes in the Middle Ages, see in particular Amino Yoshihiko and Gotō Toshihiko, "Yūjo, kugustu, shirabyōshi" (Courtesans, puppeteers, dancers), in *Asahi hyakka Nihon no rekishi*, *Chūsei* 3 (1986).

25. Amino Yoshihiko, *Nihon chūsei no hinōgyōmin to tennō*, p. 231.

26. Cf. Amino Yoshihiko, *Chūsei no hinin to yūjo* (Pariahs and prostitutes in the Middle Ages) (Tokyo: Akeshi shoten, 1994), esp. pp. 215–24.

27. Amino Yoshihiko, *Nihon chūsei no hinōgyōmin to tennō*.

28. Amino Yoshihiko, *Mōko shūrai*, pp. 109–10. On *shuku*, see Sasamoto Shōji, "Ichi, shuku, machi," in *Iwanami kōza Nihon tsūshi*, 9, *Chūsei* 3, pp. 156–61.

29. On *chōri*, see Kuroda Hideo, *Kyōkai no chūsei, Shōchō no chūsei* (The Middle Ages of borders and symbols) (Tokyo: Tōkyō daigaku shuppankai, 1986), pp. 144 et seq.

30. Amino Yoshihiko, *Mōko shūrai*, pp. 111–12. Cf. Niunoya Tetsuichi, "Hinin, kawaramono, sanjo," in *Iwanami kōza Nihon tsūshi*, 8, *Chūsei* 2, pp. 220–26.

31. On leprosy, see Yokoi Kiyoshi, *Chūsei minshū no seikatsu bunka* (Popular culture in everyday life in the Middle Ages) (Tokyo: Tōkyō daigaku shuppankai, 1975), esp. pp. 298–317.

32. Wakita Haruko, "La discrimination dans le Japon médiéval: Division du travail et statuts sociaux" (Discrimination in medieval Japan: Division of labor and social status), *Cipango, Cahiers d'études japonaises*, no. 6 (Fall 1997): 9–40.

33. The text contains characters used incorrectly for their reading as homonyms, and *ateji* (invented characters). Cf. Amino Yoshihiko, *Mōko shūrai*, p. 112.

34. Yoshie Akio, "Éviter la souillure: Le Processus de civilisation dans le Japon ancien" (Avoiding impurity: The process of civilization in ancient Japan), *Annales (Histoire, Sciences Sociales)*, no. 2 (March-April 1995): 283–306.

35. Kuroda Hideo, "Seyoku to yuya" (Ablution, charity, bath establishment), in *Asahi hyakka Nihon no rekishi*, 7, *Kamakura bukkyō* (The Buddhism of Kama-

kura) (Tokyo, 1986), p. 220. Cf. Kuroda Hideo, *Kyōkai no chūsei, Shōchō no chū-sei*, pp. 244–49.

36. Takahashi Yasuo, *Kyōto chūsei toshishi kenkyū* (Research on the urban history of Kyoto in the Middle Ages) (Kyoto: Shibunkaku, 1983). See also Takahashi Yasuo, "Kyōchū kōsho: Oyake kara shi no kūkan e" (The kōsho in the capital: From public space to private space), in Gomi Fumihiko, ed., *Asahi hyakka, Rekishi o yominaosu, 7, Chūsei no tachi to toshi, mikuro no kūkan kara* (Manors and cities in the Middle Ages: From the viewpoint of microspaces) (Tokyo, 1994), pp. 46–51. In French, cf. Nicolas Fiévé, *L'Architecture et la ville du Japon ancien: Espace architectural de la ville de Kyōto et des résidences shōgunale aux XIVᵉ et XVᵉ siècles* (Architecture and the ancient Japanese city: The architectural space of Kyoto and shogunal residences in the fourteenth and fifteenth centuries) (Paris: Maisonneuve & Larose, 1996), pp. 106–8.

37. Amino Yoshihiko, *Mōko shūrai*, pp. 33–34.

38. Ishii Susumu, "Chūsei toshi toshite no Kamakura" (Kamakura, medieval city), in *Shinpen, Nihon shi kenkyū nyūmon* (Introduction to Japanese historical research, new edition) (Tokyo: Tōkyō daigaku shuppankai, 1982). See also Gomi Fumi-hiko, "Toshi no kūkan o yomu: Emaki no naka no toshi/Kamakura. Miyako" (Reading the urban space: The cities, Kyoto, Kamakura, through illustrated scrolls), in *Asahi hyakka, Rekishi o yominaosu, 7, Chūsei no tachi to toshi, mikuro no kūkan kara*, pp. 38–45.

7. The Second Middle Ages

1. Matsumoto Shimpachirō expresses this point of view in "Nambokuchō nairan no shozentei" (Premises of civil wars in the fourteenth century), *Rekishi hyōron*, no. 11 (1947); reprinted in Matsumoto Shimpachiro, *Chūsei shakai no kenkyū* (Studies of medieval society) (Tokyo, 1956).

2. Cf. "Nambokuchō no rekishi teki imi o megutte" (On the historical significance of the Southern and Northern Courts), a debate among Nagahara Keiji, Ōsumi Kazuo, and Yokoi Kiyoshi, *Rekishi kōron* 9 (1979): 10–35.

3. Donald Keene, trans., *Essays in Idleness: The Tsurezuregusa of Kenkō* (New York: Columbia University Press, 1998), p. 173.

4. *Hōryaku kanki*, cited in *Shiryō ni yoru Nihon no ayumi: Chūsei hen* (Japanese history by the source: The Middle Ages) (Tokyo: Yoshikawa kōbunkan, 1958), pp. 167–68.

5. This section is based on Kasamatsu Hiroshi, *Tokusei rei: Chūsei no hō to kanshū* (The edicts of virtuous government: Medieval law and customs) (Tokyo: Iwan-ami shinsho, 1983).

6. Kasamatsu Hiroshi, *Tokusei rei: Chūsei no hō to saiban* (The virtuous edicts: Law and courts in the Middle Ages), in *Asahi hyakka Nihon no rekishi*, 8, Tokyo, pp. 238–39.

7. This expression, like the practice that it describes, was evidently of Chinese origin.

8. Satō Kazuhiko, "Des gens étranges à l'allure insolite: Contestation et valeur nou-velles dans le Japon médiéval" (Unusual strangers: New dissent and values in medieval Japan), *Annales (Histoire, Sciences Sociales)*, no. 2 (March–April 1995): 307–40.

9. Amino Yoshihiko, *Igyō no ōken* (Tokyo: Heibonsha, 1986), pp. 8–28.

10. Satō Kazuhiko, "Des gens étranges," pp. 312 et seq. Cf. *Tōji monjo* (Tōji archives), 5, Bunei 2, 6th lunar month (1265).

11. Satō Kazuhiko, *Nambokuchō nairanshi ron* (Essays on the history of the civil war of the Southern and Northern Courts) (Tokyo: Tōkyō daigaku shuppankai, 1979), pp. 151–52. Cf. *Kōya san monjo* (Archives of Mount Kōya), 7, Shōō 4, 9th month (1291).

12. Koiizumi Yoshiaki, *Akutō* (Tokyo: Kyōikusha, 1981), pp. 81 et seq.

13. Satō Kazuhiko, "Des gens étranges," p. 311.

14. Amino Yoshihiko, *Igyō no ōken*, pp. 123–24. See also Satō Kazuhiko, *Jiyū rōseki. Gekokujō no seikai: Chūsei nairanki no gunzō* (Arbitrary violence, the world upside down: Popular figures in the era of the medieval civil war) (Tokyo: Shogakkan, 1985), pp. 143–58.

15. Amino Yoshihiko, *Igyō no ōken*, p. 120.

16. *Hyakurenshō*, Kajō 2, 5th lunar month, 23rd day (1107): "In the capital, people of humble birth are throwing stones at each other at every crossroads: deaths have been reported."

17. Yokoi Kiyoshi, *Akutō to tsubute: Warabe to asobi* (Bandits and stone throwing: Young street people and games), in *Asahi hyakka Nihon no rekishi*, 10, Tokyo, pp. 302–3.

18. Amino Yoshihiko, *Igyō no ōken*, p. 123.

19. Yokoi Kiyoshi, *Akutō to tsubute*, p. 302.

20. Amino Yoshihiko, *Igyō no ōken*, pp. 145–47.

21. Cf. *Ōuchi shi okitegaki* (Regulations of the Ōuchi family of lords) (1487), cited by Yokoi Kiyoshi, *Akutō to tsubute*, p. 303.

22. Yokoi Kiyoshi, *Akutō to tsubute*, p. 296.

23. See Pierre F. Souyri, "Être *basara* dans le Japon médiéval" (Being *basara* in medieval Japan), *Cipango, Cahiers d'études japonaises* (November 1994): 159–80; Satō Kazuhiko, "Des gens étranges," pp. 329–38.

24. See Hayashiya Tatsusaburō and Sasaki Dōyo, *Nambokuchō no nairan to "basara" no bi* (The civil wars of the fourteenth century and the beauty of the *basara*) (Tokyo: Heibonsha, 1995).

25. Amino Yoshihiko, *Igyō no ōken*, pp.168 et seq.

26. Cited (without attribution) in Amino Yoshihiko, *Igyō no ōken*, p. 182.

27. For the sequence of events, one of the main sources is still the *Taiheiki*. Cf. Satō Kazuhiko, *Nambokuchō nairan* (Domestic troubles during the period of the Southern and Northern Courts) (Tokyo: Shogakkan, 1974), pp. 26–37.

28. *Jinnō Shōtoki*, vol. 3, p. 130 (trans.).

29. Excerpt from *Nijōgawara no rakusho* (Graffiti of Second Avenue), *Kemmu ki, Nihon shisō taikai*, vol. 22 (Tokyo: Iwanami shoten, 1981), pp. 345–46 (trans.).

30. Letter of remonstrance addressed to the emperor by Kitabatake Akiie on the eve of his death, Engen 3, 5th lunar month, 15th day (1338). Cf. Satō Kazuhiko, *Nambokuchō nairan*, pp. 86–87 (trans.).

31. Quoted by Satō Kazuhiko, *Nanbokuchō nairan*, p. 54 (trans.).

32. The Rokuhara Palace was taken on the seventh day. Iehira was a member of the shogunal army charged with putting down the imperial uprising. He transferred

his allegiance to Takauji, and this document was the proof that he had been one of the new retainers from the very beginning. Unpublished manuscript, photocopy courtesy of Satō Kazuhiko (trans.).

33. According to the *Taiheiki*, a text often quoted by, for example, Satō Kazuhiko, *Nanbokuchō nairan*, pp. 135–36.
34. Ibid., p. 136 (trans.).
35. Satō Shin'ichi, *Nambokuchō no dōran* (The wars of the Southern and Northern Courts), *Nihon no rekishi*, vol. 9 (Tokyo: Chūkōbunko, 1974), p. 259. See also Kenneth Alan Grossberg, *Japan's Renaissance: The Politics of the Muromachi Bakufu* (Cambridge, Mass.: Harvard University Press, 1981), pp. 21–27.
36. Governor of Musashi (Musashi *no kami*) was Hosokawa Yoriyuki's official title. This unpublished text from the Historical Archives, the Shiryō hensanjo, was sent to me by Satō Kazuhiko (trans.).

8. Warriors, Pirates, Peasants, and Priests

1. An episode reported by Satō Shin'ichi, *Nanbokuchō no dōran*, *Nihon no rekishi*, vol. 9 (Tokyo: Chūkōbunko, 1974), pp. 322–23.
2. *Ebisu* was a pejorative term for the not fully Japanized populations of northeastern Japan in the ancient and medieval periods. Kitabatake Akiie crossed the country from north to south to Ise with his horsemen from the northeast. Cf. Satō Kazuhiko, *Nanbokuchō nairan* (Japan in the era of the civil wars between the two courts) (Tokyo: Shogakkan, 1974), p. 88.
3. Ibid., p. 90 (trans.).
4. Miyagawa Mitsuru, "From Shōen to Chigyō: Proprietary Lordship and the Structure of Local Power," in John Whitney Hall and Toyoda Takeshi, eds., *Japan in the Muromachi Age* (Berkeley and Los Angeles: University of California Press, 1977), pp. 89–105.
5. Katsumata Shizuo, "Ikki, ligues, conjurations et révoltes dans la société médiévale japonaise" (*Ikki*, leagues, conspiracies, and revolts in medieval Japanese society), *Annales (Histoire, Sciences Sociales)*, no. 2 (March–April 1995): 373–94. Cf. Katsumata Shizuo, *Ikki* (Tokyo: Iwanami shinsho, 1982), esp. pp. 60 et seq.
6. Minegishi Sumio, "Chūsei shakai to ikki" (Medieval society and the *ikki*), in Aoki Michio, ed., *Ikki shi nyūmon* (Introduction to the history of the *ikki*), in *Ikki*, vol. 1 (Tokyo: Tōkyō daigaku shuppankai, 1981), pp. 52 et seq.
7. Satō Kazuhiko, *Nambokuchō nairan*, p. 201.
8. Katsumata Shizuo, *Ikki*, pp. 68 et seq.
9. Satō Kazuhiko, *Nambokuchō nairan*, p. 204.
10. Ibid.
11. Amino Yoshihiko, *Nihon chūsei no hinōgyōmin to tennō* (Nonfarmers and the emperor in medieval Japan) (Tokyo: Iwanami shoten, 1984), pp. 253–59.
12. Tanaka Takeo, *Wakō: Umi no rekishi* (The *wakō*: History of the sea) (Tokyo: Kyōikusha, 1982), p. 15 (trans.).
13. Tanaka Takeo, "Wakō to Higashi Ajia kōtsūken" (The *wakō* and the trade zone in east Asia), in *Nihon no shakai shi*, 1, *Rettō naigai no kōtsū to kokka* (History of

Japanese society, vol. 1, Trade and the state inside and outside the archipelago) (Tokyo: Iwanami shoten, 1987), pp. 146–47.

14. Ibid.

15. Ibid.

16. Ibid., p. 151.

17. According to the *Seishū jitsuroku* (Chronicle of King Sejong), cited by Tanaka Takeo, "Wakō to Higashi Ajia kōtsūken," p. 149.

18. Miura Keiichi, *Chūsei minshū seikatsushi no kenkyū* (Research on the history of the daily life of the working classes in the Middle Ages) (Tokyo: Shibunkaku shuppan, 1981), pp. 57–69.

19. According to the *Wamyō ruijushō*, cultivated land in Japan totaled about 862,000 *chōbu* in the early tenth century. According to the *Shūgaishō*, the country had 946,000 *chōbu* in cultivation in the early fourteenth century. The increase in farmed area was thus marginal, given the probable increase in the population. Cf. Inagaki Yasuhiko, "Chūsei no nōgyō keiei to shūshu keitai" (Medieval agricultural operations and forms of taxation), in *Kōza Nihon no rekishi*, 6, *Chūsei* 2 (Tokyo: Iwanami shoten, 1975), p. 169.

20. Karl Wittfogel, *Le Despotisme oriental* (*Asian despotism*) (Paris: Éditions de minuit, 1964); Bernard-Philippe Groslier, "La Cité hydraulique angkorienne: Exploitation ou susexploitation du sol?" (The Angkorian irrigation system: Exploitation or overexploitation of the soil?), *Bulletin de l'École française d'extrême-orient* 66 (1979): 161–202.

21. Yields must be compared with those recorded in the codes of the ancient regime. At any rate, they were almost double the optimal yield for the eighth century. Cf. Sasaki Ginya, *Muromachi bakufu*, in *Nihon no rekishi*, vol. 13 (Tokyo: Shogakkan, 1974), p. 103.

22. Cited by Sasaki Ginya, *Muromachi bakufu*, p. 104.

23. *Ōshima Okitsushima jinja monjo*, Kōchō 2, 10th lunar month, 21st day.

24. *Ōshima Okitsushima jinja monjo*, Kōei 1, 2d lunar month.

25. Tōji hyakugō *monjo o*, 141), Ōei 34, 11th lunar month, 28th day; 12th lunar month, 3d day (trans.).

26. Cf. Satō Kazuhiko, "Sōshō ikki no kiban to tenkai: Harima no kuni, Yano no shō" (The ikki in the estates: Their bases and their growth through the example of the Yano estate in Harima), in Inagaki Yasuhiko, ed., *Shōen no sekai* (The world of the estate) (Tokyo: Tōkyō daigaku shuppankai, 1973), pp. 241–70.

27. Uejima Tamotsu estimated the male adult population of Kami Kuze at one hundred people. Cf. Uejima Tamotsu, "Kyōkō shōen no nōmin to shōke no ikki" (The peasants in an estate outside Kyoto and the estate revolts), in Inagaki Yasuhiko, *Shōen no seikai*, pp. 162–63.

28. *Tōji hyakugō monjo*, Eikyō 9, 10th lunar month, 1st day (trans.).

29. Satō Kazuhiko, "Sōshō ikki no kiban to tenkai," p. 254.

30. *Ōshima Okitsushima jinja monjo*, Eini 6, 6th lunar month, 4th day (trans.).

31. H. Paul Varley, *Imperial Restoration in Medieval Japan* (New York: Columbia University Press, 1971), pp. 95 et seq. The *Jinnō Shōtōki* was translated and published by Varley as *A Chronicle of Gods and Sovereigns: Jinnō Shōtoki of Kitabatake Chikafusa* (New York: Columbia University Press, 1980).

32. See Kasahara Kazuo, "Shinbukkyō kyōdan no hatten" (The rise of groups of followers of the new Buddhism), in *Iwanami kōza Nihon no rekishi* 7, *Chūsei* 3
(Tokyo: Iwanami shoten, 1963), pp. 255 et seq.

33. The Hōonkō celebration of Shinran's death was a sort of thanksgiving for the
kind deeds performed by the master.

34. Shinran's descendants assumed the position of *iemoto*, a legitimate family with
the hereditary responsibility for transmitting a teaching.

35. On all these issues, see Martin Collcutt, "Zen and the Gozan," in Kozo Yamamura, ed., *The Cambridge History of Japan*, vol. 3: *Medieval Japan* (Cambridge:
Cambridge University Press, 1990), pp. 583–652. See also Tamamura Takeji,
"Zenshu no hatten" (Development of Zen sects), in *Iwanami kōza Nihon no rekishi*, 7, *Chūsei* 3 (Tokyo: Iwanami shoten, 1963), pp. 262–302.

36. See *Poèmes du Zen des Cinq-Montagnes*, translated from the Chinese and annotated by Alain-Louis Colas (Paris: Maisonneuve & Larose, 1991). In English, see
David Pollack, *Zen Poems of the Five Mountains* (Decatur, Ga.: Scholars Press,
1985).

9. *The Splendor and Misery of the Muromachi Century: The Culmination of the Ashikaga and the Development of Trade*

1. Cf. Hattori Shisō, *Zettaishugi ron* (Essay on absolutism) (Tokyo, 1948).

2. Sasaki Ginya, *Muromachi bakufu*, vol. 13 of *Nihon no rekishi* (Tokyo: Shogakkan,
1974), pp. 27–28.

3. Ibid., p. 67.

4. Ibid., pp. 77–78.

5. *Kanmon gyoki*, Kakitsu 1, 6th lunar month, 24th and 25th days.

6. Cf. Tanaka Takeo, "Umi: Kan shinakai to kan nihon kai" (The sea: Maritime
routes in the China Sea and the Japan Sea), in *Asahi hyakka Nihon no rekishi*, 15
(Tokyo, 1986), pp. 98–99.

7. Murai Shōsuke, "Chūsei ni okeru Higashi Ajia shochiiki to no kōtsū" (Medieval
trade among the regions of East Asia), in *Nihon no shakai shi* (History of Japanese society), vol. 1: *Rettō naigai no kōtsū to kokka* (Trade inside and outside the
archipelago and the state) (Tokyo: Iwanami shoten, 1987), pp. 120–23.

8. Tanaka Takeo, *Wakō: Umi no rekishi* (The *wakō*: History of the sea) (Tokyo:
Kyōikusha, 1982), pp. 58–59.

9. These were documents sent by China to the "king of Japan," who gave them to
shipowners or captains. The seals were numbered and in two parts. One part
stayed in the Chinese port, and the other had to be presented by the captains as
proof that they were authorized to trade. On the official trade using seals, see
Charlotte von Verschuer, *Le Commerce extérieur du Japon, des origines au XVIᵉ
siècle* (Japan's foreign trade, from the beginnings to the sixteenth century) (Paris:
Maisonneuve & Larose, 1988).

10. See Tanaka Takeo with Robert Sakai, "Japan's Relations with Overseas Countries," in John Whitney Hall and Toyoda Takeshi, eds., *Japan in the Muromachi
Age* (Berkeley and Los Angeles: University of California Press, 1977), pp. 159–78.

11. According to the *Zōjiki*, by Jinson, cited by Sasaki Ginya, *Muromachi bakufu*,
pp. 303–5.

12. Tanaka Takeo, "Umi: Kan shinakai to kan nihon kai," pp. 110–11.
13. Sasaki Ginya, *Muromachi bakufu*, pp. 296–97.
14. On Okinawa, see the analysis by Takara Kurayoshi, *Ryūkyū ōkoku* (The kingdom of the Ryukyu Islands) (Tokyo: Iwanami shinsho, 1993).
15. Ibid., p. 83.
16. Sasaki Ginya, *Muromachi bakufu*, p. 294.
17. Tanaka Takeo, "Umi: Kan shinakai to kan nihon kai," pp. 107–8 (trans.).
18. See also Denys Lombard, *Le Carrefour javanais: Essai d'histoire globale, les réseaux asiatiques* (The Javanese crossroads: Essay on global history, the Asian networks) (Paris: Éditions de l'École des hautes études en sciences sociales, 1990), vol. 2, pp. 31–48.
19. Toyoda Takeshi and Sugiyama Hiroshi, "The Growth of Commerce and the Trades," in Hall and Takeshi, *Japan in the Muromachi Age*, p. 139.
20. Toyoda Takeshi, "Za to dosō" (Guilds and money lenders), in *Iwanami kōza Nihon no rekishi*, 7, *Chūsei* 2 (Tokyo: Iwanami shoten, 1963), pp. 167–68. Cf. Sasaki Ginya, *Nihon shōnin no genryū: Chūsei no shōnintachi* (The origins of Japanese merchants: Merchants of the Middle Ages) (Tokyo: Kyōikusha, 1981), pp. 190–202.
21. Toyoda Takeshi, *A History of Pre-Meiji Commerce in Japan* (Tokyo: Kokusai bunka shinokai, 1969), pp. 19–20.
22. Sasaki Ginya, *Muromachi bakufu*, p. 48.
23. Nagahara Keiji, *Gekokujō no jidai* (The era of the lower commanding the upper), vol. 10 of *Nihon no rekishi* (History of Japan) (Tokyo: Shogakkan, 1998), p. 156.
24. Ibid., p. 46.
25. Sasaki Ginya, "Inshu" (Drinking saké), in *Ōnin no ran* (The Ōnin war), *Asahi hyakka Nihon no rekishi*, 18 (Tokyo, 1986), p. 220.
26. More precisely, its use spread, since the word itself seems to be older, dating from the early fourteenth century in the sense of "wealthy man." Cf. Nagahara Keiji, *Gekokujō no jidai*, p. 144.
27. Hayashiya Tatsusaburō, "Kyoto in the Muromachi Age," in Hall and Takeshi, *Japan in the Muromachi Age*, pp. 25–27.
28. Ibid., p. 26. See also Murai Yasuhiko, "Kinkakuji to Ginkakuji: Muromachi bunka" (The Golden Pavilion and the Silver Pavilion: The Muromachi culture), in *Asahi hyakka Nihon no rekishi*, 16, p. 140.
29. *Tamon'in nikki*, Eiroku 13, 3d lunar month, 19th day, quoted by Takahashi Masaaki, *Mizumi no kuni no chūseishi* (The country of the lake in the Middle Ages) (Tokyo: Heibonsha, 1987), p. 18 (trans.).
30. Imatani Akira, *Biwa ko to Yodo no suikei*, in *Asahi hyakka Nihon no rekishi*, 20 (Tokyo, 1987), p. 263.
31. Ibid., pp. 283–84.
32. Kayoshōza or Shifu kayochōza, a guild that took its name from the bearers of the imperial palanquin (*kayochō* or the four *shifu* guards), men attached to the court and later organized into the rice merchants' guild.
33. Imatani Akira, *Biwa ko to Yodo no suikei*, p. 278.
34. Ibid.
35. Hayashiya Tatsusaburō, ed., *Hyōgo kitazeki nyūsen nōchō* (Register of payments made by ships entering the port of Hyōgo by the northern barrier) (Tokyo: Chūō

kōron bijutsu shuppan, 1981). Analyses of this document can be found in Nagahara Keiji, *Nairan to minshū no seiki* (The civil wars and the century of people's
movements), vol. 6 of *Taikei Nihon no rekishi* (An outline of Japanese history)
(Tokyo: Shogakkan), pp. 204 et seq. See also Watanabe Norifumi, "Nihon shakai
ni okeru Setonaikai chiiki" (The Inland Sea region in Japanese society), in
Nihon no shakaishi (History of Japanese society), vol. 1: *Rettō naigai kōtsu to
kokka* (Trade inside and outside the archipelago and the state) (Tokyo: Iwanami
shoten, 1987), pp. 262 et seq. See also Imatani Akira, *Biwa ko to Yodo no suikei*,
pp. 274 et seq.

36. Sasaki Ginya, *Muromachi bakufu*, pp. 260–62.

10. The Splendor and Misery of the Muromachi Century: New Uprisings, New Culture

1. Jinson (1430–1508), dignitary of the Kōfukuji, left his "Catalogue of daily notes
kept at the Daijōin" (Daijōin nikki mokuroku), comprising texts drawn from the
archives of the Daijōin. The text quoted here is from these notes (trans.). He also
wrote his own notes on the events he witnessed.
2. Nakamura Kichiji, *Do-ikki kenkyū* (Research on the *do-ikki* revolts) (Tokyo: Azekura shobō, 1974), pp. 156–75.
3. *Do-ikki,* short for *domin-ikki*: the *domin* were people who lived in the countryside. They included not only peasants per se but also indebted low-ranking warriors. The older reading, *tsuchi ikki*, also refers to the *do-ikki*. Cf. David L. Davis,
"Ikki in Late Medieval Japan," in John W. Hall and Jeffrey P. Mass, eds., *Medieval Japan: Essays in Institutional History* (New Haven, Conn.: Yale University
Press, 1974), p. 229.
4. Inagaki Yasuhiko and Toda Yoshimi, eds., *Do-ikki to nairan* (Revolts and civil
wars), vol. 2 of *Nihon minshū no rekishi* (History of the working class in Japan)
(Tokyo: Sanseidō, 1974), pp. 276–82.
5. Cf. the detailed chronology by Nakamura Kichiji, *Do-ikki kenkyū*, pp. 676–88.
6. Katsumata Shizuo, *Ikki* (Tokyo: Iwanami shinsho, 1982), pp. 152–59.
7. Kasamatsu Hiroshi, *Tokusei rei: Chūsei no hō to kanshū* (The edicts of virtuous
government: Laws and customs in the Middle Ages) (Tokyo: Iwanami shinsho,
1983), pp. 55–60. The peasants did not, however, have a different awareness of
history than did the rest of society. During the ancient period, the court's cele-
brations of the new year had the same sense of renewal and a new start. Cf. Katsumata Shizuo, *Ikki*, pp. 152–59.
8. This is notably the case among certain postwar Marxist historians. Cf. in particular, Suzuki Ryōichi, *Nihon chūsei no nōmin mondai* (The peasant question in
medieval Japan) (Tokyo: Azekura shobō, 1971); and more recently, Inagaki Yasuhiko and Toda Yoshimi, *Do-ikki to nairan*.
9. On this famine and its relationship to the revolts, see Nagahara Keiji, *Gekokujō
no jidai*, vol. 10 of *Nihon no rekishi* (History of Japan) (Tokyo: Shogakkan, 1998),
pp. 210–22.
10. According to the *Hekizan nichiroku*, a chronicle by the Zen monk Daigyoku,
quoted by Sasaki Ginya in *Muromachi bakufu*, vol. 13 of *Nihon no rekishi*

(Tokyo: Shogakkan, 1974), pp. 212–13. Cf. Imatani Akira, Ōnin no ran (The Ōnin War), Asahi hyakka Nihon no rekishi 18 (Tokyo, 1986), pp. 203–4.

11. Many studies have looked at the story of the Niimi estate. I was inspired by Kudō Kei'ichi, Shōen no hitobito (The people of the estates) (Tokyo: Kyōikusha, 1978), pp. 164–74; and Ishii Susumu, Asahi hyakka Nihon no rekishi, 2, Chūsei no mura o aruku, jiin to shōen (About medieval villages, monasteries, and estates), pp. 60–68.

12. The expression "the three demons" (sanma) apparently came from a satirical song that cited Arima Moto'ie, the head of the guard, Karasuma Suketō, cousin of the shogun's mother, and Imamairi no Tsubone, called O'ima, Yoshimasa's nurse.

13. See H. Paul Varley, The Ōnin War: History of Its Origins and Background. With a Selective Translation of the Chronicle of Ōnin (New York: Columbia University Press, 1967).

14. According to the Ōnin ki (Ōnin chronicle) (trans.).

15. After the war, Hayashiya Tatsuaburō established the most elaborate explanation for the creation of a new culture in the fifteenth century in his Chūsei bunka no kichō (The dominant tone of medieval culture) (Tokyo: Tōkyō daigaku shuppan-kai, 1953).

16. Ichiza: originally a group or guild, gathered for a performance; later, a troupe (of actors). Yoriai: assembly; later, council or communal assembly. Ikki: "a single plan, a single goal," a league formed for a common objective.

17. Nishino Haruo, "Nō to kyōgen" (Nō and kyōgen), in Asahi hyakka Nihon no rekishi, 17 (Tokyo, 1986), p. 162.

18. Renga are linked poems. This poetic form was created in the late Heian period as a form of entertainment for the court nobility. Its first theoretician was a great aristocrat, Nijō Yoshimoto (1320–88). In the fourteenth century, the composition of renga spread among the warriors, many of them educated by monks, and in the following century, "linked poetry" became a relatively popular form of expression.

19. Sasaki Ginya, Muromachi bakufu, vol. 13 of Nihon no rekishi (Tokyo: Shogakkan, 1974), pp. 360–63; Wakita Haruko, Taikei Nihon no rekishi, 7, Sengoku daimyō (Tokyo: Shogakkan, 1988), pp. 79–83.

20. Katsumata Shizuo, "Ikki," in Asahi hyakka Nihon no rekishi, 81 (Tokyo, 1987), p. 108. Cf. Yamamoto Kichisō, "Nō to kyōgen," in Asahi hyakka Nihon no reki-shi, 17 (Tokyo, 1986), pp. 178–79.

21. Various facts reported by several sources, the most detailed of which is the Tai-heiki, ch. 27.

22. On Sasaki Dōyo and the basara phenomenon, see Satō Kazuhiko, ed., Basara daimyō no subete (All about the basara lords) (Tokyo: Shinjinbutsuōraisha, 1990); Hayashiya Tatsusaburō, Sasaki Dōyo: Nambokuchō no nairan to basara no bi (Sasaki Dōyo: The civil wars between the two courts and the basara aesthetic) (Tokyo: Heibonsha, 1995). See also Pierre F. Souyri, "Être basara dans le Japon médiéval" (Being basara in medieval Japan), Cipango, no. 3 (November 1994): 159–70.

23. Yokoi Kiyoshi, Higashiyama bunka (The Higashiyama culture) (Tokyo: Heibon-sha, 1994), pp. 176–77.

24. On dōbōshū, see Nagahara Keiji, *Gekokujō no jidai*, pp. 339–42; Murai Yasu-hiko, *Kinkakuji to Ginkakuji: Muromachi bunka* (The Golden Pavilion and the Silver Pavilion: Culture in the Muromachi period), in *Asahi hyakka Nihon no rekishi*, 16 (Tokyo, 1986), pp. 138–42.

25. Amino Yoshihiko, *Nihon ron no shiza: Rettō no shakai to kokka* (Views on dis-courses on Japan: Society and state in the archipelago) (Tokyo: Shogakkan, 1990), pp. 269–99. See also Niunoya Tetsuichi, "Hinin, karawamono, sanjo" (Nonhumans, people of the riverbanks, and wanderers), in *Iwanami kōza Nihon tsūshi*, 8, *Chūsei* 2 (Tokyo: Iwanami shoten), pp. 230–40; Yokoi Kiyoshi, *Higashi-yama bunka*, pp. 182–96.

26. Yokoi Kiyoshi, *Kawara to rakusho, oni to yōkai* (Inhabitants of the riverbanks, graffiti, monsters, and wraiths), in *Asahi hyakka Nihon no rekishi*, 13 (Tokyo, 1986), pp. 36 et seq.

27. On leprosy, see Yokoi Kiyoshi, *Chūsei minshū no seikatsu bunka* (Daily culture of people of the Middle Ages) (Tokyo: Tōkyō daigaku shuppankai, 1975), pp. 295–334.

28. See Amino Yoshihiko, *Zōho, Muen kūkai, raku: Nihon chūsei no jiyū to heiwa* (Absence of links, space without lord, and site of free trade: Freedom and peace in medieval Japan), expanded ed. (Tokyo: Heibonsha, 1987), esp. pp. 139 et seq.

29. Yokoi Kiyoshi, *Kawara to rakusho, oni to yōkai*, pp. 41–42.

30. Yokoi Kiyoshi, *Higashiyama bunka*, pp. 178 et seq.

31. Ibid., p. 141.

32. Ibid., pp. 132–33. See H. Paul Varley and George Elison, "The Culture of Tea: From Its Origins to Sen no Rikyū," in George Elison and Bardwell L. Smith, eds., *Warlords, Artists, and Commoners: Japan in the Sixteenth Century* (Hono-lulu: University of Hawaii Press, 1981), pp. 198–200.

33. Yokoi Kiyoshi, *Higashiyama bunka*, pp. 159–173.

34. H. Paul Varley, "Ashikaga Yoshimitsu and the World of Kitayama: Social Change and Shogunal Patronage in Early Muromachi Japan," in John Whitney Hall and Toyoda Takeshi, eds., *Japan in the Muromachi Age* (Berkeley and Los Angeles: University of California Press, 1977), p. 203.

35. There were two kinds of books: scrolls and booklets, both generally kept in wooden boxes; booklets that had no box were piled horizontally. See Sasaki Ginya, *Muromachi bakufu*, pp. 346–48.

36. Hyūga Susumu, cited in Murai Yasuhiko, *Kinkakuji to Ginkakuji*, p. 143.

37. Murai Yasuhiko, *Kinkakuji to Ginkakuji*, pp. 152–53.

38. Ibid., p. 153.

11. The Sengoku Period: Communes, Religious Leagues, and Neighborhood Associations

1. Gunaichō shoryōbu, ed., *Masamoto kō tabihikitsuke* (Tokyo: Yōtokusha, 1962). A good analysis can be found in Kudō Kei'ichi, *Shōen no hitobito* (The people of the estates) (Tokyo: Kyōikusha, 1978), pp. 187–217.

2. Mary Elizabeth Barry, *Hideyoshi* (Cambridge, Mass.: Harvard University Press, 1982).

3. In 1917, documents (Sugaura *monjo*) that relate almost two centuries of conflict between Sugaura and the neighboring village of Ōura were discovered in the Chinju Suga jinja (shrine). These important documents have been thoroughly researched. A good summary may be found in Imatani Akira, *Biwako to Yodo no suikei* (Lake Biwa and the Yodo River basin), in *Asahi hyakka Nihon no rekishi*, 20, Tokyo, pp. 266–71. See also Kudō Kei'ichi, *Shōen no hitobito*, pp. 143–60.

4. Tōji archives, 6, item 103, *Dai Nihon shiryō, iewake monjo*, series 10 (Tokyo: Tōkyō daigaku shiryō hensanjo).

5. Cited by Sasaki Ginya, *Muromachi bakufu*, vol. 13 of *Nihon no rekishi* (Tokyo: Shogakkan, 1974), p. 98.

6. Ōshima Okitsushima jinja *monjo*, Meiō 1, 12th lunar month, 4th day (trans.).

7. Fujiki Hisashi, "Le village et son seigneur" (The village and its lord), *Annales (Histoire, Sciences Sociales)*, no. 2 (March–April 1995): 413.

8. Cited by Katsumata Shizuo, *Tokuseirei: Chūsei no hō to saiban* (The edicts of virtuous government: Law and the courts in the Middle Ages), in *Asahi hyakka Nihon no rekishi*, 8 (Tokyo, 1986), pp. 258–60.

9. Ibid.

10. Sugaura *monjo*, Eiroku 11, 12th lunar month, 14th day (trans.).

11. *Daijō'in jisha zōjiki*, Bunmei 18, 2d lunar month, 13th day; Bunmei 18, 5th lunar month, 9th day.

12. On the great Yamashiro revolt, see Suzuki Ryōichi, *Nihon chūsei no nōmin mondai* (The peasant question during the Japanese Middle Ages) (Tokyo: Azekura shobō, 1976), esp. pp. 141–79. See also *Yamashiro kuni ikki*, published on the five-hundredth anniversary of the revolt by Nihon shi kenkyūkai, and *Rekishigaku kenkyūkai* (Tokyo: Tōkyō daigaku shuppankai, 1986).

13. Suzuki Ryōichi, *Ōnin no ran* (The Ōnin War) (Tokyo: Iwanami shinsho, 1973), pp. 166–71.

14. Nagahara Keiji, *Sengoku no dōran* (The uprisings of the Sengoku period), vol. 14 of *Nihon no rekishi* (Tokyo: Shogakkan, 1975), p. 64. See also Katsumata Shizuo, *Ikki* (Tokyo: Iwanami shinsho, 1982), pp. 98–100.

15. Nagahara Keiji, *Sengoku no dōran*, p. 67. Cf. Ikegami Hiroko, *Sengokuki no ikki* (The revolts in the Sengoku period), in *Ikki*, vol. 2: *Ikki no rekishi* (History of the revolts) (Tokyo: Tōkyō daigaku shuppankai, 1981), pp. 124–31.

16. *Jingū bunkozō, Yamanaka monjo, Iga sōkoku ikki okitegaki*. Undated document probably written between 1552 and 1568 (trans.).

17. Rennyo (1415–99) was the descendant of a daughter of Shinran who was the guardian of a funerary chapel dedicated to her father and passed on this responsibility to her descendants. They gradually gained strong influence in the sect, which gained preeminence under Rennyo's leadership. Kasahara Kazuo has written a number of works on relations between Shinran and Rennyo, including *Ran'yo no ningen zō: Shinran to Rennyo* (Figures of troubled times: Shinran and Rennyo) (Tokyo: NHK shimin daigaku, 1984). Fragments of Rennyo's letters to his followers have been translated into English. See Yamamoto Kōshō, *Shinshū seiten: The Holy Scripture of Shinshū* (Honolulu: University of Hawaii Press, 1955).

18. Fujiki Hisashi, *Ikkō ikki ron* (On the *ikkō* leagues), in *Kōza Nihon rekishi*, 4, *Chūsei* 2 (Tokyo: Tōkyō daigaku shuppankai, 1985), esp. pp. 207 et seq.

19. Nagahara Keiji, *Gekokujō ni jidai* (The epoch of the lower commanding the upper), vol. 10 of *Nihon no rekishi* (History of Japan) (Tokyo: Shogakkan, 1998), p. 435.

20. Nagahara Keiji, *Sengoku no dōran*, p. 71.

21. Ikegami Hiroko, *Sengoku ki no ikki*, pp. 98–110.

22. This expression conveys the secularization of the ideal of salvation preached by Shinran, in conformity with a trend in Japanese Buddhism, which had always — since ancient times — proposed to its followers prosperity and happiness in this world.

23. Kinryū Shizuka, *Chūsei no shūkyō to ikki* (Religion and revolt in the Middle Ages), in *Ikki*, vol. 4: *Seikatsu, bunka, shisō* (Daily life, culture, and thought) (Tokyo daigaku shuppankai, 1981), pp. 259–76.

24. Nagahara Keiji, *Sengoku no dōran*, p. 76.

25. Imatani Akira, *Ōnin no ran* (The Ōnin war), in *Asahi hyakka Nihon no rekishi*, 18 (Tokyo, 1986), p. 219.

26. Hayashiya Tatsusaburō was the foremost expert on the urban history of Kyoto between 1955 and 1980. His studies of the social structures and cultural evolution of the city between 1470 and 1570 are unequaled. The plan of Kyoto reproduced here and found in many books. For more detail, see Nicolas Fiévé, *L'Architecture et la ville du Japon ancien: Espace architectural de la ville de Kyōto et des résidences shōgunales aux XIVe et XVe siècles* (Architecture and the ancient Japanese city: The architectural space of Kyoto and shogunal residences in the fourteenth and fifteenth centuries) (Paris: Maisonneuve & Larose, 1996), fig. 42, drawn by Takahashi Yasuo. On Kyoto during this period, see also Mary Elizabeth Berry, *The Culture of Civil War in Kyoto* (Berkeley and Los Angeles: University of California Press, 1994).

27. Imatani Akira, *Ōnin no ran*, p. 222.

28. The Hokkeshū, also called the Nichiren sect, after its founder. Its teachings were based on the Lotus Sutra of the True Law, Hokkekyō. The Buddhist term for designating success in this world is *gense rikayu*, but all sects more or less promised it to their followers. Some historians have contrasted the materialism of the Hokke sect with the millenarian character of Amidism.

29. Hayashiya Tatsusaburō, *Tenka ittō*, vol. 12 of *Nihon no rekishi* (Tokyo: Chūkō bunko, 1974), pp. 45 et seq.

30. Ibid., p. 47.

31. Hayashiya Tatsusaburō, "Kyoto in the Muromachi Age," in John W. Hall and Toyoda Takeshi, eds., *Japan in the Muromachi Age* (Berkeley and Los Angeles: University of California Press, 1977), p. 31.

32. Hayashiya Tatsusaburō, *Machishū: Kyōto ni okeru "shimin" keiseishi* (The *machishū*: History of the formation of "citizens" in Kyoto) (Tokyo: Chūkōshinsho, 1964), esp. pp. 146–49.

33. Quoted in Imatani Akira, *Ōnin no ran*, p. 222 (trans.).

34. In 1529, there were twenty *sōdai* "general deputies" in Kyoto, all of them wealthy moneylenders and merchants. In the districts, the municipal administration was

led for a month at a time by *machishū* who owned houses. Cf. Hayashiya Tatsusaburō, *Tenka ittō*, pp. 48–49.

35. Hayashiya Tatsusaburō, *Tenka ittō*, pp. 51–52.

36. Literally, "the group that meets." There were also *kaigōshū*. A good analysis of
Sakai in this period in English is by V. Dixon Morris, "The City of Sakai and
Urban Autonomy," in George Alison and Bardwell L. Smith, eds., *Warlords, Art-
ists and Commoners: Japan in the Sixteenth Century* (Honolulu: University of
Hawaii Press, 1981), pp. 23–54.

37. Quoted by Takao Kazuhiko, "Kyōto, Sakai, Hakata," in *Iwanami kōza Nihon no
rekishi*, 9, *Kinsei* 1 (Tokyo: Iwanami shoten, 1963), p. 127 (trans.). On how the
Portuguese missionaries saw Sakai, see Izumi Chōichi, *Sakai, chūsei jiyū toshi*
(Sakai, a free city in the Middle Ages) (Tokyo: Kyōikuha, 1981), pp. 144–58.

38. Quoted in Hayashiya Tatsusaburō, *Tenka ittō*, p. 53 (trans.).

39. The leaders of the city, all wealthy merchants, were known for their negotiating
talents, for protecting their city against aggression, and for resolving conflicts
between warring lords. They had gone to the same tea-ceremony schools as the
lords and so knew them very well, which gave them leverage in negotiations. Cf.
Hayashiya Tatsusaburō, *Tenka ittō*, p. 56.

40. Murai Yasuhiko, *Kinkakuji to Ginkakuji: Muromachi bunka* (The Golden Pavilion and the Silver Pavilion: The Muromachi culture), in *Asahi hyakka Nihon no
rekishi*, 16 (Tokyo, 1986), pp. 157–58.

41. This was Murata Sōju, heir to Murata Jukō, the founder of the spare style of the
art of tea. The rustic tea pavilion was called a *sōan*, a thatch-roofed cottage. On
Jukō (or Shukō) and Sōju, see the excellent study by H. Paul Varley and George
Elison, "The Culture of Tea: From Its Origins to Sen no Rikyū," in George Ali-
son and Bardwell L. Smith, eds., *Warlords, Artists and Commoners: Japan in the
Sixteenth Century* (Honolulu: University of Hawaii Press, 1981), pp. 205 et seq.

42. Fragments of the theoretical writings of the tea masters Murata Jukō (1423–1502),
Takeno Jōō (1502–55), and Sen no Rikyū (1522–91) were translated into English
by Dennis Hirota in the magazine *Chanoyu Quarterly* in 1979 and 1980.

43. Hayashiya Tatsusaburō, *Tenka ittō*, pp. 50–51.

12. *The Sengoku Period: Warlords Seeking Power*

1. Reported by Nagahara Keiji, *Sengoku no dōran* (The disturbances of the Sengoku period), vol. 14 of *Nihon no rekishi* (Tokyo: Shogakkan, 1975), p. 47 (trans.).

2. On the Ōuchi, see Peter Judd Arnesen, *The Medieval Japanese Daimyo: The
Ōuchi Family's Rule of Suō and Nagato* (New Haven, Conn.: Yale University
Press, 1979).

3. To distinguish them from the Hōjō of the Kamakura period, Japanese historians
often call Sōun and his successors the Go Hōjō (the later Hōjō).

4. Trans. Such moral instructions left to descendants were a very old genre, examples of which exist from the Heian and Kamakura periods. Sōun's recommendations were, like those of others, a mixture of rules about daily living (hygiene)
and moral instruction. The document has been translated into English; see Carl

Steenstrup, "Hōjō Sōun's Twenty-One Articles," *Monumenta Nipponica* (Summer 1974).

5. On the Hōjō lords, see, for example, Sugiyama Hiroshi, *Sengoku daimyō*, vol. 11 of *Nihon no rekishi* (Tokyo: Chūkō bunko, 1974), pp. 59–90; and Nagahara Keiji, *Sengoku no dōran*, pp. 23–31.

6. This text was translated into German by Wilhelm Röhl, *Nachrichten der deutschen Gesellschaft für Natur und Völkerkunde Ostasiens*, 1959.

7. Bunkokuhō, provincial (principality) legislation. Some of these bodies of law have been translated into English in William Scott Wilson and Gregory Lee, *Ideals of the Samurai: Writings of Japanese Warriors* (Ohara Publications, 1982).

8. Nagahara Keiji, *Sengoku no dōran*, pp. 50–53.

9. Cited by Katsumata Shizuo, "Sengoku daimyō," in *Asahi hyakka Nihon no rekishi*, 23 (Tokyo, 1986), p. 4.

10. Owada Tetsuo, *Sengoku daimyō* (Tokyo: Kyōikusha, 1978), pp. 94 et seq.

11. *Ōsumi-gun monjo* no. 60, cited by Nagahara Keiji with Kozo Yamamura, "The Sengoku Daimyo and the Kandaka System," in John Whitney Hall, Nagahara Keiji, and Kozo Yamamura, eds., *Japan Before Tokugawa: Political Consolidation and Economic Growth, 1500 to 1650* (Princeton, N.J.: Princeton University Press, 1981), p. 50.

12. Ibid., table 1.2, p. 42.

13. Nagahara Keiji, *Sengoku no dōran*, pp. 221 et seq.

14. *Sugaura monjo*, Eiroku, year 11, 12th lunar month, 24th day.

15. This point of view was developed by Nakamura Kichiji in *Nihon no hōken shakai* (Feudal society in Japan) (Tokyo: Azakura shobō, 1979).

16. Jacques Le Goff, *La Civilisation de l'Occident médiéval* (Medieval civilization in the West) (Paris: Arthaud, 1984), p. 223.

17. Naitō Konan, *Nihon bunka to wa nanzo ya* (What exactly is Japanese culture?), in *Rekishi to shisō: Gendai Nihon shisō taikei*, 27 (Tokyo: Chikuma shobō, 1965).

18. Cf. the debate among Amino Yoshihiko, Nagahara Keiji, and Ozaki Masahide, "Naitō Konon no 'Ōnin no ran ni tsuite' o megutte" (About Naitō Konan and his interpretation of the Ōnin wars), in *Rekishi kōron*, 11 (Tokyo, 1981), pp. 10–37.

19. This expression is used as a chapter title in Wakita Haruko, *Sengoku daimyō*, vol. 7 of *Taikei Nihon no rekishi* (Tokyo: Shogakkan, 1988), p. 121.

GLOSSARY OF JAPANESE WORDS AND NAMES

Abe	安倍氏	Ashikaga Tadayoshi	足利直義
Adachi	安達氏	Ashikaga Takauji	足利尊氏
Adachi Yasumori	安達泰盛	Ashikaga Yoshiakira	足利義詮
Akamatsu	赤松氏	Ashikaga Yoshihisa	足利義尚
Akamatsu Mitsusuke	赤松満祐	Ashikaga Yoshimasa	足利義政
Akanabe no shō	茜部荘	Ashikaga Yoshimi	足利義視
Akasaka jō	赤坂城	Ashikaga Yoshimitsu	足利義満
Aki	安芸	Ashikaga Yoshimochi	足利義持
akutō	悪党	Ashikaga Yoshinori	足利義教
ama shōgun	尼将軍	asobime	遊女
Amako	尼子氏	Awa	阿波国
Amaterasu	天照	Awa	安房国
Amenokoyane	天児屋根	azukaridokoro	預所
Amida	阿弥陀	Azuma	吾妻／東国
ando	安堵	Azuma kagami	吾妻鏡
Antoku	安徳		
Arai Hakuseki	新井白石	bakufu	幕府
Asai	浅井氏	basara	婆娑羅
Arakawa no shō	荒川荘	bashaku	馬借
Asakura	朝倉氏	Bendōwa	弁道話
Asakura Norikage	朝倉教景	Bingo	備後国
Asakura sōteki waki	朝倉宗滴話記	Biwa	琵琶湖
ashigaru	足軽	Bizen	備前国
Ashikaga	足利氏	bunke	分家
Ashikaga Chachamaru	足利茶々丸	bunkoku hō	分国法
Ashikaga Morouji	足利師氏	Bupporyō	仏法領

bushi	武士	Fujiwara	藤原氏
bushidan	武士団	Fujiwara Machinaga	藤原道長
bushidō	武士道	Fujiwara Nobuyori	藤原信頼
Byōdōin	平等院	Fujiwara Sadaie	藤原定家
		Fujiwara Sumitomo	藤原純友
Chiba	千葉氏	Fujiwara Tadamichi	藤原忠通
chigyō	知行	Fujiwara Yorinaga	藤原頼長
chigyō koku	知行国	fukoku kyōhei	富国強兵
Chihaya jō	千早城		
chinzei tandai	鎮西探題	Gan'ami	観阿弥
chōri	長吏	geinōmin	芸能民
Chōshū	長州	gekokujō	下剋上
Chōsokabe	長曽我部氏	Gen'e	玄恵
Choson	朝鮮	genin	下人
chūsei	中世	Gion	祇園
		Go Fukakusa	後深草
dajōdaijin	太政大臣	Go Hōjō	後北条氏
Dai Nihon shi	大日本史	Go Kashiwara	後柏原
Dai Nihon komonjo	大日本古文書	Go Nara	後奈良
Daigo	醍醐	Go Saga	後嵯峨
Daijōin	大乗院	Go Sanjō	後三条
Daikakuji	大覚寺	Go Shirakawa	後白河
daimyō	大名	Go Toba	後鳥羽
Date	伊達氏	gojō	五条
Dazaifu	大宰府	gokenin	御家人
dengaku	田楽	Gokurakuji	極楽寺
Dewa	出羽国	Goseibai shikimoku	御成敗式目
do-ikki	土一揆	Gozan	五山
dōdōshū	同朋衆	Gukanshō	愚管抄
Dōgen	道元	gumi	組み
dogō	土豪	gunji	郡司
dōjō	道場	Gunsho ruijū	群書類従
dōri	道理	Gusainin	供祭人
dosō	土倉	Gyokuyō	玉葉
		Hachiman	八幡
ebisu	恵比寿	Hachimangū	八幡宮
Echigo	越後国	Hakata	博多
Echizen	越前国	hanzei	半済
Edo	江戸	Harima	播磨国
egoshū	会合衆	Hasegawa Tōhaku	長谷川等伯
Eguchi	江口	Hatakeyama	畠山氏
Eiheiji	永平寺	Hatakeyama Masanaga	畠山政長
Eisai	栄西	Hatakeyama Yoshinari	畠山義就
Eison	叡尊	Heian	平安
Engakuji	円覚寺	Heiji no ran	平治の乱
Enryakuji	延暦寺	Heike monogatari	平家物語
Etchū	越中国	Heirakuji	平楽寺
Ezo	蝦夷	henreki no sekai	遍歴の世界
		Hie jinja	日吉神社
fengjian	封建	Higashiyama	東山
fudai	譜代	higokenin	非御家人

Hiki	比企氏	Iganomono	伊賀者
Hine no shō	日根荘	igyō	異形
Hino Shigeko	日野重子	ikebana	生花
Hino Tomiko	日野富子	ikkō shū	一向宗
Hiraizumi	平泉	ikkō ikki	一向一揆
Hiroshige	広重	Imagawa	今川氏
Hitachi	常陸国	Imagawa kana mokuroku	今川仮名目録
Hōgen no ran	保元の乱	Imagawa Ujichika	今川氏親
Hōjō	北条氏	Imagawa Yoshimoto	今川義元
Hōjō Masako	北条政子	imayō	今様
Hōjō Nagatoki	北条長時	In	院
Hōjō Sadatoki	北条貞時	In no chō	院庁
Hōjō Shigetoki	北条重時	inga	因果
Hōjō Sōun	北条早雲	Insei	院政
Hōjō Tokimasa	北条時政	Ippen	一遍
Hōjō Tokimune	北条時宗	Iriyamada	入山田
Hōjō Tokiyori	北条時頼	Ise	伊勢国
Hōjō Ujitsuna	北条氏綱	Ise jingū	伊勢神宮
Hōjō Ujiyasu	北条氏康	Ise Sadachika	伊勢貞親
Hōjō Yasutoki	北条泰時	Ise Taira (Heishi)	伊勢平氏
Hōjō Yoshitoki	北条義時	Ishiguro no shō	石黒荘
Hōjōki	方丈記	Issan Ichinei	一山一寧
hōken	封建	Iwashimizu hachimangū	石清水八幡宮
hōkōshū	奉公衆	Iyo	伊予国
hokumen no bushi	北面の武士	Izu	伊豆国
Hokke shū	法華宗	Izumi	和泉国
Hokkekyōji	法華経寺	Izumo	出雲国
Honchō	本朝		
Hōnen	法然	Jishū	時宗
Honganji	本願寺	Jien	慈円
honke	本家	Jimyōin	持明院
Honnōji	本能寺	jinin	神人
Horikawa	堀川	Jinnō shōtoki	神皇正統記
Hosokawa	細川氏	jiriki	自力
Hosokawa Harumoto	細川晴元	Jinson	尋尊
Hosokawa Katsumoto	細川勝元	ji okoshi	地起し
Hosokawa Masamoto	細川政元	jitō	地頭
Hosokawa Yoriyuki	細川頼之	jissatsu	十刹
hyakushō	百姓	jiyū rōzeki	自由狼藉
Hyōgo	兵庫	jizamurai	地侍
hyōjōshū	評定衆	Jizō	地蔵
hyōrōmai	兵糧米	Jōdo shinshū	浄土真宗
		Jōdo shū	浄土宗
Ichijōtani	一乗谷	Jōei shikimoku	貞永式目
ichimi dōshin	一味同心	jōkamachi	城下町
ichimon	一門	Jōkyū no ran	承久の乱
ichinomiya	一宮	jōri	条里
Ichinotani	一の谷	Jufukuji	寿福寺
ichiza	一座		
ie no ko	家子	Kaga	加賀国
Iga	伊賀	Kai	甲斐国

Kakuichi	覚一	kō	講
kakun	家訓	Kō Moronao	高師直
Kakunyo	覚如	Koga	古河
kakushikibumi	隠規文	Kōgon	光厳
Kakushin-ni	覚信尼	Kōfukuji	興福寺
Kamakura	鎌倉	kokujin	国人
Kamakura dono	鎌倉殿	kokushi	国司
Kamegiku	亀菊	kokutai	国体
Kamigyō	上京	kōchi	公地
kamikaze	神風	Kōga	甲賀
Kami Koma	上狛	kōmin	公民
Kami Kuze	上久世	konden	墾田
Kammu Taira	桓武平氏	Kōno	河野氏
Kamo Chōmei	鴨長明	Konoe Kanetsune	近衛兼経
Kan'ami	観阿弥	konshi	懇志
Kandaka	貫高	Kōraishi	高麗史
Kanazawa Akitoki	金沢顕時	Koryŏ	高麗
Kanazawa Sanemasa	金沢実政	kosakunin	小作人
Kanazawa Sanetoki	金沢実時	kōsho	巷所
Kanō ha	狩野派	kotan	枯淡
kanrei	管領	Kōzuke	上野国
Kantō fu	関東府	Kuise	杭瀬
Kantō kubō	関東公方	Kusaba Sainin	組
Kanzaki	神崎	kusainin	楠葉西忍
Kanze	観世	kugonin	供御人
Kanze za	観世座	kugutsu	傀儡
kare sansui	枯山水	kugutsume	傀儡女
Kasuga jinja	春日神社	Kugutsu shi no ki	傀儡子記
Kawachi	河内国	Kugyō	公暁
Kawaguchi no shō	河の口荘	Kujō Kanezane	九条兼実
kawaramono	川原者	Kujō Masamoto	九条政基
Kazusa	上総国	Kujō Michiie	九条道家
kemari	蹴鞠	Kumagai Naozane	熊谷直実
kenmon taisei	権門体制	Kumano	熊野
Kenmu shikimoku	建武式目	Kumano gongen	熊野権現
kenin	家人	kumon	公文
Kenninji	建仁寺	kunishū	国衆
Kenreimon'in	建礼門院	Kuroda no shō	黒田荘
Kii	紀伊国	Kusado Sengen	草戸千軒
kinsei	近世	Kusonoki Masashige	楠木正成
kiryō no jin	器量の仁	Kuze no shō	久世荘
kishin	寄進	Kyōgen	狂言
Kiso Yoshinaka	木曽義仲	kyōkai no funsō	境界の紛争
kissa ōrai	喫茶往来		
Kitabatake Akiie	北畠顕家	Li Songgye	李成桂
Kitabatake Chikafusa	北畠親房		
Kitano jinja	北野神社	machi	町
Kitayama	北山	machishū	町衆
Kiyohara	清原氏	Madenokōji Tokifusa	万里小路時房
Kiyomizu dera	清水寺	mandokoro	政所
Kizu	木津	Mansai	満済

mappō	末法	Myōkenji	妙顕寺
Matsudaira	松平氏	myōshu	名主
Matsura	松浦氏		
Meigetsuki	明月記	Nagao Kagetora	長尾景虎
Mikawa	三河国	Nagashino	長篠
mikurya	御厨	Nagoe	名越氏
Minamoto Noriyori	源範頼	Namu Amida butsu	南無阿弥陀仏
Minamoto Sanetomo	源実朝	Namba	難波
Minamoto Tameyoshi	源為義	Nambokuchō jidai	南北朝時代
Minamoto Yoriie	源頼家	Nanzenji	南禅寺
Minamoto Yoritomo	源頼朝	Narita Gorō	成田五郎
Minamoto Yoriyoshi	源頼義	Nawa Nagatoshi	名和長年
Minamoto Yoshiie	源義家	Negoroji	根来寺
Minamoto Yoshitomo	源義朝	Nichiren	日蓮
Minamoto Yoshitsune	源義経	Nichiren shū	日蓮宗
Mineaiki	峰相記	Niimi no shō	新見荘
Ming	明	Niirayama	韮山
Mino	美濃国	Nijō kawara rakusho	二条河原落書
Mishima	三島	Nijō Yoshimoto	二条良基
Mito	水戸	Ningbo	寧波
Mitsuke	見附	Ninshō	忍性
miuchibito	御内人	Nishinomiya	西宮
Miura	三浦氏	Nishioka	西岡
miyako	京	Nitta	新田氏
miyaza	宮座	Nitta Yoshisada	新田義貞
Miyoshi	三好氏	nō	能
Miyoshi Chōkei	三好長慶	Nō'ami	能阿弥
Miyoshi Motonaga	三好元長		
Mochihito	以仁	Ōba Kagechika	大庭景親
Mokuan	黙庵	Oda Nobunaga	織田信長
mokudai	目代	Odawara	小田原
Monkan	文観	Ōe no Masafusa	大江匡房
Mōri	毛利氏	Ōgimachi	正親町
Mōri Motonari	毛利元就	Okehazama	桶狭間
Motomasa	元雅	Okitsushima	奥島
Motonobu ha	元信派	Ōmi	近江国
Mugaku Sogen	無学祖元	On'ami	音阿弥
Mujū Ichien	無住一円	Ōnin no ran	応仁の乱
mura no okibumi	村の置文	onkyū	恩給
mura okite	村掟	osa	長
Murata Jukō	村田珠光	Ōtani byōdō	大谷廟堂
Murata Sōju	村田宗珠	Ōtomo	大友氏
Muromachi	室町	Ōuchi	大内氏
Muroo	室生	Ōuchi Yoshioki	大内義興
Musashi	武蔵国	Ōuchi Yoshitaka	大内義隆
Musashi no shichitō	武蔵七党	Owari	尾張国
musha no yo	武者の世	Ōyama no shō	大山荘
Musō Soseki	夢窓疎石	Oyamato	小倭
Mutsu	陸奥国		
myō	名	rakuchū jishisen	洛中地子銭
myōden	名田	Rankei Dōryū	蘭渓道隆

rekidai hōan	歴代宝案	shiki	職
renga	連歌	shikken	執権
Rennyo	蓮如	Shimazu	島津氏
rensho	連署	Shimo Kuze	下久世
Rettō no bunkashi	列島の文化史	Shimogyō	下京
Rinzaishū	臨済宗	Shimōsa	下総国
Rokkaku dō	六角堂	Shimotsuke	下野国
Rokkaku Mitsutsuna	六角満綱	Shinano	信濃国
Rokuchō	六町	Shingon shū	真言宗
Rokuhara	六波羅	Shinkei	心敬
Rokuhara tandai	六波羅探題	Shinran	親鸞
		shintan	震旦
Sadafusa	貞成	Shinzei	信西
Sagami	相模国	shirabyōshi	白拍子
Saigyō	西行	Shirakawa	白河
Saionji	西園寺氏	Shiryō hensanjo	史料編纂所
Saitō Dōsan	齋藤道三	Shizuka Gozen	静御前
Saitō Sanemori	齋藤実盛	Sho Hashi	尚巴志
saka	坂	Sho Taikyū	尚泰久
Sakai	堺	shōen	荘園
Sakamoto	坂本	shōen sei	荘園制
sakaya	酒屋	shoin zukuri	書院造
Sakura Sōgorō	佐倉惣五郎	shōji	障子
samurai	侍	shojū	所従
samurai dokoro	侍所	Shōke no ikki	荘家の一揆
samurai dokoro no bettō	侍所の別当	Shōkokuji	相国寺
Sanjōnishi Sanetaka	三条西実隆	Shōnyo	証如
Sannō	山王	Someta	染田
Sanuki	讃岐国	shugo	守護
San'yōdō	山陽道	shugo daimyō	守護大名
sarugaku nō	**猿楽能**	shugodai	守護代
Sasaki Dōyo	佐々木道誉	shuku	宿
Satake	佐竹氏	Shun'oku Myōha	春屋妙葩
satori	悟り	sō	惣
Satsuma	薩摩国	Sō	宋氏
sei i tai shōgun	征夷大将軍	Sōami	相阿弥
seijaku	静寂	sōdai	惣代
Seiwa Genji	清和源氏	Sōkin	相金
sekkyō	説教	sōkoku	惣国
Sen Rikyū	千利休	sōroku	僧録
Sengoku	戦国	soma	杣
sengoku daimyō	戦国大名	Sōma	相馬
Sesshū	雪舟	Song	宋
Settsu	摂津国	sono	園
share	洒落	sōryōsei	惣領制
shashaku	車借	sōson	惣村
Shasekishū	沙石集	Sōtōshū	曹洞宗
Shiba	斯波氏	Sue Harukata	陶晴賢
Shiba Yoshimasa	斯波義将	Sugaura	菅浦
shijō	四条	suke	介

Sumiyoshi	住吉	tōryō	棟梁
Sunpu	駿府	Tōsandō	東山道
Suruga	駿河	Tōtōmi	遠江国
Sutoku	崇徳	Towazugatari	とわずがたり
		tozama	外様
Taiheiki	太平記	tsubute	飛礫
Taira	平氏	Tsugaru Tosan minato	津軽十三湊
Taira Koremori	平維盛	Tsurezuregusa	徒然草
Taira Kiyomori	平清盛	Tsurugaoka Hachimangū	鶴岡八幡宮
Taira Masakado	平将門		
Taira Tadamori	平忠盛	Uesugi	上杉氏
Taira Yoritsuna	平頼綱	Uesugi Kenshin	上杉謙信
Takakura	高倉	Uji	宇治
Takamochi ō	高望親王	Urabe Kaneyoshi	卜部兼好
Takeda	武田氏	ura	浦
Takeda Shingen	武田信玄	ura monjo	裏文書
Takeno Jōō	武野紹鴎	utokunin	有徳人
Tamon'in Eishun	多聞院英俊		
Tanba	丹波国	wabi	侘
Tanegashima	種子島	Wada Yoshimori	和田義盛
Tang	唐	waka	和歌
Tango no Tsubone	丹後局	Wakasa	若狭国
Tannishō	歎異抄	Wakō	倭寇
Tara no shō	太良荘	Watarai Ieyuki	度会家行
tariki	他力		
tatami	畳	Yagyū	柳生
tato	田堵	Yajima	矢島
Teika	定家	yamabushi	山伏
Tendai shū	天台宗	Yamaguchi	山口
tengu	天狗	Yamaki Kanetaka	山木兼隆
Tenjiku	天竺	Yamana	山名氏
Tenjinja	天神	Yamana Sōzen	山名宗全
Tenmon bunka	天文文化	Yamashina Tokigutsu	山科言継
Tenryūji	天竜寺／天龍寺	Yamashiro	山城国
Toba	鳥羽	Yamato	大和国
Tōdaiji	東大寺	Yanagizake	柳酒
Togashi	富樫氏	Yano no shō	矢野荘
toimaru	問丸	Yasutomi	康富
Tōji	東寺	yatsubara	奴原
Tōkaidō	東海道	yatsuko	奴
Toki	土岐氏	Yukinaga	行永
tokonoma	床の間	Yodo	淀
Tokudaiji Sanemoto	徳大寺実元	yoriai	寄合
Tokugawa	徳川氏	Yoshida Kenkō	吉田兼好
Tokugawa Mitsukuni	徳川斉昭	Yoshino	吉野
Tokugawa Yoshimune	徳川吉宗	Yuan	元
tokusei	徳政	yūgen	幽玄
tokusei ikki	徳政一揆	Yuien	唯円
tokusei rei	徳政令	Yukawa Sen'a	湯川宣阿
tone	刀禰	Yūsei	祐清

za	座
zaichō kanjin	在庁官人
zaike	在家
Zeami	世阿弥
Zen'ami	禅阿弥
Zōami	増阿弥
zen	禅
zuryō	受領

BIBLIOGRAPHY

Acta Asiatica, Bulletin of the Institute of Eastern Culture. "Studies on Bushi (Samurai)," no. 35 (1985).
———. "Studies in Japanese Legal History," no. 35 (1978).
———. "Studies in Japanese Medieval Social and Economic History." no. 44 (1983).
Amino Yoshihiko. "Les Japonais et la mer." *Annales (Histoire, Sciences Sociales),* no. 2 (March–April 1995).
———. "Le Moyen Âge japonais et quelques questions qu'il pose aux historiens aujourd'hui." *Cipango, Cahiers d'étude japonaise,* no. 3 (November 1994).
Arnesen, Peter. *The Japanese Medieval Daimyo: The Ōuchi Family's Rule of Suō and Nagato.* New Haven, Conn.: Yale University Press, 1979.
Asakawa Kan'ichi. *The Documents of Iriki.* 1929. Reprint, Tokyo: Japan Society for the Promotion of Science, 1995.
Beasley, W. G., and E. G. Pulleybank, eds. *Historians of China and Japan.* Oxford: Oxford University Press, 1961.
Berry, Mary Elizabeth. *The Culture of Civil War in Kyoto.* Berkeley and Los Angeles: University of California Press, 1994.
———. *Hideyoshi.* Cambridge, Mass.: Harvard University Press, 1982.
Berthier, François. *Le Jardin du Ryōanji: Lire le zen dans les pierres.* Paris: Éditions Adam Biro, 1989.
Brazell, Karen, trans. *The Confessions of Lady Nijō.* Stanford, Calif.: Stanford University Press, 1973.
Colas, Alain-Louis, trans. *Poèmes du zen des Cinq-Montagnes.* Paris: Maisonneuve & Larose, 1991.
Dōgen. *La Vision immédiate: Nature éveil et tradition selon le Shōbogenzō.* Translated and annotated by Bernard Faure. Paris: Éditions Le Mail, 1987.

Ducor, Jérôme. *La Vie de Zonkaku: Religieux bouddhiste japonais de XIVᵉ siècle.* Paris: Maisonneuve & Larose, 1993.

Eliseeff, Danielle. *Hideyoshi: Bâtisseur du Japon moderne.* Paris: Fayard, 1986.

Fiévé, Nicolas. *L'Architecture et la ville du Japon ancien: Espace architectural de la ville de Kyōto et des résidences shōgunales aux XIVᵉ et XVᵉ siècles.* Paris: Maisonneuve & Larose, 1996.

Frank, Bernard, trans. *Histoires qui sont maintenant du passé.* Paris: Gallimard, 1968.

Frédéric, Louis. *La Vie quotidienne au Japon au temps des samouraï, 1185–1603.* Paris: Hachette, 1968.

Fujiki Hisashi. "Le Village et son seigneur (XIVᵉ–XVIᵉ siècles), domination sur le terroir, autodéfense et justice." *Annales (Histoire, Sciences Sociales),* no. 2 (March–April 1995).

Gira, Dennis. *Le Sens de la conversion dans l'enseignement de Shinran.* Paris: Collège de France, 1985.

Girard, Frédéric. *Un moine de la secte Kegon, à l'époque de Kamakura, Myōe (1173–1232) et le journal de ses rêves.* Paris: École française d'extrême-Orient, 1990.

Giroux, Sakaé. *Zéami et ses "entretiens sur le nō."* Paris: Publications orientalistes de France, 1991.

Grossberg, Kenneth Alan. *Japan's Renaissance: The Politics of the Muromachi Bakufu.* Cambridge, Mass.: Harvard University Press, 1981.

Hall, John Whitney. *Government and Local Power in Japan, 500 to 1700: A Study Based on Bizen Province.* Princeton, N.J.: Princeton University Press, 1966.

Hall, John Whitney, and Jeffrey P. Mass, eds. *Medieval Japan: Essays in Institutional History.* New Haven, Conn.: Yale University Press, 1974.

Hall, John Whitney, Keiji Nagahara, and Kozo Yamamura, eds. *Japan Before Tokugawa: Political Consolidation and Economic Growth, 1500 to 1650.* Princeton, N.J.: Princeton University Press, 1981.

Hall, John Whitney, and Toyoda Takeshi, eds. *Japan in the Muromachi Age.* Berkeley and Los Angeles: University of California Press, 1977.

Hérail, Francine. *Histoire du Japon des origines à la fin de Meiji: Matériaux pour l'étude de la langue et de la civilisation japonaise.* Paris: Publications orientalistes de France, 1986.

Hurst III, G. Cameron. *Insei: Abdicated Sovereigns in the Politics of Late Heian, 1086–1185.* New York: Columbia University Press, 1976.

Ichien Mujū. *Collection de sable et de pierres: Shasekishū.* Trans. Hartmut O. Rotermund. Paris: Gallimard, 1979.

Joüon des Longrais, Frédéric. *Âge de Kamakura, sources, archives.* Paris: Maison franco-japonaise, 1950.

———. *L'Est et l'Ouest: Institutions du Japon et de l'Occident comparées (Six études de sociologie juridique).* Paris: Maison franco-japonaise, 1958.

Kato Suichi. *Histoire de la littérature japonaise.* Trans. E. Dale Saunders. 3 vols. Paris: Fayard/intertextes, 1984.

Katsumata Shizuo. "Ikki: Conjurations et révoltes dans la société médiévale japonaise." *Annales (histoire, sciences sociales),* no. 2 (March–April 1995).

Keene, Donald. *Essays in Idleness: The* Tsurezuregusa *of Kenkō*. New York: Columbia University Press, 1998.

Keene, Donald, ed. *Anthology of Japanese Literature: From the Earliest Era to the Mid-Nineteenth Century*. New York: Grove Press, 1999.

Keirstead, Thomas. *The Geography of Power in Medieval Japan*. Princeton, N.J.: Princeton University Press, 1992.

Lewis, Archibald. *Knights and Samurai: Feudalism in Northern France and Japan*. London: Temple Smith, 1974.

Mass, Jeffrey P. *Antiquity and Anachronism in Japanese History*. Stanford, Calif.: Stanford University Press, 1992.

———. *The Kamakura Bakufu: A Study in Documents*. Foreword by Takeuchi Rizō. Stanford, Calif.: Stanford University Press, 1976.

———. *Warrior Government and Early Medieval Japan: A Study of the Kamakura Bakufu, Shugo, and Jitō*. New Haven, Conn.: Yale University Press, 1974.

Mass, Jeffrey P., ed. *Court and Bakufu in Japan: Essays in Kamakura History*. New Haven, Conn.: Yale University Press, 1982.

Mass, Jeffrey P., and William B. Hauser, eds. *The Bakufu in Japanese History*. Stanford, Calif.: Stanford University Press, 1985.

McCullough, Helen Craig, trans. *The Taiheiki: A Chronicle of Medieval Japan*. New York: Columbia University Press, 1959.

———. *The Tale of the Heike*. Stanford, Calif.: Stanford University Press, 1988.

———. *Yoshitsune: A Fifteenth-Century Chronicle* (Gigei-ki). Stanford, Calif.: Stanford University Press, 1966.

Morris, Ivan. *The Nobility of Failure: Tragic Heroes in the History of Japan*. New York: Holt, Rinehart and Winston, 1975.

Ōka Makoto. *Poésie et poétique du Japon ancien: Cinq leçons données au Collège de France, 1994–1995*. Trans. Dominique Palmé. Paris: Maisonneuve & Larose, 1995.

Pigeot, Jacqueline. *Michiyuki-bun: Poétique de l'itinéraire dans la littérature du Japon ancien*. Paris: Maisonneuve & Larose, 1982.

Pinguet, Maurice. *La Mort volontaire au Japon*. Paris: Gallimard, 1984.

Pons, Philippe, and Pierre F. Souyri. "La Pérennité du système impérial japonais." *Le Débat*, no. 73 (January–February 1993).

Publications de la Maison franco-japonaise, ed. *Dictionnaire historique du Japon*. 20 vols. Tokyo: Kinokuniya, 1963–95.

Renondeau, Georges. *Le Bouddhisme japonais*. Paris: Albin Michel, 1965.

———. "Histoire des moine guerriers au Japon." *Mélanges publiés par l'Institut des hautes études chinoise*. Vol. 1, pp. 159–346. Paris: Presses universitaires de France, 1957.

Rotermund, Hartmut O. "La Conception des kami japonais à l'époque de Kamakura." *Annales du Musée Guimet: Revue de l'histoire des religions*, no. 182 (1972).

Sansom, George B. *A History of Japan to 1334*. Stanford, Calif.: Stanford University Press, 1958.

———. *A History of Japan, 1334–1615*. Stanford, Calif.: Stanford University Press, 1961.

Satō Kazuhiko. "Des gens étranges à l'allure insolite: Contestation et valeurs nouvelles dans le Japon médiéval." *Annales (histoire, sciences sociales)*, no. 2 (March–April 1995).

Sieffert, René, trans. *Dit des Heiké*. Paris: Publications orientalistes de France, 1978.

———. *Dit de Hōgen, Dit de Heiji*. Paris: Publications orientalistes de France, 1976.

Souyri, Pierre F. "Être basara dans le Japon médiéval: Anticonformisme et culture japonaise 'traditionnelle.'" *Cipango, Chaiers d'études japonaise*, no. 3 (November 1994).

———. "Luis Frois et l'histoire des femmes japonaise." *O Seculo cristao do Japao* [Lisbon], 1994.

———. "Une forme originale de domination coloniale? Les Japonais et le Hokkaidō avant l'époque Meiji." In *De Russie et d'ailleurs: Feux croisés sur l'histoire, pour Marc Ferro*. Institut d'études slaves, 1995.

Steenstrup, Carl. *Hōjō Shigetoki (1198–1261) and His Role in the History of Political and Ethical Ideas in Japan*. London: Curzon Press, 1979.

Toyoda Takeshi. *A History of Pre-Meiji Commerce in Japan*. Tokyo: Kokusai bunka shinkokai, 1969.

Umehara Takeshi. *La Philosophie japonaise des enfers*. Paris: Méridiens Kliencksieck, 1990.

Varley, H. Paul. *Imperial Restoration in Medieval Japan*. New York: Columbia University Press, 1971.

———. *The Ōnin War: History of Its Origins and Background, with a Selective Translation of the Chronicle of Ōnin*. New York: Columbia University Press, 1967.

———. *Warriors of Japan As Portrayed in the War Tales*. Honolulu: University of Hawaii Press, 1994.

Varley, H. Paul, Ivan Morris, and Nobuko Morris. *The Samurai*. London: Weidenfeld & Nicholson, 1970.

Vie, Michel. *Histoire du Japon des origines à Meiji*. Paris: Presses universitaires de France, 1969.

Von Verschuer, Charlotte. *Le Commerce extérieur du Japon des origines au XVIe siècle*. Paris: Maisonneuve & Larose, 1988.

Wakita Haruko. "La Discrimination dans le Japon médiéval: Division du travail et statuts sociaux." *Cipango, Cahiers d'études japonaises*, no. 6 (Fall 1997).

———. "Fêtes et communautés urbaines dans le Japon médiéval: La Fête de Gion à Kyoto." *Annales (histoire, sciences sociales)*, no. 5 (September–October 1997).

———. "La Montée du prestige impérial dans le Japon du XVIe siècle." *Bulletin de l'École française d'extrême-orient*, no. 84 (1997).

Yamamura, Kozo, ed. *Medieval Japan*. Vol. 3 of *The Cambridge History of Japan*. Cambridge: Cambridge University Press, 1981.

Yoshida Kenkō. *Les Heures oisives suivi de Kamo no Chōmei: Notes de ma cabane de moine*. Trans. Charles Grosbois, Tomiko Yoshida, and Father Sauveur Candeau. Paris: Gallimard/UNESCO, 1968.

Yoshie Akio. "Eviter la souillure: Le Processus de civilisation dans le Japon ancien." *Annales (Histoire, Sciences Sociales)*, no. 2 (March–April 1995).

Zeami. *La Traduction secrète du nō: Suivi de* Une journée de Nō. Trans. René Sieffert. Paris: Gallimard/UNESCO, 1960.

Zeami et al. *La Lande des mortifications: Vingt-cinq pièces de nō.* Trans. Armen Godel and Koichi Kano. Paris: Gallimard, 1994.

INDEX

Abe family, 23–24
Adachi family, 53
Adachi Yasumori, 103, 104
agriculture: development of, 60, 87–88, 91; dryland *vs.* wetland, 91; in eastern region, 55–56; and estate system, 85–86; and irrigation, 56, 91, 129, 184, 186, 212; productivity of, 128–29, 130, 216; and trade, 87–88, 91, 155; under warlords, 212. *See also* rice
Akamatsu family, 111, 116, 167, 168, 207
Akamatsu Mitsusuke, 147
Aki Province, 208
Akita Prefecture, 15
akutō. See bandits
Amagasaki, 158
Amagatsuya (god), 69
Amako family, 207, 208
ama shōgun (nun-shogun; Hōjō Masako), 49–52, 53, 77
Amaterasu (Sun Goddess), 3, 69, 136
Amida Buddha, 71, 72–73, 80, 82
Amida Buddhism, 70–80, 138–39, 217,

246n28; and arts, 172, 176; images of hell in, 71, 83; and leagues, 183, 192; reactions to, 74–80
Amino Yoshihiko, 14, 15, 34, 92, 98, 213, 224n37, 234n2
ancestor worship, 38
Annam, 152
Antoku, Emperor, 28, 31, 32, 71
Aomori Prefecture, 15
Arima Moto'ie, 243n12
aristocracy. *See* court nobility
artisans, 42, 92, 93, 95–96, 153, 212, 214; manufacture of firearms by, 6, 216; in urban areas, 171, 195, 198
arts, 8, 79, 83, 172, 217; and interior decor, 179–80, 201; and *kawara* society, 176–78; sponsorship of, 175–78. *See also* literature
Asai warlords, 215
Asakura family, 8, 168
Asakura Norikage, 209
Asakura Sōteki waki ("recommendations" of Asakura Norikage), 209

93, 102, 104–5, 215; in western region, 55–56, 61. *See also* land; *myōshu*
Etchū Province, 10, 47, 60
Europe: comparisons with, 2–4, 5, 33, 83, 140, 158–59, 183–84, 196, 217; contact with, 214, 216, 217; firearms from, 6, 61, 183, 205, 216, 221*n*17; population of, 224*n*38
Ezo tribes, 23–24, 46

factions, 40, 145, 161, 230*n*11; within Ashikaga family, 143–44, 203; among court nobility, 66; within families, 124, 167–68; within imperial family, 63–64; in new sects, 139; and retired emperors, 18, 27–28; among warriors, 124, 167–68
family, 38, 167, 173; and new sects, 138–39, 139; structure of, 124, 227*n*16. *See also* clans; inheritance
famine, 33, 34–35, 157, 168, 187; and peasant rebellions, 161–62, 164–65
feudalism (*hōken; feng-jian*), 118, 129, 147–48, 213–14, 216, 234*n*2; and fiefs, 54, 61; Western *vs.* Japanese, 2–3
The Fifty-five Stations of the Tōkaidō (Hiroshige), 13
firearms, 6, 61, 183, 205, 216, 221*n*17
fishermen, 92–95, 157, 158. *See also* people of the sea
Five Mountains (Gozan) system, 78–79, 102, 139–41, 153
flower arranging (*ikebana*), 170, 175, 179
France, 3, 4, 38, 83
fudai (second rank of vassals), 210–11
Fuji River, battle of, 30–31, 32, 41
Fujiwara family, 19, 52, 53, 69, 136, 145; and family structure, 227*n*16; and imperial court, 17, 18; and retired emperors, 24–28
Fujiwara Iehira, 115, 237*n*32
Fujiwara (Kiyohara) family, 31, 45, 46
Fujiwara no Kanezane, 68
Fujiwara no Michinaga, 71
Fujiwara no Nobuyori, 28
Fujiwara no Sadaie (Teika), 33, 50
Fujiwara no Sumitomo, 23
Fujiwara no Tadamichi, 27, 68
Fujiwara no Yorimichi, 24
Fujiwara no Yorinaga, 27

fukoku kyōhei (wealthy nation, strong army), 217
Fukuhara, 29–30
Fukui region, 10

Gan'ami (monk), 165
gardens, 102, 140, 170, 178, 179
geinōmin (artists), 154
gekokujō (lower commanding upper, social instability), 4, 142, 147, 170, 181–83, 202, 208, 216
Gen'ami, 178
Gen'e, 178
genin (inferiors), 37
gentry, local, 17–21, 43, 124, 182, 207, 208; and warriors, 20–21, 37
geography, knowledge of, 148, 151
Gifu region, 10
Gio (in *Heike*), 81, 82
Gion Shrine, 81, 105
Go Daigo, Emperor, 107, 109, 135, 137, 140, 154, 172; and Kenmu restoration, 112–16; rebellion of, 110–12
gods (*kami*), 92, 127, 136, 137, 146, 154, 157; and Mongol invasions, 135; and peasant leagues, 130–31, 134–35, 166
Go Fukakusa, Emperor, 63
Go Hōjō family, 203–5, 206, 208, 210–12, 247*n*3
Go Kashiwabara, Emperor, 202
gokenin (retainers), 43, 53
Gokurakuji Monastery, 74
Go Nara, Emperor, 182
Gorai Shigeru, 9
Go Saga, Emperor, 63
Go Sanjō, Emperor, 17, 24–25
Goseibai shikimoku (legal code), 3, 56–59, 89, 127
Go Shirakawa, Emperor, 18, 27–28, 82, 97, 225*n*47; and Taira family, 29, 30, 32; and Yoritomo, 44–45, 46, 52
Gotō, island of, 63, 127, 152
Go Toba, Emperor, 49, 50, 51–52, 68, 97, 105
Go Uda, Emperor, 110
government: Chikafusa on, 135–38; cloister (*insei*), 25, 27; by favorites, 168–69; and Ikkō leagues, 193, 194–95; and law, 57, 58, 59; local, 5, 183–88, 193, 194–95, 196; and mercantile capitalists, 156; provincial, 54–56; and

CPSIA information can be obtained
at www.ICGtesting.com
Printed in the USA
JSHW011230080120
3454JS00007B/222